Specifying Syntactic
Structures

Studies in Logic, Language and Information

Studies in Logic, Language and Information is the official book series of the European Association for Logic, Language and Information (FoLLI).

The scope of the series is the logical and computational foundations of natural, formal, and programming languages, as well as the different forms of human and mechanized inference and information processing. It covers the logical, linguistic, psychological and information-theoretic parts of the cognitive sciences as well as mathematical tools for them. The emphasis is on the theoretical and interdisciplinary aspects of these areas.

The series aims at the rapid dissemination of research monographs, lecture notes and edited volumes at an affordable price.

Managing editor: Robin Cooper, University of Gothenburg

Executive editor: Maarten de Rijke, University of Warwick

Editorial board:

Peter Aczel, Manchester University

Nicholas Asher, The University of Austin, Texas

Jon Barwise, Indiana University, Bloomington

John Etchemendy, CSLI, Stanford University

Dov Gabbay, Imperial College, London

Hans Kamp, Universität Stuttgart

Godehard Link, Universität München

Fernando Pereira, AT&T Bell Laboratories, Murray Hill

Dag Westerståhl, Stockholm University

Specifying Syntactic Structures

edited by
Patrick Blackburn &
Maarten de Rijke

CSLI Publications
Center for the Study of Language and Information
Stanford, California
&
FoLLI
The European Association for
Logic, Language and Information

Library of Congress Cataloging-in-Publication Data

Specifying syntactic structures/edited by Patrick Blackburn, Maarten
    de Rijke
        p. cm.
    Rev. papers originally presented at a workshop held Sept. 26–28,
1994, Centrul voor Wiskunde en Informatica, Amsterdam.
    Includes bibliographical reference and index.
    Contents: A grammar formalism and cross-serial dependencies /
Tore Burheim—On constraint-based Lambek calculi / Jochen Dürre
and Suresh Manandhar—On reducing principles to rules / Marcus
Kracht—Structural control / Natasha Kurtonina and Michael
Moortgat—Featureless HPSG / M. Andrew Moshier—On descriptive
complexity, language complexity, and GB / James Rogers—Feature
trees over arbitrary structures / Ralf Treinen—Dutch verb clustering
without verb clusters / Gertjan van Noord and Gosse Bouma—
Approaches to unification in grammar: a brief survey / Jürgen
Wedekind.
    ISBN 1-57586-085-6 (hardcover : alk. paper).ISBN 1-57586-084-8
    (pbk. : alk. paper)
        1. Grammar, Comparative and general—Syntax. I.
    Blackburn, Patrick, 1959– . II. Rijke, Maarten de.
    P291.S55 1997
    415—dc21   7-52733
                                          CIP

CSLI Publications reports new developments in the study of language,
information, and computation. In addition to lecture notes, our publications include monographs, working papers, revised dissertations, and
conference proceedings. Our aim is to make new results, ideas, and approaches available as quickly as possible. Please visit our website at
http://csli-www.stanford.edu/publications/
for comments on this and other titles, as well as for changes and cor-
rections by the author and publisher.

Contents

Contributors

PATRICK BLACKBURN is a lecturer at the department of computational linguists, University of Saarland. His research interests are logic and its applications to computation and the cognitive sciences.
Current address: Computerlinguistik, Universität des Saarlandes, D-66041 Saarbrücken, Germany. E-mail: `patrick@coli.uni-sb.de`.

GOSSE BOUMA is working as a computational linguist at the alfa-informatica department of the University of Groningen. He has done research on default unification, categorial grammar, and processing of constraint-based grammar formalisms.
Current address: Alfa-informatica Department, Groningen University, P.O. Box 716, 9700 AS Groningen, The Netherlands. E-mail: `gosse@let.rug.nl`.

TORE BURHEIM is a Ph.D. student at the department of informatics, University of Bergen. His main research interest is formal grammars, but he is also interested in most aspects of mathematical and computational linguistics.
Current address: Department of Informatics, University of Bergen, N-5020 Bergen, Norway. E-mail: `Tore.Burheim@ii.uib.no`.

JOCHEN DÖRRE is a research scientist in the Institute for Natural Language Processing at the University of Stuttgart. His research interests include logical foundations and computational properties of grammar formalisms, as well as computational semantics, and logic and constraint programming.
Current address: Institut für maschinelle Sprachverarbeitung, University of Stuttgart, Azenbergstr. 12, 70191 Stuttgart, Germany. E-mail: `Jochen.Doerre @ims.uni-stuttgart`.

MARCUS KRACHT is assistant professor at the department of mathematics of the Freie Universität Berlin. He is working in nonclassical logic and theoretical linguistics.
Current address: II. Mathematisches Institut, Freie Universität Berlin, Arnimallee 3, 14195 Berlin, Germany. E-mail: `kracht@math.fu-berlin.de`.

NATASHA KURTONINA is a a research scientist in the Center for Logic, Ghent University. Her research interests include logic, philosophy, computer science and computational linguistics.
Current address: Center for Logic, Ghent University, Rozier 44, Ghent 9000, Belgium. E-mail: `Natasha.Kurtonina@rug.ac.be`.

SURESH MANANDHAR is a research scientist at the Human Communication Research Centre of the University of Edinburgh. His broad research interests are in the logical and computational aspects of natural language processing systems. *Current address:* Language Technology Group, Human Communication Research Centre, University of Edinburgh, 2 Buccleuch Place, EH8 9LW, Scotland. E-mail: `Suresh.Manandhar@ed.ac.uk`.

MICHAEL MOORTGAT is professor of computational linguistics at the Research Institute for Language and Speech (OTS) at Utrecht University. His research interests include categorial grammar, the logical basis of grammar architectures, and applications of proof theoretic techniques in natural language processing and understanding. *Current address:* OTS, Trans 10, 3512 JK, Utrecht, The Netherlands. Email: `Michael.Moortgat@let.ruu.nl`.

M. ANDREW MOSHIER is assistant professor of mathematics and computer science at Chapman University. His current research interests are in metamathematical foundations of linguistic theory, in domain theory and in solution strategies for very large systems of non-linear equations. *Current address:* Department of Mathematics and Computer Science, Chapman University, Orange CA 92866, USA. Email: `moshier@nexus.chapman.edu`.

MAARTEN DE RIJKE is a Warwick research fellow in the department of computer science at the University of Warwick. His current research interests include logic and computation. *Current address:* Department of Computer Science, University of Warwick, Coventry CV4 7AL, England. E-mail: `mdr@dcs.warwick.ac.uk`.

JAMES ROGERS is a post-doctoral fellow at the Institute for Research in Cognitive Science at the University of Pennsylvania. His research focuses on the logical foundations of formal theories of syntax. *Current address:* IRCS, University of Pennsylvania, Suite 400C, 3401 Walnut St., Philadelphia, PA, 19104-6228, USA. E-mail: `jrogers@linc.cis.upenn.edu`.

RALF TREINEN is a research scientist at the Laboratoire de Recherche en Informatique, Université de Paris-Sud. He is working on symbolic constraint systems. *Current address:* L.R.I., Bât. 490, Université de Paris-Sud, F-91405 Orsay cedex, France. E-mail: `treinen@lri.fr`. Web: `http://www.lri.fr/~treinen`.

GERTJAN VAN NOORD is a research scientist at the alfa-informatica department of the University of Groningen. His research interests include computational linguistics, in particular natural language understanding. *Current address:* Alfa-informatica, University of Groningen, P.O. Box 716, 9700 AS Groningen, The Netherlands. E-mail: `vannoord@let.rug.nl`.

JÜRGEN WEDEKIND is a researcher at the Institute for Natural Language Processing at the University of Stuttgart. His research mostly concentrates on algorithmic problems. *Current address:* Institute for Natural Language Processing, University of Stuttgart, Azenbergstr. 12, D-70174 Stuttgart, Germany. E-mail: `juergen@ims.uni-stuttgart.de`.

Preface

During the 1980s, many computational linguists considered logic an eminently suitable medium for specifying syntactic structures. Logic, it was argued, allowed grammars to be treated as purely declarative knowledge bases, thus opening the way for clean treatments of parsing and generation. Moreover, logic was safe. Many of the knowledge representation formalisms used in Artificial Intelligence (notably semantic nets) had been criticized as incoherent. No such foundational worries beset the computational linguist who used standard logical tools.

Times change. The 1990s brought a tidal wave of interest in stochastic methods, and logical approaches lost their status as the cutting edge of research in natural language processing. Given this, it is perhaps tempting for a die-hard exponent of logic to view the 1980s as a lost golden age — but the temptation should be firmly resisted. Although the logical approach had many successes (for example, the development of the influential PATR-II system, and the rekindling of interest in categorial grammar), with the benefit of hindsight its shortcomings are equally plain. While the papers in the present collection belong to the logical tradition of grammar specification, they belong to a new wave of that tradition. Either directly or indirectly, they address the shortcomings of earlier work, and develop the logical tradition in a variety of new and important directions. The purpose of this introduction is to provide the reader with a preliminary map of this territory: what were the principal shortcomings in earlier work, and what new perspectives are offered by the papers collected here?

Painting with a very broad brush, it is possible to indicate four principal areas of discontent.

Foundational Issues. Minimally, logic was supposed to offer computational linguists a range of clean well understood formalisms, and tools (for example, model-theoretic analysis) for understanding the formalisms developed by computational linguists themselves. Additionally, logic was supposed to offer a catalogue of useful results. In retrospect, it is striking how long even quite fundamental perspectives on grammar formalisms took to emerge (for example, it took nearly a decade for the first-order perspective on feature structures to be clearly articulated) and how thin on the ground applicable results were (for example, descriptive complexity results linking logical descriptions with the Chomsky hierarchy).

Many of the papers in this collection offer deeper insight into foundational issues. For example, Moshier offers an abstract (and feature free) perspective on the foundations of Head-driven Phrase Structure Grammar (HPSG); Treinen shows how to build feature structures over structured entities and maintain decidability; both Kracht and Rogers provide (and apply) logical characterizations of context free languages; and Wedekind reconstructs a number of order-theoretic approaches to unification and proves their equivalence.

Architectural Issues. Most linguistic theories have a complex internal architecture: this is obviously true of Government and Binding theory (GB), but also of monostratal theories such as Generalized Phrase Structure Grammar (GPSG) and Lexical Functional Grammar (LFG), where trees and feature structures are linked together in non-trivial ways. However, too often logical analyses have focused exclusively on one component of the resulting system (such as the feature component) and neglected to analyse how the flow of information between the various parts of such rich architectures is regulated.

Many of the papers in this collection bear directly on this issue. For example, Dörre and Manandhar show how categorial and featural information can be combined in a simple and logically natural way; Kurtonina and Moortgat present a system in which independent categorial systems, each controlling a distinct domain of linguistic information, can communicate; while Moshier's category theoretic reconstruction of HPSG enables complex grammars to be built up out of genuinely independent modules. In general, the issues posed by entire linguistic architectures, not just isolated subsystems, are now the focus of interest.

Linguistic Issues. An often expressed complaint is that proponents of formal specification techniques make little effort to address the sort of data, or to capture the sort of ideas, that working (computational) linguists are concerned with. Too often, it seems, logical models merely cartoon the easy ideas, and leave the difficult parts unanalyzed.

Several of the papers in this collection deal explicitly with linguistic problems, or with the expressivity requirements of linguistic theories. Both Burheim (using a weak variant of LFG) and van Noord and Bouma (using a version of HPSG which produces relatively flat structures) examine the problems posed by cross-serial dependencies. Dörre and Manandhar use their hybrid system to analyse agreement phenomena in co-ordinated structures (a topic also touched on in Kracht's contribution), and both Kracht and Rogers show that large parts of the Chomskyan program can be straightforwardly captured by means of axiomatic specifications.

Statics versus Dynamics. One of the convictions most stubbornly held by proponents of logical specification can be summed up as: 'declarative good, procedural bad.' But this attitude pushes a number of important issues off the research agenda. Simply put, the dynamics of systems are both interesting and important, they *are* susceptible to logical analysis (recursion theory is no less a part of logic than model theory), and there are important links between static specifications of systems and their dynamic behaviour.

Two of the papers in this volume deal with this theme head on; in both cases the link between the static and dynamic perspectives is descriptive complexity. Roughly speaking, both Kracht and Rogers show that purely declarative specifications of sets of finite trees (namely, formulating these specifications as axiomatic stipulations) can have dynamic consequences (the trees admitted form a context free generable set). The theme is also present in Treinen's decidability results for strong feature logics. It is worth noting that a fundamental technical result underlies these three papers: the decidability of monadic second-order theories of n successors. Roughly speaking, all three authors proceed by finding linguistically useful specification languages that correspond to fragments of these theories.

Bearing these generalities in mind, let us examine the individual contributions in more detail.

A Grammar Formalism and Cross-Serial Dependencies, by *Tore Burheim.* A recurring theme in unification based approaches to grammar is the search for general principles which constrain computational power; a classic example is the off-line parseability constraint, which renders the LFG formalism decidable. In this paper, Tore Burheim explores new constraints on LFG: functional uncertainty is dispensed with, and strong restrictions are placed on the range of permissible equation schemata. However, empty right hand sides are allowed in lexical rules, and this combination of ideas leads to a neat result: the resulting system describes a full abstract family of languages. Moreover, although simple, the system has the power to capture cross-serial dependencies of the type found in Swiss German.

On Constraint-Based Lambek Calculi, by *Jochen Dörre* and *Suresh Manandhar.* This paper combines the central ideas of categorial grammar and feature logic in a strikingly simple way. Instead of building the categorial types out of unstructured atoms, they are built out of feature structures; and instead of insisting that a functor A/B must combine with an argument of type B, it is allowed to combine with any subtype of B. This change allows the well-known completeness, cut-elimination and context freeness results for Lambek calculus to be preserved in a natural way. More to the point, it also permits a linguistically natural division of labour. Categorial ideas are inherently suitable for capturing long distance dependencies and coordination; feature subsumption is inherently suitable for modeling agreement. In this system, each component deals with what it does best, and the result is a simple treatment of agreement in coordinations.

On Reducing Principles to Rules, by *Marcus Kracht*. Recent linguistic theorizing has shunned specific rules, emphasizing instead the importance of general principles. Using his 'Coding Theorem', a descriptive complexity theory result that provides a two way path between rules and principles, Kracht demonstrates that many of the leading ideas of the Chomskyan program *can* be viewed from a rule based perspective. As Kracht emphasizes, this does not mean that one *should* so view transformational grammar, nor that an ontological reduction has been effected — rather, the point is that the linguist is free to choose the appropriate perspective for the problem at hand. Kracht discusses the linguistic implications of this freedom and its methodological consequences.

Structural Control, by *Natasha Kurtonina* and *Michael Moortgat*. An important theme in recent work in categorial grammar is the use of 'structural modalities.' Taking their cue from linear logic, such modalities are used to gain fine grained control of the type system. What has been lacking, however, is a general framework for such proposals. Here, Kurtonina and Moortgat propose such a framework. Linguistic structure is viewed as being governed by a number of different logical systems, in particular, systems for precedence, dominance and dependency. Such an architecture allows fine grained control over each component; the problem is now to make these separate subsystems communicate effectively. It is here that some (novel) substructural modalities come into play: their role is to regulate the communication process, and the authors prove a number of embedding theorems which show that this goal is successfully achieved.

Featureless HPSG, by *M. Andrew Moshier*. No grammatical theory is more closely identified with feature structures than HPSG — but in this paper Moshier argues that this identification is misplaced, indeed, even dangerous. For a start, it threatens modularity: thinking solely in terms of feature geometry makes it hard, perhaps impossible, to isolate the effects of any single principle. It also makes it difficult to compare different versions of the theory — there is no obvious notion of interdefinability. Moshier's solution is to introduce an abstract class of models for HPSG specifically tailored to avoid these deficiencies. The models are category-theoretic, and Moshier shows that principles can be modeled as constraints on limits, co-limits, and commutativity.

On Descriptive Complexity, Language Complexity, and GB, by *James Rogers.* The paper discusses a powerful — and linguistically natural — method for establishing language complexity results. GB practitioners have long abandoned characterizations of natural language in terms of language complexity classes, preferring classifications in terms of principles and parameters instead. Ironically, Rogers shows that the principles themselves actually offer a key handle on language complexity: by viewing them as axiomatic constraints, one can show that large numbers of linguistic principles necessarily give rise to strongly context-free languages — in fact, any constraint specifiable in a certain language of monadic second logic has this property. The technique is applied to a significant portion of GB, both positive and negative results are established, and the significance for generative linguistics is discussed.

Feature Trees over Arbitrary Structures, by *Ralf Treinen.* Feature structures remain one of the key ingredients in unification based approaches to grammar, and the first-order analysis of feature structures has some claims to be the 'standard.' Treinen here generalizes the first-order analysis in two useful ways. Firstly, he allows feature structures to be built over structured feature symbols. Second, he allows a restricted form of quantification over features, namely quantification over those features which are defined at the root of a tree. These changes yield a more expressive (and more natural) feature description language. Moreover, if the theory of structured feature symbols is decidable, so is the entire formalism; the result is proved exhibiting a quantifier elimination algorithm.

Dutch Verb Clustering without Verb Clusters, by *Gertjan van Noord* and *Gosse Bouma.* In this paper the machinery of HPSG is adapted to allow a simple analysis of Dutch cross-serial dependencies. Arguing that previous categorial and HPSG analyses require ad-hoc methods for distinguishing verb complexes from other verbal projections, they opt for a 'flat' analysis. The key innovation is the assumption that only one rule is required to derive subordinate clauses — the rule allows for partial, unsaturated VPs. Much of the paper is devoted to showing that these modifications are consistent with Dutch word order phenomena, and the standard HPSG account of binding.

Approaches to Unification in Grammar: A Brief Survey, by *Jürgen Wedekind.* Two main currents exist in the study of feature structures: the logical, and the order-theoretic. While there are interesting and important interactions between the two, in recent years logical matters have tended to be emphasized at the expense of the order-theoretic. This article redresses the balance. It surveys the ideas and results underlying the order-theoretic results, from the ψ-terms of Aït-Kaci through to the present day. The approaches are systematically inter-related, a number of new and 'folklore' results are proved, and connections with the logical tradition are established.

To sum up, the articles collected here address a number of general concerns that nearly two decade's experience with logic-based methods have brought into focus. They show that logical methods are capable of addressing non-trivial linguistic concerns — and indeed, that viewing linguistic problems through a logical lens can lead to genuine insight. The existence of such work is testimony to the continued relevance of logical methods for natural language processing.

The papers in this collection are (updated and amended) versions of papers presented by participants of the workshop *Logic, Structures and Syntax*, held at the Centrum voor Wiskunde en Informatica (CWI), Amsterdam, the Netherlands on September 26–28, 1994. We would like the thank the Nederlandse Organisatie voor Wetenschapelijk Onderzoek (NWO) who funded this workshop as part of project NF 102/62-356, 'Structural and Semantic Parallels in Natural Languages and Programming Languages,' and Mieke Bruné, whose superb organization ensured the workshop's success. Finally, we would like to thank the authors and referees for their cooperation in the preparation of this volume.

Patrick Blackburn, Saarbrücken
Maarten de Rijke, Coventry

1

A Grammar Formalism and Cross-Serial Dependencies

Tore Burheim

ABSTRACT. First we define a unification grammar formalism called Tree Homomorphic Feature Structure Grammar. It is based on Lexical Functional Grammar (LFG), but has a strong restriction on the syntax of equations. We then show that this formalism defines a full abstract family of languages, and that it is capable of describing cross-serial dependencies of the type found in Swiss German.

1 Introduction

Due to their combination of simplicity and flexibility, unification grammars have become widely used in computational linguistics in the last fifteen years. But this flexibility reflects the fact that they are very powerful formalisms. As a result of this power, the membership problem for unification grammars in their most general form is undecidable. Therefore, most such grammars have restrictions to make them decidable, for example the *off-line parseability constraint* in LFG (Kaplan and Bresnan 1982). Even so, the membership problem is NP-complete (Barton et al. 1987) or harder for most unification formalisms. It is therefore interesting to study further restrictions on such grammars. GPSG (Gazdar et al. 1985), which was one of the first unification grammar formalisms, has only a finite number of possible feature structures and describes the class of context-free languages. From this it follows that we can decide in polynomial time if a given string is a member of the language generated by a GPSG-grammar. More recently, Keller and Weir (1995) have defined a grammar formalism where there is no common feature structure for the sentence as a whole, just feature structures annotating individual nodes of a phrase structure tree. As there are only limited possibilities of sharing information, the

Specifying Syntactic Structures
P. Blackburn and M. de Rijke, eds.
Copyright © 1997, CSLI Publications.

membership problem for this formalism can also be decided in polynomial time.

In this paper we will study a formalism that lies somewhere in between the most powerful and the most limited ones. The formalism is called Tree Homomorphic Feature Structure Grammar (THFSG), and it is based on Lexical Functional Grammar and work by Colban (1991). We show that this formalism defines a full abstract family of languages, and that it is capable of describing cross-serial dependencies of the type found in Swiss German.

What we here call unification grammars are also called attribute-value grammars, feature-structure grammars and constraint-based grammars. We may divide them into two major groups: those based on a phrase-structure backbone such as LFG and PATR, and those entirely described using feature structures such as HPSG (Pollard and Sag 1994). Here we will use a context-free phrase structure backbone and add equations to the nodes in the phrase-structure tree as is done in LFG. These equations will describe feature structures. Due to a restriction that we will impose on the equations in the grammar, the feature structures will be trees that are homomorphic images of the phrase structure tree. This homomorphism may be interesting from a computational point of view.

2 Feature Structures

One of the main characteristics of unification grammars is that they are information based. This information is inductively collected from the sentences sub-strings, sub-sub-strings, and so on. Feature structures are used to represent this information.

There are many ways of viewing, defining and describing feature structures; for example as directed acyclic graphs (Shieber 1986), as finite deterministic automata (Kasper and Rounds 1990), as models for first order logic (Smolka 1988, 1992, Johnson 1988), or as Kripke frames for modal logic (Blackburn 1994). Here we use a slightly modified version of the Kasper and Rounds (1990) definition of feature structures, and we will later use a subset of the equation schemata used by LFG to describe them.

We assume we are given two predefined sets, one of attribute symbols and one of value symbols. In a linguistic framework, attribute symbols will typically be things like *subject, object, number* and *case*, and value symbols will typically be things like *singular, plural, dative* and *accusative*.

Definition 2.1 A *feature structure* M over the set of attribute symbols A and value symbols V is a 4-tuple $\langle Q, f_D, \delta_0, \alpha \rangle$ where

- Q is a finite set of *nodes*,
- $f_D : D \to Q$ is a function, called the *name mapping function*, where D is a finite set of names,

- $\delta_0 : Q \times A \to Q$ is a partial function, called the *transition function*,
- $\alpha : Q \to V$ is a partial function, called the *atomic value function*.

We extend the transition function δ_0 to a partial function $\delta : (Q \times A^*) \to Q$ as follows: (1) For every $q \in Q$, $\delta(q, \varepsilon) = q$, (2) if $\delta(q_1, w) = q_2$ and $\delta_0(q_2, a) = q_3$ then $\delta(q_1, wa) = q_3$ for every $q_1, q_2, q_3 \in Q$, $w \in A^*$ and $a \in A$.

A feature structure is *well defined* if it is

- *atomic*: For all $q \in Q$, if $\alpha(q)$ is defined, then $\delta_0(q, a)$ is not defined for any $a \in A$.
- *acyclic*: For all $q \in Q$, $\delta(q, w) = q$ if and only if $w = \varepsilon$.
- *describable*: For all $q \in Q$ there exists an $x \in D$ and a $w \in A^*$ such that $\delta(f_D(x), w) = q$

All feature structures are required to be well defined.

We may also represent well defined feature structures as directed acyclic graphs, where all the edges are labeled with attribute symbols and some nodes without out-edges have assigned value symbols; an example is shown in Figure 2 below. In addition we name some nodes where each node may have more than one name.

Some definitions of feature structures require that they have an initial node from which one can reach every other node with the extended transition function. We prefer to use the name mapping function and to require feature structures to be describable. If instead of the name mapping function we add an initial node q_0, and replace the name mapping function by a definition of $\delta(q_0, x) = f_D(x)$ for all x such that $f_D(x)$ is defined, we get a feature structure with an initial node from a describable one with names. In the rest of the paper we will view the domain of names as implicitly defined in the name mapping function f and drop D as subscript.

We use equations to describe feature structures. Essentially, a set of equations describes the least feature structure that satisfies all the equations in the set. Let us make this precise.

A feature structure *satisfies* the equation

$$(1) \qquad\qquad x_1 w_1 = x_2 w_2$$

if and only if $\delta(f(x_1), w_1) = \delta(f(x_2), w_2)$, and the equation

$$(2) \qquad\qquad x_3 w_3 = v$$

if and only if $\alpha(\delta(f(x_3), w_3)) = v$, where $x_1, x_2, x_3 \in D$, $w_1, w_2, w_3 \in A^*$ and $v \in V$. It is worth emphasizing that $x_1 w_1 = x_2 w_2$ and $x_3 w_3 = v$ are the only two forms of equations we allow, and indeed, in the grammar formalism we will impose further restrictions.

If E is a set of equations and M is a well defined feature structure such that M satisfies every equation in E then we say that M *supports* E and we write

$$(3) \qquad\qquad M \models E.$$

If M_1 and M_2 are feature structures, we say that M_1 *subsumes* M_2, written $M_1 \sqsubseteq M_2$, if and only if for every set of equations E, if $M_1 \models E$ then $M_2 \models E$. Intuitively, if M_1 subsumes M_2 then M_2 contains all the information that M_1 contains. Two feature structures M_1 and M_2, are *equivalent* if and only if $M_1 \sqsubseteq M_2$ and $M_2 \sqsubseteq M_1$. This means that they contain the same information. Note that subsumption partially orders the classes of equivalent feature structures.

Given a set of equations E, we say that E *describes* a feature structure M if and only if $M \models E$ and for every feature structure M', if $M' \models E$ then $M \sqsubseteq M'$. Clearly, a given set of equations may describe different feature structures, but all the feature structures it describes are equivalent. Moreover, if an equation set is supported by a feature structure, then there exists a feature structure which the equation set describes. If E describes a feature structure M we write this as

$$(4) \qquad\qquad E \gg M.$$

The concepts we have introduced give us all we need to express the usual notion of unification. Let M_1 and M_2 be two well defined feature structures. Then the *unification* of M_1 and M_2, $(M_1 \sqcup M_2)$ is a feature structure such that $M_1 \sqsubseteq (M_1 \sqcup M_2)$, $M_2 \sqsubseteq (M_1 \sqcup M_2)$ and for every M' such that $M_1 \sqsubseteq M'$ and $M_2 \sqsubseteq M'$, $(M_1 \sqcup M_2) \sqsubseteq M'$. From the definition it follows that if $E_1 \gg M_1$ and $E_2 \gg M_2$ then $(E_1 \cup E_2) \gg (M_1 \sqcup M_2)$. So instead of using unification directly, we may collect equations and see if the collection describes a feature structure.

A set of equations E is *consistent* if there exists a well defined feature structure that E describes. It is possible that an equation set does not describe any well defined feature structure. We then say that the equation set is *inconsistent*. This happens, for instance, if the equation set contains both the equations $ea = v$ and $eaa = v$ for a value symbol v.

3 The Grammar Formalism

Tree Homomorphic Feature Structure Grammar[1] (THFSG) is based on LFG (Kaplan and Bresnan 1982), but is much simplified. The main differences are that we have a strong restriction on the sets of equation schemata, we treat the lexical items in almost the same way as production rules, and we do not have the completeness and coherence constraints or anything like the functional uncertainty mechanism (Kaplan et al. 1987). In short, we have tried to make the formalism as simple as possible.

---

[1]This grammar formalisms is part of a hierarchy of grammar formalisms, based on different equation formats and definitions of grammatical strings, described in Burheim (1992). What we here call THFSG is there named $RS_1 \& T_0$.

THFSG is very much like, and indeed may be seen as a generalization of, the grammar formalism $GF1$ defined by Colban (1991). There are two main differences. First, we accept empty right hand sides[2] in the lexicon rules. As we shall see, this gives us the ability to describe a full abstract family of languages, which $GF1$ does not (Burheim 1992). In addition, $GF1$ only accepts equation schemata in the format that THFSG-grammars have in their normal form.

Definition 3.1 A *Tree Homomorphic Feature Structure Grammar*, THFSG, is a 5-tuple $\langle \mathcal{K}, \mathcal{S}, \Sigma, \mathcal{P}, \mathcal{L} \rangle$ over the set of attribute symbols A and value symbols V where

- $\mathcal{K}$ is a finite set of symbols, called *categories*,
- $\mathcal{S} \in \mathcal{K}$ is a symbol, called *start symbol*,
- Σ is a finite set of symbols, called *terminals*,
- $\mathcal{P}$ is a finite set of *production rules*

$$(5) \qquad \begin{array}{ccccc} K_0 & \to & K_1 & \ldots & K_m \\ & & E_1 & & E_m \end{array}$$

where $m \geq 1$, K_0, ..., $K_m \in \mathcal{K}$, and for all i, $1 \leq i \leq m$, E_i is a finite set consisting of one and only one equation schema of the form $\uparrow a_1 \ldots a_n = \downarrow$ where $n \geq 0$ and $a_1, \ldots, a_n \in A$, and a finite number of equation schemata of the form $\uparrow a_1 \ldots a_n = v$ where $n \geq 1$, $a_1, \ldots,$ $a_n \in A$ and $v \in V$.

- $\mathcal{L}$ is a finite set of *lexicon rules*

$$(6) \qquad \begin{array}{ccc} K & \to & t \\ & & E \end{array}$$

where $K \in \mathcal{K}$, $t \in (\Sigma \cup \{\varepsilon\})$, and E is a finite set of equation schemata of the form $\uparrow a_1 \ldots a_n = v$ where $n \geq 1$, $a_1, \ldots, a_n \in A$ and $v \in V$.

The sets $\mathcal{K}$ and Σ are required to be disjoint.

As in LFG, we see that to each element on the right hand side of a production or lexicon rule, we annotate a set of equation schemata. These equation schemata differ from the equations used to describe feature structures: the schemata have up and down arrows where equations have names. The up and down arrows are *metavariables*: to get equations we instantiate the arrows to the nodes in the phrase structure tree. In the production rules, each set of equation schemata includes one and only one schema with both up and down arrows. In this schema we only allow attribute symbols on the left-hand side — none on the right-hand side. As a result of this we will later see that the described feature structure will be a tree that is a

---

[2]Empty right hand sides, or empty categories, are sometimes used in the analysis of various linguistic phenomena. For example, in LFG without functional uncertainty, empty right hand sides are used in the analysis of long-distance dependencies.

homomorphic image of the phrase structure tree, or *constituent structure* as we will call it.

We now define constituent structures and the set of grammatical strings with respect to a grammar. To define constituent structures we use tree domains. Let $\mathcal{N}_+$ be the set of all integers greater than zero. A *tree domain* D is a set $D \subseteq \mathcal{N}_+^*$ of number strings such that if $x \in D$ then all prefixes of x are also in D, and for all $i \in \mathcal{N}_+$ and $x \in \mathcal{N}_+^*$, if $xi \in D$ then $xj \in D$ for all j, $1 \leq j < i$. The *out degree* $d(x)$ of an element x in a tree domain D is the cardinality of the set $\{i \mid xi \in D, i \in \mathcal{N}_+\}$. The set of terminals of D is $term(D) = \{x \mid x \in D, d(x) = 0\}$. The elements of a tree domain are totally ordered lexicographically as follows: $x' \prec x$ if x' is a prefix of x, or there exist strings $y, z, z' \in \mathcal{N}_+^*$ and $i, j \in \mathcal{N}_+$ with $i < j$, such that $x' = yiz'$ and $x = yjz$. A tree domain may be infinite, but we restrict attention to finite tree domains.[3]

A tree domain D can be viewed as a tree graph in the following way. The elements of D are the nodes, ε is the root, and for every $x \in D$ the element $xi \in D$ is x's child number i. The terminals of D are the terminal nodes in the tree.

A tree domain describes the topology of a phrase structure tree. The representation is convenient because it provides a name for every node in the tree. We will substitute these names for the arrows used in the equation schemata.

Definition 3.2 A *constituent structure* (c-structure) based on a THFSG-grammar $G = \langle \mathcal{K}, \mathcal{S}, \Sigma, \mathcal{P}, \mathcal{L} \rangle$ is a triple $\langle D, K, E \rangle$ where

- D is a finite tree domain,
- $K : D \to (\mathcal{K} \cup \Sigma \cup \{\varepsilon\})$ is a function,
- $E : (D - \{\varepsilon\}) \to \Gamma$ is a function where Γ is the set of all sets of equation schemata in G,

such that $K(x) \in (\Sigma \cup \{\varepsilon\})$ for all $x \in term(D)$, $K(\varepsilon) = \mathcal{S}$, and for all $x \in (D - term(D))$, if $d(x) = m$ then

$$(7) \qquad \begin{array}{cccc} K(x) & \to & K(x1) & \dots & K(xm) \\ & & E(x1) & & E(xm) \end{array}$$

is a production or lexicon rule in G. The *terminal string* of a constituent structure is the string $K(x_1) \dots K(x_n)$ such that $\{x_1, \dots, x_n\} = term(D)$ and $x_i \prec x_{i+1}$ for all i, $1 \leq i < n$.

Here the function K labels the nonterminal nodes with category symbols and the terminal nodes with terminal symbols. The terminal string is a string in Σ^* since $K(x) \in (\Sigma \cup \{\varepsilon\})$ for all $x \in term(D)$. The function E assigns a set of equation schemata to each node in the tree domain.

---

[3]See Gallier (1986) for more about tree domains.

This is done such that each mother-node together with all its daughters corresponds to a production or lexicon rule. To get equations that can be used to describe feature structures we must instantiate the up and down arrows in the equation schemata from the production and lexicon rules. We substitute them with nodes from the c-structure. For this purpose we define the $'$-function such that

$$(8) \qquad E'(xi) = E(xi)[x/\!\!\uparrow, xi/\!\!\downarrow]$$

We see that the value of the function E' is a set of equations that feature structures may support.

Definition 3.3 The c-structure $\langle D, K, E \rangle$ *generates* the feature structure M if and only if

$$(9) \qquad \bigcup_{x \in (D - \{\varepsilon\})} E'(x) \gg M$$

A c-structure is *consistent* if it generates a feature structure.

The nonterminal part of the tree domain will form the name set for feature structures that this union describes. A c-structure is consistent if this union is consistent and a string is grammatical if its c-structure is consistent.

Definition 3.4 Let G be a THFSG-grammar. A string w is *grammatical* with respect to G if and only if there exists a consistent c-structure with w as the terminal string.

The set of all grammatical strings[4] with respect to a grammar G is denoted $L(G)$ and is the language that the grammar G generates. Two grammars G and G' are *equivalent* if $L(G) = L(G')$.

Example 3.5 Assume that *next* and *lex* are attribute symbols in A, and a, b, c and $\$$ are value symbols in V. Let G_1 be the THFSG-grammar $\langle \mathcal{K}, S, \Sigma, \mathcal{P}, \mathcal{L} \rangle$ where $\mathcal{K} = \{S, B, B', C, C', C''\}$, $\Sigma = \{a, b, c\}$ and $\mathcal{P}$ contains the following production rules

$$(10) \qquad S \;\rightarrow\; \begin{array}{cccc} B & C & C & B \\ \uparrow = \downarrow & \uparrow = \downarrow & \uparrow = \downarrow & \uparrow = \downarrow \end{array}$$

$$(11) \quad C \;\rightarrow\; \begin{array}{cc} C & C \\ \uparrow next = \downarrow & \uparrow next = \downarrow \end{array} \qquad C \;\rightarrow\; \begin{array}{c} C' \\ \uparrow = \downarrow \\ \uparrow next = \$ \end{array}$$

---

[4]We may have different definitions of which strings are grammatical. For grammars in normal form (see below) we may also require a c-structure to (correctly) generate a feature structure that for any two nodes x and y in the c-structure, if $\delta(f(x), w) = f(y)$ then $f(x) = f(x')$, where x' is the greatest common prefix of x and y (or in other words, x' is the closest common predecessor). If we add this constraint we get a grammar formalism that describes the class of context-free languages (Burheim 1992, Colban 1991).

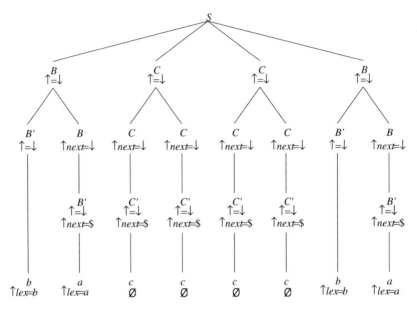

FIGURE 1 c-structure for the string "baccccba" in $L(G_1)$.

$$(12) \quad \begin{array}{ccc} B & \to & B' \quad\quad B \\ & & \uparrow = \downarrow \quad \uparrow next = \downarrow \end{array} \quad\quad\quad \begin{array}{ccc} B & \to & B' \\ & & \uparrow = \downarrow \\ & & \uparrow next = \$ \end{array}$$

Moreover, $\mathcal{L}$ contains the following lexicon rules

$$(13) \quad \begin{array}{ccc} B' & \to & a \\ & & \uparrow lex = a \end{array} \quad\quad\quad \begin{array}{ccc} B' & \to & b \\ & & \uparrow lex = b \end{array}$$

$$\begin{array}{ccc} C' & \to & c \\ & & \emptyset \end{array}$$

Figure 1 shows the c-structure for the string *baccccba*. The following are the equations we get from the left subtree after we have instantiated the up and down arrows:

$$(14) \quad \begin{array}{rcl} \varepsilon & = & 1 \\ 1 & = & 11 \\ 11 \; lex & = & b \end{array} \quad\quad\quad \begin{array}{rcl} 1 \; next & = & 12 \\ 12 & = & 121 \\ 12 \; next & = & \$ \\ 121 \; lex & = & a \end{array}$$

These are only a subset of all the equations from the c-structure. Figure 2 shows a feature structure which the c-structure generates. This shows

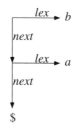

FIGURE 2 Feature-structure (without names)
for the string "baccccba" in $L(G_1)$.

that *baccccba* is grammatical with respect to G_1. The language generated
by G_1 is

(15) $$L(G_1) = \{wc^{2^n}w \mid w \in \{a,b\}^* \wedge |w| = n \wedge n \geq 1\}$$

Here we use the attribute *next* to count the length of the w substring and
the attribute *lex* to distribute information about its content.

In this grammar formalism we allow one and only one equation schema
with both up and down arrows in each set of equation schemata in the
production rules. Moreover, in this schema we only allow attribute symbols
on the left hand side — none on the right hand side. As a result the feature
structures will be trees and the domination relation in the c-structure is
preserved in the feature structure (Colban 1991). The domination relation
must not be confused with the lexicographical ordering of the nodes in
the c-structure, so let us explicitly define the domination relation on the
c-structure and the feature structure. First, for all the nodes x in the tree
domain D of a c-structure, let $x' \leq_c x$ for all prefixes x' of x. This is the
traditional predecessor relation on tree graphs. In the feature structure,
let $q' \leq_M q$ for all nodes such that $\delta(q', w) = q$ for a $w \in A^*$. Then a node
in a feature structure dominates another node if there exists an attribute
path from the first node to the second node. For any c-structure $\langle D, K, E \rangle$
which generates a feature structure M we then have

(16) $$x' \leq_c x \Rightarrow f(x') \leq_M f(x).$$

Then the name function $f : D \to Q$ is a homomorphism between the node
sets with the domination relation of those two structures (Colban 1991).

We conclude this presentation of THFSG-grammars by defining a *normal
form*.

Definition 3.6 A THFSG-grammar $G = \langle \mathcal{K}, \mathcal{S}, \Sigma, \mathcal{P}, \mathcal{L} \rangle$ is in *normal form*
if each production rule in $\mathcal{P}$ is of the form

(17) $$\begin{array}{ccc} K_0 & \to & K_1 \quad K_2 \\ & & E_1 \quad E_2 \end{array}$$

where $K_0, K_1, K_2 \in \mathcal{K}$, and each of the equation schema sets, E_1 and E_2, is a finite set consisting of one and only one equation schema of the form $\uparrow a = \downarrow$ or $\uparrow = \downarrow$ where $a \in A$, and a finite number of equation schemata of the form $\uparrow a_1 \ldots a_n = v$ where $n \geq 1$, $a_1, \ldots, a_n \in A$ and $v \in V$.

We see that a THFSG-grammar is in normal form if every production rule has exactly two elements on the right hand side and the equation schemata with both up and down arrows have no more than one attribute symbol.

Lemma 3.7 *For every* THFSG-*grammar there exist an equivalent* THFSG-*grammar in normal form.*

Proof. We show how to construct a THFSG-grammar in normal form G' for any THFSG-grammar G such that $L(G) = L(G')$. There are two constraints for grammars in normal form, one on the equation schemata, and one on the format of the production rules. First we show how to get the equation schemata right.

For each set of equation schemata E_i with an equation schema

$$(18) \qquad\qquad \uparrow a_1 \ldots a_n = \downarrow,$$

where $n > 1$ in each production rule

$$(19) \qquad\qquad \begin{matrix} K_0 & \to & K_1 & \ldots & K_i & \ldots & K_m \\ & & E_1 & & E_i & & E_m \end{matrix}$$

we replace K_i with a unique new category $K'_{i,1}$ and E_i with the set $E'_i = (E_i - \{\uparrow a_1 \ldots a_n = \downarrow\}) \cup \{\uparrow a_1 = \downarrow\}$, and add the new production rules:

$$(20) \qquad\qquad \begin{matrix} K'_{i,(j-1)} & \to & K'_{i,j} \\ & & \uparrow a_j = \downarrow \end{matrix}$$

for all j, $2 \leq j \leq n$, where $K'_{i,2} \ldots K'_{i,n-1}$ are unique new categories and $K'_{i,n} = K_i$. Now each set of equation schemata in each production rule is of the required form.

Next we must get the production rules right. First, replace each production rule

$$(21) \qquad\qquad \begin{matrix} K_0 & \to & K_1 & \ldots & K_m \\ & & E_1 & & E_m \end{matrix}$$

where $m > 2$, with the two production rules

$$(22) \qquad\qquad \begin{matrix} K_0 & \to & K_1 & K'_2 \\ & & E_1 & \uparrow = \downarrow \end{matrix}$$

(23)
$$K'_{m-1} \rightarrow \begin{array}{cc} K_{m-1} & K_m \\ E_{m-1} & E_m \end{array}$$

together with the new production rules

(24)
$$K'_i \rightarrow \begin{array}{cc} K_i & K'_{i+1} \\ E_i & \uparrow = \downarrow \end{array}$$

for all i, $2 \leq i \leq (m-2)$ where $K'_2, \ldots, K'_{m-1}$ are unique new categories.

Next, if $m = 1$ in production rule (21), replace it with the new production rule

(25)
$$K_0 \rightarrow \begin{array}{cc} K_1 & \tilde{\varepsilon} \\ E_1 & \uparrow = \downarrow \end{array}$$

and add the lexicon rule

(26)
$$\tilde{\varepsilon} \rightarrow \begin{array}{c} \varepsilon \\ \emptyset \end{array}$$

where $\tilde{\varepsilon}$ is a new category.

Now we have a grammar in normal form, and it is easy to see that we have a consistent c-structure for a string based on the original grammar if and only if we have a consistent c-structure for the same string based on the grammar in normal form. Thus $L(G) = L(G')$. $\square$

4 Full Abstract Family of Languages

When studying formal grammars we often want to study the *class of languages* that a grammar formalism defines. A class of languages $\mathcal{C}_\Gamma$ over a countable set of symbols Γ is a set of languages such that for each language $L \in \mathcal{C}_\Gamma$ there exists a finite subset Σ of Γ such that $L \subseteq \Sigma^*$. The class $\mathcal{C}_\Gamma(GF)$ of languages that a grammar formalism GF defines is the set of all languages L' over Γ such that there exists a grammar G in GF such that $L(G) = L'$.

For a given countably infinite Γ, an uncountable number of different classes of languages exist. Some of them are more natural and well-behaved than others, and of particular interest are the *full abstract families of languages* (full AFL). A full AFL is a class of languages closed under union, concatenation, Kleene closure, intersection with regular languages, string homomorphism and inverse string homomorphism[5]. The class of regular

---

[5] See Ginsburg (1975) for more about full abstract families of languages.

languages and context-free languages are both full AFL, but the class of context-sensitive languages is not since they are not closed under homomorphism (Hopcroft and Ullman 1979). Here we show that the class of languages that the grammar formalism THFSG defines,[6] $C(\text{THFSG})$, is a full abstract family of languages.

As a first step, we spell out the concepts underlying the definition of full abstract families of languages. A string homomorphism is a function $h : \Delta^* \to \Sigma^*$ such that for every $w \in \Delta^*$ and $a \in \Delta$ we have

$$(27) \qquad h(\varepsilon) \;=\; \varepsilon$$
$$(28) \qquad h(aw) \;=\; h(a)h(w).$$

A string homomorphic image of a language $L \subseteq \Delta^*$ for a string homomorphism $h : \Delta^* \to \Sigma^*$ is the language $h(L) = \{h(w) \mid w \in L\}$. The inverse string homomorphic image of a language $L' \subseteq \Sigma^*$ is the language $h^{-1}(L') = \{w \mid h(w) \in L'\}$. The concatenation of two languages L_1 and L_2 is the language $L_1 L_2 = \{w_1 w_2 \mid w_1 \in L_1 \wedge w_2 \in L_2\}$. The Kleene closure of a language L is the language $L^* = \{w_1 \ldots w_n \mid n \geq 0 \wedge w_1, \ldots, w_n \in L\}$. Union and intersection are the standard set-theoretic operations.

Lemma 4.1 $C(\text{THFSG})$ *is closed under union, concatenation and Kleene-closure.*

Proof. Let $G = \langle \mathcal{K}, \mathcal{S}, \Sigma, \mathcal{P}, \mathcal{L} \rangle$ and $G' = \langle \mathcal{K}', \mathcal{S}', \Sigma', \mathcal{P}', \mathcal{L}' \rangle$ be two THFSG-grammars and assume that $(\mathcal{K} \cap \mathcal{K}') = \emptyset$, $\mathcal{S}_0 \notin (\mathcal{K} \cup \mathcal{K}' \cup \Sigma \cup \Sigma')$, and that *first* and *next* are not used as attribute symbols in G or G'.

Union: Let $G_\cup$ be the grammar $\langle \mathcal{K} \cup \mathcal{K}' \cup \{\mathcal{S}_0\}, \mathcal{S}_0, \Sigma \cup \Sigma', \mathcal{P}'', \mathcal{L} \cup \mathcal{L}' \rangle$ where $\mathcal{P}''$ is the least set such that $(\mathcal{P} \cup \mathcal{P}') \subseteq \mathcal{P}''$ and $\mathcal{P}''$ contains the following two production rules:

$$(29) \qquad\qquad \mathcal{S}_0 \;\to\; \begin{array}{c} \mathcal{S} \\ \uparrow = \downarrow \end{array}$$

$$(30) \qquad\qquad \mathcal{S}_0 \;\to\; \begin{array}{c} \mathcal{S}' \\ \uparrow = \downarrow \end{array}$$

Then $G_\cup$ is a THFSG-grammar and it is trivial that $L(G_\cup) = L(G) \cup L(G')$.

Concatenation: Let G_c be the grammar $\langle \mathcal{K} \cup \mathcal{K}' \cup \{\mathcal{S}_0\}, \mathcal{S}_0, \Sigma \cup \Sigma', \mathcal{P}'', \mathcal{L} \cup \mathcal{L}' \rangle$ where $\mathcal{P}''$ is the least set such that $(\mathcal{P} \cup \mathcal{P}') \subseteq \mathcal{P}''$ and $\mathcal{P}''$ contains the following production rule:

$$(31) \qquad\qquad \mathcal{S}_0 \;\to\; \begin{array}{cc} \mathcal{S} & \mathcal{S}' \\ \uparrow\!first = \downarrow & \uparrow\!next = \downarrow \end{array}$$

---

[6]We assume here that Γ is the set of all symbols that we use and drop Γ as subscript in $C(\text{THFSG})$.

Then G_c is a THFSG-grammar and it is trivial that $L(G_c) = L(G)L(G')$.

Kleene-closure: Let G_* be the grammar $\langle \mathcal{K} \cup \{\mathcal{S}_0\}, \mathcal{S}_0, \Sigma, \mathcal{P}'', \mathcal{L}'' \rangle$ where $\mathcal{P}''$ is the least set such that $\mathcal{P} \subseteq \mathcal{P}''$ and $\mathcal{P}''$ contains the following production rule:

(32)
$$\mathcal{S}_0 \quad \rightarrow \quad \underset{\uparrow first\, =\, \downarrow}{\mathcal{S}} \quad \underset{\uparrow next\, =\, \downarrow}{\mathcal{S}_0}$$

Moreover is $\mathcal{L}''$ the least set such that $\mathcal{L} \subseteq \mathcal{L}''$ and $\mathcal{L}''$ contains the following lexicon rule:

(33)
$$\mathcal{S}_0 \quad \rightarrow \quad \underset{\emptyset}{\varepsilon}$$

Then G_* is a THFSG-grammar and it is trivial that $L(G_*) = L(G)^*$. $\quad\square$

To show that $\mathcal{C}(\text{THFSG})$ is closed under intersection with regular languages, string homomorphism and inverse string homomorphism, we show that $\mathcal{C}(\text{THFSG})$ is closed under NFT-mapping. Informally, a *Nondeterministic Finite Transducer* (NFT) is a nondeterministic finite state machine with an additional write tape. In addition to just reading symbols and changing states, an NFT also writes symbols on the write tape. It may write symbols and change states when reading the empty string. Formally, an NFT is a 6-tuple $M = \langle Q, \Delta, \Sigma, \delta_0, q_0, F \rangle$ where Q is a finite set of states, Δ is an input-alphabet, Σ is an output-alphabet, δ_0 is a function from $Q \times (\Delta \cup \{\varepsilon\})$ to finite subsets of $Q \times \Sigma^*$, $q_0 \in Q$ is the initial state and $F \subseteq Q$ is a set of final states.

For every $q_1, q_2, q_3 \in Q, a \in (\Delta \cup \{\varepsilon\}), w \in \Delta^*$ and $x, y \in \Sigma^*$, the extended transition function δ from $Q \times \Delta^*$ to subsets of $Q \times \Sigma^*$ is defined as the least function satisfying the following:

(34)
$$(q_1, \varepsilon) \in \delta(q_1, \varepsilon)$$

(35) $\quad (q_2, x) \in \delta(q_1, w) \wedge (q_3, y) \in \delta_0(q_2, a) \Rightarrow (q_3, xy) \in \delta(q_1, wa).$

For any NFT $M = \langle Q, \Delta, \Sigma, \delta_0, q_0, F \rangle$, the NFT-mapping M of a string $w \in \Delta^*$ and a language $L \subseteq \Delta^*$ is defined as follows:

(36)
$$M(w) \quad = \quad \{x \mid \exists q \in F : (q, x) \in \delta(q_0, w)\}$$

(37)
$$M(L) \quad = \quad \bigcup_{w \in L} M(w).$$

Furthermore, the inverse NFT-mapping M^{-1} of a string $x \in \Sigma^*$ and a language $L' \subseteq \Sigma^*$ is defined as follows:

(38)
$$M^{-1}(x) \quad = \quad \{w \mid x \in M(w)\}$$

$$(39) \qquad\qquad M^{-1}(L') \;=\; \bigcup_{w \in L'} M^{-1}(w).$$

The definition of NFT is sufficiently general to ensure that for any given NFT-mapping, the inverse NFT-mapping is also an NFT-mapping. A finite state machine is a special version of an NFT, which writes every symbol it reads, and does not change state or write anything while reading the empty string. If M is a finite state machine version of an NFT, then $M(L)$ is the intersection of L and the regular language that the finite state machine describes.

A string homomorphism $h : \Delta^* \to \Sigma^*$ can be expressed by an NFT. Let M_h be the NFT $\langle Q, \Delta, \Sigma, \delta_0, q_0, F \rangle$ such that $Q = F = \{q_0\}$ and for all $a \in \Delta$, $\delta(q_0, a) = \{(q_0, h(a))\}$. Then $h(L) = M_h(L)$ for any language $L \subseteq \Delta^*$ and the inverse string homomorphism can also be expressed with an NFT-mapping.

If we can show that the class $\mathcal{C}(\text{THFSG})$ is closed under NFT-mapping, it follows that $\mathcal{C}(\text{THFSG})$ is closed under intersection with regular languages, string homomorphism and inverse string homomorphism. We do this by first defining a grammar from a THFSG-grammar in normal form and an NFT, and then we show that this grammar generates the NFT-mapping of the language generated by the first grammar. The use of NFT-mappings to show these closure properties is inspired by Aho (1968).

Definition 4.2 Let $G = \langle \mathcal{K}, \mathcal{S}, \Delta, \mathcal{P}, \mathcal{L} \rangle$ be a THFSG-grammar in normal form, and let $M = \langle Q, \Delta, \Sigma, \delta_0, q_0, F \rangle$ be a Nondeterministic Finite Transducer. Assume that the symbols $\mathcal{S}_0$ and $\tilde{a}$ for all $a \in (\Sigma \cup \{\varepsilon\})$ are not used in G. The grammar $G_M = \langle \mathcal{K}', \mathcal{S}_0, \Sigma, \mathcal{P}', \mathcal{L}' \rangle$ for the NFT-image $M(L(G))$ is defined as follows.

Let $\mathcal{K}'$ be the set $(Q \times (\mathcal{K} \cup \Delta \cup \{\varepsilon\}) \times Q) \cup \{\tilde{a} \mid a \in (\Sigma \cup \{\varepsilon\})\} \cup \{\mathcal{S}_0\}$ and let $\mathcal{P}'$ and $\mathcal{L}'$ be the least sets such that:

(a) For all $q \in F$, the following is a rule in $\mathcal{P}'$:

$$(40) \qquad\qquad \mathcal{S}_0 \;\to\; \begin{array}{c} (q_0, \mathcal{S}, q) \\ \uparrow\,=\,\downarrow \end{array}$$

(b) For all production rules

$$(41) \qquad\qquad \begin{array}{ccc} K_0 & \to & K_1 \quad K_2 \\ & & E_1 \quad E_2 \end{array}$$

in $\mathcal{P}$ and all $q_1, q_2, q_3 \in Q$, the following is a rule in $\mathcal{P}'$:

$$(42) \qquad (q_1, K_0, q_3) \;\to\; \begin{array}{cc} (q_1, K_1, q_2) & (q_2, K_2, q_3) \\ E_1 & E_2 \end{array}$$

(c) For all lexicon rules

$$(43) \qquad\qquad K \;\;\rightarrow\;\; \begin{matrix} b \\ E \end{matrix}$$

in $\mathcal{L}$ and all $q_1, q_2 \in Q$, the following is a rule in $\mathcal{P}'$:

$$(44) \qquad (q_1, K, q_2) \;\;\rightarrow\;\; \begin{matrix} (q_1, b, q_2) \\ E \cup \{\uparrow = \downarrow\} \end{matrix}$$

(d) For all $q_1, q_2, q_3 \in Q$ and all $b \in (\Delta \cup \{\varepsilon\})$, the following are rules in P'

$$(45) \qquad (q_1, b, q_3) \;\;\rightarrow\;\; \begin{matrix} (q_1, b, q_2) \\ \uparrow = \downarrow \end{matrix} \quad \begin{matrix} (q_2, \varepsilon, q_3) \\ \uparrow = \downarrow \end{matrix}$$

$$(46) \qquad (q_1, b, q_3) \;\;\rightarrow\;\; \begin{matrix} (q_1, \varepsilon, q_2) \\ \uparrow = \downarrow \end{matrix} \quad \begin{matrix} (q_2, b, q_3) \\ \uparrow = \downarrow \end{matrix}$$

(e) For all $q_1, q_2 \in Q, b \in (\Delta \cup \{\varepsilon\})$ and $y \in \Sigma^*$, such that $(q_2, y) \in \delta_0(q_1, b)$ where $y = a_1 \ldots a_n$ for $|y| = n \geq 1$, or if $y = \varepsilon$ let $\tilde{a}_1 = \tilde{\varepsilon}$ and $n = 1$, the following is a production rule in $\mathcal{P}'$:

$$(47) \qquad (q_1, b, q_2) \;\;\rightarrow\;\; \begin{matrix} \tilde{a}_1 \\ \uparrow = \downarrow \end{matrix} \quad \cdots \quad \begin{matrix} \tilde{a}_n \\ \uparrow = \downarrow \end{matrix}$$

(f) For all $a \in (\Sigma \cup \{\varepsilon\})$, the following is a rule in $\mathcal{L}'$:

$$(48) \qquad\qquad \tilde{a} \;\;\rightarrow\;\; \begin{matrix} a \\ \emptyset \end{matrix}$$

The main idea in this definition is that if a node in a c-structure based on G with category K is the root of a sub-c-structure with x as terminal string and the NFT accepts x as input string in a state q, then there is a corresponding node in a c-structure based on G_M with category (q, K, p). This node is the root of a sub-c-structure with y as terminal string such that $(p, y) \in \delta(q, x)$, or less formally, such that the NFT may write y when reading the string x processing from state q to p (Figure 3). This is done such that the new c-structure gives a specification of how the NFT processes the input string, changes states and writes symbols. Downwards in the new c-structure we get more and more details of how the string is

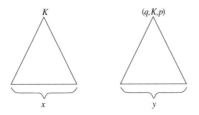

FIGURE 3 Transformation to the NFT-mappings grammar for $(p, y) \in \delta(q, x)$.

processed. In the end the grandmothers of the terminal nodes correspond to each transition step.

In the definition, part (a), (b) and (c) give us for any c-structure based on G with $w = b_1 \ldots b_n$ as terminal string, the upper part of a new c-structure based on G_M, where the upper part is isomorphic with the first c-structure except that it will have an additional root node on the top. The main point here is that the terminal nodes in the first c-structure will have corresponding nodes with possible categories

$$(49) \qquad (q_0, b_1, q_1), (q_1, b_2, q_2), \ldots, (q_{n-1}, b_n, q_n)$$

in the new one, for any sequence of states, q_0, q_1, ..., q_n where q_0 is the initial state, and q_n is a final state. This is done such that if a node has (exactly) two daughters labeled (q, K_1, q') and (q'', K_2, q'''), q' must be equal to q'' and the mother node must be labeled (q, K_0, q''') where K_0, K_1 and K_3 are the categories labeling the corresponding nodes in the first c-structure. Part (d) in the definition allows the NFT to write symbols and change states while reading the empty string. In part (e) we limit the previous parts of the definition such that all c-structures must correspond to the transition function in the NFT. This is achieved by requiring that for any symbol $b \in (\Delta \cup \{\varepsilon\})$, the triple category (q_1, b, q_2) can only label the grandmother nodes of the terminal nodes in a c-structure if in fact there exists a one step transition from state q_1 to q_2 while reading b. The daughters of this node have nonterminal categories representing the output symbols of this one step transition. The last part of the definition (f) is just the lexical complement of part (e).

Note also that the sets of equation schemata in the lexicon and production rules of the original grammar are transferred to the new grammar without any significant modification. Thus, in practice we obtain the same constraints on c-structures based on the new grammar as on the corresponding c-structures based on the original grammar.

Lemma 4.3 $\mathcal{C}(\textsc{thfsg})$ *is closed under NFT-mapping.*

Proof. Given Definition 4.2 we have to show that for all strings in $u \in \Sigma^*$,

$u \in L(G_M)$ if and only if there exist a string w in $L(G)$ and a final state $q \in F$ such that $(q, u) \in \delta(q_0, w)$.

($\Rightarrow$) Assume that we have a consistent c-structure based on G_M with u as terminal string such that $u \in L(G_M)$. (1) By induction on the height of the nodes we have from (d), (e) and (f) in Definition 4.2 that if a node with category (q, b, q') is a root of a sub-c-structure with y as terminal string, where $b \in (\Delta \cup \{\varepsilon\})$, then $(q', y) \in \delta(q, b)$. (2) By a top down induction on the c-structure we have from (a), (b), (c), and (d) in Definition 4.2 that for any horizontal node-cut of nodes labeled with triple categories

(50) $$(q_1, \beta_1, q_1'), \ldots, (q_n, \beta_n, q_n')$$

where $\beta_1, \ldots, \beta_n \in (\mathcal{K} \cup \Delta \cup \{\varepsilon\})$, that $q_i' = q_{i+1}$ for all i, $1 \leq i < n$, q_1 is the initial state and q_n' is a final state. (3) There exists a sequence of the topmost nodes with triple categories where each β_i is in $(\Delta \cup \{\varepsilon\})$ and where each node has a mother node with a category (q_i', K_i, q_i) for $K_i \in \mathcal{K}$. This sequence forms a node cut and if

(51) $$(q_0, b_1, q_1), (q_1, b_2, q_2), \ldots, (q_{n-1}, b_n, q_n)$$

are the categories labeling these nodes in lexicographical order, this sequence give us a string $w = b_1 \ldots b_n$ in Δ^*. The concatenation of the terminal strings $y_1, \ldots, y_n$ of the sub-c-structures where these nodes are the roots is u. From the definition of the extended transition function and the induction in the first part we have that $(q_n, u) \in \delta(q_0, w)$. (4) By reversing Definition 4.2 (b) and (c) it is straightforward to construct a c-structure for w based on G, and if the c-structure for u generates a feature structure so must the one for w, since we do not add any equation schemata. Then $w \in L(G)$.

($\Leftarrow$) Assume that we have a $w \in L(G)$ and a final state q such that $(q, u) \in \delta(q_0, w)$, for a string $u \in \Sigma^*$. Since $(q, u) \in \delta(q_0, w)$ there must be a processing of w of the NFT with u as output. Following the discussion of Definition 4.2 it is straightforward to construct a c-structure for u based on G_M which specifies the processing of w in M. If the c-structure for w generates a feature structure so must the new one also, since we do not add any substantial new equation schemata. Then $u \in L(G_M)$. $\square$

From Lemma 4.1 and Lemma 4.3 we have the main result in this section.

Theorem 4.4 $\mathcal{C}(\text{THFSG})$ *is a full abstract family of languages.*

5 Cross-Serial Dependencies

The last ten to fifteen years saw a revival of the discussion of whether or not natural languages could be described by context-free grammars (Gazdar and Pullum 1982). This discussion distinguishes between a grammar's capacity to describe a language *strongly*, that is, to describe the language as a structured set, or *weakly*, that is, to describe the language as a set of strings. Cross-serial dependencies are one of the main properties that were eventually used to show that context-free grammars are *not* capable of even weakly describing natural language.

Cross-serial dependencies occur in languages like

$$(52) \qquad \{xx \mid x \in \Sigma^*\}^7$$

and

$$(53) \qquad \{wa^m b^n x c^m d^n y \mid w, x, y, \in \Sigma^*, m, n \geq 1, a, b, c, d \in \Sigma\}.$$

Shieber (1985) showed that Swiss German contain cross-serial dependencies. This is due to two facts about Swiss German:

"First, Swiss German uses case-marking (dative and accusative) on objects, just as standard German does; different verbs subcategorize for objects of different case. Second, Swiss German, like Dutch, allows cross-serial order for the structure of subordinate clauses. Of critical importance is the fact that Swiss German requires appropriate case-marking to hold even within the cross-serial construction." Shieber (1985, page 334).

This occurs, for example, in the following subordinate clauses preceded by *"Jan säit das"* (*"Jan says that"*):[8]

	...mer	em Hans	es huus	hälfed	aastriiche
(54)	...we	Hans(DAT)	the house(ACC)	helped	paint

...we helped Hans paint the house.

Here the verb *hälfed* subcategorizes for an object in dative; *em Hans*, and the verb *aastriiche* subcategorizes for an object in accusative; *es huus*. Shieber shows that this dependency is robust and that it holds in quite complex clauses, as seen in this example:

	...mer	d'chind	em Hans	es huus
(55)	...we	the children(ACC)	Hans(DAT)	the house(ACC)

	haend	wele	laa	hälfe	aastriiche
	have	wanted	let	help	paint

...we have wanted to let the children help Hans paint the house.

If we change the cases of the objects then the strings become ungrammatical. Shieber (1985, page 336) specifies four claims that this construction in Swiss German satisfies:

1. "Swiss-German subordinate clauses can have a structure in which all the Vs follow all the NPs."
2. "Among such sentences, those with all dative NP's preceding all accusative NPs, and all dative-subcategorizing Vs preceding all accusative-subcategorizing Vs are acceptable."

---

[7]We assume that Σ has more than one symbol.

[8]All linguistic data is from Shieber (1985).

3. "The number of Vs requiring dative objects (for example, *hälfe*) must equal the number of dative NPs (for example, *em Hans*) and similarly for accusatives (*laa* and *chind*)."
4. "An arbitrary number of Vs can occur in a subordinate clause of this type (subject, of course, to performance constraints)."

Shieber then shows that any language that satisfies these claims cannot be context-free, since such languages allow constructions of the form $wa^m b^n x c^m d^n y$. Here we study the language L which contains strings of the form

(56) *Jan säit das mer* $N_1 \ldots N_n$ *es huus haend wele* $V_1 \ldots V_n$ *aastriiche,*

where $n \geq 1$ and

$$N_i \in \{em\ Hans,\ es\ Hans,\ d`chind\}^9$$

and $V_i \in \{hälfe,\ laa\}$ for all i, $1 \geq i \geq n$, and such that $V_i = hälfe$ if and only if $N_i = em\ Hans$.

We see that this is a subset of Swiss German with the right case marking and subcategorizing, and that it satisfies Shieber's claims. Hence it cannot be context-free. To make it easier to study we use the following homomorphism:[10]

(57)
$$
\begin{aligned}
h(Jan\ s\ddot{a}it\ das\ mer) &= x \\
h(es\ huus\ haend\ wele) &= y \\
h(aastriiche) &= z \\
h(s) &= s \quad \text{for all } s \in (N_{all} \cup V_{all}).
\end{aligned}
$$

where N_{all} is the set $\{em\ Hans,\ es\ Hans,\ d`chind\}$ and V_{all} is the set $\{hälfe,\ laa\}$. We then have that $h(L)$ is the following language:

(58) $\quad h(L) \quad = \quad \{x N_1 \ldots N_n y V_1 \ldots V_n z \mid$
$$n \geq 1 \wedge$$
$$\forall i\ 1 \leq i \leq n\ [N_i \in N_{all} \wedge V_i \in V_{all} \wedge$$
$$(V_i = h\ddot{a}lfe \iff N_i = em\ Hans)]\}$$

We construct the following THFSG-grammar $G = \langle \mathcal{K}, \mathcal{S}, \Sigma, \mathcal{P}, \mathcal{L} \rangle$ for the language $h(L)$: Let

$$
\begin{aligned}
\Sigma &= \{em\ Hans,\ es\ Hans,\ d`chind,\ h\ddot{a}lfe,\ laa, x, y, z\}, \text{ and} \\
\mathcal{K} &= \{S, VP, V, NP, N, X, Y, Z\}
\end{aligned}
$$

We have the following production rules in $\mathcal{P}$:

$$
\begin{array}{cccccc}
S & \to & X & NP & Y & VP & Z \\
& & \uparrow = \downarrow & \uparrow = \downarrow & \uparrow = \downarrow & \uparrow = \downarrow & \uparrow = \downarrow
\end{array}
$$

---

[9] For simplicity we define the constructions *em Hans*, *es Hans* and *d`chind* as atomic symbols.

[10] We can do this since our grammar formalism is closed under string homomorphism and inverse string homomorphism.

$$NP \rightarrow \begin{array}{cc} N & NP \\ \uparrow obj = \downarrow & \uparrow vcomp = \downarrow \end{array} \qquad NP \rightarrow \begin{array}{c} N \\ \uparrow obj = \downarrow \\ \uparrow vcomp = null \end{array}$$

$$VP \rightarrow \begin{array}{cc} V & VP \\ \uparrow = \downarrow & \uparrow vcomp = \downarrow \end{array} \qquad VP \rightarrow \begin{array}{c} V \\ \uparrow = \downarrow \\ \uparrow vcomp = null \end{array}$$

We have the following lexicon rules in $\mathcal{L}$:

$$N \rightarrow \begin{array}{c} em\ Hans \\ \uparrow case = DAT \end{array} \qquad N \rightarrow \begin{array}{c} es\ Hans \\ \uparrow case = ACC \end{array}$$

$$N \rightarrow \begin{array}{c} d'chind \\ \uparrow case = ACC \end{array}$$

$$V \rightarrow \begin{array}{c} la \\ \uparrow obj\ case = ACC \end{array} \qquad V \rightarrow \begin{array}{c} hälfe \\ \uparrow obj\ case = DAT \end{array}$$

$$X \rightarrow \begin{array}{c} x \\ \emptyset \end{array} \qquad Y \rightarrow \begin{array}{c} y \\ \emptyset \end{array} \qquad Z \rightarrow \begin{array}{c} z \\ \emptyset \end{array}$$

From this grammar we get that strings like *"x em Hans d'chind y hälfe laa z"* are grammatical, while a string like *"x es Hans d'chind y hälfe laa z"* is ungrammatical, because of an inconsistency in the equation set. In Figure 4 we show the c-structure and feature structure for the string

(59)   *"x d'chind em Hans y laa hälfe z"*

This is not meant as an adequate linguistic analysis, but an example of how we may collect cross-serial information with a THFSG-grammar.

6   Summary and Remarks

We have defined a grammar formalism that describes a full abstract family of languages and showed that it can weakly describe a small subset of Swiss German with cross-serial dependencies. The method used to show that THFSG describes a full abstract family of languages is of some independent interest, for it seems to be applicable to many other unification grammar formalisms with a context free phrase structure backbone. The method basically requires that the equation sets are more or less uniform in the phrase structure and that we have the possibility to add "no information" equation sets. Of course, additional constraints on how information is collected, shared and distributed in the phrase-structure tree may complicate its application in practice.

There are two potential disadvantages to THFSG. Firstly, its membership problem is NP-hard (Colban 1991). This is due to the feature structures capacity to collect and distribute information across the sen-

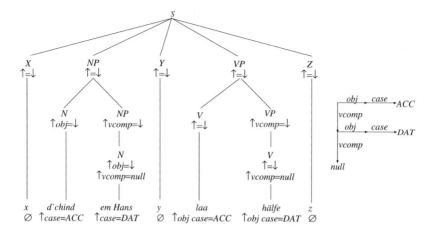

FIGURE 4 c-structure and feature structure for cross-serial dependencies

tence. This makes it possible to distribute truth-assignments uniformly for boolean expressions and then define a grammar that only accepts satisfiable expressions.

Secondly, it is not yet clear whether THFSG has enough *linguistic flexibility*. That is, will it always be possible to express linguistic phenomena in THFSG in the linguistically most natural way? After all, in THFSG we have only simple means of describing feature structures at our disposal. As a result of this, the feature structures will always be trees, and it may be argued that this is too limited compared to the much richer structures available in HPSG and LFG. On the other hand, on the string level of natural languages, cross-serial dependencies are to my knowledge the only constructions that are outside the context-free domain. Thus THFSG is a formalism that is strong enough to describe the string sets of natural languages — and not much stronger then that. Only further work can determine whether THFSG's balance between simplicity and expressivity is linguistically natural, and we refrain from drawing any strong conclusions on the issue here.

Acknowledgments

I would like to thank Tore Langholm for his advice during the work that this paper is based on, and for extensive comments on earlier versions of the paper. I would also like to thank Patrick Blackburn. Without his interest this paper would still have been collecting dust on my shelf. He also made many useful comments.

A previous version of this paper was presented at the workshop *Computational Logic for Natural Language Processing* in Edinburgh in April

1995. The workshop was jointly organized by the European Network in Language and Speech (ELSNET), the European Network in Computational Logic (COMPULOG-NET) and the Expert Advisory Group on Language Engineering Standards (EAGLES).

The final preparation of this paper has been supported by the Norwegian Research Council, grant 100437/410.

References

Aho, Alfred V. 1968. Indexed Grammars —An Extension of Context-Free Grammars. *Journal of the Association of Computing Machinery* 15(4):647–671.

Bar-Hillel, Y., M. Perles, and E. Shamir. 1961. On Formal Properties of Simple Phrase Structure Grammars. *Zeitscrift für Phonetik, Sprachwissenschaft und Kommunikationsforschung* 14:143–172.

Barton, Edward G., Robert C. Berwick, and Eric S. Ristad. 1987. *Computational Complexity and Natural Language.* Cambridge, MA: MIT Press.

Blackburn, Patrick. 1994. Structures, Languages and Translations: the Structural Approach to Feature Logic. In *Constraints, Language and Computation*, ed. C. J. Rupp, M. A. Rosner, and R. L. Johnson. 1–28. London: Academic Press.

Burheim, Tore. 1992. Regelstrukturer og tolkningsdefinisjoner. Master's thesis, Department of Informatics, University of Bergen. In Norwegian.

Colban, Erik A. 1991. *Three Studies in Computational Semantics.* Doctoral dissertation, University of Oslo.

Gallier, Jean H. 1986. *Logic for Computer Science.* New York: Harper & Row.

Gazdar, Gerald, Ewan Klein, Geoffrey Pullum, and Ivan Sag. 1985. *Generalized Phrase Structure Grammar.* Oxford: Basil Blackwell Publisher Ltd.

Gazdar, Gerald, and Geoffrey Pullum. 1982. Natural Languages and Context-Free Languages. *Linguistics and Philosophy* 4:471–504.

Ginsburg, Seymour. 1975. *Algebraic and Automata-Theoretic Properties of Formal Languages.* Amsterdam: North-Holland Publishing Company.

Hopcroft, John E., and Jeffrey D. Ullman. 1979. *Introduction to Automata Theory, Languages and Computation.* Reading, MA: Addison-Wesley Publishing Company.

Johnson, Mark. 1988. *Attribute-Value Logic and the Theory of Grammar.* CSLI Lecture Notes, No. 14. Stanford University, California, USA: Center for the Study of Language and Information.

Kaplan, Ronald M., and Joan Bresnan. 1982. Lexical Functional Grammar: A Formal System of Grammatical Representation. In *The Mental Representation of Grammatical Relations*, ed. Joan Bresnan. Cambrdige, MA: MIT Press.

Kaplan, Ronald M., John T. Maxwell, and Annie Zaenen. 1987. Functional Uncertainty. Stanford University: Center for the Study of Language and Information. CSLI Monthly 2:4.

Kasper, Robert T, and William T. Rounds. 1990. The Logic of Unification Grammar. *Linguistics and Philosophy* 13(1):35–58.

Keller, Bill, and David Weir. 1995. A Tractable Extension of Linear Indexed Grammars. In *Proceedings of the 7th Conference of the European Chapter of the Association for Computational Linguistics, EACL'95*. Association for Computational Linguistics.

Pollard, Carl, and Ivan Sag. 1994. *Head-Driven Phrase Structure Grammar*. Stanford: CSLI Publications and Chicago: University of Chicago Press.

Shieber, Stuart M. 1985. Evidence Against the Context-Freeness of Natural Language. *Linguistics and Philosophy* 8:333–343.

Shieber, Stuart M. 1986. *An Introduction to Unification-based Approaches to Grammar*. CSLI Lecture Notes, No. 4. Stanford University: Center for the Study of Language and Information. Chicago University Press.

Smolka, Gert. 1988. A Feature Logic with Subsorts. Lilog-report 33. Stuttgart: IBM-Deutschland.

Smolka, Gert. 1992. Feature Constraint Logics for Unification Grammars. *Journal of Logic Programming* 12:51–87.

2

On Constraint-Based Lambek Calculi

JOCHEN DÖRRE AND SURESH MANANDHAR

ABSTRACT. We explore the consequences of layering a Lambek calculus over an arbitrary constraint logic. A simple model-theoretic semantics for our hybrid language is provided, for which a particularly simple combination of Lambek's proof system and the proof system of the base logic is complete. In fact, the proof system for the underlying base logic can be assumed to be a black box that performs *entailment checking*. Assuming feature logic as the base logic, entailment checking amounts to a *subsumption* test, a well-known quasi-linear time decidable problem.

1 Background

In recent years there has been a growing awareness of a need to design grammar logics that incorporate both the resource sensitive nature of categorial grammars and the typed constraint-based approach of HPSG (Pollard and Sag 1987, 1994). We believe that the long-term goal of this enterprise is to provide an incremental and largely deterministic model of sentence comprehension within a constraint-based setting — something that current HPSG lacks. The constraint-based setting is important because it provides an excellent knowledge representation, engineering and structuring environment for natural language processing.

Although many fine-grained systems of categorial grammar (Moortgat and Oehrle 1993, Morrill 1992) have been developed, none directly build on unification based frameworks. In a system such as that of Moortgat (1992) for example, categories can be built using tuples containing *type, syntax* and *structure* in the spirit of UCG (Zeevat et al. 1987). However the use of feature descriptions is restricted — they cannot be employed to describe the syntax for example. The consequences of more direct (and perhaps more pragmatic) approaches remain unexplored, and this paper attempts to fill the gap.

Specifying Syntactic Structures
P. Blackburn and M. de Rijke, eds.
Copyright © 1997, CSLI Publications.

UCG (Zeevat et al. 1987) and CUG (Uszkoreit 1986) were early attempts to integrate categorial and constraint based ideas. However both lacked a rigorous model-theory. Even worse, their underlying unification-based proof system is incompatible with the straightforward model theory of feature-based categorial types (that is, where feature terms take the place of basic categories, for example $(cat: s)/(cat: np \ \& \ case: acc)$), when the following two basic assumptions (which we believe are highly desirable) are made:

1. The denotation of complex types should be composed in the same way as in standard semantics for (Lambek) categorial systems. No matter whether we use string semantics or ternary frame semantics (Došen 1992), types denote sets of objects, and a complex type A/B (or $B\backslash A$) denotes a left- (respectively right-) *residual* with respect to a join operation (or relation) $\odot$. That is, a complex type A/B (or $B\backslash A$) denotes those 'functional' objects which when joined with a B object (on the appropriate side) yield an A object.

2. Feature terms should induce a subtype ordering on categories in which more specific types denote subsets of less specific ones (for example, $[\![cat: np \ \& \ case: acc]\!] \subset [\![cat: np]\!]$).

Now, these assumptions imply, for example, that $A/B \odot B' \Rightarrow A$ ("when something is the join of A/B and B', then it is of type A") if and only if B' is a *subtype* of B. However in unification-based systems such as UCG and CUG, this sequent is derivable whenever B and B' unify. Thus there is an essential difference between the two views. Our model theory postulates an asymmetry between B and B' — namely that B' is informationally more specific than B — and takes a *subsumption-based* approach to binding. On the other hand, the approach typified by UCG and CUG postulates no such asymmetry and takes a *unification-based* approach to binding.

This paper explores the consequences of layering a Lambek calculus over an arbitrary (constraint) logic while following the subsumption-based binding approach. We provide a simple set-theoretic semantics for our hybrid language, show that the Lambek proof system carries over to this hybrid logic, and furthermore show that the proof system for the underlying base logic can be assumed to be a black box that performs *entailment checking*. Assuming feature logic as the base logic, entailment checking amounts to a *subsumption* test,[1] which is a well-known quasi-linear time decidable problem (Aït-Kaci et al. 1992, Smolka and Treinen 1994).

Section 2 reviews linguistic motivation in favor of the subsumption-based approach; this is borrowed from recent work by Bayer and Johnson

---

[1]This shouldn't be confused with the problem of satisfying subsumption constraints (as object language propositions), which is undecidable over feature structures (Dörre and Rounds 1992).

(1995). Section 3 presents the formal framework for our combined logics: a straightforward extension of Lambek's calculus with subtyping. Next, in Section 4, we define a layering of the Lambek system over arbitrary base logics; we pay special attention to the case where feature logic is chosen as the base logic. Section 5 closes with a discussion of possible limitations and raises the idea of having both subsumption-based and unification-based approaches in one system.

2 Double Coordinations

Recently, Bayer and Johnson (1995) have given an analysis of agreement phenomena in coordinations, which strongly supports the view of subsumption-based argument binding and which we review here as the primary linguistic motivation for our approach. Consider examples 1a–d.

(1)   a. Kim [$_{VP}$ [$_V$ became] [$_?$ [$_{AP}$ wealthy] and [$_{NP}$ a Republican]]]]
      b. *Kim [$_{VP}$ [$_V$ grew] [$_?$ [$_{AP}$ wealthy] and [$_{NP}$ a Republican]]]]
      c./d. Kim grew [$_{AP}$ wealthy] / * [$_{NP}$ a Republican]

Clearly, the contrast between (1a) and (1b) should be explained on the basis that *become* admits AP and NP complements, whereas no NP complement is allowed to follow *grew*. Assuming that we do not want to give coordinations a metagrammatical treatment, but attempt a phrase-structure analysis, a question arises: what category should be given a coordination such as the one in (1a)? In most 'unification-based' approaches to grammar, this kind of polymorphic coordination is accounted for by requiring that the feature structure of the coordination *subsumes* (or as a stronger condition: is the *generalization* of) all the feature structures of the coordinated elements. This is captured by a coordination rule like

$$X_0 \longrightarrow X_1 \ conj \ X_2$$
$$\text{where } X_0 \sqsubseteq X_1 \text{ and } X_0 \sqsubseteq X_2$$

(see Shieber 1992). Due to the additional assumption that types AP, NP, VP, PP are represented with the help of two binary features $\pm v$ and $\pm n$ as $\{+v, +n\}$, $\{-v, +n\}$, $\{+v, -n\}$, $\{-v, -n\}$, respectively, the polymorphic subcategorization requirement of *become* can be encoded as $+n$. Thus we may also assign category $+n$ to the coordination in (1a), because this subsumes both AP ($\{+v, +n\}$) and NP ($\{-v, +n\}$). (1b) is correctly ruled out, since *grew* requires the coordination to be $\{+n, +v\}$, and thus it cannot satisfy the subsumption constraint for the NP.

This approach to coordination, however, does not carry over to 'double coordinations' of the kind considered in Bayer and Johnson 1995. Here, in addition, the verbal part consists of a coordination:

(2)   a. * Kim [grew and remained] [wealthy and a Republican].

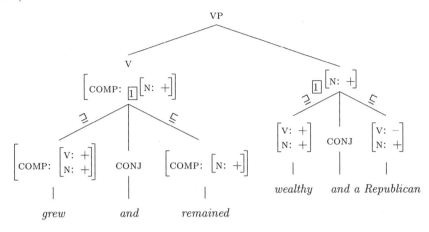

FIGURE 1 Overgeneration of the coordination rule
in a unification-based setting

Assuming a standard encoding of subcategorization information on the verb, the coordination rule here would predict a weakening (generalization) of the subcategorization requirements of two conjoined verbs (see Figure 1). With the above rule, a phrase "v_1 and v_2" would admit any complement whose type subsumes the type that v_1 selects for, as well as the one v_2 selects for. This fits with the data as long as the complement(s) have maximally specific types (that is, AP, NP, VP, or PP). However the analysis breaks down if the complement is itself a coordination. For such a double coordination construction, an analysis using the above coordination rule would lead to a complete relaxation of any subcategorization requirements (any combination of verbs could take any combination of phrases as complement), since we could simply assume that the structure $\boxed{1}$ was [] (empty information), and all subsumption and equality constraints of this analysis are trivially met.

In fact, a construction "v_1 and v_2" has to allow for just those complements that can follow v_1 by itself, and can also follow v_2 by itself; the requirements of both verbs have to be imposed together. For example, only an AP complement may follow *grew and remained*. But note that we cannot simply assume that the type requirements of the two verbs simply get unified; they may be inconsistent. This possibility is suggested by the following German sentences (cited originally by Pullum and Zwicky 1986 and Ingria 1990).

(3) a./b./c.   Er findet und hilft *Männer /*Kindern / Frauen
              he find   and help   men   children   women
                  ACC   DAT ACC   DAT   ACC+DAT

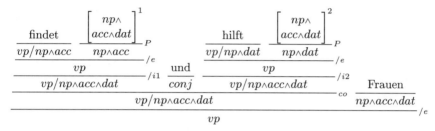

FIGURE 2 Partial proof tree showing rejection of (2) (Bayer and Johnson 1995)

$$
\begin{array}{c}
\dfrac{\dfrac{findet \quad \left[\begin{smallmatrix} np\wedge \\ acc\wedge dat \end{smallmatrix}\right]^1}{vp/np\wedge acc \quad np\wedge acc}\,P}{\dfrac{vp}{vp/np\wedge acc\wedge dat}\,{/e}}\,{/i1} \quad \dfrac{und}{conj} \quad \dfrac{\dfrac{hilft \quad \left[\begin{smallmatrix} np\wedge \\ acc\wedge dat \end{smallmatrix}\right]^2}{vp/np\wedge dat \quad np\wedge dat}\,P}{\dfrac{vp}{vp/np\wedge acc\wedge dat}\,{/e}}\,{/i2}
}{\dfrac{\dfrac{vp/np\wedge acc\wedge dat}{}\,co \qquad \dfrac{Frauen}{np\wedge acc\wedge dat}}{vp}\,{/e}}
\end{array}
$$

FIGURE 3 The LCG analysis of (3c)

Bayer and Johnson have a simple and convincing analysis of this phenomenon. They devise a simple extension to LCG (Lambek Categorial Grammar) in which basic types are replaced by propositional formulas built solely from propositional variables, ∧ (conjunction) and ∨ (disjunction). Apart from the original LCG rules, only the following two rule schemata are needed:[2]

$$\dfrac{\phi}{\psi}P, \quad \text{if } \phi \vdash \psi \text{ in propositional logic} \qquad\qquad \dfrac{A \; conj \; A}{A}co \quad \begin{array}{l}\text{Condition: no undischarged} \\ \text{hypothesis in any conjunct}\end{array}$$

The first deals with propositional formulae, the second with coordination. Now, the polymorphic verbs *become* and *remained* can simply be categorised as $vp/np \vee ap$. A coordination like *wealthy and a Republican* receives category $np \vee ap$ by using the weakening rule P twice. However, when we want to conjoin *grew* and *remained* using *co*, we need to strengthen the argument category of *remained* to be ap (see Figure 2). Thus the ungrammatical double coordination (2) is correctly rejected. Recasting the analysis in terms of logic, the fact that the subcategorization information acts as a premise of an implication — logically, functor categories can be seen as implications — is the reason why in a coordination of verbs this requirement gets strengthened (the category of the coordination becomes a common weakening of all the conjoined verb categories).

---

[2]Rules are assumed to be in the format of Natural Deduction.

$$\cfrac{\text{findet und hilft}}{vp/np \wedge acc \wedge dat} \quad \cfrac{\cfrac{\text{Männer}}{np \wedge acc}}{np \wedge (acc \vee dat)} \, P \quad \cfrac{\text{und}}{conj} \quad \cfrac{\cfrac{\text{Kindern}}{np \wedge dat}}{np \wedge (acc \vee dat)} \, P }{np \wedge (acc \vee dat)} \, co$$

FIGURE 4 The LCG analysis showing blocking of (4)

Interestingly, since subcategorization requirements are encoded as 'feature information' that must be *entailed* by the respective complement, there is no need to view different grammatical cases like *dative* and *accusative* as mutually inconsistent information. For instance, the German verb *helfen* may require an object to have dative case without disallowing it to be accusative as well; in other words, *helfen* would be specified as $vp/np \wedge dat$. Actually, this view of grammatical cases seems to be necessary to deal with the difference in grammaticality between (3c) and (4).

(4)   *Er findet und hilft Männer und Kindern.

Frauen simply needs to be of type $np \wedge acc \wedge dat$ and then the extended LCG of Bayer and Johnson 1995 correctly accepts (3c) (see Figure 3). Also, (4) is rejected (see Figure 4), since *Männer und Kindern* receives the weaker type $np \wedge (acc \vee dat)$, and hence does not match the combined requirement of *findet und hilft*.

3   Lambek Calculi with Subtyping

The general approach we take can be seen as adding Lambek slashes to some simple logical system, some *base logic*, for describing grammatical categories. However, seen from the outside the only effect of such base logics on the Lambek layer — so-to-speak the intercategorial layer — will be that they define subtype orderings between 'basic' categories. For example, we might want to allow for basic category descriptions like the above $np \wedge acc \wedge sg$ and $np \wedge acc$ (or if we want to employ feature logic $[np \, \& \, case\!: acc \, \& \, num\!: sg]$ and $[np \, \& \, case\!: acc]$) together with the stipulation that whenever something is of the former type, it is also of the latter. So before looking at Lambek systems over arbitrary base logics, we first give a rigorous treatment of the almost trivial extension to Lambek calculi where the set of basic types $\mathcal{B}$ is assumed to come with some subtype ordering $\preceq$. The combination schema defined later on, in which a base logic for the description of categories is employed, will be an instance of Lambek systems of this kind. Specifically, in the case of feature term descriptions, the subtype ordering will be the well-known feature term subsumption relation.

3.1   Syntax and Semantics

Assume as given a set of basic types $\mathcal{B} = \{b_1, b_2, \ldots\}$ on which a preorder $\preceq$ (the subtype ordering) is defined; that is, we require $\preceq \subseteq \mathcal{B} \times \mathcal{B}$ to be reflexive and transitive. If $b_1 \preceq b_2$, call b_1 a subtype of b_2 and b_2 a supertype of b_1.

Definition 3.1 The *set of formulae* $\mathcal{F}$ *of* $\mathsf{L}_{\preceq}$ is defined inductively by:

1. if b is in $\mathcal{B}$, then b is in $\mathcal{F}$;
2. if A and B are in $\mathcal{F}$, then A/B and $B\backslash A$ are in $\mathcal{F}$.

Definition 3.2   A *(string-semantic) model for* $\mathsf{L}_{\preceq}$ is a Kripke model $\langle W, \cdot, [\![\cdot]\!] \rangle$, where

1. W is a nonempty set;
2. $\cdot : W \times W \mapsto W$ is an associative operation; and
3. $[\![\cdot]\!] : \mathcal{F} \mapsto 2^W$ maps formulae to subsets of W and satisfies:
    a. $[\![b_1]\!] \subseteq [\![b_2]\!]$ whenever $b_1 \preceq b_2$;
    b. $[\![A/B]\!] = \{x \mid \forall y \in [\![B]\!] \, (x \cdot y \in [\![A]\!])\}$; and
    c. $[\![B\backslash A]\!] = \{y \mid \forall x \in [\![B]\!] \, (x \cdot y \in [\![A]\!])\}$.

We will also develop, in parallel to $\mathsf{L}_{\preceq}$, the logics resulting from extending with subtyping the variants NL, LP and NLP of Lambek's calculus. Here N abbreviates "nonassociative" and P abbreviates "with permutation". We define models for $\mathsf{NL}_{\preceq}$ (respectively $\mathsf{LP}_{\preceq}$; respectively $\mathsf{NLP}_{\preceq}$) as in Definition 3.2, but simply allowing (requiring) the second component $\cdot$ of models to be an arbitrary [respectively commutative and associative; respectively commutative] operation.

3.2   Gentzen Calculi

There is a well-known common formulation of the proof systems of all these Lambek logic variants in the form of a Gentzen sequent calculus. The (almost trivial) extension needed to cover subtyping is the same for all variants.

In Gentzen calculi, claims of the form $U \Rightarrow A$ are derived. These can be read as "formula A is derivable from the structured database U", where a structured database (or G-term) is built from formulae using the single (binary) structural connective $\odot$.

The denotation mappings $[\![\cdot]\!]$ in our models are naturally extended to G-terms by defining

$$[\![U \odot V]\!] := \{z \in W \mid \exists x, y \in W \, (z = x \cdot y \wedge x \in [\![U]\!] \wedge y \in [\![V]\!])\}.$$

(Symbols U and V will henceforth always denote G-terms.)

A *sequent* in each of our logics is a pair (U, A), written $U \Rightarrow A$, where U is a G-term and $A \in \mathcal{F}$. We call a sequent $U \Rightarrow A$ *valid*, if for all string models $\mathcal{M} = \langle W_{\mathcal{M}}, \cdot^{\mathcal{M}}, [\![\cdot]\!]^{\mathcal{M}} \rangle$, $[\![U]\!]^{\mathcal{M}} \subseteq [\![A]\!]^{\mathcal{M}}$.

$$(Ax) \frac{}{b_1 \Rightarrow b_2} \qquad \text{if } b_1 \preceq b_2$$

$$(/L) \frac{V \Rightarrow B \quad U[A] \Rightarrow C}{U[A/B \odot V] \Rightarrow C} \qquad (/R) \frac{U \odot B \Rightarrow A}{U \Rightarrow A/B}$$

$$(\backslash L) \frac{V \Rightarrow B \quad U[A] \Rightarrow C}{U[V \odot B \backslash A] \Rightarrow C} \qquad (\backslash R) \frac{B \odot U \Rightarrow A}{U \Rightarrow B \backslash A}$$

$$(Cut) \frac{V \Rightarrow A \quad U[A] \Rightarrow C}{U[V] \Rightarrow C}$$

FIGURE 5 Gentzen calculus $\mathsf{NL}_{\preceq}$

Now, the logical rules for all variant systems are the same; these rules are shown in Figure 5. The notation $U[X]$ in rules $/L$, $\backslash L$ and Cut stands for a G-term U with a distinguished occurrence of the (sub-)G-term X, and by using $U[Y]$ in the same rule we denote the result of substituting Y for that occurrence X in $U[X]$. The variations between the four logics comes from their different use of the so-called structural rules ASSOCIATIVITY and PERMUTATION, by which the G-term connective $\odot$ may be forced to obey the appropriate combination of being associative or not and being commutative or not. However, we do not assume these rules explicitly; rather, as is standard, we let them be implicit in the notion of G-term for the respective logic. This is done by viewing G-terms in a manner that is appropriate for these rules. For instance, in L the $\odot$ connective is assumed to be associative; thus for this logic we view G-terms as being (nonempty) sequences (strings) of formulas with $\odot$ denoting concatenation.

The only departure from standard Lambek calculus is the axiom scheme. It is the straightforward generalization needed to generate all valid sequents of two basic formulae.

3.3 Soundness and Completeness

Let us now check that our proof systems are indeed sound and complete. In the following completeness theorem, the case of $\mathsf{L}_{\preceq}$ follows from an argument given in Emms 1994, which shows that the product-free Lambek calculus (that is, $\mathsf{L}_{\preceq}$ where $\preceq$ is the identity) augmented by a set of additional axiom schemata R, is sound and complete with respect to the class of string-semantic models satisfying R. The proof here is a straightforward adaptation of this argument; we give it for all Lambek variants simultaneously.

Theorem 3.3 $U \Rightarrow A$ *is derivable in* $\mathsf{L}_{\preceq}$ *(respectively* $\mathsf{NL}_{\preceq}$, $\mathsf{LP}_{\preceq}$, $\mathsf{NLP}_{\preceq}$*)* *iff* $U \Rightarrow A$ *is valid (with the respective condition on the structural connective* $\odot$*).*

Proof. The direction from left to right (soundness) is shown by the usual induction on length of proofs. Validity of axiom instances directly follows from model condition (3a). For the other direction, we construct the canonical model $\mathcal{CM}$ as follows. Let $\mathcal{CM} = \langle W, \odot, \llbracket \cdot \rrbracket \rangle$ where $\langle W, \odot \rangle$ is the free algebra generated by $\odot$ over the formulas (modulo the respective structural rules) and $\llbracket \cdot \rrbracket$ is defined as

$$\llbracket A \rrbracket \quad := \quad \{u \in W \mid \vdash u \Rightarrow A\}.$$

Here $\vdash \Gamma$ stands for Γ *is derivable in the respective logical system*. Observe that due to the reflexivity of $\preceq$, all sequents derivable in the original Lambek calculus (respectively: in its variants NL, LP, NLP) are also derivable here.

1. $\mathcal{CM}$ is a model: we check the conditions *(a)–(c)* in the definition of $\llbracket \cdot \rrbracket$.
   a. Suppose $b_1 \preceq b_2$. Then $U \in \llbracket b_1 \rrbracket$ iff $\vdash U \Rightarrow b_1$, but then with Cut on $b_1 \Rightarrow b_2$, $\vdash U \Rightarrow b_2$.
   b. We need to show for all $U \in W$, $A, B \in \mathcal{F}$:

      $\vdash U \Rightarrow A/B$ iff $\forall V \in W$ ($\vdash V \Rightarrow B$ implies $\vdash U \odot V \Rightarrow A$).

      So, suppose for arbitrary U, A, B, and V, $\vdash U \Rightarrow A/B$ and $\vdash V \Rightarrow B$. The latter gives, using $/L$ on $A \Rightarrow A$, $A/B \odot V \Rightarrow A$, and hence with Cut, $\vdash U \odot V \Rightarrow A$. For the converse assume U, A, B such that the condition of the right-hand side holds. With $V = B$ we then get $\vdash U \odot B \Rightarrow A$, since $\vdash B \Rightarrow B$ is true. But then, by $/R$ we derive the required $U \Rightarrow A/B$.
   c. Symmetrical.
2. $\mathcal{CM}$ invalidates nonderivable sequents: for suppose $\nvdash U \Rightarrow A$, hence $U \notin \llbracket A \rrbracket$. But clearly $U \in \llbracket U \rrbracket$ contradicting the validity of $U \Rightarrow A$.

This completes the proof. $\square$

3.4 Some Properties of the Calculi

It is helpful to classify the occurrences of subformulas in $\mathcal{F}$-formulas and sequents into positive (polarity $= +1$) and negative (polarity $= -1$) as follows.

Definition 3.4 (Positive/negative subformula occurrences)

- A occurs *positively* in A.
- If the polarity of B in A is p and B has the form C/D or $D\backslash C$, then the polarity of that occurrence of C (respectively D) in A is p (respectively $-p$).

Next we extend the subtyping relation $\preceq$ to complex types by stipulating

(1)   if $A \preceq A'$ and $B' \preceq B$ then $A/B \preceq A'/B'$ and $B \backslash A \preceq B' \backslash A'$.

Evidently, with this definition we remain faithful to the intended meaning of subtyping, namely that it denotes the subset relation.

Lemma 3.5 *If $A \preceq B$, then for any* $\mathsf{L}_{\preceq}$ *model* $[\![A]\!] \subseteq [\![B]\!]$.

Using completeness we trivially obtain

Theorem 3.6 *If $A \preceq B$, then $\vdash A \Rightarrow B$.*

The following two derived rules make explicit the monotonicity properties of derivability with respect to subtyping on the left- and on the right-hand side. They are specializations of *Cut* taking into account Theorem 3.6. Be warned that the notation $U[A]$ stands for U with a *G-term occurrence* A (not an arbitrary subformula).

$$(\text{strengthen } L) \,\, \frac{U[B] \Rightarrow C}{U[A] \Rightarrow C} \quad \text{if } A \preceq B \qquad (\text{weaken } R) \,\, \frac{U \Rightarrow A}{U \Rightarrow B} \quad \text{if } A \preceq B$$

3.4.1   Cut Elimination

An important result is that the *Cut* rule is redundant, since from this decidability (in fact, even containment in the complexity class $\mathcal{NP}$) directly follows. *Cut*-free proofs have the nice property that the length of the proof is bounded linearly by the size of the sequent to be proven. So, let us in the following call $\mathsf{NL}_{\preceq}^{-}$ the system containing all the rules and axiom shown in Figure 5, except for the *Cut*-rule.

Theorem 3.7 (Cut Elimination) $U \Rightarrow A$ *is derivable in* $\mathsf{NL}_{\preceq}$ *iff it is derivable in* $\mathsf{NL}_{\preceq}^{-}$.

(A proof is given in the appendix.)

3.4.2   Context-Freeness

We show here that the addition of subtyping to the calculus of Lambek categorial grammars does not extend their generative capacity. A categorial grammar based on $\mathsf{L}_{\preceq}$ can always be compiled out into a (possibly much larger) Lambek categorial grammar (and hence, also into a context-free grammar).

Assume as given a system $\mathsf{L}_{\preceq} = (\mathcal{F}, \vdash_{\mathsf{L}_{\preceq}})$ and a finite alphabet $\mathcal{T}$ of lexical entities.

Definition 3.8 An $\mathsf{L}_{\preceq}$ grammar G for $\mathcal{T}$ is a pair (α, S) consisting of the lexical assignment $\alpha : \mathcal{T} \mapsto 2^{\mathcal{F}}$, such that for any $t \in \mathcal{T}$, $\alpha(t)$ is a finite set of types, and the distinguished (sentence) type $S \in \mathcal{F}$.

The language generated by G is

$$L(G) := \{t_1 \ldots t_n \in \mathcal{T}^* \mid \exists B_1 \ldots B_n \; (\vdash_{\mathsf{L}_{\preceq}} B_1 \ldots B_n \Rightarrow S \wedge \bigwedge_{i=1}^{n} B_i \in \alpha(t_i))\}$$

Theorem 3.9 (Context-Freeness) *For any* $\mathsf{L}_{\preceq}$ *grammar* G *the language* $L(G)$ *is context-free.*

(A proof is given in the appendix.)

4 Layering Lambek over Some Base Logic

We now describe how the abstract placeholder of the subtype ordering is sensibly filled in in constraint-based Lambek grammar. As explained above, we assume some specification language (or base logic) whose purpose it is to allow for more fine-grained descriptions of the basic categories. Before we proceed to describe a concrete choice of base logic, let us first consider abstractly what we demand of such a logic and how an integration with Lambek logic can be defined generally in a way exhibiting the desired properties.

Formally, we assume a base logic BL consisting of:

1. the denumerable set of formulae $\mathcal{BF}$
2. the class $\mathcal{C}$ of models $\flat$ of the form $\langle W_\flat, \llbracket \cdot \rrbracket^\flat \rangle$, where:
   a. $W_\flat$ is some nonempty set
   b. $\llbracket \cdot \rrbracket^\flat : \mathcal{BF} \mapsto 2^{W_\flat}$ maps formulae to subsets of $W_\flat$

We will be interested in logical consequence between two single formulae, that is, in the relation $\phi \models_{\mathsf{BL}} \psi \Leftrightarrow_{\mathsf{def}} \forall \flat \in \mathcal{C} \; (\llbracket \phi \rrbracket^\flat \subseteq \llbracket \psi \rrbracket^\flat)$ for all $\phi, \psi \in \mathcal{BF}$. We also assume a sound and complete deduction system $\vdash_{\mathsf{BL}}$ for answering this question. Note that $\models_{\mathsf{BL}}$ is a preorder. Now we define the layered Lambek logic $\mathsf{L(BL)}$ over some given base logic BL as follows.

Definition 4.1 The logic $\mathsf{L(BL)}$ is the logic $\mathsf{L}_{\models_{\mathsf{BL}}}$ over basic types $\mathcal{BF}$.

This means, we let $\mathsf{L(BL)}$ simply be a subtyping Lambek logic $\mathsf{L}_{\preceq}$ taking as $\preceq$ the consequence relation over BL-formulae. Thus we inherit the complete and decidable (provided $\models_{\mathsf{BL}}$ is decidable) proof system of $\mathsf{L}_{\preceq}$, but also its limited generative capacity.

Note that every formula of $\mathsf{L(BL)}$ has an outer (possibly empty) Lambek part, which composes some BL-formulae with the connectives $/$ and $\backslash$, but no BL connective may scope over formulae containing $/$ or $\backslash$ (hence the term 'layered logic').

The reader will have noticed that Bayer and Johnson's logic presented in Section 2 is a layered logic of this kind, where BL is instantiated to be propositional logic (restricted to connectives $\wedge$ and $\vee$).

It may be a bit surprising that the generative capacity is not affected by the choice of the base logic. Even if we admit full standard first-order logic, we do not exceed context-free power. We see a cause of this in the fact that there is no direct interrelation between L(BL)-models and base models. Only on the abstract level of the consequence relation $\models_{BL}$ does the notion of base model enter the conditions on L(BL)-models.[3]

The lack of a direct interrelation between L(BL)-models and base models also ensures that L(BL) enjoys a particularly simple and modular proof system. Proofs can be built by decomposing the Lambek part of a goal sequent with the usual rules until one reaches pure BL-sequents (Lambek axioms). Those are then proved in pure $\vdash_{BL}$ by *independent* proofs for each sequent; that is, the proof system $\vdash_{BL}$ can be considered a black box.

4.1 Feature Logic as Base Logic

We now consider the consequence of choosing feature logic as the base logic. For this variant of the logic to be complete, we need a proof system for deciding whether $\phi \models_{FL} \psi$, that is, for checking whether ϕ *entails* ψ. Proof systems for deciding entailment between feature constraints are well known (Aït-Kaci et al. 1992, Aït-Kaci and Podelski 1994).

We provide a simple entailment checking procedure for a restricted feature logic with the following syntax:

$$\phi, \psi \longrightarrow \quad \begin{array}{ll} x & \text{variable} \\ a & \text{atom} \\ \top & \text{top} \\ \bot & \text{bottom} \\ f : \phi & \text{feature term} \\ \exists x(\phi) & \text{existentially quantified variable} \\ \phi \,\&\, \psi & \text{conjunction} \end{array}$$

Since the semantics of feature logic is well known, we do not provide a model theoretic semantics here (see Smolka 1992 for details).

As a first step in deciding whether the entailment $\phi \models_{FL} \psi$ holds, we translate the constraints $x = \phi$ and $x = \psi$ (where x is a fresh variable) into normal form by employing a normalization procedure for feature logic (see Smolka 1992). A normal form translation of the constraint $x = \phi$ results in a constraint of the form $\exists x_0 \ldots x_n \, \phi'$, where ϕ' is a conjunction of simple constraints. In our case, these are of the form : $x = a, x = \top, x =$

---

[3] As an alternative to our model conception, consider the option of defining an L(BL)-model in a such way that it contains a base model as a part. For instance, when given a base model $\flat$, we could stipulate

$$[\![\phi]\!] = [\![\phi]\!]^{\flat} \quad \textit{for all } \phi \in \mathcal{BF}$$

instead of condition *(a)* on $[\![\cdot]\!]$ (assume $W_{\flat} \subset W$). (In our model conception such models are allowed, but not required). A consequence of this option is that certain logical be haviour of BL-formulae may get exported to the Lambek level leading to incompleteness there. For example, when BL contains a constant (or formula), say FALSE, denoting the empty set, any sequent of the form $U[\text{FALSE}] \Rightarrow A$ will be valid.

$\bot, x = f : y$. Thus, normal form translation of $x = (cat : np \,\&\, case : acc)$ gives $\exists y_0 y_1 (x = cat : y_0 \,\&\, y_0 = np \,\&\, x = case : y_1 \,\&\, y_1 = acc)$. The normal form translation, apart from providing a simplified conjunction of constraints, also decides consistency of the initial formula.

Now for the second step; by the previous remark, we can assume that both ϕ and ψ are consistent. Let $\exists x_0 \dots x_n \; \phi'$ (respectively $\exists y_0 \dots y_m \; \psi'$) denote the normal form translation of $x = \phi$ (respectively $x = \psi$). For simplicity of presentation, we assume that the existentially quantified variables $x_0 \dots x_n$ and $y_0 \dots y_m$ are disjoint. Since the existential quantification in $\exists x_0 \dots x_n \; \phi'$ is not needed in the simplification procedure, we remove this from consideration. We then apply the entailment checking procedure given in Figure 6 to $\phi' \models_{\mathsf{FL}} \exists y_0 \dots y_m \; \psi'$ calling ϕ' the *context* and $\exists y_0 \dots y_m \; \psi'$ the *guard*.

$$(SAtom) \; \frac{x = a \,\&\, \phi \models_{\mathsf{FL}} \exists y_0 \dots y_n \; \psi}{x = a \,\&\, \phi \models_{\mathsf{FL}} \exists y_0 \dots y_n \; x = a \,\&\, \psi}$$

$$(SFeat) \; \frac{x = f : y \,\&\, \phi \models_{\mathsf{FL}} \exists y_0 \dots y_n \; \psi}{x = f : y \,\&\, \phi \models_{\mathsf{FL}} \exists y_0 \dots y_n \; x = f : y \,\&\, \psi}$$

$$(SFeatExist) \; \frac{x = f : y \,\&\, \phi \models_{\mathsf{FL}} \exists y_0 \dots y_i \dots y_n \; [y/y_i]\psi}{x = f : y \,\&\, \phi \models_{\mathsf{FL}} \exists y_0 \dots y_i \dots y_n \; x = f : y_i \,\&\, \psi}$$

FIGURE 6   Entailment checking in simple feature logic

The rules given in Figure 6 are to be read from bottom to top. These rules simplify the guard with respect to the context. The rules *SAtom* and *SFeat* are self-explanatory. In rule *SFeatExist*, the notation $[y/y_i]\psi$ means replace every occurrence of y_i with y in ψ. Once the entailment checking rules terminate, entailment and disentailment can be decided by inspection.

- $\phi \models_{\mathsf{FL}} \psi$ if entailment checking of $\phi' \models_{\mathsf{FL}} \exists y_0 \dots y_m \; \psi'$ simplifies ψ' to a possibly empty conjunction of formula of the form $y_i = \top$.
- $\phi \not\models_{\mathsf{FL}} \psi$ (that is, ϕ *disentails* ψ) if entailment checking of $\phi' \models_{\mathsf{FL}} \exists y_0 \dots y_m \; \psi'$ simplifies to the form $x = a \,\&\, \phi' \models_{\mathsf{FL}} \exists y_0 \dots y_m \; x = \tau \,\&\, \psi'$ [or the form $x = \tau \,\&\, \phi' \models_{\mathsf{FL}} \exists y_0 \dots y_m \; x = a \,\&\, \psi'$] where τ is one of:
  - b with a, b distinct
  - $f : z$
- $\phi \models_{\mathsf{FL}} \psi$ is *blocked* if neither of the above two conditions hold.

This completes the basic building blocks needed to implement a proof system for a Lambek calculus with feature logic as the base logic.

5 Discussion

The initial motivation for conducting this research was the lack of a model-theoretic semantics for unification-based versions of categorial grammar, a situation which stands in sharp contrast to the apparently clear intuitions we have about the meaning of categorial types over feature terms. We were guided by the insight (or basic assumption) that a functor type A/B, may always be applied to subtypes of B (yielding an A), but not necessarily to supertypes. Combined with the idea that feature terms as basic types essentially provide a means of expressing fine-structuring of types (that is, subtyping) this led us to devise a simple model theory embodying just those assumptions. This model theory is accompanied with a subsumption-based (and equally simple) proof system. This work in a sense complements work by Dörre, König and Gabbay (to appear), in which a model-theoretic counterpart of the unification-based proof system is constructed using the paradigm of fibred semantics (see Gabbay 1994).

However there is one important issue for grammar logics that we have not yet discussed: how do we build semantic terms? As we shall see, our logic is completely neutral on this issue. We can either please the categorial grammar purist and use the Curry-Howard(-van Benthem) correspondence in which rules are viewed as recipes for cooking up lambda terms (see van Benthem 1986), or we may go the way of aficionados of HPSG and employ an additional layer in which semantic formulae are built up by unification.

The first claim is unsurprising. In a Lambek-van Benthem system, each type is paired with a semantic formula, L-rules trigger function application and R-rules lambda abstraction on these formulae. Since this in no way interferes with our extension, we can apply this method unchanged.

On the other hand, if we were to adopt a HPSG style semantics, then variable sharing across categories is needed; we cannot simply add a SEM feature to the feature structures of basic types, since no information can be 'percolated' out of local trees. Nonetheless, there is a solution. We will use the combination scheme of Dörre, König and Gabbay (to appear) to combine L(FL) with another layer of *feature constraints*. In this second feature-logical layer, unification is employed to match categories. We briefly sketch how this construction works.

Double Layering. To each basic type occurrence in an L(FL) formula associate a new variable (the *unification layer* variable). We can impose (feature) constraints on these variables. Such constraints are written as a top-level conjunction and are included as a third component of sequents. For example, writing unification-layer variables as superscripts, an HPSG-like lexical assignment for the control verb *persuade* would be of type

$$([cat{:}np]^X \setminus [cat{:}s]^S) / [cat{:}np]^Y / ([cat{:}np]^Y \setminus [cat{:}s \ \& \ vform{:}inf]^Z),$$

together with constraints on the variables X, S, Y, Z. For instance, we might require that S is constrained to be a *persuading relation* as given by:

$$S = \left[\text{CONTENT} \left[\begin{array}{ll} \text{RELATION} & persuade \\ \text{INFLUENCE} & X \\ \text{INFLUENCED} & Y \\ \text{SOA--ARG} & Z \end{array} \right] \right]$$

A proof proceeds as in the system $L(FL)$, but additionally maintains as a global environment a feature constraint Φ. Initially Φ is the conjoined feature constraints of all formulae in the goal sequent. Whenever we apply the axiom schema on some $[b_1]^X \Rightarrow [b_2]^Y$, we add $X = Y$ to Φ, normalize, and continue if the result is consistent. That is, we unify the feature graphs (encoded as the constraints) of X and Y. Thus the composition of the content structure proceeds in exactly the same way as in HPSG (or other comparable unification-based frameworks).

In short, unification-based and subsumption-based argument binding can be combined into a single logic.[4] Moreover, the logics complement each other. Speaking in HPSG terms, we now have the flexibility to choose which parts of a sign we want only to be matched and which parts we want to be unified, when we combine it with other signs in a local tree.[5]

On the processing side, we believe that the separation of a subsumption-based layer (of context-free power) and a unification-based layer offers ben-

---

[4]In much the same way, in fact, that a unification component for feature structures can be combined with a context-free grammar to yield LFG.

[5]The reader may be wondering whether variable binding could give us a simpler mechanism for information percolation. Suppose we would use the following strategy: "after having checked that the category serving as actual argument (the complement sign) is subsumed by the functor type's argument description (the respective slot of the subcat list of the head), just unify the two". Hence, variables in the subsuming type would be bound, possibly carrying that information to other parts of the functor type's structure. For instance, we could have a modifier type $\exists x[cat: x/cat: x]$ or a coordination type $\exists x[cat: x \backslash cat: x/cat: x]$, the result type of which would depend on the type(s) of its argument(s). But consider what happens when we apply that coordination type to two arguments of different types:

$$cat: (np \vee ap) \odot \exists x[cat: x \backslash cat: x/cat: x] \odot cat: np.$$

Using $/L$ and $\backslash L$ this reduces to $cat: x$ plus the two sequents $cat: np \Rightarrow cat: x$ and $cat: (np \vee ap) \Rightarrow cat: x$. Now, if we choose to first prove the first, x gets bound (globally) to np and the second sequent fails. However if we choose the other order, $x = (np \vee ap)$ and the proof succeeds. This means that our naïve proof procedure is sensitive to the order of rule application. In other words, to guarantee completeness we would have to *search* for a particular sequence of rule ordering. This is an undesirable situation and should be avoided, since it results in a vastly inefficient proof procedure.

In addition there is a *semantic problem*: it becomes rather difficult to provide a sensible semantics for categories $B \backslash A$ and A/B. In particular, what we witnessed in the example above is that the denotation of A in $B \backslash A$ (or A/B) is going to be dynamic, that is, contingent on what A actually unifies with.

efits similar to those yielded by the distinction between c-structure and f-structure in LFG. For instance, we can easily precompile the formulas of the subsumption layer into a type hierarchy of atomic symbols and thus may be able to employ efficient indexing techniques during parsing.

A final point. There are other extensions to the original Lambek calculus, many of which appear to be prerequisites for many linguistically interesting analyses; for example, Moortgat's non-directional slash operator ↑ for non-peripheral gaps, his operator ⇑ for generalized quantifiers, Morrill's multimodal and discontinuity operators, structural modalities, and so on (see Morrill 1994). We believe that our subtyping method is compatible with (at least most of) these additional devices and offers an extension that is orthogonal to them.

6 Conclusion

We have shown that a simple and happy marriage between constraint-based grammars and categorial grammars is technically feasible and has an appealingly simple model theory. Our hybrid grammar logic permits extant categorial proof systems to be carried over into the new system. Furthermore, the logic is parameterized over arbitrary (constraint) logics as long as a reasoning mechanism for determining entailment and consistency is provided. We believe that crucial to the success of this approach is the novel use of subsumption (or entailment) checking as opposed to just unification.

A   Proofs of Theorems of Section 3.4

Cut Elimination

The following lemma considers derivability of a special case of each of the two derived rules above in $\mathsf{NL}_{\preceq}^-$, laying the seed for the *Cut* elimination proof. It is stated (as is the *Cut* elimination theorem itself) with respect to derivability in $\mathsf{NL}_{\preceq}$, the weakest of the four systems, but it should be kept in mind that these facts about derivability hold a fortiori in the other systems as well.

Lemma A.1 *If $U[b_2] \Rightarrow C$ (respectively $U \Rightarrow b_1$) is derivable in $\mathsf{NL}_{\preceq}^-$ and $b_1 \preceq b_2$, then $U[b_1] \Rightarrow C$ (respectively $U \Rightarrow b_2$) is derivable in $\mathsf{NL}_{\preceq}^-$.*

Proof. By induction on the length of the proof of $\Gamma = U[b_2] \Rightarrow C$.

$n = 0$: Then $U = b_2$ and $C = b_3 \in \mathcal{BF}$ [respectively $U = b_3$]. By transitivity of $\vdash_{\mathsf{BL}}$, $b_1 \Rightarrow b_3$ ($= U[b_1] \Rightarrow C$) [respectively $U \Rightarrow b_1$] is an axiom.

$n > 0$: We distinguish cases according to the last rule used in the proof of Γ and state the bracketed cases separately:

/R: Then $C = A/B$ and there is a proof of $(U[b_2], B) \Rightarrow A$ of smaller
  length. Hence by induction hypothesis (IH) we get $(U[b_1], B) \Rightarrow$
  A and by $/R$ the required sequent.

[/R :] cannot be last step

/L: U contains distinguished occurrences of the two G-terms b_2 and
  $(A/B, V)$. Hence, either b_2 occurs in V, in which case by IH on
  $V \Rightarrow B$ the claim is shown, or $U = U[(A/B, V), b_2]$, that is, b_2
  occurs also in $U[A]$ as a G-term different from A. In this case
  the claim follows via IH on $U[A, b_2] \Rightarrow C$.

[/L :] obvious, since we get by IH $U[A] \Rightarrow b_2$.

\R, \L, [\R], **and** [\L] are completely analogous. □

Proof of the Cut Elimination Theorem. We point out what needs to be
changed in the Cut elimination proof for standard Lambek calculus (see,
for example, Došen 1988). Let the *degree* of an application of *Cut* be the
number of occurrences of connectives in the cut-formula A, the formula
eliminated by applying *Cut*. Then the standard argument goes by showing
that whenever a sequent Γ has a proof which contains exactly one application of *Cut*, which is of degree d, and this is the last step in that proof,
that is, the proof has the form

$$
(Cut) \ \frac{\begin{array}{cc} \vdots & \vdots \\ \Gamma_1 & \Gamma_2 \end{array}}{\Gamma}
$$

then by a case analysis of the two steps introducing Γ_1 and Γ_2, it follows
that Γ is derivable from the premises of those steps involving either no
Cut or only *Cut* applications of lower degree. The arguments for all the
cases carry over identically to our system except for the case where one of
Γ's premises is an axiom. So, suppose $\Gamma_1 = b_1 \Rightarrow b_2$ with b_2 being the
Cut-formula. Then $\Gamma_2 = U[b_2] \Rightarrow C$, and by Lemma A.1, $\Gamma = U[b_1] \Rightarrow C$
has a cut-free proof. But also if $\Gamma_2 = b_1 \Rightarrow b_2$ with b_1 being cut, we get
$\Gamma_1 = V \Rightarrow b_1$ and again by Lemma A.1 the claim holds. □

Context-Freeness

The following characterization of $\preceq$, which is a simple consequence of its
definition for complex types, will be useful in proving the context-freeness
theorem.

Lemma A.2 $A \preceq B$ *iff B is the result of substituting in A 0 or more
negative subformulae occurrences $b_1, \ldots, b_n$ of basic types by subtypes and
0 or more positive subformulae occurrences $b'_1, \ldots, b'_m$ by supertypes.*

Proof of the Context-freeness Theorem. We show how to construct for an
arbitrary $L_{\preceq}$ grammar $G = (\alpha, S)$ a finite set of (pure) Lambek grammars
such that $L(G)$ is the union of the languages generated by these. Since

Lambek grammars generate only context-free languages (Pentus 1994) and context-free languages are closed under union, $L(G)$ is context-free.

Let $\mathcal{B}|_\alpha$ be the (finite) subset of $\mathcal{B}$ of basic formulae occurring (as subformulae) in some $\alpha(t_i)$. Call for arbitrary $A \in \mathcal{F}$ $super^+(A)$ (respectively $super^-(A)$) the set of formulae A' such that A' is the result of replacing in A 0 or more positive (respectively negative) subformula occurrences $b_1, \ldots, b_n$ of basic types by respective supertypes from $\mathcal{B}|_\alpha$. For instance, if $\mathcal{B}|_\alpha = \{b_1, b_2\}$ where $b_1 \prec b_2$ then $super^+(b_1/(b_1/b_1)) = \{b_1/(b_1/b_1), b_1/(b_1/b_2), b_2/(b_1/b_1), b_2/(b_1/b_2)\}$. We now define

$$\overline{S} := super^-(S) = \{S_1, \ldots, S_m\}$$
$$\overline{\alpha}(t) := \{B' \mid \exists B \ B \in \alpha(t), B' \in super^+(B)\}$$

The Lambek grammars we are seeking are $G_i = (\overline{\alpha}, S_i)$ (over the Lambek type system L_{Id}) for $i = 1, \ldots, m$. We let $\overline{L}$ stand for the union of their languages and show:

$\overline{L} \subseteq L(G)$: Suppose $w = t_1, \ldots, t_n \in \overline{L}$. Then there exists a j such that w is generated by G_j, and hence there are $B'_1, \ldots, B'_n$ such that $B'_i \in \overline{\alpha}(t_i)$ and $\vdash_{\mathsf{L}_{Id}} B'_1 \ldots B'_n \Rightarrow S_j$. But then there are $B_1, \ldots, B_n$ such that $B'_i \in super^+(B_i)$ and $B_i \in \alpha(t_i)$. Since valid derivations in L_{Id} remain valid in $\mathsf{L}_{\preceq}$ we get $\vdash_{\mathsf{L}_{\preceq}} B'_1 \ldots B'_n \Rightarrow S_j$ and then with (*strengthen L*) and (*weaken R*) (due to $B_i \preceq B'_i$ and $S_j \preceq S$, see Lemma A.2) also $\vdash_{\mathsf{L}_{\preceq}} B_1 \ldots B_n \Rightarrow S$, that is, $w \in L(G)$.

$L(G) \subseteq \overline{L}$: Suppose $w \in L(G)$, that is, there are $B_1, \ldots, B_n$ such that $\vdash_{\mathsf{L}_{\preceq}} B_1 \ldots B_n \Rightarrow S$ and $B_i \in \alpha(t_i)$. Assume Δ is a proof of this sequent in $\mathsf{L}_{\preceq}$ and relies on the axiom instances $b_1 \Rightarrow b'_1, \ldots, b_k \Rightarrow b'_k$ (that is, $b_i \preceq b'_i$). If we replace these instances by $b'_1 \Rightarrow b'_1, \ldots, b'_k \Rightarrow b'_k$, but keep the rest of the proof structure, we obtain an L_{Id} proof of a sequent $B'_1 \ldots B'_n \Rightarrow S'$, where $B'_i \in super^+(B_i)$ for $i = 1, \ldots, n$ and $S' \in super^-(S)$ (note that the left-hand sides of axioms appear as subformulae in positive occurrences on left-hand sides or negative occurrences on right-hand sides of derived sequents). Hence $B'_i \in \overline{\alpha}(t_i)$ for all $1 \leq i \leq n$ and $S' = S_j$ for some $1 \leq j \leq m$, implying that w is generated by G_j. $\square$

References

Aït-Kaci, Hassan, and Andreas Podelski. 1994. Functions as Passive Constraints in LIFE. *ACM Transactions on Programming Languages and Systems* 16(4):1–40.

Aït-Kaci, Hassan, Gert Smolka, and R. Treinen. 1992. A Feature-Based Constraint System for Logic Programming with Entailment. Research report. Saarbrücken, Germany: German Research Center for Artificial Intelligence (DFKI).

Bayer, Sam, and Mark Johnson. 1995. Features and Agreement. In *Proceedings of the 33nd Annual Meeting of the ACL, Massachusetts Institute of Technology.* Cambridge, Mass.

Dörre, Jochen, Esther König, and Dov Gabbay. to appear. Fibred Semantics for Feature-based Grammar Logic. *Journal of Logic, Language and Information.* Special Issue on Language and Proof Theory.

Dörre, Jochen, and William C. Rounds. 1992. On Subsumption and Semi-Unification in Feature Algebras. *Journal of Symbolic Computation* 13:441–461.

Došen, Kosta. 1988. Sequent Systems and Groupoid Models I. *Studia Logica* 47:353–385.

Došen, Kosta. 1992. A Brief Survey of Frames for the Lambek Calculus. *Zeitschrift für mathematische Logik und Grundlagen der Mathematik* 38:179–187.

Emms, Martin. 1994. Completeness Results for Polymorphic Lambek Calculus. In *Lambek Calculus: Multimodal and Polymorphic Extensions, DYANA-2 deliverable R1.1.B*, ed. Michael Moortgat. ESPRIT, Basic Research Project 6852, September.

Gabbay, D. M. 1994. Labelled Deductive Systems, vol 1 (3rd intermediate draft). Technical Report MPI-I-94-223. Saarbrücken, Germany: Max Planck Institut. 1st draft Manuscript 1989; 2nd intermediate draft, CIS-Bericht 90-22, CIS, University of Munich, 1990; to appear. Oxford University Press.

Ingria, Robert J. P. 1990. The Limits of Unification. In *Proceedings of the 28th Annual Meeting of the ACL, University of Pittsburgh*, 194–204. Pittsburgh, PA.

Moortgat, Michael. 1992. Labelled Deductive Systems for Categorial Theorem Proving. Working paper. Utrecht, The Netherlands: OTS, Rijksuniversiteit Utrecht. Also in P. Dekker and M. Stokhof (eds.) *Proceedings of the Eighth Amsterdam Colloquium.*

Moortgat, Michael, and Dick Oehrle. 1993. Lecture Notes on Categorial Grammar. Lecture notes. Lisbon, Portugal: Fifth European Summer School in Language, Logic and Information, August.

Morrill, Glyn. 1994. *Type Logical Grammar: Categorial Logic of Signs.* Kluwer.

Morrill, Glyn. 1992. Categorial Formalisation of Relativisation, Pied Piping, Islands and Extraction Sites. Technical Report LSI-92-23-R. Barcelona, Spain: Department de Llenguatges i sistemes informátics, Universitat Politécnica de Catalunya, September.

Pentus, Mati. 1994. Language Completeness of the Lambek Calculus,. In *Proceedings of Logic in Computer Science.* Paris.

Pollard, Carl, and Ivan Andrew Sag. 1987. *Information-Based Syntax and Semantics: Volume 1 Fundamentals.* Lecture Notes, Vol. 13. Stanford, CA: Center for the Study of Language and Information.

Pollard, Carl, and Ivan Andrew Sag. 1994. *Head-Driven Phrase Structure Grammar.* Chicago: University of Chicago Press and Stanford: CSLI Publications.

Pullum, Geoffrey K., and Arnold M. Zwicky. 1986. Phonological Resolution of Syntactic Feature Conflict. *Language* 62(4):751–773.

Shieber, Stuart M. 1992. *Constraint-Based Grammar Formalisms.* Cambridge, Mass.: MIT Press.

Smolka, Gert. 1992. Feature Constraint Logics for Unification Grammars. *Journal of Logic Programming* 12:51–87.

Smolka, Gert, and Ralf Treinen. 1994. Records for Logic Programming. *Journal of Logic Programming* 18(3):229–258.

Uszkoreit, Hans. 1986. Categorial Unification Grammar. In *11th International Conference on Computational Linguistics, COLING-86.*

van Benthem, Johan. 1986. *Essays in Logical Semantics.* Dordrecht: Reidel.

Zeevat, Henk, Ewan Klein, and Jonathan Calder. 1987. An Introduction to Unification Categorial Grammar. In *Edinburgh Working Papers in Cognitive Science*, ed. Nicholas J. Haddock, Ewan Klein, Glyn Morrill. 195–222. Centre for Cognitive Science, University of Edinburgh.

3

On Reducing Principles to Rules

Marcus Kracht

ABSTRACT. According to the research principles of the tradition established by Noam Chomsky, one should always try to get rid of construction specific rules. In *Bare Phrase Structure* he has carried this out to the extreme for the basic generative component now known as X-bar-syntax. Based on this example, we will examine the dialectics between specific rules and conditions on rules or *principles*. We will show that there is a two-way reduction, one from rules to conditions on rules, and the other from conditions on rules to specific rules. As an effect of this reduction, a particular linguistic theory can be presented alternatively as a set of rules or as an axiomatic extension of the logical theory of all phrase structure trees — or in fact a suitable mixture of the two. Although this reduction is a purely formal one — and therefore less interesting for a linguist subscribing to the Principles and Parameters approach — it offers the possibility to draw on a large array of results both from logic and from ordinary formal language theory.

1 Introduction

In physics, and in science generally, we seek simple and elegant laws; laws that hold without exception and which each explain a great variety of facts. Chomsky, and many other linguists with him, have stressed that linguistics should not be different in this respect. Of course, if linguistics were only a so-called *soft* science we might not be able to expect laws to be 100% valid — we might have to allow for exceptions. However Chomsky has insisted that linguistics deals with a real object, the *language faculty*, and that we can expect hard results about this object. Chomsky 1980 successfully defends the place of linguistics in science and its particular mode of inquiry. Furthermore, in Chomsky 1986b he has reminded us of the fact that there is a difference between language the way it presents itself to us (for example, in the form of grammatical judgments) and the

Specifying Syntactic Structures
P. Blackburn and M. de Rijke, eds.
Copyright © 1997, CSLI Publications.

way it is realized and manipulated internally. The former has been called E-language, the latter I-language.

Probably few people dispute that this distinction is reasonable and that we can have nontrivial results about the I-language. However, quite often the insistence that it is I-language that we should be interested in has been abused to shake off critics. One example that concerns us here is the reduction of principles to rules as undertaken in Kracht 1995b. Remarking on this technique Chomsky writes (p.c.)

[...] there is no nontrivial concept of weak generation, hence of weak generative capacity, for any theory of language that has been seriously proposed. Nor is there any explanatory gap that would be filled if such a notion were constructed. That is to say, there is no reason to believe that any such notion has the slightest relevance to natural language.

This passage at least implicitly uses the abovementioned distinction. The argument is that if the I-language does not make explicit use of a property then this property is of questionable interest in linguistics. I agree with the first two sentences, but not with the last. Any theory about I-language (or natural language for that matter) has to meet the facts, and these facts are — in standard practice — facts about E-language. Any attempt to systematize the latter will help in this process of evaluation. Even if we do not make any attempts to elucidate the structure of I-language, the description of E-language may be worth pursuing. What is more, we should welcome any result that mediates between various theoretical descriptions of language, be they of I-language or simply of E-language. The reason is the following. If in the course of inquiry we have to discuss problems concerning our theories, how do we settle the dispute? In the absence of any other knowledge we will probably try to evaluate the theories as far as possible, see where they differ and try to see which one is correct. To do this requires skill. For how do we know the consequences of a theory, if, as has been pointed out on numerous occasions, GB is so highly modular that small changes in one component can have bewildering global effects? It might be trivial to evaluate the effects given a specific construction, but who can foresee the *precise overall effect* of such changes? And who knows the exact limits of this enterprise in full? These are serious questions, and an answer is called for.

Perhaps this is not a problem for linguists. After all, linguists are interested mainly in empirical questions. Maybe such problems should be relegated to mathematics. However, Chomsky claims (p.c.)

The problem of formalization is, in my opinion, not a very interesting one. It's an easy matter to formalize a theory, but also a pointless exercise, which is why it is not undertaken in the natural sciences (even in mathematics, until recently). When the need arises within a research program, the gap can easily be filled (as it was in mathematics, when it became useful). The reason why it is pointless to formalize is that in doing so, we must make arbitrary decisions in areas where we do not know the answers, and that is simply a waste of time — though easy enough to do.

Although I half agree with these remarks, there is problem. In these remarks Chomsky essentially identifies *mathematics* with *formalization*. By doing so, Chomsky simply erects a strawman which he then successfully dismantles.

It's easy enough, though mistaken, to identify mathematics with formalization. Nearly all mathematics is formal in some sense — after all, typically lots of formulae get used. And if mathematics is not formal then what else is? However, formalization within mathematics, in the sense referred to by Chomsky in the above quotation, was a special development of the last century, aimed at placing mathematics on indisputable foundations. This did change mathematics since it tightened the requirements of what is to be counted a proof. Nonetheless, in everyday mathematics formalisation in the strict sense is absent: only *precision and clarity* are required. Much work in linguistics lacks both, and it is a noble task to look for remedies.

The distinction between formalisation and precision is well worth emphasizing. Strict formalization is often seen in linguistics. There is still the idea around in linguistics (and other sciences) that more symbols means more precision. This is both false and dangerous, and Chomsky is right to criticize it.

However, mathematicians do not present their assumptions and theorems as formal systems. They would be unreadable like this. Mathematics is *not* the art of formalization. The latter is only a craft within it. Rather, mathematics is a special form of inquiry, which explores the absolutely necessary conclusions of certain assumptions. If presented with a theory a mathematician would ask questions like *What are the models of this theory?* or *To what theory might this one be equivalent under suitable interpretation?* or *What are the consequences of this theory?* Usually, as is demonstrated by group theory for example, a system of classifying the structures of interest is developed as a result of mathematical investigations — thus one learns more and more about the structure of these objects and the power of the theory. It is in this sense that mathematics is extremely useful for all sciences — including linguistics.

This paper is not intended to be an abstract debate on the role of mathematics in linguistics. Rather, I will illustrate the utility of mathematics by discussing in some detail the special relation between *principles* and *rules*. I will show how rules can be reduced to principles, and how principles can be reduced to rules. The prime example used throughout is *X-bar-syntax*.

Lately, in Chomsky 1995, we have witnessed the total elimination of specific rules in favour of principles. We will analyse this particular solution and point at some difficult problems concerning the overall strategy. We will show that the particular form of Principles and Parameters Theory deriving from GB has its limits in that it cannot reduce certain phenomena to principles. In short, mathematics will provide us with a high level view of the architecture of transformational grammar,[1] and will enable us indicate some of its problematic features.

This paper describes research that has been carried out in part in the Innovationskolleg INK II/A12 'Formale Modelle kognitiver Komplexität' funded by the DFG. I wish to thank Noam Chomsky, Carsten Grefe, Werner Simon, Juan Uriagereka and Christian Wartena for discussions on this matter.

2   X-bar-Syntax

We begin by recalling X-bar-syntax in the particular form it reached in the 1980s with the work of Stowell (see Stowell 1981). X-bar-syntax provides a rudimentary analysis of sentences. It consists of a list of primitive categories, n, v, infl, comp, and nowadays a variety of functional categories such as agr–s, neg and so on. Their number is limited and can be seen as being derived from properties of the lexical items. Languages may or may not vary in their inventory of basic categories. Each category can project a phrase. By that we mean, roughly, that each category symbol not on a leaf of a syntactic tree can be traced to a leaf of the tree.[2] The totality of nodes thus corresponding to a given leaf form a subset of the tree which is linearly ordered by the dominance relation. This is called the *projection line* of the lexical item or leaf. Each node within that line is a *projection* of the leaf. In addition, projections have different *levels*, three for each category. Going up the tree, levels may not decrease.[3]

Notation and terminology is as follows. With comp being a basic category, $comp^0$ is a zero-level projection, also called the *lexical* or *minimal* level projection, $comp^1$, comp′ or $\overline{comp}$ the *first-level* or *intermediate* projection and $\overline{\overline{comp}}$, comp″ or compp the *second-level* or *phrasal* projection. With categories getting more complex, we will follow the GPSG-convention of writing them in the form of attribute-value pairs. The category $\overline{\overline{comp}}$

---

[1] A note on terminology. A multitude of approaches to linguistics have been advanced by Chomsky. I use the cover term *transformational grammar* to refer to all of these theories. In particular, this term covers GB, the Principles and Parameters framework and the Minimalist Program.

[2] This is a nontrivial fact corresponding to the requirement of strict endocentricity of constructions. But this is only an exposition of X-bar syntax, not an explanation of why it is the way it is.

[3] Again, this is a nontrivial assumption.

would be written in this notation as follows.

$$\begin{bmatrix} \text{CAT} & : & \text{comp} \\ \text{LEVEL} & : & 2 \end{bmatrix}$$

We assume the following X-bar rules, in traditional notation:

(u)	X''	$\rightarrow$	X'		X'	$\rightarrow$	X^0
(pp)	X''	$\rightarrow$	Y''	X''	X''	$\rightarrow$	X'' Y''
(pi)	X''	$\rightarrow$	Y''	X'	X''	$\rightarrow$	X' Y''
(ii)	X'	$\rightarrow$	Y''	X'	X'	$\rightarrow$	X' Y''
(iz)	X'	$\rightarrow$	Y''	X^0	X'	$\rightarrow$	X^0 Y''
(zz)	X^0	$\rightarrow$	Y^0	X^0	X^0	$\rightarrow$	X^0 Y^0

This schema is just *one* of the possibilities. Specifically, we have chosen a form of X-bar-syntax that holds throughout the derivation, not just at D-structure. We remain uncommitted with respect to this choice. The variables X and Y each stand for any particular choice of basic category.[4]

On the basis of these rules we can define what I want to call the *centricity role* of a node. There are four types of centricity roles, namely *head*, *complement*, *specifier* and *adjunct*. In each rule, one of the daughters is called the *head*. The head is of the same category as the mother. The other daughter (if there is one) is called a *complement* if one of the rules (iz) has been applied, *specifier* if one of the rules (pi) has been applied, and *adjunct* in all other cases.

Immediately, a problem appears. Nothing prevents us from choosing $X = Y$, in which case we cannot tell which is the head.[5] However, we can also move to a fully articulated X-bar syntax by introducing explicit *centricity* roles. In attribute-value notation, we have a feature CENT with values head, comp, spec, adct. To keep notation short, we will use booleans.

First one needs to introduce the centricity grammar. It is based on the *head grammar*, which itself only distributes the headness role.

(u)	$\top$	$\rightarrow$	head						
(b)	$\top$	$\rightarrow$	¬head	head		$\top$	$\rightarrow$	head	¬head

---

[4]A notational point. Chomsky 1986a uses in his exposition the variable X to denote both X and Y, Sternefeld 1991 lets Y'' appear to both sides in a rule, but hastens to add that this means it can appear on either side but not on both. Both are very unhelpful ways of stating the facts. Incidentally, many have followed Chomsky in using X just as a piece of ink to which the level symbols are tagged rather than as genuine variables.

[5]Fanselow 1991 is the only place where I have found this problem being discussed. In his view there can be only one head, and to identify it means that one has to resort to a more complex definition. However, if we assume that there are no base generated adjuncts of phrases and minimal projections, then the problematic case appears only at s-structure and LF. It has then been produced by movement. It is clear that the adjoined constituent cannot be called a head. As long as the derivational history can be recovered, it is then in principle possible to say which daughter is the head and which one is not.

(See Kracht 1995b for more details.) Here, $\top$ is a constant for the unit, that is, the element which is always true. As a consequence of this notation, the value of the mother is totally unimportant for determining the centricity role of a node. The roles comp, adct and spec are added by stating that all four centricity roles are exclusive. This completes the definition of the centricity grammar. In the rules (b), we are allowed to specialize ¬head to any of the three roles adct, comp and spec. Thus, effectively the centricity grammar makes no real distinction between adjuncts, complements and specifiers.

On top of the centricity grammar we can now define the X-bar syntax. Namely, we say that (i) the category value is passed from the mother to the head daughter, (ii) the levels are defined as follows: the level goes one down if there is no adjunct, otherwise it is the same at the mother and the head daughter. The non-head has level 0 if it is adjunct to a zero-level head, and is phrasal otherwise. We can see that with the centricity grammar introduced, the levels are redundant. Notice that GPSG and HPSG make use of the centricity roles, although it seems that GPSG would rather regard the notion of a head as epiphenomenal. The complete phrase structure rules (without levels), when put into (order irrelevant) attribute value notation, are like this:

$$\begin{bmatrix} \text{CENT} & : & 1 \\ \text{CAT} & : & \alpha \end{bmatrix} \rightarrow \begin{bmatrix} \text{CENT} & : & \text{head} \\ \text{CAT} & : & \alpha \end{bmatrix} \begin{bmatrix} \text{CENT} & : & \neg\text{head} \\ \text{CAT} & : & \beta \end{bmatrix}$$

In Chomsky 1995 a bold attempt is made at eliminating X-bar syntax by apparently reducing it to its bare minimum. The attack is chiefly directed towards the level grammar. We have already seen that it is in principle dispensible, but it is worthwhile to see Chomsky's solution here. If we put adjunction aside for the moment, we see that X-bar syntax mainly provides a reason for there being a single complement and a single specifier. We can achieve the same by saying that in a projection line the lowest node is lexical and the highest one is phrasal. Assuming that we can always identify heads (for example by banning the rules $X^0 \rightarrow X^0\ X^0$ and $X'' \rightarrow X''\ X''$) we can identify the level of each node. However, since the levels are not intrinsic characteristics of single nodes, but are in fact relational, the level of a node can only be recovered given a suitably large context. If we want to abandon the restrictions posed by the levels on how to rewrite these level-projections, we encounter the problem that we have to stipulate that without adjunction any projection line has length three. (Kayne 1994, by the way, achieves this by pairing linear order with asymmetric c-command.)

Chomsky is now led to assume that this restriction must be lifted. Given that eventually there will be no explicit distinction between specifier, (adjunct and) complement, this is most sensible, because it allows for the standard recursion within phrases (for example, it allows, contra Kayne, any number of base generated X'-adjuncts, to use the old terminology). Furthermore, every rule must now be branching. Chomsky now codes trees as sets in the following way. We define a function t on binary branching trees with explicit marking of a head, and a function h which will define the head of the entire tree. If the tree τ consists only of a single node, carrying the lexical entry α, then $t(\tau) := \alpha$ and $h(\tau) := \alpha$. This is the ground clause; for the inductive clause suppose that we have a tree τ consisting of two immediate subtrees σ_1 and σ_2. We now need to know which of σ_1 and σ_2 is the head. This is given to us by the assumption that the heads are explicitly marked. Suppose the node y_1, the root of σ_1, is the head. Then

$$\begin{aligned} t(\tau) &:= \{h(\tau), \{t(\sigma_1), t(\sigma_2)\}\} \\ h(\tau) &:= h(\sigma_1). \end{aligned}$$

There is the possibility that both terms are equal, in which case the set reduces to $\{\alpha, \{t(y_1)\}\}$. On the assumption that trees are strictly binary branching, we can nevertheless recover the original tree. However, this does not seem to be an intended effect. If σ_2 is the head, then $h(\tau)$ has to be defined as $h(\sigma_2)$. Furthermore, since in the bare structure we need no levels, it is possible to use the head as a label. Thus for the structure *the book* we have the following code

$$\{the, \{the, book\}\}$$

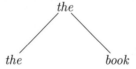

Notice that nothing is assumed about the relative order of the elements. Thus, with the set notation, everything is derived from the lexicon.

Now, in order to incorporate adjunction, Chomsky uses a trick. Rather than using the term $\{h(\sigma_1), \{t(\sigma_1), t(\sigma_2)\}\}$ he now defines (for σ_1 the head of τ)

$$t(\tau) := \{\langle h(\sigma_1), h(\sigma_1)\rangle, \{t(\sigma_1), t(\sigma_2)\}\}.$$

Thus, rather than using the lexical entry of the head of the construction as a marker of the head of construction, he just uses the pair $\langle h(\sigma_1), h(\sigma_1)\rangle$. Given the typical definition of a pair $\langle x, y\rangle$ as the set $\{\{x\}, \{x, y\}\}$ we get

$$t(\tau) = \{\{h(\sigma_1)\}\}, \{t(\sigma_1), t(\sigma_2)\}\}.$$

This encoding can also be used to give labels to each node in a tree; simply identify the label of x with $t(\downarrow x)$, where $\downarrow x$ is the constituent rooted at x. Seen this way, each node label is actually also a code of the structure of the constituent underneath that node. This explains why movement can never go down in a tree, only upwards. (This was pointed out to me by

Juan Uriagereka, who refers to this as the *Grandmother Problem*.) Moving down would mean inserting some nodes into the tree, whereby all labels further up would fail to correctly encode the structure of the tree. Thus we have an explanation of why already built structure resists manipulation. This explanation, however, is conditional on an analysis of movement as a process that takes place in time, as does real movement. As much as I agree with this — since it means that the term *movement* is well chosen as a metaphor — it is precisely that interpretation that Chomsky rejects. We will not pursue such issues further here.[6]

3   The Human Computational System

In order to understand the motivation of *Bare Phrase Structure* one has explain the framework in which it has been put, namely the *Minimalist Program* of Chomsky 1993. There Chomsky explores the consequences of the assumption that a linguistic theory should employ only those concepts that follow — as Chomsky puts it — with *virtual necessity* from the fact that the language faculty mediates between sound and meaning. The difference between the Minimalist Program and the aims of Chomsky 1995 is that in the latter he is more concerned with minimizing the additional components of the representation itself rather than the global architecture of the theory. The latter contains now two so-called *interfaces*, namely (from syntax to) the *articulatory-perceptual* system (A-P) and (from syntax to) the *intentional-conceptual* system (C-I). Ideally, what we observe as nontrivial properties of the grammar should be consequences of conditions imposed by the two systems.

Chomsky assumes that there is one and only one lexicon, that there is a single computational system (C_{HL}) and that both together derive representations that are fed to the two systems A-P and C-I. D-structure and s-structure have been abandoned, mainly because by definition a level of representation must serve the purpose of checking nontrivial properties, and if there is nothing to check at these levels, they cannot be called levels of representation. It is formally possible (and sometimes also useful for comparison) to think that D- and S-structure are there nevertheless, but that nothing is checked there. But while this is possible, from an explanatory point of view we would loose something. Namely, it is a specific conceptual advance in the Minimalist Program that conditions on representations must be motivated by external demands. The computational system is free to derive any structure it can, but those which violate output conditions,

---

[6]Another relevant question is why the representation should be in terms of sets, as presented here. Such labellings should be excluded on economical grounds since they code what is present in the structure anyway.

that is, those which give rise to problems at the interface, are filtered out because the systems to which they are sent are unable to handle them.

The computational system operates as follows. It draws from the lexicon a multiset (Chomsky uses the term *numeration*, but this is practically the same thing) and composes the items into trees via an operation called *Merge*, performing on its way some other nontrivial operations (forming chains, moving items, and so on). There is no point at which the former D-structure can be said to be present. In that sense it has really been abandoned. Thus, C_{HL} may draw the multiset $\{reads, the, book\}_m{}^7$ and then form a tree-term

$$\{the, \{the, book\}\},$$

identifying *the* as the head of the phrase (due to properties derived from the lexical entry itself). It may then continue to incorporate the verb into the tree to yield

$$\{reads, \{reads, \{the, \{the, book\}\}\}\}.$$

The notation leaves a lot of things unseen. The entry for *book* contains extra features, as do the verb and the determiner. In particular, all items are inserted with full morphological specification, for example, for case, gender, and so on (though that is not a necessary assumption in the Minimalist Program). Features come in two classes, *interpretable features* and *uninterpretable features*. Uninterpretable features (for example, Case) must be seen as genuinely syntactic, that is, they belong to C_{HL} and must therefore disappear before the (derived) structure is presented at the interface. Interpretable features are allowed to survive the derivation, because the C-I component does not reject them (as it would with the uninterpretable ones). At the cost of misrepresenting the original proposal we can picture the elimination of features as follows. A feature FEAT can have several values, $val_1, \ldots, val_n$. C_{HL} operates by moving features; if that feature is connected with a constituent then that constituent is taken along with that feature.

A note on terminology is actually necessary here. Features in the Minimalist Program are by intention pairs [FEAT : val]. However, there is also talk of the Case-feature of a DP. Here, we use the following convention. Only CASE is the feature, while the pair [CASE : nom], say, is an *elementary feature-structure*. An item can get rid of its elementary feature-structure [FEAT : val_i] either by moving into the specifier of or by adjoining to the

---

[7]The subscript m is used to identify this as a multiset. Recall that in a multiset the number of occurrences of an element matters, not however the order in which they are listed. In the present example the multiset is not different from the mere set, but in the following example, it is:

$$\{the, pope, wrote, the, book\}_m.$$

head of a functional projection carrying [FEAT : val$_i$]. The word order variation is derived by assuming that features are either *strong* or *weak* and that at the point at which the structure is prepared for the articulatory interface, only elementary feature structures corresponding to weak features are stripped off (this point is called *Spell-Out*). If strong feature-value pairs remain, A-P cannot process it and the derivation is said to *crash*; that is, it terminates with no output.

The Spell-Out point can be equated with S-structure. However, in the new system Spell-Out can take place at any point in the derivation, though of course many of the attempts at Spell-Out will yield a crash. Thus, with the numeration fixed we can have many Spell-Out points. Notice, however, that in GB there need not be a single S-structure for a given D-structure. The difference with the Minimalist Program is only that in the latter the derivational component does not identify itself the S-structure; rather, the S-structure is identified indirectly as those points of Spell-Out which do not yield a crashing derivation. The identification is thus made into an interface condition.

Of course, there must be the possibility of having several S-structures for a given D-structure; otherwise it is not clear, for example, why Scrambling in Germanic languages or Rightward Movement can be optional. Notice, however, that in the original system the apparent options for Spell-Out quickly reduce to one and only one point. Thus, strictly interpreted, free word order in Germanic languages receives no explanation. The Minimalist Program, although accounting for cross language variation, has no explanation for such language internal variation.

The distinctive feature of the Minimalist Program is the use of global and abstract principles that have no equivalent in GB and the Principles and Parameters framework. First, there is the principle *Procrastinate*, which simply forbids any movement. The reason why there is movement at all is that this principle has lowest priority and can be overridden. Second, there is the principle *Greed* which says that movement must result in a benefit. Originally, *Greed* required the benefit to be for the item that is being moved. Thus, an item may only move if it itself receives a benefit from doing so. In particular, this benefit lies in getting rid of a feature. If in the course of a derivation we are before (a non crashing) Spell-Out point then we can only move if we thereby strip off a strong feature, because there is another chance after Spell-Out and the latter is preferred by *Procrastinate*. By moving an element it may serve to check a strong feature of another element, as has been noted in Čavar and Wilder 1994, who call this phenomenon *Early altruism*. This principle is compatible with Greed. For movement need not be beneficial exclusively for the element that is being moved; side effects for other elements are allowed to occur.

To save the whole process from overgenerating, Chomsky also employs a set of economy principles, namely the requirement that (i) only shortest moves may be made, and (ii) the fewest number of steps must be chosen. The first is a condition for convergence (that is, the derivation will otherwise crash). The second is covered by another principle called *Economy*. In the Minimalist Program it assumed a specific form, namely as the transderivational constraint that one must choose the shortest possible derivation.

The actual wording of these constraints or principles has given rise to a lot of confusion. There have been debates about the compatibility of these economy principles, but we will refrain from commenting on them. Suffice it to say that it is still unclear how economy can be properly formulated to meet the facts of language.

4   Principles as Axioms as Rules

I have argued at length in Kracht 1995a that it is possible to reduce principles of grammar to axioms within a special kind of modal logic which has been dubbed the *constituent logic*, **CL**. That much may in this context be granted, since axioms and principles are of similar nature. Rogers 1994 has conducted similar investigations, using a second order logic over structures with successor functions. These two approaches are similar in spirit, and there seem to be deeper connections, which are however not fully understood.

In this section I will briefly outline the syntax and semantics of **CL**. **CL** is in fact a variety of special languages, each a fragment of dynamic logic. Recall from Harel 1984 or Goldblatt 1987 that dynamic logic has two types of well-formed expressions, propositions and programs. There are denumerably many propositional variables, $var = \{p_1, p_2, \ldots\}$, denumerably many propositional constants, $con = \{c_1, c_2, \ldots\}$, the usual boolean connectives $\wedge, \vee, \neg, \rightarrow$, any fixed number of elementary *programs*, $prg = \{\pi_1, \pi_2, \ldots, \pi_m\}$, the program connectives $\cup, \circ, ^*$, and finally the test ? and the brackets $[-], \langle - \rangle$. If α and β are programs, so is α^*, $\alpha \cup \beta$ and $\alpha \circ \beta$. If ϕ is a proposition, ϕ? is a program. Finally, if α is a program and ϕ a proposition, then $[\alpha]\phi$ and $\langle \alpha \rangle \phi$ are both propositions.

A *frame model* is a triple $\langle f, \beta, \eta \rangle$ where $\beta : var \cup con \rightarrow \wp(f)$ and $\eta : prg \rightarrow \wp(f \times f)$. Both β and η can be extended over all propositions and programs as follows.

$$\begin{aligned}
\beta(\neg\phi) &:= f - \beta(\phi) & \beta(\phi \wedge \psi) &:= \beta(\phi) \cap \beta(\psi) \\
\beta(\phi \vee \psi) &:= \beta(\phi) \cup \beta(\psi) \\
\eta(\phi?) &:= \{\langle x, x \rangle | x \in \beta(\phi)\} & \eta(\alpha \cup \delta) &:= \eta(\alpha) \cup \eta(\delta) \\
\eta(\alpha \circ \delta) &:= \eta(\alpha) \cdot \eta(\delta) & \eta(\alpha^*) &:= \eta(\alpha)^* \\
\beta([\alpha]\phi) &:= \{x | (\forall y)(\langle x, y \rangle \in \eta(\alpha) \rightarrow y \in \beta(\phi))\} \\
\beta(\langle \alpha \rangle \phi) &:= \{x | (\exists y)(\langle x, y \rangle \in \eta(\alpha) \wedge y \in \beta(\phi))\}
\end{aligned}$$

Here, we have made use of the relation composition $\cdot$, and Kleene Star, *, which are defined as follows.

$$R \cdot S \quad := \quad \{\langle x, z\rangle | (\exists y)(\langle x, y\rangle \in R \text{ and } \langle y, z\rangle \in S)\}$$
$$R^* \quad := \quad id \cup R \cup R \cdot R \cup R \cdot R \cdot R \cup \dots$$

It would take too much to explain more about dynamic logic in general, instead I will now turn to the logic(s) **CL**. The specialty is that we assume two different types of programs: features and orientation programs. Of the latter there are only three or four, depending on necessity. They serve to look around inside the syntactic tree. We assume that our models are ordered trees (in the sense that for each node the set of daughters is linearly ordered) with each node being a feature structure consisting of possibly stacked attribute-value pairs. The tree relations are *one step down*, *one step left* and *one step right* and the fourth one is *one step up*. They are abbreviated by *down*, *left*, *right* and *up*. Instead of $\langle down\rangle$ we write $\Diamond$, and instead of $[down]$ we write $\Box$. The symbols $\Diamond$, $\boxminus$, $\Diamond$ and $\boxminus$, $\Diamond$, $\Box$ should be self-explanatory. We assume any fixed number of features $\text{FEAT}_1, \dots, \text{FEAT}_m$ and a finite set of constants. **CL** has axioms which force the interpretation of *down*, *left* and *right* to form an ordered tree. Moreover, any formula stacking the orientation programs inside feature-programs will be false; thus we have axioms of the form $[\text{FEAT}_i \circ down]\bot$. Finally, each feature is deterministic, that is, the relations corresponding to these features are partial functions. This is easy to axiomatize.

Almost any particular grammar using some finite set of features can be rewritten as an axiomatic extension of **CL**. This has been demonstrated in Kracht 1995a. Moreover, assume that the trees of the grammars have an upper bound n on the number of daughters for a single node. Furthermore, let $\mathbf{CL}_n$ be the extension of **CL** by an axiom stating that the bound is n. Then the following is a theorem (Kracht 1995b).

Theorem 4.1 (Coding Theorem) *Let Λ be an extension of $\mathbf{CL}_n$ by finitely many axioms. The finite trees characterized by Λ can be generated by a context-free grammar iff Λ is axiomatizable by finitely many constant formulae over $\mathbf{CL}_n$.*

This theorem is called the Coding Theorem because the method by which it is proved is by enriching the language with constants, which stand for certain properties of nodes. A grammar that distributes a constant exactly at those nodes that satisfy a property P is called a *syntactic code* of P. To enforce a condition P on a given grammar G one first writes a code H for P; then H is fused with G. This fusion is a straightforwardly definable procedure. This theorem establishes a strong correspondence between two ways of characterizing the structures of a language, either directly via axioms (alias universal principles) or indirectly by a generating system (alias grammar).

It is important not to underestimate the fact that such a grammar can generate these structures directly — for a given logic, after all, it may not be clear how to build correct models. On the other hand, axiomatic extensions of **CL** are expressible also in a fragment of second-order logic with only universal prefixes for predicate variables. For the latter it is known that the validity of sentences can be checked on a finite model in polynomial time. So, at least from this perspective, **CL** is not too difficult a language.

An informal account of the ideas underlying the proof of the coding theorem may be of interest to some readers, for the proof itself is technically demanding. Following Kracht 1995b we start with a grammar that has only *n*-ary branching rules and is completely arbitrary, that is, all rules are admitted.[8] Basically, it is clear that any kind of local dependency (mother-daughter and sister-sister) can be encoded into the rule system by just throwing away all those rules not conforming to these dependencies. For example, if there is a law stating that a feature FEAT should be instantiated to a value at a given node iff it is instantiated to that same value at the mother, then simply throw away all rules in which mother and daughter do not agree in the value of FEAT. In order to handle the non-local dependencies we must introduce additional features. For example, if an axiom requires a node to agree with its *grandmother* with respect to FEAT then we add a new feature N-FEAT together with the axiom that the N-FEAT-value of a node should agree with the FEAT-value of the mother, and another to require that the FEAT-value of a node should be identical to the N-FEAT-value of the mother. This clearly encodes *grandmother-granddaughter-agreement.* Similarly, *spec-head-agreement* would require the addition of an extra feature. However, it is not always necessary to introduce new features. In the second case, we also have *mother-head-daughter-agreement* for the original feature, and so the dependency from the specifier to the zero-level head of the phrase proceeds through a series of local dependencies. The latter can thus be coded into the grammar directly, without additional features. Thus, what the result above comes down to is the observation that, at the cost of having to add new features, we can extend the range of dependencies considerably to include — for example — what is known in LFG as functional uncertainty, and many other relations.

As it turns out, there are types of principles which do not correspond to constant axioms because they force the grammar to be non-context free. A familiar construction are the cross-serial dependencies.[9] Despite the fact

---

[8]Here we need the finite branching assumption. Without it the set of rules would be infinite.

[9]In Kracht 1995a it is shown how simple grammars for such cross-serial-dependencies can be reduced to axioms. In the present circumstances it is however not necessary to know how this particular solution works.

that they cannot be reduced to context-free grammars, there are some more powerful grammars to which they too can be reduced. Particularly suitable in this respect are *definite clause grammars*, or DCGs for short. A rule in a DCG may for our purposes just be of the form $F \rightarrow G_1 \ldots G_m$, where F and G_i, $1 \leq i \leq m$, are feature-structures. A DCG is context-free iff it can be written using a finite number of such feature-structures. (This is not to say that it must use finitely many symbols, only that up to syntactic distinguishability it uses finitely many.) Characteristically, DCGs allow for more than that, yet they too can encode only strictly local dependencies. The same trick may therefore be used with DCGs to show that non-local dependencies can be reduced to local dependencies at the cost of introducing new features.

Theorem 4.2 *Let n be a natural number and Λ be an extension of* $\mathbf{CL}_n$ *by finitely many axioms. The finite trees characterized by Λ can be generated by a definite clause grammar.*

This result shows that it is one and the same thing to speak of an axiomatic system and to speak of definite clause grammars. However, the correspondence is not entirely straightforward. First, only finitely axiomatizable logics may be considered (which form a sublattice of the entire lattice of extensions). Secondly, there may be logics which are not determined by their finite models. So the translation from logic to grammar and back may yield a *stronger logic*. In the case of context-free grammars, however, there is no danger of that happening.

5   Transformations and their Stratification

That logics correspond to DCGs shows rather directly that GPSG- and HPSG-style grammars can be directly analysed as axiomatic extensions of the constituent logic. The same holds for LFG, even with functional uncertainty; this was demonstrated in Kracht 1995a. Thus, with the exception of transformational grammar and categorial grammar, we are able to translate back and forth between grammars and logics describing their parse trees, and thus can analyse these theories and compare them on — so to speak — neutral territory.

However, it is possible to use the same methods for transformational grammar as well. All that is needed is a way of reducing movement. For, since transformations operate on structures to produce new structures, we must find a way to let a single structure represent all there is to the derivational history of a structure once generated by the base component (if there is any). So, we need to flatten out the derivations in such a way that we can talk about a single structure rather than a sequence of them. Let us call the process of reducing transformational grammars *stratification*.

There are versions of transformational grammar that are stratified, for example Koster 1986 and Brody 1995. The latter also raises many points against derivational analyses, some of which overlap with those given below. It should be stressed that the point we are making is a formal one, not one pertaining to the empirical coverage of any theory, and less also to the internal structure of the theory. We could, as does Brody, simply argue in favour of a stratified account by pointing at economy principles, which should favour a movement-free account. We will not do that; the reader is referred to the quoted book instead. Moreover, although there is talk of evidence against a stratified account, we will show that from a purely descriptive point of view there is no way to decide which of the two is more adequate, because they are reducible to each other.

We assume that transformations are simply *movement* operations. There is no deletion in the sense of removing structure, only in the sense of marking an element as phonetically empty. (Thus after deletion, the structure is still there but will not be pronounced.) Now, using a trick akin to abstract incorporation we can encode LF into s-structure.[10] All this is fairly standard. If we want to pursue the reduction to **CL** we must, however, also get rid of indices. To do that we assume that the structure of a trace is (almost) isomorphic to that of the antecedent. This was in fact proposed in Chomsky 1993 but is rejected in Chomsky 1995. Commenting on a structure where a noun is incorporated into a verb which itself has raised he notes

In all such cases it is possible to formulate the desired result in terms of outputs. For example, in the movement-case, one can appeal to the (plausible) assumption that the trace is a copy, so the intermediate V-trace includes within it a record of the local $V \to N$ raising. But surely this is the wrong move. The relevant chains at LF are (N, t_N) and (V, t_V), and in these the locality relation by successive raising is not represented.

I fail to see why this is the wrong move. Nobody knows what the structure of traces is at LF. It can only be deduced with the help of assumptions on the global architecture of the grammatical system and the structure of representation(s). Further, notice that even if there is every reason to believe that the current program is on the right track, one should still acknowledge the importance of this reduction of indices. If the purpose is to compare different theories of grammar with respect to their empirical predictions, then in absence of any hard evidence for LF and its structure, appeal to its 'evident' properties is illegitimate. Transformationalists may be granted their different levels, whether they are in fact part of the human symbolic system or not — but they must be prepared to accept comparison

---

[10]Recall that s-structure is nonexistent in the minimalist program. Nevertheless, we may regard it as identical to the Spell-Out point. What is important is that we need to encode the surface alignment of the lexical items.

to theories without them. To give a crude example, all symbolic processes can be described by using natural numbers and recursive functions. This means that anything can be reduced to a game played with numbers. This however is no ontological claim; all that is claimed is the existence of a faithful encoding of a symbolic process into a process involving numbers. Mathematically this is advantageous because a recursion theorist can then go on studying recursive functions on natural numbers only. What numbers *are* is not the problem of a recursion theorist.

There are alternative ways to express the same facts which also do not make use of movement. One very attractive proposal is that we should think in terms of links or reentrant structures, as for example in HPSG. Instead of copying material we just make or add a link from the antecedent to the trace or conversely, analogous to manipulating a pointer structure in a computer. Notice that reentrant structures are more economical representations than the ones standardly used in transformational grammar.

Now assume that traces are copies, isomorphic to their antecedents with the exception that one is marked as a trace the other as antecedent. Since there are no indices there must be independent ways to identify the trace-antecedent pairs. In the GB this was possible due to two facts. One was that there were limits on the distance between trace and antecedent and the other was that within these limits many landing sites for the antecedent were ruled out as improper. The latter restrictions can be coded by additional features (such as whether the item originated in an A-position, a case-position, and so on). The former are formulated in terms of mutual command. In Kracht 1993 I have shown what relations are relevant for the usual cases in GB. I put aside a proof that all these relations can be encoded as **CL**-programs (easy) even with the by now standard distinction between nodes and segments of a category (less easy, but still straightforward). Moreover, I will also omit the proof that the fact that trace and antecedent are related to each other via a relation R remains valid throughout all subsequent levels, so that we can check whether trace and antecedent are R-related at any level, thus at S-structure. (The latter is a nontrivial property of the command relations in syntax and the way adjunction works, and a proof of that fact is not entirely straightforward.)

If all these assumptions are granted, all versions of GB can be stratified. But what about the Minimalist Program? Here we have no straightforward definitions of domains, but only certain principles on when and where to move. I can see no direct way to state an axiom to account for the requirement that a derivation must be optimal among all competing ones, nor an axiom to the effect that the fewest number of steps is being made. However, the cases for which these principles have been invented, can (in my opinion) be accounted for. Certainly the other principles, *Greed, Procrastinate* and *Shortest Steps* can be given an axiomatic encoding. To see this, consider first Shortest Steps. It says that an element must move to the closest possible landing site. Since landing sites are identified by their category (and some features), this requirement boils down to a command relation between trace and antecedent in the sense of Kracht 1993. Namely, for every trace there must be an antecedent within a certain command domain of the trace. In order to specify what the antecedent must look like given the trace, we say that a feature structure α is a *minor* of τ if (i) all elementary feature-value pairs of α are in τ, (ii) if τ contains strong features then some pair [FEAT : val] such that FEAT is strong is contained in τ but not α, (iii) some pair [FEAT : val] is contained in τ but not in α. (Here, α *contains* [FEAT : val] if $\alpha \models \langle \text{feat} \rangle \text{val}$. (i) encodes the fact that the antecedent is obtained by nibbling off structure from τ, (ii) is Procrastinate, (iii) is Greed.) So, finally, Shortest Steps says that given an occurrence of a structure τ in a tree that contains a feature, there exists within some command domain of τ a unique α which is a minor of τ.

One should take this formalization with a grain of salt, though. First, the domain extension has to be taken into account. That is to say, domains change in the course of derivation. Second, there are versions of Procrastinate that do not allow an encoding as proposed above. We might for example minimize over the length of derivations leading to a Spell-Out point. These issues tend to get very intricate when one looks at the possible ramifications. It is nevertheless a plausible hypothesis that while local economy principles can be replaced by axioms on the structure (or output filters), transderivational economy principles generally cannot.

6 An Analysis of Bare Phrase Structure

Let us now return to the reduction of X-bar syntax to bare phrase structure. Consider the case where we start out with an articulated X-bar grammar using categories, levels and centricity roles. Trees are binary branching, so we work over $\mathbf{CL}_2$. Let us introduce new features JOI and DIR, with values $+$ and $-$. Technically, they can be defined as follows.

$$\begin{array}{lcl} [\text{JOI} : +] & \leftrightarrow & \Diamond\text{adct} \\ [\text{JOI} : -] & \leftrightarrow & \neg\Diamond\text{adct} \\ [\text{DIR} : +] & \leftrightarrow & \Diamond(\text{head} \wedge \neg\Diamond\top) \\ [\text{DIR} : -] & \leftrightarrow & \Diamond(\text{head} \wedge \neg\Diamond\top) \end{array}$$

In words, JOI encodes whether or not a node is an upper segment, that is, resulted from adjoining to its daughter. DIR encodes the position of the head. [DIR : +] states that the head is to the left, while [DIR : $-$] states that it is to the right. In terms of these features it is possible to recover the category of the mother from that of its daughters, by simply passing up the category of the head daughter.[11] The directionality feature tells us which of the two is the head. Furthermore, the mother node can tell whether or not it is the result of adjunction. Thus we can recover also the phrase level in the following way. We know that a completed phrase is a non-head (if it is not the root), and that going up from the highest non-adjoined node within it we have level 2; however, we want to express this in terms of the primitives JOI and DIR rather than the centricity roles. Note that head is definable as follows:

$$\text{head.} \leftrightarrow .\neg\Diamond\top \wedge \Diamond[\text{DIR} : +] \vee \neg\Diamond\top \wedge \Diamond[\text{DIR} : -] \vee \neg\Diamond\top.^{[12]}$$

In other words, we are a head if we are on the left and the mother has its head on the left hand side, or we are on the right hand side and the mother has its head there too. We introduce the constants u–seg and l–seg, standing for *being an upper segment* and *being a lower segment*. Then we have

$$\begin{aligned} \text{u–seg} &\leftrightarrow [\text{JOI} : -] \\ \text{l–seg} &\leftrightarrow \neg\Diamond\top \vee \Diamond(\text{head} \wedge \text{u–seg}). \end{aligned}$$

Now we can recover the levels by saying that *level: 2* or *phrasal* means either being the root or a non-adjoined non-head or else, on going up until the next non-head, every node must be adjoined. This can be defined in **CL**:

$$\text{phr.} \leftrightarrow .\neg\Diamond\top \vee \langle((\text{head?}); (\neg\text{u–seg?}); up)^*\rangle(\text{u–seg} \wedge \neg\text{head}).$$

Being lexical — or zero-level — and *being first-level* can also be defined. A zero-level category is either non-adjoined and preterminal (or terminal in Chomsky's new version, but this is really unimportant) or adjoined and travelling down adjoined nodes we will eventually meet a non-adjoined preterminal:

$$\text{lex.} \leftrightarrow .\langle((\text{head?}); \neg\text{l–seg?}); down)^*\rangle\Box\bot.$$

Finally, a node is *level: 1* iff it is $\neg\text{lex} \wedge \neg\text{phr}$. A node may be both lexical and phrasal.

---

[11]Talk of feature passing is meant to be metaphorical. It is totally irrelevant for the result whether we talk of passing a feature up, passing it down, or whether we phrase this as principles of feature agreement.

[12]Technically, the root is herewith also classified as a head. This is done for purely technical reasons, and has no further implications.

Notice that here we have used the upgoing modality. Elsewhere in Kracht 1995a I have shown that practically speaking this modality is unnecessary. This requires explanation. Notice that the coding results really show that there is a close link between features and expressive power of the language that we use to express the principles. In other words, all we are doing is to boost up the non-logical symbolism to compensate for the fact that certain strong constructors are not present, such as Kleene Star and others. The less expressive power, the more additional basic constants or feature-constructs we must add to ensure a proper formulation of the principles. At present our aim is to use as few constants or constructors as possible, and this means that we may be forced to use a stronger language to define the otherwise explicit constants.

There still remain the centricity roles. Being adct means being a daughter of a non-lower segment. spec is the highest non-adjunct that is not a comp and comp is a non-adjunct sister of a lexical head.

$$\begin{aligned} \text{adct} \quad &. \leftrightarrow . \quad \neg\text{head} \land \Diamond(\neg\text{l–seg}) \\ \text{comp} \quad &. \leftrightarrow . \quad \Diamond(\text{head} \land \text{u–seg} \land \text{lex}) \lor \Diamond(\text{head} \land \text{u–seg} \land \text{lex}) \\ \text{spec} \quad &. \leftrightarrow . \quad \neg\text{comp} \land \neg\text{head} \land \Diamond(\text{l–seg} \land \text{phr}). \end{aligned}$$

Suppose now that the following axiom holds

(†) $\qquad\qquad\qquad$ head $\lor$ spec $\lor$ comp $\lor$ adct.

Then immediately we would get the same X-bar syntax back again. However, Chomsky's aim in this case is to get rid of such axioms since they put global constraints on the representation within the syntactic component so he dismisses it, with the consequence that we have a fifth type of centricity role, which might suitably be translated as *base generated intermediate adjunct*. This is because there can be any number of intermediate level nodes with feature [JOI : $-$]. It is *not* an axiom that there are exactly five of them, this follows already from the way things are set up, that is, it is a theorem. Chomsky on the other hand redefines the notion of a specifier to include this fifth type of a centricity role (and so he gets back (†) as a theorem).

Let us summarize what we have got so far. We can code a traditional phrase structure tree as follows. (i) The category is labelled only at the leaves, (ii) all other nodes are of four types only, indicating whether they are adjoined or not and whether the head daughter is found on the left or on the right. Lifting the ban on base generated intermediate adjunction we can observe that there are absolutely no restrictions left on the representation, so any tree satisfying (i) and (ii) is legitimate.

Notice, by the way, that the way in which these trees are represented according to Chomsky 1995 is highly inefficient, because it introduces great deal of redundancy. To copy the head into the mother given that a lexicon contains hundreds of thousands of words, is a waste of memory. Instead, the two distinctive features are enough. It's true that they do not derive from the lexicon, but then neither do the sets in the set notation. I should also point out that in using sets Chomsky also gets rid of representations of order in the structure. Presumably, ordering should be derivable from other properties. I have no stance on that here, but I'd like to point out that rather than *sets*, it seems that *lists* are the primitives out of which everything is formed (at least in a computer). I do not know of any compelling argument that information is stored in the form of a set rather than a list. In the case at hand we have two options. (i) List all rules twice, (ii) disconnect linear order in the string from the physical alignment and let the latter be explicitly encoded by another feature REAL, where

[REAL : +] means that the daughters are aligned in the same way as coded, and [REAL : −] that they are aligned in opposite order.

But now let us return to the bare phrase structure. What is still worrying is the fact that we need the additional features for adjunction and head positioning. Ultimately, we may want to get rid of them, thus turning to a representation which is just a set encoding the constituent structure. The idea presented by Chomsky is to derive it from independent principles of grammar. This, however, requires a rather deep analysis of the total system. Let us illustrate how it can be performed. Suppose that we start with the multiset $\{book, the, read\}_m$. It is a fact that determiners select nouns.[13] So we project a structure $\{the, \{the, book\}\}$, assuming the difference between sets and multisets to be irrelevant at the structural level. We know where the head is, and that there is a complement. Next we project a structure

$$\{read, \{read, \{the, \{the, book\}\}\}\}.$$

The head is *read*, from subcategorization. Suppose now that the complement moves for checking. Then we the following structure

$$\{\langle read, read\rangle, \{\{the, \{the, book\}\}, \{read, \{read, \underline{t}\}\}\}\}.$$

Next we must assume the verb to have been raised, and so on. If we follow this process close enough and ensure that trace-antecedent relations are recoverable after stratification, then a suitably complex definition will capture the notion of head position and adjoinedness.

We shall not pursue this further but simply note that in addition to there being a genuine concern in spotting the redundancies of the system there is much of shadow boxing as well. We can make the representation compact in the way suggested, but the price we pay is that the control structure will be complex. Thus, this is the opposite of the Coding Method, where we seek to reduce control structure and explode the feature system instead. There is an antagonism between explicit symbolism and the power of the language in which principles are being formulated. Powerful languages require very complicated control structures so that they can be executed correctly, whence a reduction of the explicit symbolism increases the complexity of the control structure. This would require spelling out the control strategy rather carefully; this has not been undertaken in the Minimalist Program. On the other hand, control can be identified with structure in a rather precise way. Recall from Kracht 1995b the idea of

---

[13]It is unclear where to place this requirement. It is probably not part of the lexicon because it is a regular fact of language, at least if we assume it correct that NPs should be seen as DPs. The selection facts, be they universal (that is, part of UG) or language particular, as many propose (for example, Laka 1991) do not belong to the computational system qua transformational component but qua structure building process (although the two are now non-distinct).

a *memory*. We may forget as suggested the category labels in the representation, but while parsing a sentence these labels must be recorded somewhere. A rule based grammar of X-bar syntax has them present in each node (whence the redundancy), while for bare phrase structure we need to compute them. However, rather than recomputing them all the time we will simply store them in a *memory*. The amount of extra storage needed to correctly parse sentences is called the *size* of memory. This just measures in the finite case the distance from this grammar to a context-free grammar performing the same analysis. A final note. Chomsky's particular reduction of the level grammar to properties of C_{HL}, in particular the visibility properties of projections, is not without major problems, as has been pointed out by Gaertner 1995.

7 Why Rules are Sometimes Better

Most of the data discussed in the transformational tradition consists of alignment facts. Very little is being said about agreement, although at present — in the Minimalist Program — agreement seems to be given a major role in the theory. Another aspect of language receiving marginal attention in transformational grammar is coordination. Many rival theories owe their success to substantial progress in analyzing coordination (for example GPSG, HPSG, combinatorial categorial grammar). Here we will be concerned with agreement in the context of coordination and show that none of the theories has a good answer to the phenomena at hand. Worse still, it seems that this particular phenomenon cannot be incorporated into any current framework other than by making a list of possible combinations. Certainly, at a low level these facts can be accommodated in any framework — but they do not conform with any higher level principle.

Before we begin outlining the facts let us make clear that there is a fundamental difference between individual noun phrases and the coordinated structure as regards agreement. In a construction $[np_1 \ and \ np_2]_3$ the conjuncts wear their own marking directly on their sleeves; the coordinated noun phrase itself is nowhere marked directly for its agreement features, since the coordinator does not show any overt agreement. Hence, we can test the intrinsic character of the noun phrase only by the fact that it agrees with verbs or other elements in the construction. Lack of a one-to-one-correspondence between the agreement forms of the subject and the agreement forms of the verb may therefore obscure the facts somewhat.

Let us present the data, starting from the most simple facts. In English, a noun phrase such as *Mary and John* is plural, while both *Mary* and *John* itself are singular. On the other hand, *Mary or John* is (or may at least be) singular. In German, in similar constructions, I would accept both singular and plural, though the acceptance varies with the contextualization. But with *entweder ... oder* (exclusive or) judgments are clear: the coordinated noun phrase must be singular. In languages where there is in addition to singular and plural also a dual, matters are naturally a bit more complex. There may be straightforward semantic explanations for this behaviour, so that one may be inclined to simply not regard this as a syntactic phenomenon. In the Minimalist Program one may see this as a problem of LF.

But let's proceed further. Baker 1992 discusses a peculiar agreement phenomenon of Mohawk, exemplified in the next two sentences, which appear as (20a,b) in the reference.

(1)   John wa'-t-hy-atskahu-' ne   Uwari.
        John ate.masc.dual   with   Mary.

(2)   John tanu Uwari wa'-t-hy-atskahu-'.
        John and Mary   ate.masc.dual.

Observe that the verb shows *dual* agreement in both cases. In their German translations (1) differs from (2) in that the verb is plural in (2) and singular in (1).

(1')   Karl und Maria aßen.
        Karl and Mary ate.plur.

(2')   Karl aß mit Maria.
        Karl ate.sing with Mary.

The facts of German are readily explained. The subject in (1') is plural while singular in (2'). However, the Mohawk agreement system disconnects the notion of subject and agreement target of the verb. The consequences of this may be far reaching, but we have not considered what they will be.

There is another simple construction, in Latin, in which we can see a morphological agreement in gender between subject and verb, namely in predicative constructions.

(3)   Carolus est magnus.
        Karl is big.

(4)   Maria non est magna.
        Mary is not big.

If we insert a coordinated noun phrase, we can detect from the attributive adjective which gender the noun phrase must have. It turns out that (i) if both noun phrases agree in gender, the coordinated noun phrase will agree with both, (ii) if they disagree, then masculine wins over feminine in case of humans, while in case of things the one nearer to the verb wins.[14] For example we have

---

[14]See Bayer and Lindauer 1974. Facts are a bit obscured by the fact that they speak of persons and things rather than syntactic gender. To be fair, intuitions in coordination, especially with respect to number agreement, seem to be driven by semantic consider-

(5)   Murus et porta fulmine icta est.
        Wall-m.sg and door-f.sg by lightning struck-f.sg been-sg.
        Wall and door have been struck by a lightning.

(6)   In oratorem omnium ora atque oculi conversi erant.
        Towards speaker of-all faces-n.pl and eyes-m.pl directed-m.pl were.
        Everybody's faces and eyes were directed towards the speaker.

Indeed, in the case of things, agreement is with the nearest conjunct, not with the conjoined noun phrase. Notice in passing that these facts might be solved by the analysis provided by Munn 1993. Munn assumes that in coordinated structures the coordinator (for example, *and*) projects a so-called *boolean phrase* which in turn is adjoined to the first conjunct. This solution has a number of advantages. It can explain why in Arabic the verb agrees with the first conjunct in a VSO structure. How we reconcile this with the standard facts — that coordinated structures are nonsingular even when the individual coordinated elements are singular — is left unexplained.

All constructions show a dependency between three items. For example, in the coordinated construction np_1 *and* np_2, the two noun phrases np_1 and np_2 and the conjunction are interrelated. We find that the value of the feature PLU can be calculated for English with the following list.

	−	+
−	+	+
+	+	+

It may be tempting to dismiss this problem by saying that in coordinated structures of this kind we can safely assume that the result is plural, so no real dependency is observed. However, in languages with a dual, the table is as follows if we assume that it faithfully reflects the cardinality (i. e. 1, 2, and more than two).[15]

---

ation. It may very well be the case that due to the lack of the specifically problematic constructions there are no clear syntactic judgments, and that they get replaced by semantic considerations. This applies for example to the cases of constructions such as *Johan oder Maria* (English: *John or Mary*). Since there is the possibility that we mean both rather than one, we expect to find either of (i) and (ii).

    (i) Johan oder Maria hat dies getan.
       John or Mary has done this.
    (ii) Johan oder Maria haben dies getan.
       John or Mary have done this.

I find (ii) less acceptable, but with the right context it might also be ok.

[15]Note that zero has no proper home in any of the number systems. The analysis in terms of cardinality is therefore not accurate. It seems that in many languages two contrasts are melted into one, namely one between one individual and several, and the other between a specified amount and an unspecified amount. Consider, for example, the quantifier *all*, which shows plural agreement.

	s	d	p
s	d	p	p
d	p	p	p
p	p	p	p

Here the marking of the conjunct depends on the marking of the individual noun phrases. Moreover, this relation is a ternary relation (since it is a function on two arguments) but it cannot be reduced to a binary relation. The same holds with respect to gender marking.

Nothing lets us conclude that transformational grammar can handle ternary relations — unless they arise from phrase structure rules. Let us see why this is so. We have in the pre-Minimalist tradition the basic phrase-structure component called X-bar syntax. There is no indication as to how coordination can fit into it, since coordination is basically a polymorphous construction. (See Keenan and Faltz 1985 for extensive arguments.) Moreover, apart from distributing levels and categories, X-bar syntax did not provide special mechanisms to account for agreement. Surely, most people will agree that in principle a rule based grammar could be written to encode these facts about coordination in languages, although none of the accounts I am familiar with (including that of Gazdar et al. 1985) are fully correct. The problem is that the grammars take it for granted that agreement can be regulated by identity criteria. For example, in GPSG it is part of the head-feature percolation mechanism which distributes the PLU-value from mother to head. Since in coordinated NPs both noun phrases are heads, it can never happen that they are singular while the mother is plural. This gap is due to the focus on subject-verb agreement, plainly visible also in the Minimalist Program. Be it with the help of transformations which move items into checking position or without, the Minimalist Program, just as any of its predecessors, relies on an identity check with respect to agreement. This gets subject-verb agreement (almost) right but leaves the difficult cases of coordinated NPs out of discussion. To add to the complication, the cases of disagreement that Baker gives in the quoted paper show that identity checks are insufficient for those languages which treat a comitative phrase as if it was a coordinated conjunct of the subject.

Some of the problems can be solved by allowing the feature GENDER to take a *set* of gender values. The gender conflict can then be handled by realization rules on these sets. In Latin, we will let the set {masc, fem}, {masc, neut} come out as masculine agreement, while {fem, neut} will be feminine. (We disregard here for simplicity the distinction between people and things.) However, such additional symbolism would be no less stipulative than simple phrase structure rules if not backed by additional evidence. In fact, such evidence may come from the semantics of such coordinated structures, and in particular from a theory of plurals.[16] For on the one hand syntax requires (at least in some languages) that noun phrases have a gender, but what gender a group of different people, or a combination of people and things should have, is a highly conventional affair. Groups, however, may as a first approximation be analysed as sets, so sets of gender values qualify as syntactic reflexes from that perspective. It is at least intuitively clear that under such an interpretation a unification account of gender is incorrect. A proof of that needs careful investigation, however.

There are other cases of apparent disagreement. For example, plural neuter subjects in Greek cause singular agreement on the verb (see Kaegi 1972). There are many more such examples, but on the whole they do not pose problems of a similar sort for GB. If ϕ-features are transmitted to the verb, we will simply posit a special realization rule for the verb to assure it comes out singular. Or we may deny that neuter are plural, at least as concerns the agreement feature transmitted to the verb. In the case at hand, the latter approach is at least historically correct. Namely, the ending in the nominative neuter plural was originally a feminine in a collective singular ending in -$\overline{\alpha}$.

8 Gains of the Coding Method

Proving intertranslatability between logical systems, grammars and syntactic theories does not amount to saying that syntactic theories have to be translated into rules. Nor does it mean that there is an ontological reduction of one to the other. But it does tell us how to recast theories if we need to. There is a lot to say in favour of establishing such techniques — even though Chomsky and many others see no significance in them. For a start, even if two theories are notational variants, depending on the problem at hand it may be easier to work with one rather than the other. Also, transformational grammar has persistently been a model of sentence production; the design of parsing or recognition procedures is typically thought of as a secondary problem.[17] However, in formal language theory there is a lot of serious work on parsing; connecting with that work directly may be a much better strategy than starting afresh. In principle-based parsing, however, the strategy has been that even in the context-free case, principles allow much better parsing algorithms to be

---

[16]The latter subject has attracted much more research and various proposals have been made (see Baker 1992 and references therein). There have been debates particularly about the role of indices in connection with agreement. The additional twist in the problems raised here comes from an interaction with basic syntactic constructions.

[17]Notice also the word *generative* in transformational generative grammar. To be fair, many syntactic theories begin with the production side, and it is not our aim to criticise this qua research strategy. Rather, we want to emphasize that a full theory of language must also be able to explain our abilities as listeners in addition to those as speakers.

derived (see for example Berwick 1991). That can only be so if languages form a proper subset of the context-free languages. But from the angle of complexity all that matters is the inherent combinatorial complexity of the problem itself, abstracting away as much as possible from its particular presentation. Thus additional research into the complexity of the human language presented within GB-theory is made redundant by the possibility of giving a formal translation into rule systems. Although this translation results in an explosion of the underlying feature system, this does not affect the complexity class. Moreover, the exact factor by which the feature system gets expanded can also be determined given any theory $\mathbf{CL}_n \oplus \Phi$, Φ constant. Thus, if we end up with a context-free grammar (which is the case surprisingly often) then we can make use of the standard techniques for CFGs.

Matters tend to be less favorable if the reduction does not end up in a context-free grammar. However, not all is lost. In any case we can use a result of Fagin 1974 (which can also be found in Ebbinghaus and Flum 1995), which states that universal second-order sentences of the form $(\forall \overline{P})\phi(\overline{P})$ where $\phi(\overline{P})$ is first-order can be checked on finite structures in polynomial time. If in addition there is a constant c such that for a given input string there is a parse tree with at most $c \cdot n$ terminal nodes, then there is a parsing strategy which requires at most exponential time. It proceeds as follows; first guess a tree or a directed acyclic graph with at most $c \cdot n$ leaves such that the yield with null elements erased is the original string. (This is the exponential part.) Then check all principles on that structure. This result is less spectacular, but one might hope to have substantially better results if one makes use of the specific characteristics of syntactic theories (as opposed to just arbitrary axiomatic extensions). Notice that the Minimalist Program allows to deduce that there is a constant c of the required kind. This is so because each overt element has a bounded number of features, and so there is a bound on the number of movements for each element.[18]

Another problem area where the method is useful is in deciding the adequacy or the equivalence of syntactic theories. Here we say that a theory is *adequate* in a given sense if it is *equivalent to the real grammar* in that sense, where the real grammar — so to speak — is the one in our heads. Several degrees of adequacy for a grammar have been distinguished, weak adequacy if it admits the correct strings, strong adequacy if it admits the same structures, and finally explanatory adequacy. The latter is difficult to define, let alone make rigorous in a mathematical sense. Although it has been emphasized over and over that explanatory adequacy is the most

---

[18] For that we must work with the reentrant structures à la HPSG and not with copy movement. Otherwise the bound on the number of nodes is far too large.

important thing we should look for, the other criteria should not at all be regarded useless. It is legitimate to ask whether two given theories differ weakly or strongly or in any other sense. If, for example, natural languages are not context-free then any syntactic theory predicting that they are is simply wrong.

In this way, questions of generative complexity, perhaps in terms of a given language hierarchy, are of some importance for the actual inquiry into language. These questions, even though not of the same fundamental nature, are nevertheless surprisingly tricky to answer and will hopefully add substance to the claim that theories of language are not so easy to analyse. First of all, it is known that weak equivalence of context-free grammars is undecidable, while strong equivalence evidently is decidable. (You just have to define a bijection between the nonterminals that preserves the rules in both directions.) The first question is certainly the most interesting one, because acceptability of surface strings is the most readily accessible empirical data. Strong equivalence, on the other hand, is uninteresting because it takes into account structure about which we have only indirect evidence (empty elements, unary rules). In between the two, however, we can recognize a third kind of equivalence, namely the question of whether two grammars generate the same bracketed strings. Although to analyse strings into bracketed structures requires syntactic skill, it may be considered a fairly theory-neutral affair. It has the great advantage of being decidable, as has been shown in McNaughton 1967. To generalize this in absence of context-freeness is a real challenge.

However, be it transformational grammar, GPSG or other formalisms, one of their main characteristics is the internal architecture of the system. GPSG is not just about context-free grammars, it also tries to detect global mechanisms and properties such as head- versus foot-features, metarules, defaults, and so on. Our system for translating between axioms and rules immediately shows a way to encode the facts once we have been able to spell them out in sufficient detail. This gives a lot of insight into the way in which the feature system of language (or UG) should be designed without going through many painful details as in Pollard and Sag 1987, to give just one example.

Take again the example of agreement in coordination. It is a simple matter to write down the axiom concerning the distribution of number features (or ϕ-features in general) once we know the facts themselves. It is equally simple to refine any grammar without ϕ-feature assignment into a grammar that distributes them correctly. But it is rather difficult to incorporate these insights into a syntactic formalism that has an articulate inner structure. The Coding Method is a method that mechanically incorporates any facts about language into a rule system. The problematic aspect of it is that it disrespects totally the architecture of the theories; in other words, it is in itself rather simple minded. On the other hand, if that is so, it is not clear how the given architecture is justifiable. For example, it is a complete mystery as to why certain features are classified as head-features and others as foot-features, and why the particular percolation mechanisms are the way they are. We have demonstrated above that PLU cannot be a head-feature although it is classified as such in the standard reference Gazdar et al. 1985. So, we need independent criteria for what is to count as a head-feature, or else give up the head-feature convention in its present form. Thus, the Coding Method may be used to determine the particular mode of percolation for a given feature and thus ultimately connect GPSG up with the empirical data in a systematic and less ad hoc fashion.

References

Baker, Mark. 1992. Unmatched Chains and the Representation of Plural pronouns. *Journal of Semantics* 1:33–74.

Bayer, Karl, and Joseph Lindauer. 1974. *Lateinische Grammatik*. München: Oldenbourg.

Berwick, Robert C. 1991. Principle-Based Parsing. In *Foundational Issues in Natural Language Processing*, ed. Peter Sells, Stuart M. Shieber, and Thomas Wasow. 31–81. MIT Press.

Brody, Michael. 1995. *Lexico-Logical Form — a Radically Minimalist Theory*. Linguistic Inquiry Monographs, No. 27. MIT Press.

Ćavar, Damir, and Chris Wilder. 1994. Word order variation, verb movement, and economy principles. *Studia Linguistica* 48:46–86.

Chomsky, Noam. 1980. *Rules and Representations*. Columbia University Press.

Chomsky, Noam. 1986a. *Barriers*. Cambrigde (Mass.): MIT Press.

Chomsky, Noam. 1986b. *Knowledge of Language. Its Nature, Origin and Use*. New York: Praeger.

Chomsky, Noam. 1993. A Minimalist Program for Linguistic Theory. In *The View from Building 20: Essays in Honour of Sylvain Bromberger*, ed. K. Hale and Keyser S. J. 1–52. MIT Press.

Chomsky, Noam. 1995. Bare Phrase Structure. In *Government and Binding Theory and the Minimalist Program*, ed. Gert Webelhuth. 385–439. Blackwell.

Ebbinghaus, Hans-Dieter, and Jörg Flum. 1995. *Finite Model Theory*. Perspectives in Mathematical Logic. Springer.

Fagin, Ronald. 1974. Generalized first-order spectra and polynomial-time recognizable sets. In *Complexity of Computation, SIAM-AMS Proceedings*, ed. R. M. Karp, 43–73.

Fanselow, Gisbert. 1991. *Minimale Syntax*. Groninger Arbeiten zur germanistischen Linguistik, No. 32. Rijksuniversiteit Groningen.

Gaertner, Hans-Martin. 1995. Has Bare Phrase Structure Theory superseded X-Bar Theory? In *FAS Papers in Linguistics*, ed. Artemis Alexiadou et. al. 22–35. Forschungsschwerpunkt Allgemeine Sprachwissenschaft, Berlin.

Gazdar, Gerald, Ewan Klein, Geoffrey Pullum, and Ivan Sag. 1985. *Generalized Phrase Structure Grammar*. Oxford: Blackwell.

Goldblatt, Robert I. 1987. *Logics of Time and Computation*. CSLI Lecture Notes, No. 7. CSLI.

Harel, D. 1984. Dynamic Logic. In *Handbook of Philosophical Logic*, ed. Dov M. Gabbay and Franz Guenthner. 497–604. Reidel.

Kaegi, Adolf. 1972. *Griechische Schulgrammatik*. Weidmann Verlag.

Kayne, Richard S. 1994. *The Antisymmetry of Syntax*. Linguistic Inquiry Monographs, No. 25. MIT Press.

Keenan, Edward L., and Leonard M. Faltz. 1985. *Boolean Semantics for Natural Language*. Synthese Language Library, No. 23. Dordrecht: Reidel.

Koster, Jan. 1986. *Domains and Dynasties: the Radical Autonomy of Syntax*. Dordrecht: Foris.

Kracht, Marcus. 1993. Mathematical Aspects of Command Relations. In *Proceedings of the EACL 93*, 240–249.

Kracht, Marcus. 1995a. Is there a genuine modal perspective on feature structures? *Linguistics and Philosophy* 18:401–458.

Kracht, Marcus. 1995b. Syntactic Codes and Grammar Refinement. *Journal of Logic, Language and Information* 4:41–60.

Laka, Itziar. 1991. Negation in syntax: on the nature of functional categories and projections. *International Journal of Basque Linguistics and Philology* 25:65–138.

McNaughton, Robert. 1967. Parenthesis Grammars. *Journal of the Association for Computing Machinery* 14:490–500.

Munn, Alan B. 1993. *Topics in the Syntax and Semantics of Coordinate Structures*. Doctoral dissertation, University of Maryland.

Pollard, Carl, and Ivan A. Sag. 1987. *Information-Based Syntax and Semantics, Part I*. CSLI Lecture Notes, No. 13. CSLI.

Rogers, James. 1994. *Studies in the Logic of Trees with Applications to Grammar Formalisms*. Doctoral dissertation, Department of Computer and Information Sciences, University of Delaware.

Sternefeld, Wolfgang. 1991. *Syntaktische Grenzen. Chomskys Barrierentheorie und ihre Weiterentwicklungen*. Opladen: Westdeutscher Verlag.

Stowell, Tim. 1981. *Elements of Phrase Structure*. Doctoral dissertation, MIT.

4

Structural Control

Natasha Kurtonina and Michael Moortgat

ABSTRACT. In this paper we study Lambek systems as *grammar logics*: logics for reasoning about structured linguistic resources. The structural parameters of precedence, dominance and dependency generate a cube of resource-sensitive categorial type logics. From the pure logic of residuation **NL**, one obtains **L**, **NLP** and **LP** in terms of Associativity, Commutativity, and their combination. Each of these systems has a dependency variant, where the product is split up into a left-headed and a right-headed version.

We develop a theory of systematic communication between these systems. The communication is two-way: we show how one can fully recover the structural discrimination of a weaker logic from within a system with a more liberal resource management regime, and how one can reintroduce the structural flexibility of a stronger logic within a system with a more articulate notion of structure-sensitivity.

In executing this programme we follow the standard logical agenda: the categorial formula language is enriched with extra control operators, so-called structural modalities, and on the basis of these control operators, we prove embedding theorems for the two directions of substructural communication. But our results differ from the Linear Logic style of embedding with $S4$-like modalities in that we realize the communication in both directions in terms of a *minimal* pair of structural modalities. The control devices $\diamondsuit, \square^{\downarrow}$ used here represent the pure logic of residuation for a family of unary multiplicatives: they do not impose any restrictions on the binary accessibility relation interpreting the unary modalities, unlike the $S4$ operators which require a transitive and reflexive interpretation. With the more delicate control devices we can avoid the model-theoretic and proof-theoretic problems one encounters when importing the Linear Logic modalities in a linguistic setting.

Specifying Syntactic Structures
P. Blackburn and M. de Rijke, eds.
Copyright © 1997, CSLI Publications.

1   Logics of Structured Resources

This paper is concerned with the issue of *communication* between categorial type logics of the Lambek family. Lambek calculi occupy a lively corner in the broader landscape of resource-sensitive systems of inference. We study these systems here as grammar logics. In line with the 'Parsing as Deduction' slogan, we present the key concept in grammatical analysis — *well-formedness* — in logical terms, i.e. grammatical well-formedness amounts to *derivability* in our grammar logic. In the grammatical application, the resources we are talking about are linguistic expressions — multidimensional form-meaning complexes, or *signs* as they have come to be called in current grammar formalisms. These resources are structured in a number of grammatically relevant dimensions. For the sake of concreteness, we concentrate on three types of linguistic structure of central importance: linear order, hierarchical grouping (constituency) and dependency. The structure of the linguistic resources in these dimensions plays a crucial role in determining well-formedness: one cannot generally assume that changes in the structural configuration of the resources will preserve well-formedness. In logical terms, we are interested in structure-sensitive notions of linguistic inference.

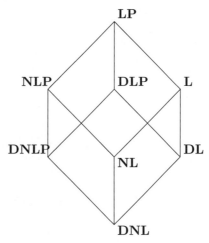

FIGURE 1   Resource-sensitive logics: precedence, dominance, dependency

Figure 1 charts the eight logics that result from the interplay of the structural parameters of precedence, dominance and dependency. The systems lower in the cube exhibit a more fine-grained sense of structure-sensitivity; their neighbours higher up loose discrimination for one of the structural parameters we distinguish here.

Let us present the essentials (syntactically and semantically) of the framework we are assuming before addressing the communication problem. For a full treatment of the multimodal categorial architecture, the reader can turn to Moortgat 1996a and references cited there. Consider the standard language of categorial type formulae $\mathcal{F}$ freely generated from a set of atomic formulae $\mathcal{A}$: $\mathcal{F} ::= \mathcal{A} \mid \mathcal{F}/\mathcal{F} \mid \mathcal{F} \bullet \mathcal{F} \mid \mathcal{F}\backslash\mathcal{F}$. The most general interpretation for such a language can be given in terms of Kripke style relational structures — ternary relational structures $\langle W, R^3 \rangle$ in the case of the binary connectives (cf. Došen 1992). W here is to be understood as the set of linguistic resources (signs) and the accessibility relation R as representing linguistic composition. From a ternary frame we obtain a model by adding a valuation V sending prime formulae to subsets of W and satisfying the clauses below for compound formulae.

$$V(A \bullet B) = \{z \mid \exists x \exists y [Rzxy \,\&\, x \in V(A) \,\&\, y \in V(B)]\}$$
$$V(C/B) = \{x \mid \forall y \forall z [(Rzxy \,\&\, y \in V(B)) \Rightarrow z \in V(C)]\}$$
$$V(A\backslash C) = \{y \mid \forall x \forall z [(Rzxy \,\&\, x \in V(A)) \Rightarrow z \in V(C)]\}$$

With no restrictions on R, we obtain the pure logic of residuation known as **NL**.

RES(2) $A \to C/B \quad\Longleftrightarrow\quad A \bullet B \to C \quad\Longleftrightarrow\quad B \to A\backslash C$

And with restrictions on the interpretation of R, and corresponding structural postulates, we obtain the systems **NLP**, **L** and **LP**. Below we give the structural postulates of Associativity (A) and Permutation (P) and the corresponding frame conditions $F(A)$ and $F(P)$. Notice that the structural discrimination gets coarser as we impose more constraints on the interpretation of R. In the presence of Permutation, well-formedness is unaffected by changes in the linear order of the linguistic resources. In the presence of Associativity, different groupings of the linguistic resources into hierarchical constituent structures has no influence on derivability.

(A) $A \bullet (B \bullet C) \longleftrightarrow (A \bullet B) \bullet C$
$F(A)$ $(\forall xyz \in W) \; \exists t.Rxyt \,\&\, Rtzu \Leftrightarrow \exists v.Rvyz \,\&\, Rxvu$
(P) $A \bullet B \to B \bullet A$
$F(P)$ $(\forall xyz \in W) \; Rxyz \Leftrightarrow Rxzy$

What we have said so far concerns the upper face of the cube of Figure 1. To obtain the systems at the lower face, we split the connective $\bullet$ into left-headed $\bullet_l$ and right-headed $\bullet_r$, taking into account the asymmetry between heads and dependents. It is argued in Moortgat and Morrill 1991 that the dependency dimension should be treated as orthogonal in principle to the functor/argument asymmetry. The distinction between left-headed $\bullet_l$ and right-headed $\bullet_r$ (and their residual implications) makes the type language articulate enough to discriminate between head/complement configurations, and modifier/head or specifier/head configurations. A determiner, for example, could be typed as $np/_r n$. Such a declaration naturally accounts for the fact that determiners act semantically as functions from n-type meanings to np-type meanings, whereas in the form dimension they should be treated as dependent on the common noun they are in construction with, so that they can derive their agreement properties from the head noun.

In the Kripke models, the lower plane of Figure 1 is obtained by moving from unimodal to multimodal (in this case: bimodal) frames $\langle W, R_l^3, R_r^3 \rangle$, with a distinct accessibility relation for each product. Again, we have the pure (bimodal) logic of residuation **DNL**, with an arbitrary interpretation for R_l^3, R_r^3, and its relatives **DNLP**, **DL**, **DLP**, obtained by imposing associativity or (dependency-preserving!) commutativity constraints on the frames. The relevant structural postulates are given below. The distinction between the left-headed and right-headed connectives is destroyed by the postulate (D).

(A_l) $A \bullet_l (B \bullet_l C) \longleftrightarrow (A \bullet_l B) \bullet_l C$

(A_r) $A \bullet_r (B \bullet_r C) \longleftrightarrow (A \bullet_r B) \bullet_r C$

$(P_{l,r})$ $A \bullet_l B \longleftrightarrow B \bullet_r A$

(D) $A \bullet_l B \longleftrightarrow A \bullet_r B$

It will be clear already from the foregoing that in presenting the grammar for a given language, we will in general not be in a position to restrict ourselves to one particular type logic — we want to have access to the combined inferential capacities of the different logics, without destroying their individual characteristics. For this to be possible we need a theory of systematic *communication* between type systems. The structural postulates presented above do not have the required granularity for such a theory of communication: they globally destroy structure sensitivity in one of the relevant dimensions, whereas we would like to have *lexical control* over resource management. Depending on the direction of communication, one can develop two perspectives on controlled resource management. On the one hand, one would like to have control devices to license limited access to a more liberal resource management regime from within a system with a higher sense of structural discrimination. On the other hand, one would like to impose constraints on resource management in systems where such constraints are lacking by default. For discussion of linguistic phenomena motivating these two types of communication, the reader can turn to the papers in Barry and Morrill 1990 where the licensing perspective was originally introduced, and to Morrill 1994 where apart from licensing of structural relaxation one can also find discussion of constraints with respect to the associativity dimension. We give an illustration for each type of control, drawing on the references just mentioned.

Licensing Structural Relaxation. For the licensing type of communication, consider type assignment to relative pronouns like *that* in the sentences below.

$$\text{the book that John read}$$
$$\text{the book that John read yesterday}$$
$$\mathbf{L} \vdash \ r/(s/np), np, (np\backslash s)/np \Rightarrow r$$
$$\mathbf{L} \nvdash \ r/(s/np), np, (np\backslash s)/np, s\backslash s \Rightarrow r$$
$$\mathbf{NL} \nvdash \ (r/(s/np), (np, (np\backslash s)/np)) \Rightarrow r$$

Suppose first we are dealing with the associative regime of $\mathbf{L}$, and assign the relative pronoun the type $r/(s/np)$, abbreviating $n\backslash n$ as r, i.e. the pronoun looks to its right for a relative clause body missing a noun phrase. The first example is derivable[1] (because 'John read np' indeed yields s), the second is not (because the hypothetical np assumption in the subderivation 'John read yesterday np' is not in the required position adjacent to the verb 'read'). We would like to refine the assignment to the relative pronoun to a type $r/(s/np^\sharp)$, where $np^\sharp$ is a noun phrase resource which has access to Permutation in virtue of its $\cdot^\sharp$ decoration. Similarly, if we change the default regime to $\mathbf{NL}$, already the first example fails on the assignment $r/(s/np)$ with the indicated constituent bracketing: although the hypothetical np in the subcomputation '((John read) np)' finds itself in the right position with respect to linear order requirements, it cannot satisfy the direct object role for 'read' being outside the clausal boundaries. A refined assignment $r/(s/np^\sharp)$ here could license the marked $np^\sharp$ a controlled access to the structural rule of Associativity which is absent in the $\mathbf{NL}$ default regime.

Imposing Structural Constraints. For the other direction of communication, we take an example from Morrill 1994 which again concerns relative clause formation, but this time in its interaction with coordination. Assume we are dealing with an associative default regime, and let the conjunction particle 'and' be polymorphically typed as $(X\backslash X)/X$. With the instantiation $X = s/np$ we can derive the first example. But, given Associativity and an instantiation $X = s$, nothing blocks the ungrammatical second example: 'Melville wrote Moby Dick and John read np' derives s, so that withdrawing the np hypothesis indeed gives s/np, the type required for the relative clause body.

$$\text{the book that Melville wrote and John read}$$
$$\mathbf{L} \vdash r/(s/np), np, (np\backslash s)/np, (X\backslash X)/X, np, (np\backslash s)/np \Rightarrow r \ \ (X = s/np)$$
$$\text{*the book that Melville wrote Moby Dick and John read}$$
$$\mathbf{L} \vdash r/(s/np), np, (np\backslash s)/np, np, (X\backslash X)/X, np, (np\backslash s)/np \Rightarrow r \ \ (X = s)$$

To block this violation of the so-called Coordinate Structure Constraint,

---

[1]The Appendix gives axiomatic and Gentzen style presentation of the logics under discussion.

while allowing Across-the-Board Extraction as exemplified by our first example, we would like to refine the type assignment for the particle 'and' to $(X \backslash X^b)/X$, where the intended interpretation for the marked X^b now would be the following: after combining with the right and the left conjuncts, the $\cdot^b$ decoration makes the complete coordination freeze into an island configuration which is inaccessible to extraction under the default associative resource management regime.

Minimal Structural Modalities. Our task in the following pages is to give a logical implementation of the informal idea of decorating formulas with a label $(\cdot)^\sharp$ or $(\cdot)^b$, licensing extra flexibility or imposing a tighter regime for the marked formulae. The original introduction of the licensing type of communication in Barry and Morrill 1990 was inspired by the modalities '!,?' of Linear Logic — unary operators which give marked formulae access to the structural rules of Contraction and Weakening, thus making it possible to recover the full power of Intuitionistic or Classical Logic from within the resource sensitive linear variants. On the proof-theoretic level, the '!,?' operators have the properties of $S4$ modalities. It is not self-evident that $S4$ behaviour is appropriate for substructural systems *weaker* than Linear Logic — indeed Venema 1993 has criticised an $S4$ '!' in such settings for the fact that the proof rule for '!' has undesired side-effects on the meaning of other operators. On the semantic level it has been shown in Versmissen 1993 that the $S4$ regime is incomplete with respect to the linguistic interpretation which was originally intended for the structural modalities — a subalgebra interpretation in a general groupoid setting, cf. Morrill 1994 for discussion.

Given these model-theoretic and proof-theoretic problems with the use of Linear Logic modalities in linguistic analysis, we will explore a different route and develop an approach attuned to the specific domain of application of our grammar logics — a domain of structured linguistic resources.

Moortgat 1995 proposes an enrichment of the type language of categorial logics with *unary* residuated operators, interpreted in terms of a *binary* relation of accessibility. These operators will be the key devices in our strategy for controlled resource management. If we were talking about temporal organization, $\Diamond$ and $\Box^\downarrow$ could be interpreted as future possibility and past necessity, respectively. But in our grammatical application, R^2 just like R^3 is to be interpreted in terms of structural composition. Where a ternary configuration $(xyz) \in R^3$ interpreting the product connective abstractly represents putting together the components y and z into a structured configuration x in the manner indicated by R^3, a binary configuration $(xy) \in R^2$ interpreting the unary $\Diamond$ can be seen as the construction of the sign x out of a structural component y in terms of the building instructions referred to by R^2.

$$\text{RES}(1) \qquad \diamond A \to B \iff A \to \square^\downarrow B$$

$$\begin{aligned} V(\diamond A) &= \{x \mid \exists y (R^2 xy \,\wedge\, y \in V(A))\} \\ V(\square^\downarrow A) &= \{x \mid \forall y (R^2 yx \,\Rightarrow\, y \in V(A))\} \end{aligned}$$

From the residuation laws RES(1) one directly derives the monotonicity laws below and the properties of the compositions of $\diamond$ and $\square^\downarrow$:

$$A \to B \quad \text{implies} \quad \diamond A \to \diamond B \quad \text{and} \quad \square^\downarrow A \to \square^\downarrow B$$

$$\diamond \square^\downarrow A \to A \qquad A \to \square^\downarrow \diamond A$$

In the Appendix, we present the sequent logic for these unary operators. It is shown in Moortgat 1995 that the Gentzen presentation is equivalent to the axiomatic presentation, and that it enjoys Cut Elimination. For our examples later on we will use decidable sequent proof search.

Semantically, the pure logic of residuation for $\diamond, \square^\downarrow$ does not impose any restrictions on the interpretation of R^2. As in the case of the binary connectives, we can add structural postulates for $\diamond$ and corresponding frame constraints on R^2. With a reflexive and transitive R^2, one obtains an $S4$ system. Our objective here is to show that one can develop a systematic theory of communication, both for the licensing and for the constraining perspective, in terms of the *minimal* structural modalities, i.e. the pure logic of residuation for $\diamond, \square^\downarrow$.

Completeness. The communication theorems to be presented in the following sections rely heavily on semantic argumentation. The cornerstone of the approach is the completeness of the logics compared, which guarantees that syntactic derivability $\vdash A \to B$ and semantic inclusion $V(A) \subseteq V(B)$ coincide for the classes of models we are interested in. For the $\mathcal{F}(/, \bullet, \backslash)$ fragment, Došen 1992 shows that **NL** is complete with respect to the class of all ternary models, and **L**, **NLP**, **LP** with respects to the classes of models satisfying the frame constraints for the relevant packages of structural postulates. The completeness results are obtained on the basis of a simple canonical model construction which directly accommodates bimodal dependency systems with $\mathcal{F}(/_i, \bullet_i, \backslash_i)$ $(i \in \{l, r\})$. And it is shown in Moortgat 1995 that the construction also extends unproblematically to the language enriched with $\diamond, \square^\downarrow$ as soon as one realizes that $\diamond$ can be seen as a 'truncated' product and $\square^\downarrow$ its residual implication.

Definition 1.1 Define the canonical model for mixed (2,3) frames as $\mathcal{M} = \langle W, R^2, R_i^3 \rangle$, where

W is the set of formulae $\mathcal{F}(/_i, \bullet_i, \backslash_i, \diamond, \square^\downarrow)$

$R_i^3(A, B, C)$ iff $\vdash A \to B \bullet_i C$, $R^2(A, B)$ iff $\vdash A \to \diamond B$

$A \in V(p)$ iff $\vdash A \to p$.

The Truth Lemma then states that, for any formula ϕ, $\mathcal{M}, A \models \phi$ iff $\vdash A \to \phi$. Now suppose $V(A) \subseteq V(B)$ but $\not\vdash A \to B$. If $\not\vdash A \to B$ with the canonical valuation on the canonical frame, $A \in V(A)$ but $A \notin V(B)$ so $V(A) \not\subseteq V(B)$. Contradiction.

We have to check the Truth Lemma for the new compound formulae $\diamond A$, $\square^\downarrow A$. Below the direction that requires a little thinking.

($\diamond$) Assume $A \in V(\diamond B)$. We have to show $\vdash A \to \diamond B$. $A \in V(\diamond B)$ implies $\exists A'$ such that $R^2 A A'$ and $A' \in v(B)$. By inductive hypothesis, $\vdash A' \to B$. By Isotonicity for $\diamond$ this implies $\vdash \diamond A' \to \diamond B$. We have $\vdash A \to \diamond A'$ (by Definition R^2) in the canonical frame. By Transitivity, $\vdash A \to \diamond B$.

($\square^\downarrow$) Assume $A \in V(\square^\downarrow B)$. We have to show $\vdash A \to \square^\downarrow B$. $A \in V(\square^\downarrow B)$ implies that $\forall A'$ such that $R^2 A' A$ we have $A' \in V(B)$. Let A' be $\diamond A$. $R^2 A' A$ holds in the canonical frame since $\vdash \diamond A \to \diamond A$. By inductive hypothesis we have $\vdash A' \to B$, i.e. $\vdash \diamond A \to B$. By Residuation this gives $\vdash A \to \square^\downarrow B$.

Apart from global structural postulates we will introduce in the remainder of this paper 'modal' versions of such postulates — versions which are relativized to the presence of $\diamond$ control operators. The completeness results extend to these new structural postulates. Syntactically, they consist of formulas built up entirely in terms of the $\bullet$ operator and its truncated one-place variant $\diamond$. This means they have the required shape for a generalized Sahlqvist-van Benthem theorem and frame completeness result which is proved in Kurtonina 1995:

If $R_\diamond : A \to B$ is a modal version of a structural postulate, then there exists a first order frame condition effectively obtainable from $R_\diamond$, and any logic $\mathcal{L} + R_\diamond$ is complete if $\mathcal{L}$ is complete.

Embedding Theorems: the Method in General. In the sections that follow, we consider pairs of logics $\mathcal{L}_0, \mathcal{L}_1$ where $\mathcal{L}_0$ is a 'southern' neighbor of $\mathcal{L}_1$. Let us write $\mathcal{L}\diamond$ for a system $\mathcal{L}$ extended with the unary operators $\diamond, \square^\downarrow$ with their minimal residuation logic. For the 12 edges of the cube of Figure 1, we define embedding translations $(\cdot)^\flat : \mathcal{F}(\mathcal{L}_0) \mapsto \mathcal{F}(\mathcal{L}_1\diamond)$ which impose the structural discrimination of $\mathcal{L}_0$ in $\mathcal{L}_1$ with its more liberal resource management, and $(\cdot)^\sharp : \mathcal{F}(\mathcal{L}_1) \mapsto \mathcal{F}(\mathcal{L}_0\diamond)$ which license relaxation of structure sensitivity in $\mathcal{L}_0$ in such a way that one fully recovers the flexibility of the coarser $\mathcal{L}_1$.

Our strategy for obtaining the embedding results is quite uniform. It will be helpful to present the recipe first in abstract terms, so that in the following sections we can supply the particular ingredients with reference to the general scheme. The embedding theorems have the format shown below. We call $\mathcal{L}$ the source logic, $\mathcal{L}'$ the target.

$$\mathcal{L} \vdash A \to B \quad \text{iff} \quad \mathcal{L}' \Diamond(+\mathcal{R}_\diamond) \vdash A^\natural \to B^\natural$$

For the constraining perspective, $(\cdot)^\natural$ is $(\cdot)^\flat$ with $\mathcal{L} = \mathcal{L}_0$ and $\mathcal{L}' = \mathcal{L}_1$. For the licensing type of embedding, $(\cdot)^\natural$ is $(\cdot)^\sharp$ with $\mathcal{L} = \mathcal{L}_1$ and $\mathcal{L}' = \mathcal{L}_0$. The embedding translation $(\cdot)^\natural$ decorates critical subformulae in the target logic with the operators $\Diamond, \Box^\downarrow$. The translations are defined on the product • of the source logic: their action on the implicational formulas is fully determined by the residuation laws. A • configuration of the source logic is mapped to the *composition* of $\Diamond$ and the product of the target logic. The elementary compositions are given below (writing ∘ for the target product). They mark the product as a whole, or one of the subtypes with the $\Diamond$ control operator.

$$\Diamond(- \circ -) \qquad ((\Diamond-) \circ -) \qquad (- \circ (\Diamond-))$$

Sometimes the modal decoration in itself is enough to obtain the required structural control. We call these cases pure embeddings. In other cases realizing the embedding requires the addition of $\mathcal{R}_\diamond$ — the modalized version of a structural rule package discriminating $\mathcal{L}$ from $\mathcal{L}'$. Typically, this will be the case for communication in the licensing direction: the target logics lack an option for structural manipulation that is present in the source.

The proof of the embedding theorems comes in two parts.

($\Rightarrow$: Soundness of the Embedding.) The ($\Rightarrow$) half is the easy part. Using the Lambek-style axiomatization of 5.1 we obtain this direction of the embedding by a straightforward induction on the length of derivations in $\mathcal{L}$.

($\Leftarrow$: Completeness of the Embedding.) For the proofs of the ($\Leftarrow$) part, we reason semantically and rely on the completeness of the logics compared. To show that $\vdash A^\natural \to B^\natural$ in $\mathcal{L}'\Diamond$ implies $\vdash A \to B$ in $\mathcal{L}$ we proceed by contraposition. Suppose $\mathcal{L} \nvdash A \to B$. By completeness, there is an $\mathcal{L}$ model $\mathcal{M} = \langle F, V \rangle$ falsifying $A \to B$, i.e. there is a point a such that $\mathcal{M}, a \models A$ but $\mathcal{M}, a \nvDash B$. We obtain the proof for the ($\Leftarrow$) direction in two steps.

> *Model construction.* From $\mathcal{M}$, we construct an $\mathcal{L}'\Diamond$ model $\mathcal{M}' = \langle F', V' \rangle$. For the valuation, we set $V'(p) = V(p)$. For the frames, we define a mapping between the R^3 configurations in F and corresponding mixed $R^{2'}, R^{3'}$ configurations in F'. We make sure that the mapping reflects the properties of the translation schema, and that it takes into account the different frame conditions for F and F'.

> *Truth preservation lemma.* We prove that for any $a \in W \cap W'$, $\mathcal{M}, a \models A$ iff $\mathcal{M}', a \models A^\natural$, i.e. that the construction of $\mathcal{M}'$ is truth preserving.

Now, if $\mathcal{M}$ is a countermodel for $A \to B$, so is $\mathcal{M}'$ for $A^\natural \to B^\natural$. Soundness then leads us to the conclusion that $\mathcal{L}'\Diamond \not\vdash A^\natural \to B^\natural$.

With this proof recipe in hand, the reader is prepared to tackle the sections that follow. Recovery of structural discrimination is the subject of §2. In §3 we turn to licensing of structural relaxation. In §4 we reflect on general logical and linguistic features of the proposed architecture, signaling some open questions and directions for future research.

2   Imposing Structural Constraints

Let us first look at the embedding of more discriminating logics within systems with a less fine-grained sense of structure sensitivity. Modal decoration, in this case, serves to block structural manipulation that would be available by default. The section is organized as follows. In §2.1, we give a detailed treatment of a representative case for each of the structural dimensions of precedence, dominance and dependency. This covers the edges connected to the pure logic of residuation, **NL**. With minor adaptations the embedding translations of §2.1 can be extended to the remaining edges, with the exception of the four associative logics at the right back face of the cube. We present these generalizations in §2.2. This time we refrain from fully explicit treatment where extrapolation from §2.1 is straightforward. The remaining systems are treated in §2.3. They share associative resource management but differ in their sensitivity for linear order or dependency structure. We obtain the desired embeddings in these cases via a tactical maneuver which combines the composition of simple translation schemata and the reinstallment of Associativity via *modally controlled* structural postulates.

2.1   Simple Embeddings

Associativity

Consider first the pair **NL** versus **L**$\Diamond$. Let us subscript the symbols for the connectives in **NL** with 0 and those of **L** with 1. The **L** family $/_1, \bullet_1, \backslash_1$ has an associative resource management. We extend **L** with the operators $\Diamond, \Box^\downarrow$ and recover control over associativity by means of the following translation.

Definition 2.1 The translation $\cdot^\flat : \mathcal{F}(\mathbf{NL}) \mapsto \mathcal{F}(\mathbf{L}\Diamond)$ is defined as follows.

$$
\begin{aligned}
p^\flat &= p \\
(A \bullet_0 B)^\flat &= \Diamond(A^\flat \bullet_1 B^\flat) \\
(A/_0 B)^\flat &= \Box^\downarrow A^\flat /_1 B^\flat \\
(B\backslash_0 A)^\flat &= B^\flat \backslash_1 \Box^\downarrow A^\flat
\end{aligned}
$$

Proposition 2.2 $\mathbf{NL} \vdash A \to B$ *iff* $\mathbf{L}\Diamond \vdash A^\flat \to B^\flat$.

Proof. ($\Rightarrow$) Soundness of the embedding. For the left-to-right direction we use induction on the length of derivations in **NL** on the basis of the Lambek-

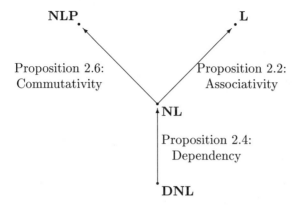

NLP

L

Proposition 2.6:
Commutativity

Proposition 2.2:
Associativity

NL

Proposition 2.4:
Dependency

DNL

FIGURE 2 Imposing constraints: precedence, dominance, dependency

style axiomatization given in the Appendix, where apart from the identity axiom and Transitivity, the Residuation rules are the only rules of inference. Assume $A \bullet_0 B \to C$ is derived from $A \to C/_0 B$ in **NL**. By inductive hypothesis, $\mathbf{L} \vdash A^\flat \to (C/_1 B)^\flat$, i.e. (†) $A^\flat \to \Box^\downarrow C^\flat /_1 B^\flat$. We have to show (‡) $\mathbf{L} \vdash (A \bullet_1 B)^\flat \to C^\flat$, i.e. $\Diamond(A^\flat \bullet_1 B^\flat) \to C^\flat$. By RES(2) we have from (†) $A^\flat \bullet_1 B^\flat \to \Box^\downarrow C^\flat$ which derives (‡) by RES(1). For the other side of the residuation inferences, assume $A \to C/_0 B$ is derived from $A \bullet_0 B \to C$. By inductive hypothesis, $\mathbf{L} \vdash (A \bullet_1 B^\flat) \to C^\flat$, i.e. (‡) $\Diamond(A^\flat \bullet_1 B^\flat) \to C^\flat$. We have to show $\mathbf{L} \vdash A^\flat \to C/_1 B^\flat$, i.e. (†) $A^\flat \to \Box^\downarrow C^\flat /_1 B^\flat$. By RES(1) we have from (‡) $A^\flat \bullet_1 B^\flat \to \Box^\downarrow C^\flat$ which derives (†) by RES(2). The residual pair $(\bullet_0, \backslash_0)$ is treated in a fully symmetrical way.

($\Leftarrow$) Completeness of the embedding. We apply the method outlined in §1. From a falsifying model $\mathcal{M} = \langle W, R_0^3, V \rangle$ for $A \to B$ in **NL** we construct $\mathcal{M}' = \langle W', R_1^3, R_\diamond^2, V' \rangle$. We prove that the construction is truth preserving, so that we can conclude from Soundness that $\mathcal{M}'$ falsifies $A^\flat \to B^\flat$ in $\mathbf{L}\Diamond$.

Model Construction. Let W_1 be a set such that $W \cap W_1 = \emptyset$ and $f : R_0^3 \mapsto W_1$ a bijection associating each triple $(abc) \in R_0^3$ with a fresh point $f((abc)) \in W_1$. $\mathcal{M}'$ is defined as follows:

$$
\begin{aligned}
W' &= W \cup W_1 \\
R_1 &= \{(a'bc) \mid \exists a. R_0 abc \wedge f((abc)) = a'\} \\
R_\diamond &= \{(aa') \mid \exists bc. R_0 abc \wedge f((abc)) = a'\} \\
V'(p) &= V(p)
\end{aligned}
$$

The following picture will help the reader to visualize how the model construction relates to the translation schema.

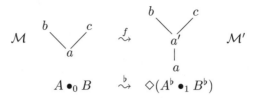

$$A \bullet_0 B \quad \overset{b}{\leadsto} \quad \Diamond(A^b \bullet_1 B^b)$$

We have to show that $\mathcal{M}'$ is an appropriate model for $\mathbf{L}$, i.e. that the construction of $\mathcal{M}'$ realizes the frame condition for associativity:

$$F(A) \qquad \forall xyzw \in W'(\exists t(R_1wxt \wedge R_1tyz) \Longleftrightarrow \exists t'(R_1wt'z \wedge R_1t'xy))$$

$F(A)$ is satisfied automatically because, by the construction of $\mathcal{M}'$, there are no $x, y, z, w \in W'$ that fulfill the requirements: for every triple $(xyz) \in R_1^3$, the point x is chosen fresh, which implies that no point of W' can be both the root of one triangle and a leaf in another one.

Lemma: Truth Preservation. By induction on the complexity of A we show that for any $a \in W$

$$\mathcal{M}, a \models A \quad \text{iff} \quad \mathcal{M}', a \models A^b$$

We prove the biconditional for the product and for one of the residual implications.

($\Rightarrow$). Suppose $\mathcal{M}, a \models A \bullet_0 B$. By the truth conditions for $\bullet_0$, there exist b, c such that (i) R_0abc and (ii) $\mathcal{M}, b \models A$, (iii) $\mathcal{M}, c \models B$. By inductive hypothesis, from (ii) and (iii) we have (ii') $\mathcal{M}', b \models A^b$ and (iii') $\mathcal{M}', c \models B^b$. By the construction of $\mathcal{M}'$, we conclude from (i) that there is a fresh $a' \in W_1$ such that (iv) $R_\diamond aa'$ and (v) $R_1a'bc$. Then, from (v) and (ii',iii') we have $\mathcal{M}', a' \models A^b \bullet_1 B^b$ and from (iv) $\mathcal{M}', a \models \Diamond(A^b \bullet_1 B^b)$.

($\Leftarrow$). Suppose $\mathcal{M}', a \models \Diamond(A^b \bullet_1 B^b)$. From the truth conditions for $\bullet_1, \Diamond$, we know there are $x, y, z \in W'$ such that (i) $R_\diamond ax$, (ii) R_1xyz and (iii) $\mathcal{M}', y \models A^b$ and $\mathcal{M}', z \models B^b$. In the construction of $\mathcal{M}'$ the function f is a bijection, so that we can conclude that the configuration (i,ii) has a unique pre-image, namely (iv) R_0ayz. By inductive hypothesis, we have from (iii) $\mathcal{M}, y \models A$, and $\mathcal{M}, z \models B$, which then with (iv) gives $\mathcal{M}, a \models A \bullet_0 B$.

($\Rightarrow$). Suppose (i) $\mathcal{M}, a \models A \backslash_0 B$. We have to show $\mathcal{M}', a \models A^b \backslash_1 \Box^\downarrow B^b$. Suppose we have (ii) R_1yxa such that $\mathcal{M}', x \models A^b$. It remains to be shown that $\mathcal{M}', y \models \Box^\downarrow B^b$. Suppose we have (iii) $R_\diamond zy$. It remains to be shown that $\mathcal{M}', z \models B^b$. The configuration (ii,iii) has a unique pre-image by the construction of $\mathcal{M}'$, namely R_0zxa. By inductive hypothesis from (ii) we have $\mathcal{M}, x \models A$ which together with (i) leads to $\mathcal{M}, z \models B$ and, again by inductive hypothesis $\mathcal{M}', z \models B^b$, as required.

($\Leftarrow$). Suppose (i) $\mathcal{M}', a \models A^b \backslash_1 \Box^\downarrow B^b$. We have to show that $\mathcal{M}, a \models A \backslash_0 B$. Suppose we have (ii) R_0cba such that $\mathcal{M}, b \models A$. To be shown is whether $\mathcal{M}, c \models B$. By the model construction and inductive hypothesis we have $R_\diamond cc'$, $R_1 c'ba$ and $\mathcal{M}', b \models A^\flat$. Hence by (i) $\mathcal{M}', c \models \Box^\downarrow B^\flat$ and therefore $\mathcal{M}', c \models B^\flat$. By our inductive hypothesis this leads to $\mathcal{M}, c \models B$, as required. $\square$

Illustration: Islands. For a concrete linguistic illustration, we return to the Coordinate Structure Constraint violations of §1. The translation schema of Def 2.1 was originally proposed by Morrill 1995, who conjectured on the basis of this schema an embedding of **NL** into **L** extended with a pair of unary 'bracket' operators closely related to $\diamond, \Box^\downarrow$. Whether the conjecture holds for the bracket operators remains open. But it is easy to recast Morrill's analysis of island constraints in terms of $\diamond, \Box^\downarrow$. We saw above that on an assignment $(X\backslash X)/X$ to the particle 'and', both the grammatical and the illformed examples are **L** derivable. Within **L**$\diamond$, we can refine the assignment to $(X\backslash\Box^\downarrow X)/X$. The relevant sequent goals now assume the following form (omitting the associative binary structural punctuation, but keeping the crucial $(\cdot)^\circ$):

(†)   the book that Melville wrote and John read
L $\vdash$ $r/(s/np), (np, (np\backslash s)/np, (X\backslash\Box^\downarrow X)/X, np, (np\backslash s)/np)^\circ \Rightarrow r$
(‡)   *the book that Melville wrote Moby Dick and John read
L$\diamond$ $\not\vdash$ $r/(s/np), (np, (np\backslash s)/np, np, (X\backslash\Box^\downarrow X)/X, np, (np\backslash s)/np)^\circ \Rightarrow r$

The $(X\backslash\Box^\downarrow X)/X$ assignment allows the particle 'and' to combine with the left and right conjuncts in the associative mode. The resulting coordinate structure is of type $\Box^\downarrow X$. To eliminate the $\Box^\downarrow$ connective, we have to close off the coordinate structure with $\diamond$ (or the corresponding structural operator $(\cdot)^\circ$ in the Gentzen presentation) — recall that $\diamond\Box^\downarrow X \to X$. For the instantiation $X = s/np$, the Across-the-Board case of extraction (†) works out fine; for the instantiation $X = s$, the island violation (‡) fails because the hypothetical gap np assumption finds itself outside the scope of the $(\cdot)^\circ$ operator.

Dependency

For a second straightforward application of the method, we consider the dependency calculus **DNL** of Moortgat and Morrill 1991 and show how it can be embedded in **NL**. Recall that **DNL** is the pure logic of residuation for a bimodal system with asymmetric products $\bullet_l, \bullet_r$ for left-headed and right-headed composition respectively. The distinction between left- and right-headed products can be recovered within **NL**$\diamond$, where we have the unary residuated pair $\diamond, \Box^\downarrow$ next to a symmetric product $\bullet$ and its implications. For the embedding translation $(\cdot)^\flat$, we label the head subtype of a product with $\diamond$. The residuation laws then determine the modal decoration of the implications.

Definition 2.3 The embedding translation $(\cdot)^\flat : \mathcal{F}(\mathbf{DNL}) \mapsto \mathcal{F}(\mathbf{NL}\Diamond)$ is defined as follows.

$$p^\flat = p$$

$$
\begin{array}{llll}
(A \bullet_l B)^\flat & = & \Diamond A^\flat \bullet B^\flat & \quad (A \bullet_r B)^\flat & = & A^\flat \bullet \Diamond B^\flat \\
(A /_l B)^\flat & = & \Box^{\downarrow}(A^\flat / B^\flat) & \quad (A /_r B)^\flat & = & A^\flat / \Diamond B^\flat \\
(B \backslash_l A)^\flat & = & \Diamond B^\flat \backslash A^\flat & \quad (B \backslash_r A)^\flat & = & \Box^{\downarrow}(B^\flat \backslash A^\flat)
\end{array}
$$

Proposition 2.4 $\mathbf{DNL} \vdash A \to B$ *iff* $\mathbf{NL}\Diamond \vdash A^\flat \to B^\flat$.

Proof. ($\Rightarrow$: Soundness of the embedding.) The soundness half is proved by induction on the length of the derivation of $A \to B$ in $\mathbf{DNL}$. We trace the residuation inferences under the translation mapping for the pair $(\bullet_l, /_l)$. The remaining cases are completely parallel.

$$
\mathbf{DNL} \quad \frac{A \bullet_l B \to C}{A \to C /_l B} \quad \rightsquigarrow \quad \frac{(A \bullet_l B)^\flat \to C^\flat}{A^\flat \to (C /_l B)^\flat}
$$

$$
\rightsquigarrow \quad \frac{\dfrac{\Diamond A^\flat \bullet B^\flat \to C^\flat}{\Diamond A^\flat \to C^\flat / B^\flat}}{A^\flat \to \Box^{\downarrow}(C^\flat / B^\flat)} \quad \mathbf{NL}
$$

($\Leftarrow$: Completeness of the embedding.) Suppose $\mathbf{DNL} \not\vdash A \to B$. By completeness, there is a model $\mathcal{M} = \langle W, R_l^3, R_r^3, V \rangle$ falsifying $A \to B$. From $\mathcal{M}$, we want to construct a model $\mathcal{M}' = \langle W', R_\bullet^3, R_\Diamond^2, V' \rangle$ which falsifies $A^\flat \to B^\flat$. Then from soundness we will be able to conclude $\mathbf{NL}\Diamond \not\vdash A^\flat \to B^\flat$.

Model Construction. Let W, W_l, W_r be disjoint sets and $f : R_l^3 \mapsto W_l$ and $g : R_r^3 \mapsto W_r$ bijective functions. $\mathcal{M}'$ is defined as follows:

$$
\begin{array}{lll}
W' & = & W \cup W_l \cup W_r \\
R_\bullet & = & \{(ab'c) \mid \exists b.R_l abc \wedge f((abc)) = b'\} \cup \\
& & \quad \{(abc') \mid \exists c.R_r abc \wedge g((abc)) = c'\} \\
R_\Diamond & = & \{(c'c) \mid \exists ab.R_r abc \wedge g((abc)) = c'\} \cup \\
& & \quad \{(b'b) \mid \exists ac.R_l abc \wedge f((abc)) = b'\} \\
V'(p) & = & V(p)
\end{array}
$$

We comment on the frames. For every triple $(abc) \in R_l^3$, we introduce a fresh b' and put the worlds $a, b, b', c \in W'$, $(b'b) \in R_\Diamond^2$ and $(ab'c) \in R_\bullet^3$. Similarly, for every triple $(abc) \in R_r^3$, we introduce a fresh c' and put the worlds $a, b, c, c' \in W'$, $(c'c) \in R_\Diamond^2$ and $(abc') \in R_\bullet^3$. In a picture (with dotted lines for the dependent daughter for R_l, R_r):

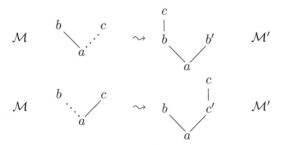

Lemma: Truth Preservation. By induction on the complexity of A, we show that for any $a \in W$, $\mathcal{M}, a \models A$ iff $\mathcal{M}', a \models A^\flat$. We prove the biconditional for the left-headed product. The other connectives are handled in a similar way.

($\Rightarrow$). Suppose $\mathcal{M}, a \models A \bullet_l B$. By the truth conditions for $\bullet_l$, there exist b, c such that (i) $R_l abc$ and (ii) $\mathcal{M}, b \models A$, (iii) $\mathcal{M}, c \models B$. By the construction of $\mathcal{M}'$, we conclude from (i) that there is a fresh $b' \in W'$ such that (iv) $R_\diamond^2 b'b$ and (v) $R_\bullet^3 ab'c$. By inductive hypothesis, from (ii) and (iii) we have $\mathcal{M}', b \models A^\flat$ and $\mathcal{M}', c \models B^\flat$. Then, from (iv) we have $\mathcal{M}', b' \models \Diamond A^\flat$ and from (v), $\mathcal{M}', a \models \Diamond A^\flat \bullet B^\flat$.

($\Leftarrow$). Suppose $\mathcal{M}', a \models \Diamond A^\flat \bullet B^\flat$. From the truth conditions for $\bullet, \Diamond$, we know there are $d', d, e \in W'$ such that (i) $R_\diamond^2 d'd$, (ii) $R_\bullet^3 ad'e$ and (iii) $\mathcal{M}', d \models A^\flat$ and $\mathcal{M}', e \models B^\flat$. From the construction of $\mathcal{M}'$, we may conclude that $d' = b', d = b, e = c$, since every triple $(abc) \in R_l^3$ is keyed to a fresh world $b' \in W'$. So we actually have (i') $R_\diamond^2 b'b$, (ii') $R_\bullet^3 ab'c$ and (iii') $\mathcal{M}', b \models A^\flat$ and $\mathcal{M}', c \models B^\flat$. (i') and (ii') imply $R_l^3 abc$. By inductive hypothesis, we have from (iii') $\mathcal{M}, b \models A$, and $\mathcal{M}, c \models B$. But then $\mathcal{M}, a \models A \bullet_l B$. $\square$

Illustration. Below are two instances of lifting in **DNL**. The left one is derivable, the right one is not.

$$\frac{\dfrac{\dfrac{A^\flat \Rightarrow A^\flat}{(A^\flat)^\diamond \Rightarrow \Diamond A^\flat} \Diamond R \qquad B^\flat \Rightarrow B^\flat}{\dfrac{((A^\flat)^\diamond, \Diamond A^\flat \backslash B^\flat)^\bullet \Rightarrow B^\flat}{\dfrac{(A^\flat)^\diamond \Rightarrow B^\flat / (\Diamond A^\flat \backslash B^\flat)}{\dfrac{A^\flat \Rightarrow \Box^\downarrow (B^\flat / (\Diamond A^\flat \backslash B^\flat))}{A \Rightarrow B /_l (A \backslash_l B)} {}_{\cdot\flat}} \Box^\downarrow R} /R} \backslash L}$$

$$\frac{\dfrac{\dfrac{?}{\dfrac{((A^\flat)^\diamond, \Box^\downarrow(A^\flat \backslash B^\flat))^\bullet \Rightarrow B^\flat}{\dfrac{(A^\flat)^\diamond \Rightarrow B^\flat / \Box^\downarrow(A^\flat \backslash B^\flat)}{A^\flat \Rightarrow \Box^\downarrow(B^\flat / \Box^\downarrow(A^\flat \backslash B^\flat))} \Box^\downarrow R} /R}}{A \Rightarrow B /_l (A \backslash_r B)} {}_{\cdot\flat}}$$

Commutativity

We can exploit the strategy for modal embedding of the dependency calculus to recover control over Permutation. Here we look at the pure case: the embedding of **NL** into **NLP$\Diamond$**. In §2.2 we will generalize the result to the other cases where Permutation is involved. For the embedding, choose one of the (asymmetric) dependency product translations for • in **NL**. Permutation in **NLP** spoils the asymmetry of the product. Whereas one could read the ◇ label in the cases of Definition 2.3 as a head marker, in the present case ◇ functions as a marker of the first daughter.

Definition 2.5 The embedding translation $\cdot^\flat$: $\mathcal{F}(\mathbf{NL}) \mapsto \mathcal{F}(\mathbf{NLP}\diamond)$ is defined as follows.

$$
\begin{aligned}
p^\flat &= p \\
(A \bullet B)^\flat &= \diamond A^\flat \otimes B^\flat \\
(A/B)^\flat &= \square^\downarrow(A^\flat \!\circ\!\!-\! B^\flat) \\
(B \backslash A)^\flat &= \diamond B^\flat \!-\!\!\circ A^\flat
\end{aligned}
$$

Proposition 2.6 $\mathbf{NL} \vdash A \to B$ *iff* $\mathbf{NLP}\diamond \vdash A^\flat \to B^\flat$.

Proof. (Sketch.) The ($\Rightarrow$) part again is proved straightforwardly by induction on the length of the derivation of $A \to B$ in **NL**. We leave this to the reader.

For the ($\Leftarrow$) direction, suppose $\mathbf{NL} \not\vdash A \to B$. By completeness, there is a model $\mathcal{M} = \langle W, R^3_\bullet, V \rangle$ falsifying $A \to B$. From $\mathcal{M}$, we now have to construct a *commutative* model $\mathcal{M}' = \langle W', R^3_\otimes, R^2_\diamond, V' \rangle$ which falsifies $A^\flat \to B^\flat$. From soundness we will conclude that $\mathbf{NLP}\diamond \not\vdash A^\flat \to B^\flat$.

The construction of the frame for $\mathcal{M}'$ in this case proceeds as follows. For every triple $(abc) \in R^3_\bullet$, we introduce a fresh b' and put the worlds $a, b, b', c \in W'$, $(b'b) \in R^2_\diamond$ and both $(ab'c), (acb') \in R^3_\otimes$. The construction makes the frame for $\mathcal{M}'$ commutative. But because every commutative triple $(ab'c)$ depends on a fresh $b' \in W' - W$, the commutativity of $\mathcal{M}'$ has no influence on $\mathcal{M}$. For the valuation, we set $V'(p) = V(p)$. Now for any $a \in W \cap W'$, we can show by induction on the complexity of A that $\mathcal{M}, a \models A$ iff $\mathcal{M}', a \models A^\flat$ which then leads to the proof of the main proposition in the usual way. $\square$

Illustration. In Figure 3 we first give a theorem of **NL**, followed by a non-theorem. We compare their image under $\cdot^\flat$ in **NLP**◇. And we notice that the second example *is* derivable in **NLP**.

2.2 Generalizations

The results of the previous section can be extended with minor modifications to the five edges that remain when we keep the Associativity face for §2.3.

What we have done in Proposition 2.4 for the pair **DNL** versus **NL**◇ can be adapted straightforwardly to the commutative pair **DNLP** versus **NLP**◇. Recall that in **DNLP**, the dependency products satisfy head-preserving commutativity $(P_{l,r})$, whereas in **NLP** we have simple commutativity (P).

$$\cfrac{\cfrac{\cfrac{\cfrac{\cfrac{\cfrac{\cfrac{B^\flat \Rightarrow B^\flat \quad A^\flat \Rightarrow A^\flat}{(A^\flat \!\circ\!\!-\! B^\flat, B^\flat)^\otimes \Rightarrow A^\flat}\ \circ\!\!-\!L}{((\Box^\downarrow(A^\flat \!\circ\!\!-\! B^\flat))^\diamond, B^\flat)^\otimes \Rightarrow A^\flat}\ \Box^\downarrow L}{(\Box^\downarrow(A^\flat \!\circ\!\!-\! B^\flat))^\diamond \Rightarrow A^\flat \!\circ\!\!-\! B^\flat}\ \circ\!\!-\!R}{\Box^\downarrow(A^\flat \!\circ\!\!-\! B^\flat) \Rightarrow \Box^\downarrow(A^\flat \!\circ\!\!-\! B^\flat)}\ \Box^\downarrow R}{(\Box^\downarrow(A^\flat \!\circ\!\!-\! B^\flat))^\diamond \Rightarrow \Diamond\Box^\downarrow(A^\flat \!\circ\!\!-\! B^\flat)}\ \Diamond R \quad A^\flat \Rightarrow A^\flat}{\cfrac{\cfrac{((\Box^\downarrow(A^\flat \!\circ\!\!-\! B^\flat))^\diamond, \Diamond\Box^\downarrow(A^\flat \!\circ\!\!-\! B^\flat)\!\!-\!\!\circ A^\flat)^\otimes \Rightarrow A^\flat}{(\Box^\downarrow(A^\flat \!\circ\!\!-\! B^\flat))^\diamond \Rightarrow A^\flat \!\circ\!\!-\!(\Diamond\Box^\downarrow(A^\flat \!\circ\!\!-\! B^\flat)\!\!-\!\!\circ A^\flat)}\ \circ\!\!-\!R}{\Box^\downarrow(A^\flat \!\circ\!\!-\! B^\flat) \Rightarrow \Box^\downarrow(A^\flat \!\circ\!\!-\!(\Diamond\Box^\downarrow(A^\flat \!\circ\!\!-\! B^\flat)\!\!-\!\!\circ A^\flat))}\ \Box^\downarrow R}\ \!-\!\!\circ L}{\mathbf{NL} \vdash A/B \Rightarrow A/((A/B)\backslash A)}\ .\flat$$

$$\cfrac{\cfrac{\cfrac{?}{((\Box^\downarrow(A^\flat \!\circ\!\!-\! B^\flat))^\diamond, \Box^\downarrow(A^\flat \!\circ\!\!-\!(\Diamond B^\flat \!\!-\!\!\circ A^\flat)))^\otimes \Rightarrow A^\flat}}{(\Box^\downarrow(A^\flat \!\circ\!\!-\! B^\flat))^\diamond \Rightarrow A^\flat \!\circ\!\!-\!(\Box^\downarrow(A^\flat \!\circ\!\!-\!(\Diamond B^\flat \!\!-\!\!\circ A^\flat)))}\ \circ\!\!-\!R}{\cfrac{\Box^\downarrow(A^\flat \!\circ\!\!-\! B^\flat) \Rightarrow \Box^\downarrow(A^\flat \!\circ\!\!-\!(\Box^\downarrow(A^\flat \!\circ\!\!-\!(\Diamond B^\flat \!\!-\!\!\circ A^\flat))))}{\mathbf{NL} \not\vdash A/B \Rightarrow A/(A/(B\backslash A))}\ .\flat}\ \Box^\downarrow R$$

$$\cfrac{\cfrac{\cfrac{\cfrac{\cfrac{B \Rightarrow B \quad A \Rightarrow A}{(A \!\circ\!\!-\! B, B)^\otimes \Rightarrow A}\ \circ\!\!-\!L}{(B, A \!\circ\!\!-\! B)^\otimes \Rightarrow A}\ P}{A \!\circ\!\!-\! B \Rightarrow B \!\!-\!\!\circ A}\ \!-\!\!\circ R \quad A \Rightarrow A}{(A \!\circ\!\!-\!(B \!\!-\!\!\circ A), A \!\circ\!\!-\! B)^\otimes \Rightarrow A}\ \circ\!\!-\!L}{\cfrac{(A \!\circ\!\!-\! B, A \!\circ\!\!-\!(B \!\!-\!\!\circ A))^\otimes \Rightarrow A}{\mathbf{NLP} \vdash A \!\circ\!\!-\! B \Rightarrow A \!\circ\!\!-\!(A \!\circ\!\!-\!(B \!\!-\!\!\circ A))}\ \circ\!\!-\!R}\ P$$

FIGURE 3 A theorem and a non-theorem

$$P_{l,r}: \quad A \otimes_l B \longleftrightarrow B \otimes_r A$$
$$P: \quad A \otimes B \to B \otimes A$$

Accommodating the commutative products, the embedding translation is that of Proposition 2.4: $\Diamond$ marks the head subtype.

Definition 2.7 The translation $(\cdot)^\flat : \mathcal{F}(\mathbf{DNLP}) \mapsto \mathcal{F}(\mathbf{NLP}\Diamond)$ is defined as follows:

$$p^\flat = p$$

$$
\begin{array}{llll}
(A \otimes_l B)^\flat & = & \Diamond A^\flat \otimes B^\flat & \quad (A \otimes_r B)^\flat & = & A^\flat \otimes \Diamond B^\flat \\
(A \!\multimap_l\! B)^\flat & = & \Box^\downarrow(A^\flat \!\multimap\! B^\flat) & \quad (A \!\multimap_r\! B)^\flat & = & A^\flat \!\multimap\! \Diamond B^\flat \\
(B \!\multimap_l\! A)^\flat & = & \Diamond B^\flat \!\multimap\! A^\flat & \quad (B \!\multimap_r\! A)^\flat & = & \Box^\downarrow(B^\flat \!\multimap\! A^\flat)
\end{array}
$$

Proposition 2.8 $\mathbf{DNLP} \vdash A \to B$ *iff* $\mathbf{NLP}\Diamond \vdash A^\flat \to B^\flat$.

For the proof of the ($\Leftarrow$) direction, we combine the method of construction of Proposition 2.4 with that of Proposition 2.6. For a configuration $R_l^\otimes abc$ in $\mathcal{M}$, we take fresh b' and put the configurations $R_\Diamond b'b, R_\otimes ab'c, R_\otimes acb'$ in $\mathcal{M}'$. Similarly, for a configuration $R_r^\otimes abc$ in $\mathcal{M}$, we take fresh c' and put the configurations $R_\Diamond c'c, R_\otimes abc', R_\otimes ac'b$ in $\mathcal{M}'$. The commutativity property of $\otimes$ is thus realized by the construction.

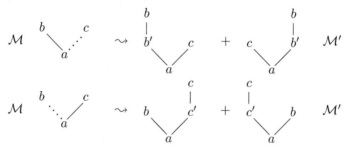

Let us check the truth preservation lemma. This time a configuration ($\star$) in $\mathcal{M}'$ does not have a unique pre-image: it can come from $R_l^\otimes xyz$ or $R_r^\otimes xzy$. But because of head-preserving commutativity (DP), these are both in $\mathcal{M}$.

($\star$)

$$
\begin{array}{c}
y \\
| \\
z \diagdown \quad y' \\
\diagdown \diagup \\
x
\end{array}
$$

Similarly, the embedding construction presented in Prop 2.6 for the pair **NL** versus **NLP**$\Diamond$ can be generalized directly to the related pair **DNL** versus **DNLP**$\Diamond$. This time, we want the embedding translation to block the structural postulate of *head-preserving* commutativity in **DNLP**. The translation below invalidates the postulate by uniformly decorating with $\Diamond$, say, the left subtype of a product.

Definition 2.9 Define $(\cdot)^\flat : \mathcal{F}(\mathbf{DNL}) \mapsto \mathcal{F}(\mathbf{DNLP}\diamond)$ as follows.

$$p^\flat = p$$

$$
\begin{aligned}
(A \bullet_l B)^\flat &= \diamond A^\flat \otimes_l B^\flat & (A \bullet_r B)^\flat &= \diamond A^\flat \otimes_r B^\flat \\
(A/_l B)^\flat &= \Box^\downarrow (A^\flat \circ\!\!-_l B^\flat) & (A/_r B)^\flat &= \Box^\downarrow (A^\flat \circ\!\!-_r B^\flat) \\
(B\backslash_l A)^\flat &= \diamond B^\flat -\!\circ_l A^\flat & (B\backslash_r A)^\flat &= \diamond B^\flat -\!\circ_r A^\flat
\end{aligned}
$$

We then have the following proposition. The proof is entirely parallel to that of Proposition 2.6 before.

Proposition 2.10 $\mathbf{DNL} \vdash A \to B$ *iff* $\mathbf{DNLP}\diamond \vdash A^\flat \to B^\flat$.

The method of Proposition 2.2 generalizes to the following cases with some simple changes.

Definition 2.11 Define the translation $(\cdot)^\flat : \mathcal{F}(\mathbf{NLP}) \mapsto \mathcal{F}(\mathbf{LP}\diamond)$ as follows.

$$
\begin{aligned}
p^\flat &= p \\
(A \otimes B)^\flat &= \diamond(A^\flat \otimes B^\flat) \\
(A\circ\!\!-B)^\flat &= \Box^\downarrow A^\flat \circ\!\!-B^\flat \\
(B-\!\circ A)^\flat &= B^\flat -\!\circ\Box^\downarrow A^\flat
\end{aligned}
$$

Proposition 2.12 $\mathbf{NLP} \vdash A \to B$ *iff* $\mathbf{LP}\diamond \vdash A^\flat \to B^\flat$.

The only difference with Proposition 2.2 is that the product in input and target logic are commutative. Commutativity is realized automatically by the construction of $\mathcal{M}'$.

Proposition 2.13 $\mathbf{DNL} \vdash A \to B$ *iff* $\mathbf{DL}\diamond \vdash A^\flat \to B^\flat$.

Proposition 2.14 $\mathbf{DNLP} \vdash A \to B$ *iff* $\mathbf{DLP}\diamond \vdash A^\flat \to B^\flat$.

2.3 Composed Translations

The remaining cases concern the right back face of the cube, where we find the systems **DL**, **L**, **LP**, and **DLP**. These logics share associative resource management, but they differ with respect to one of the remaining structural parameters — sensitivity for linear order (**L** versus **LP**, **DL** versus **DLP**) or for dependency structure (**DL** versus **L**, and **DLP** versus **LP**). We already know how to handle each of the structural dimensions individually. We use this knowledge to obtain the embeddings for systems with shared Associativity. Our strategy has two components. First we neutralize direct appeal to Associativity by taking the composition of the translation schema blocking Associativity with the schema responsible for control in the structural dimension which discriminates between the source and target logics. This first move does *not* embed the source logic, but its non-associative neighbor. The second move then is to reinstall associativity in terms of $\diamond$ modally controlled versions of the Associativity postulates.

Associative Dependency Calculus. We work out the 'rear attack' maneuver first for the pair **DL** versus **L**. In **DNL** we have no restrictions on

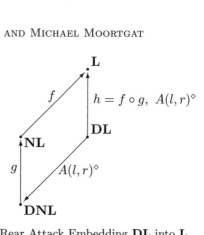

FIGURE 4 Rear Attack Embedding **DL** into **L**.

the interpretation of $\bullet_l, \bullet_r$. In **DL** we assume $\bullet_l, \bullet_r$ are interpreted on (bi-modal) associative frames, and we have structural associativity postulates $A(l), A(r)$ on top of the pure logic of residuation for $\bullet_l, \bullet_r$. In **L** we cannot discriminate between $\bullet_l$ and $\bullet_r$ — there is just one $\bullet$ operator, which shares the associative resource management with its dependency variants. The objective of the embedding is to recover the distinction between left- and right-headed structures in a system which has only one product connective.

$$A(l): \quad (A \bullet_l B) \bullet_l C \longleftrightarrow A \bullet_l (B \bullet_l C)$$
$$A(r): \quad A \bullet_r (B \bullet_r C) \longleftrightarrow (A \bullet_r B) \bullet_r C$$

For the embedding translation, we *compose* the mappings of Definition 2.3 — embedding **DNL** into **NL** — and Definition 2.1 — embedding **NL** into **L**.

Definition 2.15 Define the translation $\cdot^\flat : \mathcal{F}(\textbf{DNL}) \to \mathcal{F}(\textbf{ML}\diamond)$ as follows:

$$p^\flat = p$$
$$\begin{aligned}
(A \bullet_l B)^\flat &= \diamond(\diamond A^\flat \bullet B^\flat) & (A \bullet_r B)^\flat &= \diamond(A^\flat \bullet \diamond B^\flat) \\
(A/_l B)^\flat &= \Box^\downarrow(\Box^\downarrow A^\flat / B^\flat) & (A/_r B)^\flat &= \Box^\downarrow A^\flat / \diamond B^\flat \\
(B\backslash_l A)^\flat &= \diamond B^\flat \backslash \Box^\downarrow A^\flat & (B\backslash_r A)^\flat &= \Box^\downarrow(B^\flat \backslash \Box^\downarrow A^\flat)
\end{aligned}$$

From the proof of the embedding of **NL** into **L** we know that $\diamond$ neutralizes the effects of the associativity of $\bullet$ in the target logic **L**: the frame condition for Associativity is satisfied vacuously. To realize the desired embedding of **DL** into **L**, we reinstall modal versions of the associativity postulates.

$$A(l)^\diamond: \quad \diamond(\diamond\diamond(\diamond A \bullet B) \bullet C) \longleftrightarrow \diamond(\diamond A \bullet \diamond(\diamond B \bullet C))$$
$$A(r)^\diamond: \quad \diamond(A \bullet \diamond\diamond(B \bullet \diamond C)) \longleftrightarrow \diamond(\diamond(A \bullet \diamond B) \bullet \diamond C).$$

Figure 4 is a graphical illustration of the interplay between the composed translation schema and the modal structural postulate. f is the translation schema $(\cdot)^\flat$ of Definition 2.1, g that of Definition 2.3.

Modalized Structural Postulates: Frame Completeness. The modalized structural postulates $A(l, r)^\circ$ introduce a new element into the discussion. Semantically, these postulates require frame constraints correlating the binary and ternary relations of structural composition. Fortunately we know, from the generalized Sahlqvist-van Benthem Theorem and frame completeness result discussed in §1, that from $A(l, r)^\circ$ we can effectively obtain the relevant first order frame conditions, and that completeness of $\mathbf{L}\Diamond$ extends to the system augmented with $A(l, r)^\circ$. We check completeness for $A(l)^\circ$ here as an illustration — the situation for $A(r)^\circ$ is entirely similar. Figure 5 gives the frame condition for $A(l)^\circ$.

The models for $\mathbf{L}\Diamond$ are structures $\langle W, R^2_\Diamond, R^3_\bullet, V \rangle$. Now consider ($\Rightarrow$) in Figure 5 below. Given the canonical model construction of Definition 1.1 the following are derivable by the definition of $R^2_\Diamond, R^3_\bullet$:

$$a \to \Diamond b, \quad e \to \Diamond f,$$
$$b \to c \bullet d, \quad f \to g \bullet h,$$
$$c \to \Diamond e, \quad g \to \Diamond i.$$

From these we can conclude $\vdash a \to \Diamond(\Diamond\Diamond(\Diamond i \bullet h) \bullet d))$, i.e.

$$a \in V(\Diamond(\Diamond\Diamond(\Diamond i \bullet h) \bullet d))),$$

given the definition of the canonical valuation ($\star$). For ($\ddagger$) we have to find b', c', d', e', f' such that

$$a \to \Diamond b', \quad d' \to \Diamond e',$$
$$b' \to c' \bullet d', \quad e' \to f' \bullet d,$$
$$c' \to \Diamond i, \quad f' \to \Diamond h.$$

Let us put

$$f' = \Diamond h,$$
$$e' = f' \bullet d = \Diamond h \bullet d,$$
$$d' = \Diamond e' = \Diamond(\Diamond h \bullet d),$$
$$c' = \Diamond i,$$
$$b' = c' \bullet d' = \Diamond i \bullet \Diamond(\Diamond h \bullet d).$$

These imply $\vdash a \to \Diamond(\Diamond i \bullet \Diamond(\Diamond h \bullet d))$, i.e., $a \in V(\Diamond(\Diamond i \bullet \Diamond(\Diamond h \bullet d)))$ can be shown to follow from ($\star$). Similarly for the other direction.

Now for the embedding theorem.

Proposition 2.16 $\mathbf{DL} \vdash A \to B$ *iff* $\mathbf{L}\Diamond + A(l, r)^\circ \vdash A^\flat \to B^\flat$.

Model Construction. Suppose $\mathbf{DL} \not\vdash A \to B$. Then there is a model $\mathcal{M} = \langle W, R_l, R_r, V \rangle$ where $A \to B$ fails. From $\mathcal{M}$ we construct $\mathcal{M}'$ as follows. For every triple $(abc) \in R_l$ we take fresh a', b' and put $(aa') \in R_\Diamond, (a'b'c) \in R_\bullet, (b'b) \in R_\Diamond$. Similarly, for every triple $(abc) \in R_r$ we take fresh a', c' and put $(aa') \in R_\Diamond, (a'bc') \in R_\bullet, (c'c) \in R_\Diamond$.

We have to check whether $\mathcal{M}'$ is an appropriate model for $\mathbf{L}\Diamond + A(l, r)_\Diamond$, specifically, whether the frame condition of Figure 4 is satisfied. Sup-

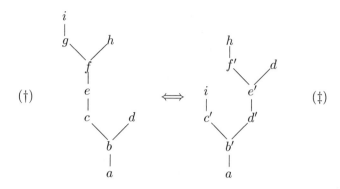

$$F(A(l)^\diamond) : \quad \exists bcefg(R_\diamond ab \wedge R_\bullet bcd \wedge R_\diamond ce \wedge R_\diamond ef \wedge R_\bullet fgh \wedge R_\diamond gi) \Longleftrightarrow$$
$$\exists b'c'd'e'f'(R_\diamond ab' \wedge R_\bullet b'c'd' \wedge R_\diamond c'i \wedge R_\diamond d'e' \wedge R_\bullet e'f'd \wedge R_\diamond f'h)$$

FIGURE 5 Frame condition for $A(l)^\diamond$.

pose ($\ddagger$) holds, and let us check whether ($\dagger$). Note that a configuration $R_\diamond ab', R_\bullet b'c'd', R_\diamond c'i$ can only hold in $\mathcal{M}'$ if in $\mathcal{M}$ we had $R_l aid'$ ($\star$). And a configuration $R_\diamond d'e', R_\bullet e'f'd, R_\diamond f'h$ can be in $\mathcal{M}'$ only if in $\mathcal{M}$ we had $R_l d'hd$ ($\star\star$). The frame for $\mathcal{M}$ is associative. Therefore, from ($\star, \star\star$) we can conclude $\mathcal{M}$ also contains a configuration $R_l aed, R_l eih$ for some $e \in W$. Applying the $\mathcal{M}'$ construction to that configuration we obtain ($\dagger$). Similarly for the other direction.

From here on, the proof of Proposition 2.16 follows the established path.

Generalization. The rear attack strategy can be generalized to the remaining edges. Below we simply state the embedding theorems with the relevant composed translations and modal structural postulates. We give the salient ingredients for the construction of $\mathcal{M}'$, leaving the elaboration as an exercise to the reader.

Consider first embedding of **L** into **LP**. The discriminating structural parameter is Commutativity. For the translation schema, we compose the translations of Definition 2.11 and Definition 2.5. Associativity is reinstalled in terms of the structural postulate $A_\otimes^\diamond$.

$$A_\otimes^\diamond: \quad \diamond(\diamond\diamond(\diamond A \otimes B) \otimes C) \longleftrightarrow \diamond(\diamond A \otimes \diamond(\diamond B \otimes C))$$

Definition 2.17 The embedding translation $(\cdot)^\flat : \mathcal{F}(\mathbf{L}) \mapsto \mathcal{F}(\mathbf{LP}\diamond)$ is defined as follows.

$$\begin{aligned}
p^\flat &= p \\
(A \bullet B)^\flat &= \diamond(\diamond A^\flat \otimes B^\flat) \\
(A/B)^\flat &= \Box^\downarrow(\Box^\downarrow A^\flat \multimapinv B^\flat) \\
(B\backslash A)^\flat &= \diamond B^\flat \multimapinv \Box^\downarrow A^\flat
\end{aligned}$$

Proposition 2.18 $\mathbf{L} \vdash A \to B$ *iff* $\mathbf{LP}\diamond + A_\otimes^\diamond \vdash A^\flat \to B^\flat$.

Semantically, the commutativity of $R_\otimes$ is realized via the construction of $\mathcal{M}'$, as in the case of Proposition 2.6:

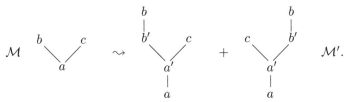

For the pair **DL** versus **DLP**, again Commutativity is the discriminating structural parameter, but now in a bimodal setting. We compose the translations for the embedding of **DNLP** into **DLP** and **DNL** into **DNLP**. The structural postulates $A^\diamond_{\otimes_l}$ and $A^\diamond_{\otimes_r}$ are the dependency variants of $A^\diamond_\otimes$ above.

$$A^\diamond_{\otimes_l}: \quad \diamond(\diamond\diamond(\diamond A \otimes_l B) \otimes_l C \longleftrightarrow \diamond(\diamond A \otimes_l \diamond(\diamond B \otimes_l C))$$
$$A^\diamond_{\otimes_r}: \quad \diamond(\diamond\diamond(\diamond A \otimes_r B) \otimes_r C \longleftrightarrow \diamond(\diamond A \otimes_r \diamond(\diamond B \otimes_r C))$$

Definition 2.19 The embedding translation $(\cdot)^\flat : \mathcal{F}(\mathbf{DL}) \mapsto \mathcal{F}(\mathbf{DLP}\diamond)$ is defined as follows.

$$p^\flat = p$$

$$
\begin{array}{ll}
(A \bullet_l B)^\flat = \diamond(\diamond A^\flat \otimes_l B^\flat) & (A \bullet_r B)^\flat = \diamond(\diamond A^\flat \otimes_r B^\flat) \\
(A/_l B)^\flat = \square^\downarrow(\square^\downarrow A^\flat \circ\!-_l B^\flat) & (A/_r B)^\flat = \square^\downarrow(\square^\downarrow A^\flat \circ\!-_r B^\flat) \\
(B\backslash_l A)^\flat = \diamond B^\flat -\circ_l \square^\downarrow A^\flat & (B\backslash_r A)^\flat = \diamond B^\flat -\circ_r \square^\downarrow A^\flat
\end{array}
$$

Proposition 2.20 $\mathbf{DL} \vdash A \to B$ *iff* $\mathbf{DLP}\diamond + (A^\diamond_{\otimes_l}, A^\diamond_{\otimes_r}) \vdash A^\flat \to B^\flat$.

Finally, for the pair **DLP** versus **LP**, the objective of the embedding is to recapture the dependency distinctions. We compose the translations of Definition 2.11 and Definition 2.7. The modal structural postulates $A(l,r)^\diamond_\otimes$ are obtained from $A(l,r)^\diamond$ by replacing $\bullet$ by $\otimes$.

Definition 2.21 The embedding translation $\cdot^\flat : \mathcal{F}(\mathbf{DLP}) \mapsto \mathcal{F}(\mathbf{LP}\diamond)$ is defined as follows.

$$p^\flat = p$$

$$
\begin{array}{ll}
(A \otimes_l B)^\flat = \diamond(\diamond A^\flat \otimes B^\flat) & (A \otimes_r B)^\flat = \diamond(A^\flat \otimes \diamond B^\flat) \\
(A\circ\!-_l B)^\flat = \square^\downarrow(\square^\downarrow A^\flat \circ\!- B^\flat) & (A\circ\!-_r B)^\flat = \square^\downarrow A^\flat \circ\!- \diamond B^\flat \\
(B-\circ_l A)^\flat = \diamond B^\flat -\circ \square^\downarrow A^\flat & (B-\circ_r A)^\flat = \square^\downarrow(B^\flat -\circ \square^\downarrow A^\flat)
\end{array}
$$

Proposition 2.22 $\mathbf{DLP} \vdash A \to B$ *iff* $\mathbf{LP}\diamond + A(l,r)^\diamond_\otimes \vdash A^\flat \to B^\flat$.

2.4 Constraining Embeddings: Summary

We have completed the tour of the landscape and shown that the connectives $\diamond, \square^\downarrow$ can systematically reintroduce structural discrimination in logics where on the level of the binary multiplicatives such discrimination is destroyed by global structural postulates. In Figure 6 we label the edges of the cube with the numbers of the embedding theorems.

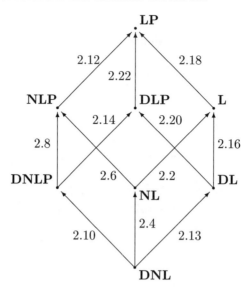

FIGURE 6 Embedding translations: recovering resource control

3   Licensing Structural Relaxation

In the present section we shift the perspective: instead of using modal decorations to *block* structural options for resource management, we now take the more discriminating logic as the starting point and use the modal operators to recover the flexibility of a neighboring logic with a more liberal resource management regime from within a system with a more rigid notion of structure-sensitivity.

Licensing of structural relaxation has traditionally been addressed (both in logic Došen 1992 and in linguistics Morrill 1994) in terms of a single universal $\Box$ modality with $S4$ type resource management. Here we stick to the minimalistic principles set out at the beginning of this paper, and realize also the licensing embeddings in terms of the pure logic of residuation for the pair $\Diamond, \Box^{\downarrow}$ plus modally controlled structural postulates. In §3.1 we present an external strategy for modal decoration: in the scope of the $\Diamond$ operator, products of the more discriminating logics gain access to structural rules that are inaccessible in the non-modal part of the logic. In §3.2 we develop a complementary strategy for internal modal decoration, where modal versions of the structural rules are accessible provided one or all of the immediate substructures are labeled with $\Diamond$. We present linguistic considerations that will affect the choice for the external or internal approach.

3.1 Modal Labeling: External Perspective

Licensing structural relaxation is simpler than recovering structural control: the target logics for the embeddings in this section *lack* an option for structural manipulation which can be reinstalled straightforwardly in terms of a modal version of the relevant structural postulate. We do not have to design specific translation strategies for the individual pairs of logics, but can do with one general translation schema.

Definition 3.1 We define a general translation schema $(\cdot)^\sharp : \mathcal{F}(\mathcal{L}_1) \mapsto \mathcal{F}(\mathcal{L}_0 \Diamond)$ embedding a stronger logic $\mathcal{L}_1$ into a weaker logic $\mathcal{L}_0$ extended with $\Diamond, \Box^{\downarrow}$ as follows.

$$
\begin{aligned}
p^\sharp &= p \\
(A \bullet_1 B)^\sharp &= \Diamond(A^\sharp \bullet_0 B^\sharp) \\
(A/_1 B)^\sharp &= \Box^{\downarrow} A^\sharp /_0 B^\sharp \\
(B\backslash_1 A)^\sharp &= B^\sharp \backslash_0 \Box^{\downarrow} A^\sharp
\end{aligned}
$$

The embedding theorems we are interested in now have the general format shown below, where $\mathcal{R}_\Diamond$ is (a package of) the modal translation(s) $A^\sharp \to B^\sharp$ of the structural rule(s) $A \to B$ which differentiate(s) $\mathcal{L}_1$ from $\mathcal{L}_0$.

$$
\mathcal{L}_1 \vdash A \to B \quad \text{iff} \quad \mathcal{L}_0 \Diamond + \mathcal{R}_\Diamond \vdash A^\sharp \to B^\sharp
$$

We look at the dimensions of dependency, precedence and dominance in general terms first, discussing the relevant aspects of the model construction. Then we comment on individual embedding theorems.

Relaxation of Dependency Sensitivity. For a start let us look at a pair of logics $\mathcal{L}_0, \mathcal{L}_1$, where $\mathcal{L}_0$ makes a dependency distinction between a left-dominant and a right-dominant product, whereas $\mathcal{L}_1$ cannot discriminate these two. There are two ways of setting up the coarser logic $\mathcal{L}_1$. Either we present $\mathcal{L}_1$ as a bimodal system where the distinction between right-dominant $\bullet_r$ and left-dominant $\bullet_l$ collapses as a result of the structural postulate (D).

$$
\mathcal{L}_1: \quad A \bullet_r B \longleftrightarrow A \bullet_l B \tag{D}
$$

Or we have a unimodal presentation for $\mathcal{L}_1$ and pick an arbitrary choice of the dependency operators for the embedding translation. We take the second option here, and realize the embedding translation as indicated below.

$$
\begin{aligned}
p^\sharp &= p \\
(A \bullet B)^\sharp &= \Diamond(A^\sharp \bullet_r B^\sharp) \\
(A/B)^\sharp &= \Box^{\downarrow} A^\sharp /_r B^\sharp \\
(B\backslash A)^\sharp &= B^\sharp \backslash_r \Box^{\downarrow} A^\sharp
\end{aligned}
$$

Relaxation of dependency sensitivity is obtained by means of a modally controlled version of (D). Corresponding to the structural postulate $(D_\Diamond)$

we have the frame condition $F(D_\diamond)$ as a restriction on models for the more discriminating logic.

$\mathcal{L}_0$: $\quad \diamond(A \bullet_r B) \longleftrightarrow \diamond(A \bullet_l B)$ $\hfill (D_\diamond)$

$F(D_\diamond)$: $\quad (\forall xyz \in W_0)\ \exists t(R_\diamond xt \wedge R_r tyz) \Leftrightarrow \exists t'(R_\diamond xt' \wedge R_r t'yz).$

Model Construction. To construct an $\mathcal{L}_0$ model $\langle W_0, R_\diamond^2, R_l^3, R_r^3, V_0 \rangle$ from a model $\langle W_1, R_1^3, V_1 \rangle$ for $\mathcal{L}_1$ we proceed as follows. For every triple $(xyz) \in R_1$ we take fresh points x_1, x_2, put x, x_1, x_2, y, z in W_0 with $(xx_1) \in R_\diamond$, $(x_1yz) \in R_l$ and $(xx_2) \in R_\diamond$, $(x_2yz) \in R_r$.

To show that the generated model $\mathcal{M}_0$ satisfies the required frame condition $F(D_\diamond)$, assume there exists $b \in W_0$ such that $R_\diamond ab$ and $R_r bcd$. Such a configuration has a unique pre-image in $\mathcal{M}_1$ namely $R_1 acd$. By virtue of the construction of $\mathcal{M}_0$ this means there exists $b' \in W_0$ such that $R_\diamond ab'$ and $R_l b'cd$, as required for $F(D_\diamond)$.

Truth preservation of the model construction is unproblematic. The proof of the following proposition then is routine.

Proposition 3.2 $\mathbf{NL} \vdash A \to B$ *iff* $\mathbf{DNL}\diamond + D_\diamond \vdash A^\sharp \to B^\sharp$.

Relaxation of Order Sensitivity. Here we compare logics $\mathcal{L}_1$ and $\mathcal{L}_0$ where the structural rule of Permutation is included in the resource management package for $\mathcal{L}_1$, but not in that of $\mathcal{L}_0$. Controlled Permutation is reintroduced in $\mathcal{L}_0$ in the form of the modal postulate $(P_\diamond)$. The corresponding frame condition on $\mathcal{L}_0$ models $\mathcal{M}_0$ is given as $F(P_\diamond)$.

$\mathcal{L}_1$: $\quad A \bullet_1 B \longleftrightarrow B \bullet_1 A$ $\hfill (P)$
$\mathcal{L}_0$: $\quad \diamond(A \bullet_0 B) \longleftrightarrow \diamond(B \bullet_0 A)$ $\hfill (P_\diamond)$

$F(P_\diamond)$: $\quad (\forall xyz \in W_0)\ \exists t(R_\diamond xt \wedge R_0 tyz) \Rightarrow \exists t'(R_\diamond xt' \wedge R_0 t'zy).$

To generate the required model $\mathcal{M}_0$ from $\mathcal{M}_1$ we proceed as follows. If $(xyz) \in R_1$ we take fresh x_1, x_2 and put both $(xx_1) \in R_\diamond$ and $(x_1yz) \in R_0$ and $(xx_2) \in R_\diamond$ and $(x_2zy) \in R_0$.

We have to show that the generated model $\mathcal{M}_0$ satisfies $F(P_\diamond)$. Assume there exists $b \in W_0$ such that $R_\diamond ab$ and $R_0 bcd$. Because of the presence of Permutation in $\mathcal{L}_1$ this configuration has two pre-images, $R_1 acd$ and $R_1 adc$. By virtue of the construction algorithm for $\mathcal{M}_0$ each of these guarantees there exists $b' \in W_0$ such that $R_\diamond ab'$ and $R_0 xdc$.

Proposition 3.3 $\mathbf{NLP} \vdash A \to B$ *iff* $\mathbf{NL}\diamond + P_\diamond \vdash A^\sharp \to B^\sharp$.

Relaxation of Constituent Sensitivity. Next compare a logic $\mathcal{L}_1$ where Associativity obtains with a more discriminating logic without global Associativity. We realize the embedding by introducing a modally controlled form of Associativity $(A_\diamond)$ with its corresponding frame condition $F(A_\diamond)$.

$$\mathcal{L}_1: \quad A \bullet_1 (B \bullet_1 C) \longleftrightarrow (A \bullet_1 B) \bullet_1 C \tag{A}$$
$$\mathcal{L}_0: \quad \diamond(A \bullet_0 \diamond(B \bullet_0 C)) \longleftrightarrow \diamond(\diamond(A \bullet_0 B) \bullet_0 C) \tag{$A_\diamond$}$$

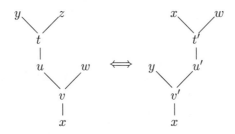

$$F(A_\diamond): \quad (\forall xyzw \in W_0)\, \exists tuv(R_\diamond xv \land R_0 vuw \land R_\diamond ut \land R_0 tyz) \Leftrightarrow$$
$$\exists t'u'v'(R_\diamond xv' \land R_0 v'yu' \land R_\diamond u't' \land R_0 t'zw).$$

The model $\mathcal{M}_0$ is generated from $\mathcal{M}_1$ in the familiar way. For every triple $(xyz) \in R_1$, we take a fresh point x', and put $x, x', y, z \in W_0$, with $(xx') \in R_\diamond$ and $(x'yz) \in R_0$.

We have to show that the frame condition $F(A_\diamond)$ holds in the generated model. Suppose (†) $R_\diamond ab$ and $R_0 bcd$ and (‡) $R_\diamond ce$ and $R_0 efg$. We have to show that there are $x, y, z \in W_0$ such that $R_\diamond ax$ and $R_0 xfy$ and $R_\diamond yz$ and $R_0 zgd$. Observe that the configurations (†) and (‡) both have unique pre-images in $\mathcal{M}_1$, $R_1 acd$ and $R_1 cfg$ respectively. Because R_1 is associative, there exists $y \in W_1$ such that $R_1 afy$ and $R_1 ygd$. But then, by the construction of $\mathcal{M}_0$, also $y \in W_0$ and there exist $x, z \in W_0$ such that $R_\diamond ax$, $R_0 xfy$, $R_\diamond yz$ and $R_0 zgd$, as required.

Proposition 3.4 $\mathbf{L} \vdash A \to B$ *iff* $\mathbf{NL}\diamond + A_\diamond \vdash A^\sharp \to B^\sharp$.

Generalizations. The preceding discussion covers the individual dimensions of structural organization. Generalizing the approach to the remaining edges of Figure 1 does not present significant new problems. Here are some suggestions to assist the tenacious reader who wants to work out the full details.

The embeddings for the lower plane of Figure 1 are obtained from the parallel embeddings in the upper plane by doubling the construction from a unimodal product setting to the bimodal situation with two dependency products.

Embeddings between logics sharing associative management, but differing with respect to order or dependency sensitivity require modal associativity $A_\diamond$ in addition to $P_\diamond$ or $D_\diamond$ for the more discriminating logic: as we have seen in §2, the external $\diamond$ decoration on product configurations pre-empts the conditions of application for the non-modal associativity postulate. We have already come across this interplay between the translation schema and modal structural postulates in §2.3. For the licensing type of embedding, concrete instances are the embedding of **LP** into $\mathbf{L}\diamond + A_\diamond + P_\diamond$, and the embedding of **L** into $\mathbf{DL}\diamond + A_\diamond + D_\diamond$.

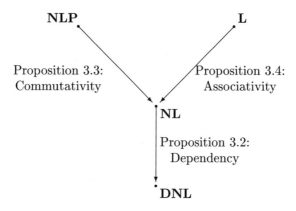

FIGURE 7 Licensing structural relaxation:
precedence, dominance, dependency.

External Decoration: Applications. Linguistic application for the external strategy of modal licensing will be found in areas where one wants to induce structural relaxation in a configuration from the outside. The complementary view, where a subconfiguration induces structural relaxation in its context, is explored in §3.2 below. For the outside perspective, consider a non-commutative default regime with $P_\diamond$ for the modal extension. Collapse of the directional implications is underivable, $\nvdash A/B \longleftrightarrow B\backslash A$, but the modal variant below is. In general terms: a lexical assignment $A/\square^{\downarrow}\diamond B$ will induce commutativity for the argument subtype.

$$\cfrac{\cfrac{\cfrac{\cfrac{B \Rightarrow B \quad (A)^{\circ} \Rightarrow \diamond A}{((A/B,B)^{\bullet})^{\circ} \Rightarrow \diamond A} \; /L}{((B,A/B)^{\bullet})^{\circ} \Rightarrow \diamond A} \; P_{\diamond}}{(B,A/B)^{\bullet} \Rightarrow \square^{\downarrow}\diamond A} \; \square^{\downarrow}R}{A/B \Rightarrow B\backslash\square^{\downarrow}\diamond A} \; \backslash R$$

Similarly, in the context of a non-associative default regime with $A_{\diamond}$ for the modal extension, one finds the following modal variant of the Geach rule, which remains underivable without the modal decoration.

$$\cfrac{\cfrac{\cfrac{\cfrac{\cfrac{\cfrac{\cfrac{C \Rightarrow C \quad (\square^{\downarrow}B)^{\circ} \Rightarrow B}{(\square^{\downarrow}B/C,C)^{\bullet})^{\circ} \Rightarrow B} \; /L \quad (A)^{\circ} \Rightarrow \diamond A}{((A/B,((\square^{\downarrow}B/C,C)^{\bullet})^{\circ})^{\bullet})^{\circ} \Rightarrow \diamond A} \; /L}{((((A/B,\square^{\downarrow}B/C)^{\bullet})^{\circ},C)^{\bullet})^{\circ} \Rightarrow \diamond A} \; A_{\diamond}}{(((A/B,\square^{\downarrow}B/C)^{\bullet})^{\circ},C)^{\bullet} \Rightarrow \square^{\downarrow}\diamond A} \; \square^{\downarrow}R}{((A/B,\square^{\downarrow}B/C)^{\bullet})^{\circ} \Rightarrow \square^{\downarrow}\diamond A/C} \; /R}{(A/B,\square^{\downarrow}B/C)^{\bullet} \Rightarrow \square^{\downarrow}(\square^{\downarrow}\diamond A/C)} \; \square^{\downarrow}R}{A/B \Rightarrow \square^{\downarrow}(\square^{\downarrow}\diamond A/C)/(\square^{\downarrow}B/C)} \; /R$$

3.2 Modal Labeling: the Internal Perspective

The embeddings discussed in the previous section license special structural behaviour by *external* decoration of product configurations: in the scope of the $\diamond$ operator the product gains access to a structural rule which is unavailable in the default resource management of the logic in question. In view of the intended linguistic applications of structural modalities we would like to complement the external modalization strategy by an *internal* one where a structural rule is applicable to a product configuration provided one of its subtypes is modally decorated. In fact, the examples of modally controlled constraints we gave at the beginning of this paper were of this form. For the internal perspective, the modalized versions of Permutation and Associativity take the form shown below.

$(P'_{\diamond})$ $\quad \diamond A \bullet B \longleftrightarrow B \bullet \diamond A$

$(A'_{\diamond})$ $\quad A_1 \bullet (A_2 \bullet A_3) \longleftrightarrow (A_1 \bullet A_2) \bullet A_3$ (provided $A_i = \diamond A, 1 \leq i \leq 3$)

We prove embedding theorems for internal modal decoration in terms of the following translation mapping, which labels positive (proper) sub-formulae with the modal prefix $\diamond\square^{\downarrow}$ and leaves negative subformulae un-decorated.

Definition 3.5 Define embedding translations

$$(\cdot)^+, (\cdot)^- : \mathcal{F}(\mathcal{L}_1) \mapsto \mathcal{F}(\mathcal{L}_0 \Diamond)$$

for positive and negative formula occurrences as follows.

$$
\begin{aligned}
(p)^+ &= p & (p)^- &= p \\
(A \bullet_1 B)^+ &= \Diamond\Box^{\downarrow}(A)^+ \bullet_0 \Diamond\Box^{\downarrow}(B)^+ & (A \bullet_1 B)^- &= (A)^- \bullet_0 (B)^- \\
(A/_1 B)^+ &= \Diamond\Box^{\downarrow}(A)^+/_0(B)^- & (A/_1 B)^- &= (A)^-/_0\Diamond\Box^{\downarrow}(B)^+ \\
(B\backslash_1 A)^+ &= (B)^-\backslash_0\Diamond\Box^{\downarrow}(A)^+ & (B\backslash_1 A)^- &= \Diamond\Box^{\downarrow}(B)^+\backslash_0(A)^-
\end{aligned}
$$

The theorems embedding a stronger logic $\mathcal{L}_1$ into a more discriminating system $\mathcal{L}_0$ now assume the following general form, where $\mathcal{R}'_\Diamond$ is the modal version of the structural rule package discriminating between $\mathcal{L}_1$ and $\mathcal{L}_0$.

Proposition 3.6 $\mathcal{L}_1 \vdash A \to B$ iff $\mathcal{L}_0 \Diamond + \mathcal{R}'_\Diamond \vdash A^+ \to B^-$.

As an illustration we consider the embedding of **L** into **NL**$\Diamond$ which involves licensing of Associativity in terms of the postulate $(A'_\Diamond)$. The frame construction method we employ is completely general: it can be used unchanged for the other cases of licensing embedding one may want to consider.

The proof of the ($\Rightarrow$) direction of Proposition 3.6 is by easy induction. We present a Gentzen derivation of the Geach rule as an example. The type responsible for licensing $A'_\Diamond$ in this case is $\Diamond\Box^{\downarrow}(B/C)^+$.

$$
\cfrac{
  \cfrac{
    \cfrac{
      \cfrac{
        \cfrac{
          \cfrac{
            \cfrac{C^+ \Rightarrow C^-}{(\Box^{\downarrow}C^+)^\circ \Rightarrow C^-} \; L\Box^{\downarrow}
          }{\Diamond\Box^{\downarrow}C^+ \Rightarrow C^-} \; L\Diamond \qquad \cfrac{\dots}{\Diamond\Box^{\downarrow}B^+ \Rightarrow B^-}
        }{\Diamond\Box^{\downarrow}B^+/C^-, \Diamond\Box^{\downarrow}C^+ \Rightarrow B^-} \; L/
      }{((\Box^{\downarrow}(\Diamond\Box^{\downarrow}B^+/C^-))^\circ, \Diamond\Box^{\downarrow}C^+) \Rightarrow B^-} \; L\Box^{\downarrow} \qquad \cfrac{\dots}{\Diamond\Box^{\downarrow}A^+ \Rightarrow A^-}
    }{(\Diamond\Box^{\downarrow}A^+/B^-, ((\Box^{\downarrow}(\Diamond\Box^{\downarrow}B^+/C^-))^\circ, \Diamond\Box^{\downarrow}C^+)) \Rightarrow A^-} \; L/
  }{
    \cfrac{
      \cfrac{
        ((\Diamond\Box^{\downarrow}A^+/B^-, (\Box^{\downarrow}(\Diamond\Box^{\downarrow}B^+/C^-))^\circ), \Diamond\Box^{\downarrow}C^+) \Rightarrow A^-
      }{((\Diamond\Box^{\downarrow}A^+/B^-, \Diamond\Box^{\downarrow}(\Diamond\Box^{\downarrow}B^+/C^-)), \Diamond\Box^{\downarrow}C^+) \Rightarrow A^-} \; A'_\Diamond
    }{\Diamond\Box^{\downarrow}A^+/B^- \Rightarrow (A^-/\Diamond\Box^{\downarrow}C^+)/\Diamond\Box^{\downarrow}(\Diamond\Box^{\downarrow}B^+/C^-)} \; L\Diamond \; R/, R/
  }
}{(A/B)^+ \Rightarrow ((A/C)/(B/C))^-} \; (\cdot)^+, (\cdot)^-
$$

For the ($\Leftarrow$) direction, we proceed by contraposition. Suppose $\mathbf{L} \not\vdash A \to B$. Completeness tells us there exists an **L** model $\mathcal{M}_1 = \langle W_1, R_1, V_1 \rangle$ with a point $a \in W$ such that $\mathcal{M}_1, a \models A$ but $\mathcal{M}_1, a \not\models B$. From $\mathcal{M}_1$ we want to construct an **NL**$\Diamond + A'_\Diamond$ model $\mathcal{M}_0 = \langle W_0, R_\Diamond, R_0, V_0 \rangle$ such that $A^+ \to B^-$ fails. Recall that R_0 has to satisfy the frame conditions for the modal versions $A'_\Diamond$ of the Associativity postulate. We give one instantiation below.

$$(A'_\Diamond) \quad \Diamond A \bullet_0 (B \bullet_0 C) \longleftrightarrow (\Diamond A \bullet_0 B) \bullet_0 C$$

($\dagger$) $(\forall xyzw \in W_0)\exists tu(R_0xtu \wedge R_\diamond ty \wedge R_0uzw) \Leftrightarrow$
$\qquad \exists t'u'(R_0xu'w \wedge R_0u't'z \wedge R_\diamond t'y)$

The model construction proceeds as follows. We put the falsifying point $a \in W_0$, and for every triple $(xyz) \in R_1$ we put $x, y, z \in W_0$ and $(xyz) \in R_0$, $(yy) \in R_\diamond$, $(zz) \in R_\diamond$.

We have to show that the model construction realizes the frame condition ($\dagger$) (and its relatives) in $\mathcal{M}_0$. Suppose $\exists xy(R_0axy \wedge R_\diamond xb \wedge R_0ycd)$. By the model construction, $x = b$, so R_0aby which has the pre-image R_1aby. The pre-image of R_0ycd is R_1ycd. The combination of these two R_1 triangles satisfies the Associativity frame condition of $\mathbf{L}$, so that we have a point t such that $R_1atd \wedge R_1tbc$. Again by the model construction, this means in $\mathcal{M}_0$ we have $\exists z, t(R_0tzc \wedge R_\diamond zb \wedge R_0atd)$, as required.

The central Truth Preservation Lemma now is that for any $a \in W_1 \cap W_0$,

$$\mathcal{M}_1, a \models A \quad \text{iff} \quad \mathcal{M}_0, a \models A^+ \quad \text{iff} \quad \mathcal{M}_0, a \models A^-.$$

We concentrate on the $(\cdot)^+$ case — the $(\cdot)^-$ case is straightforward.

($\Rightarrow$) Suppose $\mathcal{M}_1, a \models A \bullet_1 B$. We have to show that $\mathcal{M}_0, a \models \Diamond\Box^\downarrow A^+ \bullet_0 \Diamond\Box^\downarrow B^+$. By assumption, there exist b, c such that R_1abc, and $\mathcal{M}_1, b \models A$, $\mathcal{M}_1, c \models B$. By inductive hypothesis and the model construction algorithm,

we have in $\mathcal{M}_0$

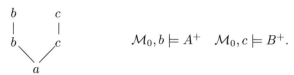

$$\mathcal{M}_0, b \models A^+ \quad \mathcal{M}_0, c \models B^+.$$

Observe that if x is the only point accessible from x via $R_\diamond$ (as is the case in $\mathcal{M}_0$), then for any formula ϕ, $x \models \phi$ iff $x \models \Diamond\phi$ iff $x \models \Box^\downarrow\phi$ iff $x \models \Diamond\Box^\downarrow\phi$. Therefore, from the above we can conclude $\mathcal{M}_0, b \models \Diamond\Box^\downarrow A^+$ and $\mathcal{M}_0, c \models \Diamond\Box^\downarrow B^+$, hence $\mathcal{M}_0, a \models \Diamond\Box^\downarrow A^+ \bullet_0 \Diamond\Box^\downarrow B^+$.

($\Leftarrow$) Suppose $\mathcal{M}_0, a \models \Diamond\Box^\downarrow A^+ \bullet_0 \Diamond\Box^\downarrow B^+$. We show that $\mathcal{M}_1, a \models A \bullet_1 B$. By assumption, there exist b, c such that $R_0 abc$, and $\mathcal{M}_0, b \models \Diamond\Box^\downarrow A^+$, $\mathcal{M}_0, c \models \Diamond\Box^\downarrow B^+$. In $\mathcal{M}_0$ all triangles are such that the daughters have themselves and only themselves accessible via $R_\diamond$. Using our observation again, we conclude that $\mathcal{M}_0, b \models A^+$, $\mathcal{M}_0, c \models B^+$, and by inductive assumption $\mathcal{M}_1, a \models A \bullet B$.

We leave the implicational formulas to the reader.

Comment: Full Internal Labeling. Licensing of structural relaxation is implemented in the above proposal via modal versions of the structural postulates requiring at least *one* of the internal subtypes to be $\Diamond$ decorated. It makes good sense to consider a variant of internal licensing, where one requires *all* relevant subtypes of a structural configuration to be modally decorated — depending on the application one has in mind, one could choose one or the other. Embeddings with this property have been studied for algebraic models by Venema 1993, Versmissen 1993. In the terms of our minimalistic setting, modal structural postulates with full internal labeling would assume the following form.

$(P''_\diamond) \quad \Diamond A \bullet \Diamond B \longleftrightarrow \Diamond B \bullet \Diamond A$
$(A''_\diamond) \quad \Diamond A \bullet (\Diamond B \bullet \Diamond C) \longleftrightarrow (\Diamond A \bullet \Diamond B) \bullet \Diamond C$

One obtains the variant of the embedding theorems for full internal labeling on the basis of the modified translation $(\cdot)^{++}$ which marks *all* positive subformulae with the modal prefix $\Diamond\Box^\downarrow$. (Below we abbreviate $\Diamond\Box^\downarrow$ to μ.) In the model construction, one puts $(xx) \in R_\diamond$ (and nothing more) for every point x that has to be put in W_0.

$$
\begin{aligned}
(p)^{++} &= \mu p & (p)^- &= p \\
(A \bullet_1 B)^{++} &= \mu(\mu(A)^{++} \bullet_0 \mu(B)^{++}) & (A \bullet_1 B)^- &= (A)^- \bullet_0 (B)^- \\
(A/_1 B)^{++} &= \mu(\mu(A)^{++}/_0(B)^-) & (A/_1 B)^- &= (A)^-/_0\mu(B)^{++} \\
(B\backslash_1 A)^{++} &= \mu((B)^-\backslash_0\mu(A)^{++}) & (B\backslash_1 A)^- &= \mu(B)^{++}\backslash_0(A)^-
\end{aligned}
$$

Proposition 3.7 $\mathcal{L}_1 \vdash A \to B$ *iff* $\mathcal{L}_0\Diamond + \mathcal{R}''_\diamond \vdash A^{++} \to B^-$.

Illustration: Extraction. For a concrete linguistic illustration of $\Diamond\Box^\downarrow$ labeling licensing structural relaxation, we return to the example of extraction from non-peripheral positions in relative clauses. The example below becomes derivable in $\mathbf{NL}\Diamond + (A'_\Diamond, P'_\Diamond)$ given a modally decorated type assignment $r/(s/\Diamond\Box^\downarrow np)$ to the relative pronoun, which allows the hypothetical $\Diamond\Box^\downarrow np$ assumption to find its appropriate location in the relative clause body via controlled Associativity and Permutation. We give the relevant part of the Gentzen derivation, abbreviating $(np\backslash s)/np$ as tv.

$$\ldots \text{that } ((\text{John read}) \text{ yesterday})$$
$$\mathbf{NL}\Diamond + (A'_\Diamond, P'_\Diamond) \vdash (r/(s/\Diamond\Box^\downarrow np), ((np, (np\backslash s)/np), s\backslash s)) \Rightarrow r$$

$$\cdots$$

$$
\cfrac{
\cfrac{
\cfrac{
\cfrac{
\cfrac{
\cfrac{
\cfrac{
\cfrac{
((np, (tv, np)), s\backslash s) \Rightarrow s
}{
((np, (tv, (\Box^\downarrow np)^\Diamond)), s\backslash s) \Rightarrow s
} L\Box^\downarrow
}{
(((np, tv), (\Box^\downarrow np)^\Diamond), s\backslash s) \Rightarrow s
} A'_\Diamond
}{
((np, tv), ((\Box^\downarrow np)^\Diamond, s\backslash s)) \Rightarrow s
} A'_\Diamond
}{
((np, tv), (s\backslash s, (\Box^\downarrow np)^\Diamond)) \Rightarrow s
} P'_\Diamond
}{
(((np, tv), s\backslash s), (\Box^\downarrow np)^\Diamond) \Rightarrow s
} A'_\Diamond
}{
(((np, tv), s\backslash s), \Diamond\Box^\downarrow np) \Rightarrow s
} L\Diamond
}{
((np, tv), s\backslash s) \Rightarrow s/\Diamond\Box^\downarrow np
} R/
$$

Comparing this form of licensing modal decoration with the treatment in terms of a universal $\Box$ operator with $S4$ structural postulates, one observes that on the proof-theoretic level, the $\Diamond\Box^\downarrow$ prefix is able to mimic the behaviour of the $S4$ $\Box$ modality, whereas on the semantic level, we are not forced to impose transitivity and reflexivity constraints on the interpretation of $R_\Diamond$. With a translation $(\Box A)^\sim = \Diamond\Box^\downarrow (A)^\sim$, the characteristic T and 4 postulates for $\Box$ become valid type transitions in the pure residuation system for $\Diamond, \Box^\downarrow$, as the reader can check.

T: $\Box A \to A \rightsquigarrow \Diamond\Box^\downarrow A \to A$

4:   $\Box A \to \Box\Box A \rightsquigarrow \Diamond\Box^\downarrow A \to \Diamond\Box^\downarrow\Diamond\Box^\downarrow A$

4   Discussion

In this final section, we reflect on some general logical and linguistic aspects of the proposed architecture, and raise a number of questions for future research.

Linear Logic and the Sublinear Landscape. In order to obtain controlled access to Contraction and Weakening, Linear Logic extends the formula language with operators which on the proof-theoretic level are governed by an $S4$-like regime. The 'sublinear' grammar logics we have studied show a higher degree of structural organization: not only the multiplicity of the resources matters, but also the way they are put together into structured configurations. These more discriminating logics suggest more delicate instruments for obtaining structural control. We have presented embedding theorems for the licensing and for the constraining perspective on substructural communication in terms of the pure logic of residuation for a set of unary multiplicatives $\Diamond, \Box^{\downarrow}$. In the frame semantics setting, these operators make more fine-grained structural distinctions than their $S4$ relatives which are interpreted with respect to a transitive and reflexive accessibility relation. But they are expressive enough to obtain full control over grammatical resource management. Our minimalistic stance is motivated by linguistic considerations. For reasons quite different from ours, and for different types of models, a number of recent proposals in the field of Linear Logic proper have argued for a decomposition of the '!,?' modalities into more elementary operators. For comparison we refer the reader to Bucalo 1994, Girard 1995.

The Price of Diamonds. We have compared logics with a 'standard' language of binary multiplicatives with systems where the formula language is extended with the unary logical constants $\Diamond, \Box^{\downarrow}$. The unary operators, one could say, are the price one has to pay to gain structural control. Do we really have to pay this price, or could one faithfully embed the systems of Figure 1 *as they stand*? For answers in a number of specific cases, one can turn to van Benthem 1991.

A question related to the above point is the following. Our embeddings compare the logics of Figure 1 pairwise, adding a modal control operator for each translation. This means that self-embeddings, from $\mathcal{L}$ to $\mathcal{L}'$ and back, end up two modal levels higher, a process which reaches equilibrium only in languages with infinitely many $\Diamond, \Box^{\downarrow}$ control operators. Can one stay within some finite modal repertoire? We conjecture the answer is positive, but a definitive result would require a deeper study of the residuation properties of the $\Diamond, \Box^{\downarrow}$ family.

Pure Embeddings Versus Modal Structural Rules. The embedding results presented here are globally of two types. One type — what we have called the pure embeddings — obtains structural control solely in terms of the modal decoration added in the translation mapping. The other type adds a relativized structural postulate which can be accessed in virtue of the modal decoration of the translation. For the licensing type of communication, the second type of embedding is fully natural. The target logic, in these cases, does not allow a form of structural manipulation which is available in the source logic: in a *controlled* form, we want to regain this flexibility. But the distinction between the two types of embedding does not coincide with the shift from licensing to constraining communication. We have seen in §2.3 that imposing structural constraints for logics sharing associative resource management requires modalized structural postulates, in addition to the modal decoration of the translation mapping. In these cases, the $\Diamond$ decoration has accidentally damaged the potential for associative rebracketing: the modalized associativity postulates repair this damage. We leave it as an open question whether one could realize pure embeddings for some of the logics of §2.3. A related question can be raised for the same family of logics under the licensing perspective: in these cases, we find not just the modal structural postulate for the parameter which discriminates between the logics, but in addition modal associativity, again because the translation schema has impaired the normal rebracketing.

Uniform Versus Customized Translations. Another asymmetry that may be noted here is our implementation of the licensing type of communication in terms of a uniform translation schema, versus the constraining type of embeddings where the translations are specifically tailored towards the particular structural dimension one wants to control. Could one treat the constraining embeddings of §2 also in terms of a uniform translation scheme? And if so, would such a scheme be cheaper or more costly than the individual schemes in the text?

Complexity. A final set of questions relates to issues of computational complexity. For many of the individual logics in the sublinear cube complexity results (pleasant or unpleasant) are known. Do the embeddings allow transfer of such results to systems where we still face embarrassing open questions (such as: the issue of polynomial complexity for $\mathbf{L}$)? In other words: what is the computational cost of the translations and modal structural postulates proposed? We conjecture that modalized versions of structural rules have the same computational cost as corresponding structural rules themselves.

Embeddings: Linguistic Relevance. We close with a remark for the reader with a linguistics background. The embedding results presented in this paper may seem somewhat removed from the daily concerns of the working grammarian. Let us try to point out how our results can contribute to the foundations of grammar development work. In the literature of the past five years, a great variety of 'structural modalities' has been introduced, with different proof-theoretic behaviour and different intended semantics. It has been argued that the defects of particular type systems (either in the sense of overgeneration, or of undergeneration) can be overcome by refining type assignment in terms of these structural modalities. The accounts proposed for individual linguistic phenomena are often ingenious, but one may legitimately ask what the level of generality of the proposals is. The embedding results of this paper show that the operators $\Diamond, \Box^{\downarrow}$ provide a general theory of structural control for the management of linguistic resources.

Postscript. We use this opportunity to add some pointers to linguistic applications of the theory of resource control that have appeared since this paper was originally written. Phenomena of *head adjunction* are studied in Kraak 1995 in an analysis of French cliticization. Modal decoration is used to enrich the lexical type assignments with head feature information. Feature 'checking' is performed by the base logic for $\Diamond, \Box^{\downarrow}$, whereas distributivity principles for the $\Diamond$ operator take care of the 'projection' of the head feature information. The same machinery is used in Moortgat 1996b to modally enforce verb cluster formation as it arises in the Dutch verb raising construction. In Versmissen 1996, the modal operators are used to systematically project or erase *word order domains* in the sense of Reape 1989. This thesis also shows how one can implement an *HPSG*-style theory of Linear Precedence Constraints in terms of modal control over non-directional **LP** lexical type assignments.

5 Appendix: Axiomatic and Gentzen Presentation

In this Appendix we juxtapose the axiomatic and the Gentzen formulations of the logics under discussion. The Lambek and Došen style axiomatic presentations are two equivalent ways of characterizing $\Diamond, \Box^{\downarrow}, \bullet, /$ and $\bullet, \backslash$ as residuated pairs of operators. For the equivalence between the axiomatic and the Gentzen presentations, see Moortgat 1995. This paper also establishes a Cut Elimination result for the language extended with $\Diamond, \Box^{\downarrow}$.

Definition 5.1 (Lambek-style axiomatic presentation)

$$A \to A \qquad \frac{A \to B \quad B \to C}{A \to C}$$

$$\Diamond A \to B \iff A \to \Box^{\downarrow} B$$

$$A \to C/B \iff A \bullet B \to C \iff B \to A \backslash C$$

Definition 5.2 (Došen style axiomatization)

$$A \to A \qquad \frac{A \to B \quad B \to C}{A \to C}$$

$$\Diamond \Box^{\downarrow} A \to A \qquad A \to \Box^{\downarrow} \Diamond A$$

$$A/B \bullet B \to A \qquad A \to (A \bullet B)/B$$

$$B \bullet B \backslash A \to A \qquad A \to B \backslash (B \bullet A)$$

$$\frac{A \to B}{\Diamond A \to \Diamond B} \qquad \frac{A \to B}{\Box^{\downarrow} A \to \Box^{\downarrow} B}$$

$$\frac{A \to B \quad C \to D}{A/D \to B/C} \qquad \frac{A \to B \quad C \to D}{A \bullet C \to B \bullet D} \qquad \frac{A \to B \quad C \to D}{D \backslash A \to C \backslash B}$$

The formulations of Definition 5.1 and Definition 5.2 give the pure residuation logic for the unary and binary families. The logics of Figure 1 are then obtained by adding different packages of structural postulates, as discussed in §1.

Definition 5.3 (Gentzen presentation) Sequents $\Gamma \Rightarrow A$ with Γ a structured database of linguistic resources, A a formula. Structured databases are inductively defined as terms $\mathcal{T} ::= \mathcal{F} \mid (\mathcal{T}, \mathcal{T})^m \mid (\mathcal{T})^\circ$, with binary $(\cdot, \cdot)^m$ or unary $(\cdot)^\circ$ structural connectives corresponding to the (binary, unary) logical connectives. We add resource management mode indexing for logical and structural connectives to keep families with different resource management properties apart. This strategy goes back to Belnap 1982 and has been applied to *modal* display logics in Kracht 1996, Wansing 1992, two papers which are related in a number of respects to our own efforts.

$$[\text{Ax}]\frac{}{A \Rightarrow A} \qquad \frac{\Gamma \Rightarrow A \quad \Delta[A] \Rightarrow C}{\Delta[\Gamma] \Rightarrow C}[\text{Cut}]$$

$$[\text{R}\Diamond]\frac{\Gamma \Rightarrow A}{(\Gamma)^\circ \Rightarrow \Diamond A} \qquad \frac{\Gamma[(A)^\circ] \Rightarrow B}{\Gamma[\Diamond A] \Rightarrow B}[\text{L}\Diamond]$$

$$[\text{R}\Box^\downarrow]\frac{(\Gamma)^\circ \Rightarrow A}{\Gamma \Rightarrow \Box^\downarrow A} \qquad \frac{\Gamma[A] \Rightarrow B}{\Gamma[(\Box^\downarrow A)^\circ] \Rightarrow B}[\text{L}\Box^\downarrow]$$

$$[\text{R}/_m]\frac{(\Gamma, B)^m \Rightarrow A}{\Gamma \Rightarrow A/_m B} \qquad \frac{\Gamma \Rightarrow B \quad \Delta[A] \Rightarrow C}{\Delta[(A/_m B, \Gamma)^m] \Rightarrow C}[\text{L}/_m]$$

$$[\text{R}\backslash_m]\frac{(B, \Gamma)^m \Rightarrow A}{\Gamma \Rightarrow B\backslash_m A} \qquad \frac{\Gamma \Rightarrow B \quad \Delta[A] \Rightarrow C}{\Delta[(\Gamma, B\backslash_m A)^m] \Rightarrow C}[\text{L}\backslash_m]$$

$$[\text{L}\bullet_m]\frac{\Gamma[(A, B)^m] \Rightarrow C}{\Gamma[A \bullet_m B] \Rightarrow C} \qquad \frac{\Gamma \Rightarrow A \quad \Delta \Rightarrow B}{(\Gamma, \Delta)^m \Rightarrow A \bullet_m B}[\text{R}\bullet_m]$$

Structural postulates, in the axiomatic presentation, have been presented as transitions $A \to B$ where A and B are constructed out of formula variables $p_1, \ldots, p_n$ and logical connectives $\bullet_m$, $\Diamond$. For structure variables $\Delta_1, \ldots, \Delta_n$ and structural connectives $(\cdot, \cdot)^m$, $(\cdot)^\circ$, define the structural equivalent $\sigma(A)$ of a formula A as indicated below (cf Kracht 1996):

$$\sigma(p_i) = \Delta_i \quad \sigma(A \bullet_m B) = (\sigma(A), \sigma(B))^m \quad \sigma(\Diamond A) = (\sigma(A))^\circ$$

The transformation of structural postulates into Gentzen rules allowing Cut Elimination then is straightforward: a postulate $A \to B$ translates as the Gentzen rule

$$\frac{\Gamma[\sigma(B)] \Rightarrow C}{\Gamma[\sigma(A)] \Rightarrow C}$$

In the cut elimination algorithm, one shows that if a structural rule precedes a Cut inference, the order of application of the inferences can be permuted, pushing the Cut upwards. See Došen 1989 for the case of global structural rules, Moortgat 1995 for the $\Diamond$ cases.

In the multimodal setting, structural rules are relativized to the appropriate resource management modes, as indicated by the mode index. An example is given below (for k a commutative and l an associative regime). Where no confusion is likely to arise, in the text we use the conventional symbols for different families of operators, rather than the official mode indexing on one generic set of symbols.

$$\frac{\Gamma[(\Delta_2, \Delta_1)^k] \Rightarrow A}{\Gamma[(\Delta_1, \Delta_2)^k] \Rightarrow A}[P] \qquad \frac{\Gamma[((\Delta_1, \Delta_2)^l, \Delta_3)^l] \Rightarrow A}{\Gamma[(\Delta_1, (\Delta_2, \Delta_3)^l)^l] \Rightarrow A}[A]$$

$$cf \ A \bullet_k B \to B \bullet_k A \qquad\qquad cf \ A \bullet_l (B \bullet_l C) \to (A \bullet_l B) \bullet_l C$$

References

Barry, G. and G. Morrill (ed.). 1990. *Studies in Categorial Grammar*. Edinburgh Working Papers in Cognitive Science, Vol 5. CCS, Edinburgh.

Belnap, N.D. 1982. Display Logic. *Journal of Philosophical Logic*, 11:375–417.

van Benthem, J. 1991. *Language in Action. Categories, Lambdas, and Dynamic Logic*. Studies in Logic. Amsterdam: North-Holland.

Bucalo, A. 1994. Modalities in Linear Logic Weaker than the Exponential "Of Course": Algebraic and Relational Semantics. *Journal of Logic, Language and Information*, 3(3):211–232.

Došen, K. 1992. A Brief Survey of Frames for the Lambek Calculus. *Zeitschr. f. math. Logik und Grundlagen d. Mathematik* 38:179–187.

Došen, K. 1988, 1989. Sequent Systems and Groupoid Models. *Studia Logica* 47:353–385, 48:41–65.

Došen, K. 1992. Modal Translations in Substructural Logics. *Journal of Philosophical Logic* 21:283–336.

Dunn, J.M. 1991. Gaggle Theory: an Abstraction of Galois Connections and Residuation, with Applications to Negation, Implication, and Various Logical Operators. In *Logics in AI. JELIA Proceedings*, ed. J. van Eijck. Berlin: Springer.

Dunn, M. 1993. Partial Gaggles Applied to Logics with Restricted Structural Rules. In *Substructural Logics*, ed. K. Došen and P. Schröder-Heister. Oxford.

Girard, J.-Y. 1995. Light Linear Logic: Extended Abstract. Manuscript, LMD, Marseille.

Kraak, E. 1995. French Object Clitics: a Multimodal Analysis. In *Formal Grammar*, ed. G. Morrill and D. Oehrle. 166–180.

Kracht, M. 1996. Power and Weakness of the Modal Display Calculus. In *Proof Theory of Modal Logic*, ed. H. Wansing. Dordecht: Kluwer.

Kurtonina, N. 1995. *Frames and Labels. A Modal Analysis of Categorial Inference*. Doctoral dissertation, OTS, Utrecht and ILLC, Amsterdam.

Kurtonina, N. and M. Moortgat. 1994. Controlling Resource Management. Esprit BRA Dyana-2 Deliverable R1.1.B, 45–62.

Lambek, J. 1958. The Mathematics of Sentence Structure. *American Mathematical Monthly* 65:154–170.

Lambek, J. 1988. Categorial and Categorical Grammar. In *Categorial Grammars and Natural Language Structures*, ed. D. Oehrle, Bach and Wheeler. Dordrecht.

Moortgat, M. 1995. Multimodal Linguistic Inference. *Bulletin of the IGPL* 3(2–3):371–401. (To appear in *Journal of Logic, Language and Information*.)

Moortgat, M. 1996a. Categorial Type Logics. Chapter 2 in *Handbook of Logic and Language*, ed. J. van Benthem and A. ter Meulen. Elsevier.

Moortgat, M. 1996b. Labeled Deduction in the Composition of Form and Meaning. In *Logic, Language and Reasoning. Essays in Honor of Dov Gabbay, Part I*, ed. H.J. Ohlbach and U. Reyle. Dordrecht: Kluwer.

Moortgat, M. and G. Morrill. 1991. Heads and Phrases. Type Calculus for Dependency and Constituent Structure. Manuscript, OTS Utrecht.

Moortgat, M. and R. Oehrle. 1993. *Logical Parameters and Linguistic Variation. Lecture Notes on Categorial Grammar*. 5th European Summer School in Logic, Language and Information. Lisbon.

Moortgat, M. and R.T. Oehrle. 1994. Adjacency, Dependency and Order. *Proceedings 9th Amsterdam Colloquium*, 447–466.

Morrill, G. 1994. *Type Logical Grammar*. Dordrecht: Kluwer.

Morrill, G. 1995. Discontinuity in Categorial Grammar. *Linguistics and Philosophy* 18:175–219.

Morrill, G. and R.T. Oehrle (ed.). 1995. *Formal Grammar*. Proceedings of the Conference of the European Summer School in Logic, Language and Information. Barcelona.

Reape, M. 1989. A Logical Treatment of Semi-Free Word Order and Bounded Discontinuous Constituency. In *Proceedings of the Fourth Conference of the European Chapter of the Association for Computational Linguistics*, Manchester, 103–115.

Venema, Y. 1995. Meeting Strength in Substructural Logics. *Studia Logica* 54:3–32.

Versmissen, K. 1993. Categorial Grammar, Modalities and Algebraic Semantics. In *Proceedings EACL93*. 377–383.

Versmissen, K. 1996. *Grammatical Composition. Modes, Models and Modalities*. Ph.D. Dissertation. OTS Utrecht.

Wansing, H. 1992. Sequent Calculi for Normal Modal Propositional Logics. ILLC Report LP-92-12.

5

Featureless HPSG

M. Andrew Moshier

ABSTRACT. Feature structures have played an important part in the development of HPSG and other linguistic theories. Yet they are at odds with concerns for modularity in the formalization of grammar. The paper presents an argument that the standard formalizations of HPSG cannot possibly capture such foundational concepts as the Head Feature Principle as independent principles. Rather, in standard formalizations, HPSG principles must be stated in terms of a fixed feature geometry, the details of which necessarily depend on arguments about the interaction of principles. Thus in order to formalize a specific principle, the linguist must already have formalized its interactions with other principles.

The latter part of the paper presents an alternative formalism for HPSG that addresses the issue of modularity. As demonstrated here, HPSG principles stated in this formalism exhibit independence in a substantive technical sense: there can be models (of the same formal language) that satisfy one principle, but not another. The formalism is based on the idea that HPSG principles are mostly about commutativity of composed functions (usually this is rendered in terms of token identity), and so can be stated in a language of category-theoretic constraints, i.e., constraints that are invariant under equivalences of categories.

1 Introduction

Head-driven Phrase Structure Grammar (HPSG), as a formal theory of language, raises two interesting questions: (i) what constitutes a model of the theory, and prior to that, (ii) what role should the models play in the linguistic enterprise of HPSG. To date, (i) has been answered essentially by assuming that feature structures or some closely similar structures must figure in models of HPSG. In that case, the model theory of HPSG fits into the broader theory of feature structures and feature logics. For example,

Specifying Syntactic Structures
P. Blackburn and M. de Rijke, eds.
Copyright © 1997, CSLI Publications.

King (1989, 1994) attempts to make sense of the various equivalent characterizations of feature structures as they pertain to models of HPSG. King
pays particular attention to the difference between token identity and type
identity. Moshier and Pollard (1994) extend the standard definition of feature structure to include "set-valued" nodes in a way that captures the
partial information needed to handle indices in HPSG. Other works on feature structures (e.g, Aït-Kaci and Nasr 1986, Backofen and Smolka 1993,
Blackburn 1994, Carpenter 1992, Johnson 1988, Moshier 1988 and Kasper
and Rounds 1990), have influenced the current meta-theory of HPSG, even
though they are not directly concerned with that theory of grammar. In
any case, the feature structure research pertains to HPSG precisely on the
assumption that a model of HPSG involves feature structures. But that
assumption does not address (ii), the logically prior question, in any way.
This, it seems to me, has led to a naïve approach to the meta-theory of
HPSG that has had serious effects on the development of the theory.

One role of models that seems to be unquestioned because of its ob-
viousness is to ensure consistency. That is, a theory without models is
inconsistent (or so the logicians tell us). So to establish the consistency of
HPSG, a model must be given. But to a logician, consistency is in some
ways the least interesting reason for constructing models. (Consider the
fact that, pace Gödel, one cannot construct a model of Peano arithmetic
without first assuming the consistency of a theory at least as strong.) Far
more interestingly, models provide a powerful tool for establishing independence, non-entailment and relative consistency. Consider Cohen's proof of
the independence of the generalized continuum hypothesis (GCH) from the
axioms of Zermelo-Fraenkel set theory Cohen (1966). It is a model theoretic proof. The fact that ZF with the negation of the GCH is consistent
(more precisely, is as consistent as ZF itself) is established by constructing
a model of $ZF + \neg GCH$. Indeed, the whole set theory enterprise of the last
four decades mainly concerns, on the purely technical side, construction of
models to establish various independence facts, and of course, the study of
the construction techniques themselves.

Pollard and Sag seem to be asking for a similar idea of independence in
HPSG:

> With such theories [LFG and GB], HPSG shares a concern about matters
> of modularity of design and the deduction of particular facts from the complex
> interaction of general principles.
>
> (Pollard and Sag (1987) p. 6)

It is difficult to imagine how one might deduce facts from interactions of
principles without a notion of independence, which is to say, a notion of
the consequences of individual principles.

Consider whether it even makes sense to discuss models of the Head

Feature Principle (HFP) in which the Subcategorization Principle fails. More generally, consider whether it makes sense to discuss models of the HPF at all? Clearly not. One has only to inspect any two contemporary versions of HPSG (e.g., Pollard and Sag 1994, Cooper 1990, Henschel 1991, Keller 1995 or Rentier 1994) to see that the Head Feature Principle cannot be stated without first deciding on certain details of feature geometry. But the relevant decisions are based entirely on the interaction of the HFP with other principles. For example, the exact placement of the HEAD feature has to do with linguistic claims that selectional restrictions, binding theory and the HFP interact in certain ways.

How do we understand the relationship, for example, between the HFP of Pollard and Sag (1987) and the HFP of Pollard and Sag (1994)? Between these two versions of HPSG, the geometry of feature structures differs radically. In the earlier version, the principle requires token identity for the paths

SYN|LOC|HEAD

and

DTRS|HD-DTR|SYN|LOC|HEAD

of every "headed phrase." In the later version, the principle requires token identity for the paths SYNSEM|LOC|HEAD and HD-DTR|SYNSEM|LOC|HEAD of every "headed phrase." But the reconfiguration of features between these versions has nothing to do with the intended meaning of the HFP. Rather the move from SYN and SEM to a single feature SYNSEM has to do more directly with refinements of the theory of subcategorization.

An HPSG practitioner seems justified in referring to the HFP as a coherent notion, yet each has a different feature geometry in mind, whence a different statement of the HFP. It is impossible to regard any less than the entire complex of principles (as well as rules, and perhaps even lexicon) as a *formally* intelligible theory. There is no sense in claiming a particular fact about language to be a consequence of the interaction, say, between the HFP and the Trace Principle as distinct from a consequence of the entire version of HPSG into which these two principles are embedded. This, because the individual principles are meaningless without a fixed feature geometry, and the feature geometry depends crucially on claims about the interaction between principles.

Put in a more practical way, HPSG lacks a notion of modularity regarding principles. Revision of the Subcategorization Principle causes revision of the HFP, and in fact of all other principles. So even if one is not concerned with the model theory of HPSG, but only with more mundane problems of "grammar engineering," contemporary HPSG is problematic. Again it is difficult to imagine how particular principles can be regarded as interacting modules when the modules cannot be specified without first specifying their interactions.

Many apparently inconsequential choices of appropriateness conditions and subsort relations are made out of the necessity of fixing a feature geometry. For example, the sort *agreement* for a grammar of English might possess two features NUMBER and PERSON which have values in the sorts *number* and *person* so that *number* has subsorts *singular* and *plural*, and *person* has subsorts *1*, *2* and *3*. Or *agreement* might possess two subsorts *singular* and *plural* so that *singular* has three subsorts *1s*, *2s* and *3s* and *plural* has three subsorts *1p*, *2p* and *3p*. Or, ... Surely, it makes no substantive difference to the linguistics which of these we choose, since in all cases we are saying that there are six different values that *agreement* can take. Yet a grammarian must choose one of these in order to write an HPSG grammar of English. Because the feature structures obtained under one choice are incommensurate with those obtained under another choice, the grammarian cannot give a formal justification for the intuition that the choice somehow doesn't matter.

It would be a service to linguistics in general, and HPSG in particular, if a notion of interdefinability were available for versions of a linguistic theory. That is, suppose there were two competing versions of HPSG. If it were the case that a model of the first version could always be constructed from a model of the second, and vice versa, then we would know that the two have essentially the same models, hence the same consequences.[1]

These considerations lead me to suspect that feature structures are not only unnecessary for HPSG, but are a hindrance to distilling the linguistic claims of the theory from the details of representation. Feature structures obstruct our view of (i) the consequences of individual principles, (ii) the role of feature geometry in enforcing certain interactions between principles, and (iii) the notions of equivalence and interdefinability required for linguistic theories.

Linguistics has enjoyed a long tradition of limiting the expressive power of a formalism in order to capture a smaller class of grammars that presumably still contains the grammars for all potential human languages. This was part of the motivation for GPSG, out of which grew HPSG. But somehow this motivation has been lost in HPSG. It can be recovered in a less familiar way by noting that the sorts of constraints one posits in HPSG have to do mostly with "token identity." If we read these sorts of constraints as commutativity conditions (that is, two different paths lead to the same place), then HPSG begins to look like a system of category

---

[1] Actually, the equivalence of two theories would require more than just constructions of models in both directions. It would also require that the categories of models be equivalent. But this gets ahead of the game. I return to the notion of equivalence for theories after categories of models are defined.

theoretic constraints. Thus, I propose to formalize HPSG only using elementary, category-theoretic properties. I mean this in a precise sense. As usual, an elementary property is one definable in first-order logic. A category-theoretic property is a property of categories that is preserved under equivalence. This is in analogy with topological properties (those preserved under homeomorphism), group theoretic properties (those preserved under isomorphism), and even logical properties of models (those preserved under automorphisms of the universe). It is beyond the scope of this introduction to give a precise definition of equivalence, but roughly it means that HPSG cannot distinguish between models except on the basis of facts having do so with commutativity. At the least, the formalization developed here has an advantage over current HPSG meta-theory in that "token identity," a notoriously messy notion at best, is replaced by the much better understood mathematical notion of commutativity.

In the remainder of this paper, I set out a formal notion of an HPSG theory and of models for such a theory. My main concern is to provide a better meta-theory for investigating independence of principles and enforcement of interactions between principles. The models of a theory form a category, complete with a useful notion of a morphism between models. With this, we can state precisely what it means for two theories to be equivalent: they are equivalent if the categories of their models are equivalent as categories.

To limit the scope of this paper, I only consider how properly to formulate and model HPSG principles and the "ID schemata," leaving the lexicon to a later paper. As my main concern here is to understand how models can explicate the interactions amongst principles, this limiting of scope seems prudent. I trust that the reader will recognize that the ideas put forth here will generalize to the other parts of a full grammar in HPSG as well.

2 Category Theory

To remind the reader, a *category* is a model of the first-order theory of composition — with function composition serving as the paradigm. There are many equivalent axiomatizations, but the intuition is quite simple. Every *arrow* (the elements of a category, corresponding to functions) has a specified *domain* and *codomain* (or range). Writing $f : A \to B$ to assert that f is an arrow with domain A and codomain B, a category requires that arrows compose if and only if their codomain and domain match correctly: if $f : B \to C$ and $g : A \to B$ are arrows, then there is an arrow $f \circ g : A \to C$. Also, if $f \circ g : A \to C$ is defined for arrows f and g, then there must be some B so that $f : B \to C$ and $g : A \to B$. The entities that can serve as domains and codomains are called *objects*. When defined, composition is associative: $f \circ (g \circ h) = (f \circ g) \circ h$. In addition, a category requires that every object have an identity arrow. So if B is an object — that is to say. if there is some arrow $f : B \to C$ or $g : A \to B$ — then there is also an arrow $\mathrm{id}_B : B \to B$ (depending only on B) for which $h \circ \mathrm{id}_B = h$ for all $h : B \to C'$ and $j = \mathrm{id}_B \circ j$ for all $j : A' \to B$.

A few example categories will help to illustrate the idea:

- The category **Set** of sets and arbitrary functions. The arrows are arbitrary functions between specified sets (the objects). Compositions and identities are the usual.

- The category **Grp** of groups and group homomorphisms. The arrows are group homomorphisms, i.e., structure preserving maps, between specified groups (the objects). Again compositions and identities are the usual.

- The category **Top** of topological spaces and continuous maps.

- The category **Rel** of sets and relations. In this case, the arrows are binary relations between specified sets. Composition is defined by $a(S \circ R)c$ if and only if there exists b so that aRb and bSc.

- Any transitive, reflexive relation $\preceq \subseteq X \times X$ on a set X yields a category. The objects are the elements of X. There is exactly one arrow from x to y provided that $x \preceq y$.

The last two examples illustrate that the arrows of a category need not correspond to functions. Nevertheless, the first three are more typical: objects are defined to be structured sets (groups, topologies, etc.) and arrows are functions that preserve that structure in a suitable way (homomorphisms, continuous maps, etc.). The category of sets illustrates that the "structure" can be vacuous. The reader who is unfamiliar with the basic concepts of category theory will find a very accessible introduction in Pierce (1991).

For any category $\mathcal{A}$, let $|\mathcal{A}|$ denote the collection of objects of the category. And for $A, B \in |\mathcal{A}|$, let $\mathcal{A}(A, B)$ denote the collection of arrows from A to B.

A *functor* from category $\mathcal{A}$ to $\mathcal{B}$ is a structure preserving map from $\mathcal{A}$ to $\mathcal{B}$. The structure of a category is precisely the composition of arrows and the identity arrows. Thus, a functor F from $\mathcal{A}$ to $\mathcal{B}$ is a map from arrows in $\mathcal{A}$ to arrows in $\mathcal{B}$ so that (i) $F(\mathrm{id}_A)$ is an identity arrow and (ii) $F(f \circ g) = F(f) \circ F(g)$ whenever $f \circ g$ is defined. According to (i), it is reasonable to write $F(A)$ for an object $A \in |\mathcal{A}|$.

For any category $\mathcal{A}$, an $\mathcal{A}$-*diagram* is a triple $D = (G, A, f)$ where G is a directed graph, and A and f label vertices and edges so that each vertex v is labeled by an object $A_v \in |\mathcal{A}|$ and each edge e from v to v' is labeled by an arrow $f_e \in \mathcal{A}(A_v, A_{v'})$. Let $E(v, v')$ denote the set of edges in G from v to v', and let $G(v, v')$ denote the set of paths in G from vertex v to vertex v'. The labeling of edges in G determines, for each $p \in G(v, v')$, an arrow $f_p : A_v \to A_{v'}$. That is, if $\langle\rangle$ denotes the empty path from v to v, then $f_{\langle\rangle} = \mathsf{id}_{A_v}$. If $\langle e_0, \dots, e_{n-1}\rangle \in G(v, v')$ and $e_n \in E(v', v'')$, then $f_{\langle e_0, \dots, e_n\rangle} = f_{e_n} \circ f_{\langle e_0, \dots, e_{n-1}\rangle}$.

A directed graph G determines a category $[G]$ with vertices as objects and paths as arrows. Composition is defined by concatenation of paths. Thus, an $\mathcal{A}$-diagram (G, A, f) determines a functor $L : [G] \Rightarrow \mathcal{A}$ by $L(p) = f_p$. Conversely, every functor $L : [G] \Rightarrow \mathcal{A}$ determines an $\mathcal{A}$-diagram (G, A, f) by $A_v = L(v)$ and $f_e = L(\langle e\rangle)$. Each $\mathcal{A}$-diagram (G, A, f) and functor $F : \mathcal{A} \Rightarrow \mathcal{B}$ determine a $\mathcal{B}$-diagram $F(G, A, f) = (G, B, g)$ where $B_v = F(A_v)$ and $g_e = F(f_e)$. That is, if $L : [G] \Rightarrow \mathcal{A}$ is the functor determined by (G, A, f), then (G, B, g) is the diagram determined by $F \circ L$.

Say that $\mathcal{A}$-diagram (G, A, f) *commutes* provided that for every two vertices v and v', and every two paths $p, q \in G(v, v')$, it is the case that $f_p = f_q$. Clearly, if (G, A, f) commutes and $F : \mathcal{A} \Rightarrow \mathcal{B}$ is a functor, then the $\mathcal{B}$-diagram $F(G, A, f)$ commutes also.

By a *model of HPSG*,[2] I understand a functor $M : \mathcal{H} \Rightarrow \mathcal{A}$, meeting various conditions. Here, $\mathcal{H}$ is a formally defined category of the form $[H]$ for a directed graph H in which both vertices and edges are certain strings over fixed alphabets. Thus, $\mathcal{H}$ takes the place of a formal language for HPSG. If $\mathcal{A}$ is **Set**, the category of sets and functions, then a model of HPSG is a **Set**-diagram. So M sends objects of $\mathcal{H}$ to sets and arrows of $\mathcal{H}$ to functions. The objects of $\mathcal{H}$ correspond to the names of sorts, so they are symbols like *sign* and *synsem*. The arrows of $\mathcal{H}$ correspond to paths of features, so they are symbols like HEAD and SYNSEM|LOC. Additionally, sort names are closed under certain syntactic constructions, e.g, $\mathsf{L}[\sigma]$ is a sort name whenever σ is. Similarly, arrows are closed under syntactic constructions including path concatenation.

The codomain of a model is the "semantic" category in which $\mathcal{H}$ is interpreted. Again, if $\mathcal{A}$ is **Set**, then a model M picks out sets as the interpretations of sort names, and functions as the interpretations of feature paths and other arrows in $\mathcal{H}$. The requirement that M be a functor ensures that the interpretation of a composite arrow in $\mathcal{H}$ must be interpreted as the composition of the interpretations of its constituent arrows.

For the reader wishing to avoid some of the category-theoretic overhead, or simply wishing for a more concrete example on which to hang intuitions, little that I write in this paper is significantly harmed by supposing that $\mathcal{A}$ is indeed **Set**. In Section 2.2, however, I argue that the choice between equivalent categories has no effect on models up to equivalence. This result shows that HPSG depends on a weaker meta-theory than set theory.

In order to model HPSG, for each sort σ there must be corresponding

---

[2]Throughout this paper, I will use the term "a model of HPSG" to mean, more precisely, a model of a specific version of the principles of HPSG.

sorts that represent lists of σ and sets of σ. This means that for a model $M : \mathcal{H} \Rightarrow \mathcal{A}$, (i) $\mathcal{H}$ must be a rich enough vocabulary to say things about lists and sets, (ii) $\mathcal{A}$ must have suitable interpretations of lists and sets, and (iii) M must carry the vocabulary of $\mathcal{H}$ over to its interpretation in $\mathcal{A}$, correctly interpreting lists and sets. We consider these three points one at a time.

In Section 2.1, the formal apparatus needed to specify $\mathcal{H}$ are developed; in Section 2.3, constraints on models having to do with the faithful interpretation of notions such as product and list are defined. Section 2.2 is essentially a digression in which I discuss the strength of the set theory that is assumed for the remainder of the paper. Specifically, I argue that the semantic domain $\mathcal{A}$ may be assumed to be an elementary topos. As the theory of elementary toposes is weaker than that of standard set theories, this digression speaks to the question of the required logical strength of a linguistic meta-theory.

2.1 Formal Categories for HPSG

In this section, I consider how to specify the "vocabulary" category $\mathcal{H}$ that serves as the domain of a model. $\mathcal{H}$ should be defined formally, that is, as a sort of formal language. Also, $\mathcal{H}$ should have a rich enough vocabulary to express facts involving, at least, lists and sets. Third, something akin to HPSG's appropriateness conditions should determine the particular $\mathcal{H}$.

Let S and L be disjoint sets. Then a *formal category over alphabets S and L* is a category of the form $[H]$ for some directed graph H satisfying the following conditions:

1. the vertices of H are drawn from S^*;
2. the edges of H are drawn from L^*.

I write $p : \sigma \to_H \tau$ to indicate that p is a path from σ to τ in H, or equivalently p is an arrow in $[H](\sigma, \tau)$, but then omit the subscript H whenever it is clear. Also, I denote concatenation of paths p followed by q as $p|q$. Thus, $q \circ p = p|q$ in $[H]$. An edge e in H can be identified with the path $\langle e \rangle$, so that $e : \sigma \to \tau$ is the same as $\langle e \rangle : \sigma \to \tau$.

Formal categories provide a means of discussing composition of arrows. But other operations are also important in HPSG. For example, HPSG requires "lists of signs" and "lists of synsems," and well as "sets of synsems."

Let BO (basic objects) and BA (basic arrows) be disjoint, infinite sets. I denote members of BO by lower-case italic strings, e.g, *sign*, and members of BA by strings of small capitals, e.g., PHON. I use s, t, u as meta-variables for BO and f, g, h as meta-variables for BA. Define sets SO (symbols for objects) and SA (symbols for arrows) as follows.

$$SO = \{\mathsf{id}, \diamond, , (\mathrm{comma}), \langle, \rangle, \pi, \pi', \mathsf{nil}, \mathsf{cons}, \ni, \ni', \Lambda, [,]\}$$
$$SA = \{1, \times, \mathsf{L}, \mathsf{P}, \mathsf{M}, [,]\}$$

Throughout the remainder of this discussion, assume that BO and SO are disjoint and that BA and SA are disjoint.

The main purpose of defining the notion of a formal category is to help distinguish between name and meaning, a distinction which is often lost in theoretical linguistics. In particular, formal categories are intended as the *domains* of functors. For example, suppose that $\mathcal{H}$ is a formal category, and suppose that $M : \mathcal{H} \Rightarrow \mathbf{Set}$ is a functor. Then one understands M as yielding the *meanings* of the formal objects and arrows that comprise $\mathcal{H}$. Thus, $M(\sigma)$ is the meaning of object the σ of $\mathcal{H}$. Now suppose that $p : \sigma \to \tau$ and $q : \sigma \to \tau$ are distinct arrows in $\mathcal{H}$. Then it is reasonable to ask whether, according to M, these are names for the same arrow, i.e., whether $M(p) = M(q)$. But note that if p and q were not distinct in $\mathcal{H}$, then such a proposition would be vacuous. So, we are committed to a formal category in which there are potentially many names for the same linguistic entity. Indeed, the formalization of a theory will, in part, be concerned with making claims of identity of the form $M(p) = M(q)$ where p and q are distinct.

An important role in such identities is played by "canonical names." For example, if $p : \sigma \to \tau$ and $p' : \tau \to \sigma$ are arrows, then one may ask whether $M(p|p')$ is the identity on $M(\sigma)$. We can render this as the proposition that $M(p|p') = M(\mathsf{id})$, where $\mathsf{id} : \sigma \to \sigma$ is a certain arrow in $\mathcal{H}$ that we insist be interpreted as an identity. In words, id is the canonical name for an identity.

With the understanding that a formal category is essentially a category of names, one can require that a formal category have canonical names for all of the objects and arrows that may be involved in formalizing a linguistic theory. That is, one can require various "closure" properties of formal categories to provide a rich enough vocabulary. Suppose that $\mathcal{H} = [H]$ is a formal category over $BO \cup SO$ and $BA \cup SA$. Then

Formal Identities. $\mathcal{H}$ has *formal identities* provided that $\mathsf{id} : \sigma \to \sigma$ is an edge in H for all $\sigma \in |\mathcal{H}|$. Formal identities provide canonical names for identity arrows.

Formal Terminals. $\mathcal{H}$ has a *formal terminal* provided that

1. $1 \in |\mathcal{H}|$; and
2. $\sigma \in |\mathcal{H}|$ implies $\diamond : \sigma \to 1$ is an edge.

A formal terminal provides canonical names relating to a nullary product. This is most useful in formalizing "constants" as arrows $c : 1 \to \sigma$.

Formal Products. $\mathcal{H}$ has *formal products* provided that

1. $\sigma, \tau \in |\mathcal{H}|$ implies that $[\sigma \times \tau] \in |\mathcal{H}|$, and that $\pi : [\sigma \times \tau] \to \sigma$ and $\pi' : [\sigma \times \tau] \to \tau$ are edges; and

2. if $p : \rho \to \sigma$ and $q : \rho \to \tau$ are paths, then $\langle p, q \rangle : \rho \to [\sigma \times \tau]$ is an edge.

Formal products are important to HPSG because HPSG involves some "functions" of more than one argument. These can be given names as paths, say from $\sigma \times \tau$ to ρ.

Formal Lists. If $\mathcal{H}$ has formal products, then $\mathcal{H}$ *has formal lists* provided that

1. $\sigma \in |\mathcal{H}|$ implies that $\mathsf{L}[\sigma] \in |\mathcal{H}|$ and that $\mathsf{nil} : 1 \to \mathsf{L}[\sigma]$ and $\mathsf{cons} : [\sigma \times \mathsf{L}[\sigma]] \to \mathsf{L}[\sigma]$ are edges; and
2. if $p : 1 \to \tau$ and $q : [\sigma \times \tau] \to \tau$ are paths, then $\mathsf{fold}[p, q] : \mathsf{L}[\sigma] \to \tau$ is an edge.

A formal list provides canonical names for the principle arrows that define the characteristics of lists. Specifically, nil and cons are canonical names for the empty list constant and the usual "cons" for lists. On the other hand, $\mathsf{fold}[p, q]$ yields canonical names for arrows defined on lists by the category-theoretic analog of primitive recursion.

Formal Powers. $\mathcal{H}$ has *formal powers* provided that

1. $\sigma \in |\mathcal{H}|$ implies that $\mathsf{P}[\sigma], \mathsf{M}[\sigma] \in |\mathcal{H}|$ and that the following are both edges: $\ni : \mathsf{M}[\sigma] \to \mathsf{P}[\sigma]$ and $\ni' : \mathsf{M}[\sigma] \to \sigma$; and
2. if $l : \rho \to \tau$ and $r : \rho \to \sigma$ are paths, then $\Lambda[l, r] : \tau \to \mathsf{P}[\sigma]$ is an edge.

Formal powers yield canonical names for the objects and arrows involved in characterizing "power sets." The idea is that $\mathsf{P}[\sigma]$ is to be interpreted as (the category theoretic analogue of) the power set of the interpretation of σ, while $\mathsf{M}[\sigma]$ is to be interpreted as the the inverse of the membership relation for σ and $\mathsf{P}[\sigma]$. In **Set**, $\mathsf{M}[\sigma]$ can be the set of pairs (X, a) where X is a subset of the meaning of σ, a is a member of the meaning of σ and $a \in X$. The arrows derive from the fundamental idea that relations between two sets A and B are in exact correspondence with functions from A to the powerset of B. Thus $\ni$ and $\ni'$ are canonical names for the "legs" of the membership relation — in sets, $\ni$ is interpreted as the map that sends (X, a) to X, $\ni'$ is interpreted as the map that sends (X, a) to a. Furthermore, $\Lambda[l, r] : \tau \to \mathsf{P}[\sigma]$ is interpreted as follows. In sets, let S, T and R be the meanings of σ, τ and ρ. Then $\Lambda[l, r]$ is interpreted as the map sending $t \in T$ to $\{s \in S \mid \exists x \in R.l(x) = t \wedge r(x) = s\}$.

I refer to a formal category with formal identities, formal terminal, formal products, formal lists and formal powers as a *formal HPSG category*. Because a formal HPSG category $\mathcal{H}$ is of the form $[H]$ for a unique directed graph depending only on $\mathcal{H}$, it makes sense to refer to an arrow in $\mathcal{H}$ as an *edge* provided that it is of the form $\langle e \rangle$ for an edge e in H.

The following abbreviations are useful in a formal HPSG category:

- For $f : \sigma \to \tau$ and $g : \sigma' \to \tau'$, abbreviate $\langle \pi | f, \pi' | g \rangle$ as $(f \times g)$.
- For $f : \sigma \to \tau$, abbreviate $\mathsf{fold}[\mathsf{nil}, \mathsf{cons} \circ (f \times \mathsf{id})]$ as $\mathsf{map}[f]$.
- Abbreviate $\Lambda[\mathsf{id}, \mathsf{id}]$ as $\{\_\}$.
- Abbreviate $\Lambda[\diamond, \mathsf{id}]$ as U.

In light of the discussion about canonical names in a formal category, it is important to ensure that the names that we wish to regard as canonical are not accidentally used for other purposes. Nothing in the definitions so far will prevent, for example, a formal category from including an arrow $\mathsf{id} : \sigma \to \tau$ for distinct σ and τ. This, however, would be contrary to our understanding that id is supposed to name identities. Call a formal HPSG category $\mathcal{H}$ *definite* provided that all of the canonical names defined above do not occur in the category except as required by the definition of formal HPSG categories. More thoroughly, $\mathcal{H}$ is definite provided that all of the following hold.

Formal Identities. If $\mathsf{id} : \sigma \to \tau$ is an edge, then $\sigma = \tau$.

Formal Terminals. If $\diamond : \sigma \to \tau$ is an edge, then $\tau = 1$.

Formal Products. If $[w \times w'] \in |\mathcal{H}|$, then $w, w' \in |\mathcal{H}|$. If $\pi : \rho \to \sigma$ is an edge then $\rho = [\sigma \times \tau]$ for some τ; and if $\pi' : \rho \to \tau$ is an edge, then $\rho = [\sigma \times \tau]$ for some σ. Also, if $\langle p, q \rangle : \rho \to \rho'$ is an edge, then $\rho' = [\sigma \times \tau]$, and $p : \rho \to \sigma$ and $q : \rho \to \tau$ are paths for some σ and τ.

Formal Lists. If $\mathsf{L}[w] \in |\mathcal{H}|$, then $w \in |\mathcal{H}|$. If $\mathsf{nil} : \rho \to \tau$ is an edge, then $\rho = 1$ and $\tau = L[\sigma]$ for some σ. If $\mathsf{cons} : \rho \to \tau$ is an edge, then $\rho = [\sigma \times \mathsf{L}[\sigma]]$ and $\tau = L[\sigma]$ for some σ. If $\mathsf{fold}[p, q] : \rho \to \tau$ is an edge, then for some $\sigma \in |\mathcal{H}|$, $\rho = \mathsf{L}[\sigma]$, and $p : 1 \to \tau$ and $q : [\sigma \times \tau] \to \tau$ are paths.

Formal Powers. $\mathsf{P}[w] \in |\mathcal{H}|$ if and only if $\mathsf{M}[w] \in |\mathcal{H}|$. If $\mathsf{P}[w] \in |\mathcal{H}|$, then $w \in |\mathcal{H}|$. If $\ni : \rho \to \tau$ is an edge, then $\rho = \mathsf{M}[\sigma]$ and $\tau = \mathsf{P}[\sigma]$ for some σ. If $\ni' : \rho \to \tau$ is an edge, then $\rho = \mathsf{M}[\tau]$. If $\Lambda[l, r] : \tau \to v$ is an edge, then there exist $\sigma, \rho \in |\mathcal{H}|$ so that $v = \mathsf{P}[\sigma]$ and $r : \rho \to \sigma$ and $l : \rho \to \tau$ are paths.

Definiteness simply means that all objects and arrows present in $\mathcal{H}$ that involve the names id, $\diamond$, π, $\langle p, q \rangle$ and so on are present only because of the conditions on formal HPSG categories.

Now consider how to specify a definite formal HPSG category. Such a specification must involve the introduction of names for objects and arrows. Naturally, arrows must be accompanied by the specification of their domains and codomains. In spirit, HPSG introduces arrows with domain and codomain specifications via *appropriateness conditions*, which specify that certain features exist for certain sorts. I seek a formal counterpart to these. In HPSG, a typical appropriateness condition can be rendered as

$$s : \begin{bmatrix} f_0 & \tau_0 \\ \vdots & \vdots \\ f_{n-1} & \tau_{n-1} \end{bmatrix}$$

where s is a basic sort name, f_0 through f_{n-1} are feature names, and τ_0 through τ_{n-1} are expressions that are intended, somewhat informally, to denote other sorts. For example,

$$sign : \begin{bmatrix} \text{PHON} & \mathsf{L}(\textit{phon-string}) \\ \vdots & \vdots \\ \text{SYNSEM} & \textit{synsem} \end{bmatrix}$$

appears in Pollard and Sag (1994) — henceforth PS94 — as an appropriateness condition for the sort *sign*. Notice that the symbol to the left of the colon is always a "basic" sort, never of the form, e.g., $\mathsf{L}(\sigma)$, and that the features are always "basic," never of the form $p|q$.

Another part of the specification of HPSG has to do with subsort ordering. The sorts are regarded as being partially ordered. In a formal HPSG category, this idea is also taken up by arrows, so that σ is a subsort of τ if there is an arrow (with certain additional properties) from σ to τ. So, in order to specify that σ_0 through σ_n are all subsorts of τ, one needs a means of specifying the existence of arrows $f_i : \sigma_i \to \tau$. In other words, the subsort relations can be specified in a manner that is essentially the same as an appropriateness condition, except that the arrows are running backward.

In both cases, standard appropriateness conditions and subsort relations, the essential information conveyed consists of a "basic" sort and a finite list (actually, a set because order doesn't matter and repetitions are not allowed) of pairs (f, τ), each consisting of a "basic" arrow f and a sort τ. What distinguishes a standard appropriateness condition from the information needed to specify subsorts is the directionality of the features.

Define an *appropriateness condition for formal HPSG category* $\mathcal{H}$ to be a triple $\alpha = (s, \phi, d)$ where

1. $s \in BO$,
2. ϕ is a finite set of pairs in $BA \times |\mathcal{H}|$;
3. and $d \in \{\mathbf{f}, \mathbf{b}\}$. Here d is intended to indicate the direction that arrows are supposed to run.

If $d = \mathbf{f}$, then α is called a *forward appropriateness condition*, otherwise α is called a *backward appropriateness condition*. I will abbreviate a forward appropriateness condition in keeping with the standard HPSG notation by writing

$$s : \begin{bmatrix} f_0 & \tau_0 \\ \vdots & \vdots \\ f_{n-1} & \tau_{n-1} \end{bmatrix}$$

and, dually, a backward appropriateness condition by writing

$$\begin{bmatrix} \tau_0 & f_0 \\ \vdots & \vdots \\ \tau_{n-1} & f_{n-1} \end{bmatrix} : s.$$

Define the *extent* of $\alpha = (s, \phi, d)$, denoted by $E(\alpha)$ as follows.

$$E(s, \phi, d) = \begin{cases} \{(s, f, \tau) \mid (f, \tau) \in \phi\} & \text{for } d = \mathbf{f} \\ \{(\tau, f, s) \mid (f, \tau) \in \phi\} & \text{for } d = \mathbf{b}. \end{cases}$$

Define the *focus* of α, denoted by $F(\alpha)$, to be $\{s\}$.

Suppose that $\mathcal{H}$ is a formal HPSG category and α is an appropriateness condition for $\mathcal{H}$, then let $\mathcal{H} + \alpha$ denote the least formal HPSG category containing $\mathcal{H}$ so that $F(\alpha) \subseteq |\mathcal{H} + \alpha|$ and for every $(\sigma, f, \rho) \in E(\alpha)$, it is the case that $f : \sigma \to \rho$ is an edge in $\mathcal{H} + \alpha$. Because all of the conditions defining formal HPSG categories are inductive, $\mathcal{H} + \alpha$ is guaranteed to exist. Also, $\mathcal{H} + \alpha = \mathcal{H}$ whenever the triples in $E(\alpha)$ already correspond to edges in $\mathcal{H}$.

Lemma 2.1 *If $\mathcal{H}$ is a definite formal HPSG category and α is an appropriateness condition for $\mathcal{H}$, then $\mathcal{H} + \alpha$ is a definite formal HPSG category.*

Proof. Suppose to the contrary that $\text{id} : \sigma \to \tau$ is an arrow in $[H'] = \mathcal{H} + \alpha$ and $\sigma \neq \tau$. Let H'' be the graph obtained by removing exactly the single edge $\text{id} : \sigma \to \tau$ from H'. Then $[H'']$ is still a formal HPSG category. On the assumption that $\mathcal{H}$ is definite, $\text{id} : \sigma \to \tau$ is not an arrow of $\mathcal{H}$. So $\mathcal{H} \subseteq [H'']$. $E(\alpha)$ contains no triples of the form $(\sigma, \text{id}, \tau)$, so all triples in $E(\alpha)$ correspond to edges in H'. But this contradicts the definition of $\mathcal{H} + \alpha$. All other cases are proved similarly. $\square$

This lemma shows that a formal HPSG category defined by a sequence of appropriateness conditions has no spurious arrows or objects that are of the forms required by the closure conditions on formal HPSG categories.

Lemma 2.2 *Let $\mathcal{H}$ be a formal HPSG category. Suppose that $\alpha_0, \ldots, \alpha_{n-1}$ and $\beta_0, \ldots, \beta_{m-1}$ are sequences so that each α_i is an appropriateness condition for $\mathcal{H} + \alpha_0 + \ldots + \alpha_{i-1}$ and each β_j is an appropriateness condition for $\mathcal{H} + \beta_0 + \ldots + \beta_{j-1}$. Then*

$$\mathcal{H} + \alpha_0 + \ldots + \alpha_{n-1} = \mathcal{H} + \beta_0 + \ldots + \beta_{m-1}$$

if and only if

$$E(\alpha_0) \cup \ldots \cup E(\alpha_{n-1}) = E(\beta_0) \cup \ldots \cup E(\beta_{m-1})$$

and

$$F(\alpha_0) \cup \ldots \cup F(\alpha_{n-1}) = F(\beta_0) \cup \ldots \cup F(\beta_{m-1}).$$

Proof. Let

$$
\begin{aligned}
\mathcal{G}_i &= \mathcal{H} + \alpha_0 + \ldots + \alpha_{i-1} \\
U_i &= E(\alpha_0) \cup \ldots \cup E(\alpha_{i-1}) \\
V_i &= F(\alpha_0) \cup \ldots \cup F(\alpha_{i-1}).
\end{aligned}
$$

By induction on i, $\mathcal{G}_i$ is the least formal HPSG category containing $\mathcal{H}$ so that (i) $V_i \subseteq |\mathcal{G}_i|$ and (ii) for every $(\sigma, f, \tau) \in U_i$, it is the case that $f : \sigma \to \rho$ is an arrow of $\mathcal{G}_i$.

Subclaim. *Suppose that $\mathcal{G}'$ is a formal HPSG category, U' is a set of triples of the form (σ, f, ρ) and $V' \subseteq BO$ so that $\mathcal{G}'$ is the least formal HPSG category containing $\mathcal{H}$ in which $V' \subseteq |\mathcal{G}'|$ and for each $(\sigma, f, \rho) \in U'$, it is the case that $f : \sigma \to \rho$ is an arrow of $\mathcal{G}'$. Furthermore, suppose that α is an appropriateness condition for $\mathcal{G}'$. Let $\mathcal{H}'$ be the least formal HPSG category containing $\mathcal{H}$ so that $V' \cup F(\alpha) \subseteq |\mathcal{H}'|$ and for each $(\sigma, f, \rho) \in U' \cup E(\alpha)$, it is the case that $f : \sigma \to \rho$ is an arrow of $\mathcal{G}'$. Then $\mathcal{G}' + \alpha = \mathcal{H}'$.*

The proof of the subclaim is by induction on the rank of arrows and objects in $\mathcal{G}' + \alpha$ and in $\mathcal{H}'$. As usual, define rank as the least ordinal at which an element appears in the construction of the category.

By the inductive hypothesis, $\mathcal{G}_i$ is the least formal HPSG category containing $\mathcal{H}$ so that $V_i \subseteq |\mathcal{G}_i|$ and for each $(\sigma, f, \rho) \in U_i$, it is the case that $f : \sigma \to \rho$ is an arrow in $\mathcal{G}_i$. Thus by the subclaim, $\mathcal{G}_{i+1} = \mathcal{G}_i + \alpha_{i+1}$ is indeed the least formal HPSG category containing $\mathcal{H}$ so that $V_{i+1} \subseteq |\mathcal{G}_{i+1}|$ and for every $(\sigma, f, \tau) \in U_{i+1}$, it is the case that $f : \sigma \to \rho$ is an arrow of $\mathcal{G}_{i+1}$. From this, the result follows easily. $\square$

This lemma shows that the order of presentation of a sequence of appropriateness conditions does not matter, so long as all sort names appearing in α_{i+1}, except possibly the lone member of $F(\alpha)$, are already present in $\mathcal{H} + \alpha_0 + \ldots + \alpha_i$.

2.2 Semantic Categories for HPSG

In parallel to the formal categories of HPSG, the semantic categories (the codomains of models) must support notions of lists and sets. Of course, the category of sets and maps does exactly this. Thus for the sake of simplicity, I assume for the first part of this section that the codomain of a model of HPSG is **Set**. Nevertheless, it is worth considering whether **Set** is necessary. Put another way, it is worth considering what properties of **Set** are needed to formalize HPSG. In this section, I consider just those properties of **Set** that are relevant to interpretations of formal HPSG categories. As it happens, all such properties hold of any elementary topos with a natural numbers object. Thus, we could just as well assume that the semantic category is any elementary topos. I will not exploit topos theory in this paper except to make this point.

Topos theory replaces axioms to do with the binary membership relation ($\in$) with axioms to do with arrows in a category. The axioms of topos theory correspond to a singleton axiom (ensuring that a topos is not empty), an ordered pair axiom, a comprehension schema, and a power object axiom. In addition, because HPSG concerns lists, I assume that a topos satisfies a form of the infinity axiom that facilitates the use of lists. Significantly, full comprehension, hence replacement, is not assumed to hold in a topos. Analogues of the union and empty set axioms of set theory are derivable from the axioms of topos theory. Also, a version of the axiom of choice may be formulated but, not surprisingly, HPSG makes no use of it.

Consider the following constructions in **Set**.

Terminal. Let $T = \{\emptyset\}$.

Binary Products. For any sets X and Y, let

$$X \times Y = \{(a, b) \mid a \in X \,\&\, b \in Y\}$$

Finite Limits. For finite **Set**-diagram $D = (G, X, f)$ where the vertices of G are $0, \ldots, n-1$, let

$$\lim(D) = \{\mathbf{a} \in X_0 \times \ldots \times X_{n-1} \mid \forall i, j < n \forall e \in G(i, j).f_e(a_i) = a_j\}$$

In case $n = 0$, let $() = \{\emptyset\}$, so that $\lim(\emptyset, \emptyset, \emptyset) = \{\{\emptyset\}\}$.

Powers. For any set X, let $\mathsf{P}[X]$ be the power set of X, and let

$$\mathsf{M}[X] = \{(x, a) \mid x \subseteq X \,\&\, a \in x\}.$$

Lists. For any set X, let $\mathsf{L}[X]$ be the set of finite sequences of elements of X.

Clearly, all of the above can be constructed in any model of set theory. Also the singleton $\{\emptyset\}$ and binary products are special cases of finite limits.

Suppose that, in the course of formalizing some part of a linguistic theory, we claim that the product of sets X and Y is needed. That is, we state some constraint on signs as a constraint involving $X \times Y$. Then surely, it can make no difference to the theory whether we state such a constraint on $X \times Y$ or on $Y \times X$. Nor for that matter can such a linguistic constraint depend on how we define ordered pairs in a model of set theory (is (a, b) defined to be $\{a, \{a, b\}\}$ or $\{\{a\}, \{a, b\}\}$?). Likewise, if a linguistic theory involves a singleton set, then surely any singleton set will do, and similarly for all of the above constructions. Simply put, the linguistic claims of a theory do not (it would seem, in principle) depend on how we choose to represent various constructions on sets. Thus, we can profit by making explicit what is meant by a "construction on sets," while purposefully avoiding choices about representation.

In the following descriptions, let $\mathcal{A}$ be any category.

Terminals. Say that $T \in |\mathcal{A}|$ is a *terminal* provided that for all $B \in |\mathcal{A}|$, there is exactly one arrow $h : B \to T$.

In **Set**, an object is a terminal if and only if it is a singleton set. In elementary topos theory, existence of a terminal takes the place of existence of an empty set, in that it guarantees a non-empty universe.

Binary Products. Say that $C \in |\mathcal{A}|$ is a *product of $A \in |\mathcal{A}|$ and $B \in |\mathcal{A}|$* provided that there exist arrows $p : C \to A$ and $q : C \to B$ so that for any two arrows $f : D \to A$ and $g : D \to B$, there is a unique $h : D \to C$ for which $f = ph$ and $g = qh$.

In **Set**, a set Z is a product of X and Y if and only if it has the same cardinality as $X \times Y$. In elementary topos theory, existence of binary products takes the place of existence of ordered pairs.

In the remainder of this paper, I assume that a category with binary products is equipped with a map $\times$ from pairs of objects to products, so that $(A \times B)$ denotes a specific product of A and B, and with arrows $\pi_{A,B} : (A \times B) \to A$ and $\pi'_{A,B} : (A \times B) \to B$ denoting the projections. For arrows $f : A \to A'$ and $g : B \to B'$, let

$$(f \times g) : (A \times B) \to (A' \times B')$$

denote the arrow determined by the equations

$$\pi_{A',B'} \circ (f \times g) = f \circ \pi_{A,B}$$
$$\pi'_{A',B'} \circ (f \times g) = g \circ \pi'_{A,B}$$

Finite Limits. Let $D = (G, A, f)$ be a finite $\mathcal{A}$-diagram. Then say that $C \in |\mathcal{A}|$ is a *limit* of D provided that there exist arrows $\eta_v : C \to A_v$ for each vertex v in G so that

1. $\eta_{v'} = f_p \circ \eta_v$ for each path $p \in G(v, v')$ and
2. if $\epsilon_v : B \to A_v$ are arrows for each vertex v for which $\epsilon_{v'} = f_p \circ \epsilon_v$ whenever $p \in G(v, v')$, then there is a unique $h : B \to C$ so that $\epsilon_v = \eta_v \circ h$ for all vertices v.

In **Set**, a set X is a limit of $D = (G, A, f)$ if and only if it has the same cardinality as $\lim(D)$. In elementary topos theory, the existence of finite limits replaces the comprehension axioms of traditional set theory. It allows definitions of "sub-objects" by finite conjunctions of equations. Like comprehension, the existence of limits for all finite diagrams can be axiomatized by a recursive axiom schema consisting of one axiom for each finite directed graph. Any category in which limits exist for all finite diagrams is called a *cartesian category*. In particular, **Set** is cartesian.

Powers. The distinguishing property of power sets with respect to functions is the fact that binary relations from X to Y correspond exactly to maps from X to the power set of Y. In **Set**, let $R : X \vdash Y$ indicate that

R is a binary relation from set X to set Y, and let $\mathbf{Rel}(X,Y)$ denote the collection of binary relations from X to Y. Consider $R : X \vdash Y$, and any map $h : Z \to X$. Form a new relation $h_R : Z \vdash Y$ by taking $a \; h_R \; c$ if and only if $h(a) \; R \; c$. Thus, the relation $R : X \vdash Y$ determines a function from $\mathbf{Set}(Z,X)$ to $\mathbf{Rel}(Z,Y)$ given by $h \mapsto h_R$. Now let P be the power set of Y and let $M : P \vdash Y$ be the inverse subset relation: $Y' \; M \; y$ if and only if $y \in Y'$. M is *universal* in the sense that for every Z, the function $h \mapsto h_M$ from $\mathbf{Set}(Z,P)$ to $\mathbf{Rel}(Z,Y)$ is a bijection: given $R : Z \vdash Y$ define m_R by $z \mapsto \{y \in Y \mid zRy\}$ — clearly, $m_{h_M} = h$ for every $h : Z \to P$ and $(m_R)_M = R$ for every $R : Z \vdash Y$. From a category-theoretic view, the existence of this universal relation $M : P \vdash Y$ characterizes the power set of Y.

In a cartesian category, call any pair of maps

$$I \xrightarrow{\;q\;} B$$
$$\left. p \right\downarrow$$
$$A$$

a *table* from A to B. In $\mathbf{Set}$, think of I as an index set into a table listing the relation

$$R = \{(p(i), q(i)) \mid i \in I\}.$$

Say that such a table is *irredundant* provided that for any other table

$$I' \xrightarrow{\;q'\;} B$$
$$\left. p' \right\downarrow$$
$$A$$

there is at most one arrow $h : I' \to I$ for which $p' = ph$ and $q' = qh$. In $\mathbf{Set}$, a table is irredundant provided that the table represented by p and q contains no repeated entries: if $(p(i), q(i)) = (p(j), q(j))$ then $i = j$.

For an object A in $\mathcal{A}$, say that the table t below

$$M \xrightarrow{\;m\;} A$$
$$\left. n \right\downarrow$$
$$P$$

is a *universal relation to A* provided that (i) t is irredundant and (ii) for every irredundant table

$$I \xrightarrow{\;q\;} A$$
$$\left. p \right\downarrow$$
$$B$$

there are unique morphisms $h : B \to P$ and $k : I \to M$ so that (a) $q = mk$ and $hp = nk$ and (b) if $hp' = nk'$, then there exists a unique $g : I' \to I$ so that $p' = pg$ and $k' = kg$.

If

$$M \xrightarrow{\; m \;} A$$
$$\downarrow n$$
$$P$$

is a universal relation to A, then P is called a *power object for A* and M is a *membership object for A*.

In **Set**, universal relations have P and M with the same cardinalities as power sets and membership relations (taken as sets). Existence of all universal relations replaces the power set axiom of traditional set theory.

A cartesian category is called a *topos* if there is a universal relation for each object. In particular, **Set** is a topos.

Lists. For object A in a category with binary products and a terminal object T, say that $n : T \to L$ and $c : (A \times L) \to L$ *define lists for A* provided that for any two arrows $a_0 : T \to B$ and $m : (A \times B) \to B$, there exists a unique arrow $h : L \to B$ so that

$$a_0 = h \circ n$$
$$m \circ (\mathrm{id}_A \times h) = h \circ c$$

In this definition, n is understood as the arrow from a terminal (singleton) that picks out the empty list, and c as the "cons" arrow. Furthermore, for arrows $a_0 : T \to B$ and $m : A \times B \to B$, the unique $h : L \to B$ determined by them is understood as an arrow defined by primitive recursion: a_0 is the basic case, m is the recursive case.

If for each object A of $\mathcal{A}$, there are arrows n and c defining lists for A, then say that all lists exist in $\mathcal{A}$.

In **Set**, lists are defined for any set X by any set of the same cardinality as $\mathsf{L}[X]$. The existence of lists in a category replaces the axiom of infinity in traditional set theory. In particular, the maps $0 : 1 \to \omega$ (defined by $\emptyset \mapsto 0$) and $+1 : 1 \times \omega \to \omega$ (defined by $(\emptyset, n) \mapsto n + 1$) define list for the terminal $1 = \{\emptyset\}$.

One kind of limit is of particular use. Suppose that $f_1 : A_1 \to A_0$ and $f_2 : A_2 \to A_0$ are arrows. Then a limit of

$$A_1$$
$$\downarrow f_1$$
$$A_2 \xrightarrow{\; f_2 \;} A_0$$

consists of three arrows $\eta_i : B \to A_i$ so that (i) $\eta_0 = f_1 \eta_1 = f_2 \eta_2$ and (ii) if $\gamma_i : C \to A_i$ are arrows so that $\gamma_0 = f_1 \gamma_1 = f_2 \gamma_2$, then there is a unique arrow $h : C \to B$ so that $\gamma_i = \eta_i \circ h$ for $i = 0, 1, 2$. A limit of a pair of arrows like f_1 and f_2 is called a *pullback of f_1 and f_2*.

In **Set**, suppose that f_1 is an inclusion map for $A_1 \subseteq A_0$ and $f_2 : A_2 \to A_0$ is any function to A_0. Then the set

$$B = \{a \in A_2 \mid f_2(a) \in A_1\}$$

is the object of a pullback with η_2 being the inclusion of $B \subseteq A_2$, and η_1 being the restriction of f_2 to B.

Although it is beyond the scope of this paper to prove these, several other useful constructions are definable in any topos (whence in **Set**). For example, every topos $\mathcal{A}$ is also *co-cartesian* — the category formed from $\mathcal{A}$ by reversing the direction of all arrows is cartesian. This is important for HPSG in at least two special cases. First, HPSG requires existence of co-products to model certain sorts, e.g., *sign* is typically defined as a disjoint union of other sorts. Co-products take the place of disjoint unions in a topos. Second, HPSG requires the existence of an initial object[3] as the counterpart to the empty set.

In any topos (more generally, in any exponential category) if $n : T \to L$ and $c : (A \times L) \to L$ defines lists for A, then there is a natural "concatenation" arrow $k : (L \times L) \to L$ for L satisfying

$$
\begin{aligned}
k \circ (n \times \mathrm{id}_L) &= \pi_{T,L} \\
k \circ (c \times \mathrm{id}_L) &= c \circ (\mathrm{id}_A \times k) \circ \alpha
\end{aligned}
$$

where $\alpha : ((A \times L) \times L) \to (A \times (L \times L))$ is the evident isomorphism between $((A \times L) \times L)$ and $(A \times (L \times L))$.

Also, union, intersection and difference are definable for each power object, but their construction in a topos is beyond this paper.

2.3 Interpretations of Formal HPSG Categories

Suppose that $\mathcal{H}$ is a formal HPSG category. Then an *interpretation* of $\mathcal{H}$ in category $\mathcal{A}$ is a functor $I : \mathcal{H} \Rightarrow \mathcal{A}$ for which the following properties hold.

Formal Identities. $I(\mathrm{id} : \sigma \to \sigma)$ is the identity for $I(\sigma)$.

Formal Terminal. $I(1)$ is a terminal object.

Formal Products. $I((\sigma \times \tau))$ is a product of $I(\sigma)$ and $I(\tau)$. $I(: \to)$ and $I(\pi' : [\sigma \times \tau] \to \tau)$ are the corresponding projections. For $p : \rho \to \sigma$ and $q : \rho \to \tau$,

$$
\begin{aligned}
I(p : \rho \to \sigma) &= I(\langle p, q \rangle \mid \pi : \rho \to \sigma) \\
I(q : \rho \to \tau) &= I(\langle p, q \rangle \mid \pi' : \rho \to \tau)
\end{aligned}
$$

---

[3] I is *initial* in a category provided that there is exactly one arrow $\square_A : I \to A$ for each object A. In **Set**, $\emptyset$ is the only initial object.

Formal Lists. $I(\text{nil} : 1 \to \mathsf{L}[\sigma])$ and $I(\text{cons} : (\sigma \times \mathsf{L}[\sigma]) \to \mathsf{L}[\sigma])$ define lists for $I(\sigma)$. For $p : 1 \to \tau$ and $q : (\sigma \times \tau) \to \tau$,

$$I(p : 1 \to \tau) = I(\text{nil}|\text{fold}[p, q] : 1 \to \tau)$$
$$I([\text{id} \times \text{fold}[p, q]]|q : (\sigma \times \mathsf{L}[\sigma]) \to \tau)$$
$$= I(\text{cons}|\text{fold}[p, q] : (\sigma \times \mathsf{L}[\sigma]) \to \tau)$$

Formal Powers. $I(\ni : \mathsf{M}[\sigma] \to \mathsf{P}[\sigma])$ and $I(\ni' : \mathsf{M}[\sigma] \to \sigma)$ constitute a universal relation to $I(\sigma)$.

For $p : \rho \to \tau$ and $q : \rho \to \sigma$, the following holds. Let

$$
\begin{array}{ccc}
A & \xrightarrow{\;\;g\;\;} & I(\mathsf{M}[\sigma]) \\
\downarrow{\scriptstyle f} & & \downarrow{\scriptstyle I(\ni)} \\
I(\tau) & \xrightarrow[I(\Lambda[p,q])]{} & I(\mathsf{P}[\sigma])
\end{array}
$$

be a pullback of $I(\Lambda[p, q] : \tau \to \mathsf{P}[\sigma])$ and $I(\ni : \mathsf{M}[\sigma] \to \mathsf{P}[\sigma])$. Then for every irreducible table

$$
t = \begin{array}{c}
B \xrightarrow{\;\;f'\;\;} I(\sigma) \\
{\scriptstyle g'}\downarrow \phantom{B \xrightarrow{\;\;f'\;\;} I(\sigma)} \\
I(\tau) \phantom{\xrightarrow{\;\;f'\;\;} I(\sigma)}
\end{array}
$$

if there is an arrow $h : I(\rho) \to B$ so that $I(p : \rho \to \tau) = f'h$ and $I(q : \rho \to \sigma) = g'h$, then there is also an arrow $h' : A \to B$, so that $f = f'h'$ and $g = g'h'$.

As an aside, I am not convinced that HPSG actually needs universal relations, but my current understanding of the Trace Principle leaves me no choice, as P[*local*] is just what is needed to formalize a notion of "set of local values." I am willing to assume universal relations as the expedient way to make sense of principles involving "set of" as they are presently formulated, but I will not be surprised to see a reformulation of HPSG do away with sets altogether, hence effectively replace topos theory with a still weaker meta-theory.

In this section, I have developed the necessary ideas of category theory to make the name/meaning distinction precise as it relates to formalizations of HPSG. In particular, I have defined the notion of a formal HPSG category, providing for a precisely defined vocabulary of sort names and arrow names in which to formalize HPSG, along with a notion of how such a category is to be interpreted in a category such as **Set**. I have also argued that, in fact, one may safely use topos theory as a weaker meta-theory than standard set theory, because this formalization of HPSG depends only on properties definable in any elementary topos with list objects.

What remains is to develop a system of constraints on interpretations that reflect the sorts of constraints necessary to pick out certain interpretations as models of HPSG. That is, having a basic vocabulary $\mathcal{H}$ and an understanding of how it may be interpreted, we must now provide a system by which to differentiate between interpretations. The next section concerns the definition of such a system.

3   Constraints on Interpretations: Theories and Models of HPSG

A version of HPSG (here called a *theory*) involves a specific formal HPSG category $\mathcal{H}$. This formalizes the vocabulary of the theory. But a theory also constrains the interpretations of that vocabulary. To state precisely what constitutes a model of HPSG, we must, therefore, formalize the various kinds of constraint that can comprise a theory.

The formal constraints needed for HPSG principles fall into six kinds: *vocabulary constraints*, corresponding to the appropriateness conditions of contemporary HPSG; *co-limit constraints*, corresponding roughly to subsort conditions in a sort hierarchy; *limit constraints*, corresponding to definitions such as "headed phrase" that are not usually regarded as separate sorts; *commutativity constraints*, corresponding to "token identity" constraints; *left factor constraints*, corresponding to sub-sort restrictions in appropriateness conditions; and *right factor constraints*, corresponding to assertions about dependence of one feature on another (as in HEAD with respect to SYNSEM).

Of these kinds of constraints, vocabulary constraints are unusual. They serve no purpose except to require that $\mathcal{H}$ have certain basic arrows and sorts. Traditional logic would have it that such requirements come prior to any statements of formal constraints in an object language ($\mathcal{H}$) because they are in effect establishing vocabulary of the object language. But in practice it is convenient to regard the establishment of new vocabulary as part of the process of formulating a theory. So the definitions here reflect that convenience by taking the specification of vocabulary as another kind of constraint, on an equal footing with the other kinds.

The system of formal constraints devised here associates a language of constraints $L(\mathcal{H})$ with each formal HPSG category $\mathcal{H}$, and a binary relation $\models_\mathcal{H}$ between interpretations $I : \mathcal{H} \Rightarrow \mathbf{Set}$ and elements of $L(\mathcal{H})$. Then an $\mathcal{H}$-theory is any set drawn from $L(\mathcal{H})$. A *model of $\mathcal{H}$-theory T* is an interpretation $I : \mathcal{H} \Rightarrow \mathbf{Set}$ so that $I \models_\mathcal{H} \theta$ for every $\theta \in T$. In contrast to standard approaches to HPSG meta-theory, the language $L(\mathcal{H})$ involves no logical connectives at all. Each $\theta \in L(\mathcal{H})$ is a primitive constraint. This simplifies the semantics of $L(\mathcal{H})$ considerably, and eliminates much of the complexity of proof theory.

Vocabulary Constraints. $\alpha \in L(\mathcal{H})$ whenever α is an appropriateness condition for $\mathcal{H}$ for which $\mathcal{H} + \alpha = \mathcal{H}$. In words, the vocabulary specified by α is required to be present in $\mathcal{H}$. The members of $L(\mathcal{H})$ of this form are called *vocabulary constraints*. Their only purpose is to introduce names of sorts and features into a theory.

Limit and Co-Limit Constraints. $(\alpha, D, i) \in L(\mathcal{H})$ whenever $\alpha = (s, \phi, d)$ is a non-empty appropriateness condition for $\mathcal{H}$, D is a finite $\mathcal{H}$-diagram in which s never appears as a vertex label, i is a map sending members of ϕ to vertices in D so that the vertex $i(f, \tau)$ is labeled τ, and $\mathcal{H} + \alpha = \mathcal{H}$. Members of $L(\mathcal{H})$ of this form are called *co-limit constraints* when α is backward and *limit constraints* when α is forward.

Co-limit constraints are needed to formalize sub-sort relations in HPSG. For example, the assertion that *sign* consists of disjoint subsorts *phrase* and *word* is here formalized by a co-limit constraint. Limit constraints are needed to formalize sub-collections defined by comprehension schemata, such as *trace* as that sub-collection of *sign* for which PHON is empty, SLASH is the singleton consisting of the value of the feature LOCAL, etc.

Commutative Diagrams. $D \in L(\mathcal{H})$ whenever D is an $\mathcal{H}$-diagram. Constraints of this form are called *commutative diagrams*.

Commutative diagrams are needed to specify conditions that are usually regarded as *token identities*. For example, the Head Feature Principle (head features of headed phrases are token identical to their head daughter's head features) is stated as a commutative diagram.

Right Factors. $(f : \sigma \to \tau) \preceq (g : \sigma \to \rho) \in L(\mathcal{H})$ whenever $f : \sigma \to \tau$ and $g : \sigma \to \rho$ are arrows of $\mathcal{H}$. A member of $L(\mathcal{H})$ of this form is called a *right factor constraint*.

Right factors are needed to specify what is standardly called "feature geometry." For example, in standard HPSG the linguistic claim that "local" features are always available for subcategorization restrictions translates into the feature geometric requirement that the feature LOCAL be found under the feature SYNSEM. Here, this claim translates into a right factor constraint.

Left Factors. $(f : \sigma \to \tau) \succeq (g : \rho \to \tau) \in L(\mathcal{H})$ whenever $f : \sigma \to \tau$ and $g : \rho \to \tau$ are arrows of $\mathcal{H}$. A member of $L(\mathcal{H})$ of this form is called a *left factor constraint*.

Left factor constraints are needed for so-called "sub-sort" restrictions. For example, that there are no complements of a head marker phrase is rendered by restricting the COMP-DTR feature to the empty list when it applies to head marker phrases. This is formalized as a left factor constraint.

The semantics of $L(\mathcal{H})$ is defined as follows.

Vocabulary Constraints. $I \models_{\mathcal{H}} \alpha$ always holds, provided that $\alpha \in L(\mathcal{H})$. In light of the requirements for membership in $L(\mathcal{H})$, this apparently vacuous constraint effectively restricts the formal HPSG category on which a theory is based.

Co-Limit Constraints. For a co-limit constraint $(\alpha, D, i) \in L(\mathcal{H})$ where

$$
\alpha = \begin{bmatrix} \tau_0 & f_0 \\ \vdots & \vdots \\ \tau_{n-1} & f_{n-1} \end{bmatrix} : s
$$

and $D = (G, \rho, p)$, and interpretation I, the relation $I \models_{\mathcal{H}} (\alpha, D, i)$ holds provided that there is a co-limit $\langle \eta_v : I(\rho_v) \to I(s) \rangle_{v \in |G|}$ of the **Set**-diagram ID so that for each $k < n$, $\eta_{i(f_k, \tau_k)} = I(f_k : \tau_k \to s)$. This constraint requires that the arrows $f_k : \tau_k \to s$ introduced by the backward appropriateness condition α be interpreted as the corresponding legs of a co-limit of D.

Limit Constraints. For a limit constraint $(\alpha, D, i) \in L(\mathcal{H})$ where

$$
\alpha = s : \begin{bmatrix} f_0 & \tau_0 \\ \vdots & \vdots \\ f_{n-1} & \tau_{n-1} \end{bmatrix}
$$

and $D = (G, \rho, p)$, and interpretation I, the relation $I \models_{\mathcal{H}} (\alpha, D, i)$ holds provided that there is a limit $\langle \eta_v : I(s) \to I(\rho_v) \rangle_{v \in |G|}$ of the **Set**-diagram ID so that for each $k < n$, $\eta_{i(f_k, \tau_k)} = I(f_k : s \to \tau_k)$. This constraint requires that the arrows $f_k : s \to \tau_k$ introduced by the forward appropriateness condition α be interpreted as the corresponding legs of a limit of D.

Commutative Diagrams. For commutative diagram D and interpretation I, the relation $I \models_{\mathcal{H}} D$ holds provided that the **Set**-diagram ID commutes. That is, for each two paths p and q in D having the same source and destination, $ID(p) = ID(q)$.

Right Factor Constraints. For right factor constraint

$$
(f : \sigma \to \tau) \preceq (g : \sigma \to \rho)
$$

and interpretation I, the relation

$$
I \models_{\mathcal{H}} (f : \sigma \to \tau) \preceq (g : \sigma \to \rho)
$$

holds provided that there exists an arrow $h : I(\tau) \to I(\rho)$ for which

$$
hI(f : \sigma \to \tau) = I(g : \sigma \to \rho).
$$

Left Factor Constraints. For left factor constraint

$$
(f : \sigma \to \tau) \succeq (g : \rho \to \tau)
$$

and interpretation I, the relation

$$I \models_{\mathcal{H}} (f : \sigma \to \tau) \succeq (g : \rho \to \tau)$$

holds provided that there exists an arrow $h : I(\sigma) \to I(\rho)$ for which

$$I(f : \sigma \to \tau) = I(g : \rho \to \tau)h.$$

For co-limit and limit constraints (α, D, i), if i is determined by α and D, then I omit it. This occurs when each τ in the appropriateness condition α appears once as a label in D. Furthermore, I write $((s, \phi, d), \emptyset)$ to abbreviate the case where the diagram D has (i) ϕ as the set of vertices, (ii) no arrows, and (iii) each vertex (f, τ) labeled τ. In words, the diagram D is a discrete diagram determined by ϕ.

A *well-formed constraint* is any member of $L(\mathcal{H})$ for any definite HPSG category $\mathcal{H}$. Similarly, a *well-formed vocabulary constraint* is any vocabulary constraint in any $L(\mathcal{H})$, and so on. For a set of well-formed constraints T, say that T is meaningful in $\mathcal{H}$ provided that $T \subseteq L(\mathcal{H})$.

The following examples will illustrate the semantics of constraints.

Vocabulary Constraints. An example vocabulary constraint:

$$sign : \begin{bmatrix} \text{PHON } \mathsf{L}[\textit{phon-string}] \\ \text{HEAD } \textit{head} \end{bmatrix}$$

This is meaningful in any formal HPSG category $\mathcal{H}$ where PHON labels an edge from the vertex labeled $sign$ to the vertex labeled $\mathsf{L}[\textit{phon-string}]$ and HEAD labels an edge from the vertex labeled $sign$ to the vertex labeled $head$. It is satisfied by any interpretation of such an $\mathcal{H}$.

Co-Limit Constraints. An example co-limit constraint:

$$\left(\begin{bmatrix} \textit{phrase } \text{PHRASE} \\ \textit{word } \text{WORD} \end{bmatrix} : sign, \emptyset \right)$$

This constraint is meaningful in any $\mathcal{H}$ where PHRASE : $phrase \to sign$ and WORD : $word \to sign$ are arrows. An interpretation of $\mathcal{H}$ satisfies this constraint provided that $sign$ is interpreted as a coproduct of $phrase$ and $word$ and PHRASE and WORD are interpreted as the corresponding injections. In **Set**, this asserts that $sign$ is (isomorphic to) a disjoint union of $phrase$ and $word$, but it makes no claims about how such disjoint unions are represented.

Limit Constraints. An example limit constraint:

$$\left(\begin{array}{l} hdd\text{-}phr : \begin{bmatrix} \text{HP} & \textit{phrase} \\ \text{HP-DTRS} & \textit{headed-struct} \end{bmatrix}, \\[2em] \qquad\qquad\qquad\qquad\qquad \textit{phrase} \\ \qquad\qquad\qquad\qquad\qquad\quad \Big\downarrow \text{DTRS} \\ \textit{headed-struct} \xrightarrow[\text{HEADED-STRUCT}]{} \textit{const-struct} \end{array} \right)$$

This is meaningful in any $\mathcal{H}$ where

HP : *hdd-phr* → *phrase*,

HP-DTRS : *hdd-phr* → *headed-struct*,

DTRS : *phrase* → *const-struct*,

HEADED-STRUCT : *headed-struct* → *const-struct*

are all arrows. An interpretation satisfies this constraint provided that

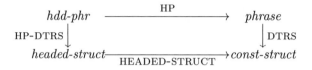

is a pullback. In fact, if we follow the version of HPSG in PS94, this is essentially how headed phrases are defined (translating, of course, from informal set theoretic language): a headed phrase is a phrase (the arrow labeled HP formalizes "is a") whose DTRS feature is a headed structure (the arrow labeled HEADED-STRUCT formalizes the second "is a"). The arrow labeled HP-DTRS is essentially the restriction of DTRS to *hdd-phr*.

Commutative Diagrams. An example commutative diagram:

$$
\begin{array}{ccc}
hdd\text{-}phr & \xrightarrow{\;\;\text{HD-DTR}\;\;} & sign \\
{\scriptstyle\text{HP}|\text{PHRASE}}\Big\downarrow & & \Big\downarrow{\scriptstyle\text{HEAD}} \\
sign & \xrightarrow[\text{HEAD}]{} & \text{HEAD}
\end{array}
$$

This is meaningful in any $\mathcal{H}$ where the sort names and arrows appearing as labels are present. An interpretation $I : \mathcal{H} \Rightarrow \mathcal{A}$ satisfies this condition provided that $I(\text{HD-DTR}|\text{HEAD}) = I(\text{HP}|\text{PHRASE}|\text{HEAD})$. This is a formal rendering of the Head Feature Principle according to PS94.

Left and Right Factor Constraints. Here are example right and left factor constraints:

$$(\text{HMK}|\text{HD-DTR} : hd\text{-}mark\text{-}struct \to sign) \succeq (\text{PHRASE} : phrase \to sign)$$

$$(\text{SYNSEM} : sign \to synsem) \preceq (\text{HEAD} : sign \to head).$$

Informally, the first holds in an interpretation where the head daughter of a head marker structure is a phrase, and the second holds in an interpretation where "head" information is part of "synsem" information. If HEAD is regarded as picking out exactly the information in a sign that is shared between a headed phrase and its head daughter, and SYNSEM is regarded as picking out exactly the information in a sign that can be selected for, then this constraint claims that any information shared between a headed phrase and its head daughter can be selected for.

For a definite formal HPSG category $\mathcal{H}$, category $\mathcal{A}$ and $\mathcal{H}$-theory T, the category $\mathbf{Mod}_{\mathcal{H}}^{\mathcal{A}}(T)$ of models of T in $\mathcal{A}$ has models $I : \mathcal{H} \Rightarrow \mathcal{A}$ as objects, and natural transformations between models as arrows. That is, for $I : \mathcal{H} \Rightarrow \mathcal{A}$ and $J : \mathcal{H} \Rightarrow \mathcal{A}$ a *natural transformation* is an $|\mathcal{H}|$ indexed family $\langle \eta_\sigma \rangle_{\sigma \in |\mathcal{H}|}$ of arrows in $\mathcal{A}$ so that for every arrow $p : \sigma \to \tau$ in $\mathcal{H}$, the following diagram commutes

$$
\begin{array}{ccc}
I(\sigma) & \xrightarrow{\eta_\sigma} & J(\sigma) \\
I(p) \downarrow & & \downarrow J(p) \\
I(\tau) & \xrightarrow{\eta_\tau} & J(\tau)
\end{array}
$$

With the definition of $\mathbf{Mod}_{\mathcal{H}}^{\mathcal{A}}(T)$, we can state precisely what it means for two versions of HPSG to be equivalent. Clearly, if T is an $\mathcal{H}$-theory, then there is has a minimal $\mathcal{H}'$ for which T is an $\mathcal{H}'$-theory. Call this category $\mathcal{H}(T)$. Now, two theories T and U are *equivalent in* $\mathcal{A}$ provided that $\mathbf{Mod}_{\mathcal{H}(T)}^{\mathcal{A}}(T)$ is equivalent as a category to $\mathbf{Mod}_{\mathcal{H}(U)}^{\mathcal{A}}(U)$. In light of the constraints on interpretations, $\mathbf{Mod}_{\mathcal{H}(T)}^{\mathcal{A}}(T)$ is, in fact, empty if $\mathcal{A}$ does not have the necessary finite limits and universal relations. It is not the case, however, that $\mathcal{A}$ must actually be a topos. Nevertheless, I conjecture that equivalence can actually be settled in toposes. That is, say that T and U are *equivalent* if and only if they are equivalent in all categories. The conjecture is that T and U are equivalent if and only if they are equivalent in all toposes.

4 The Principles

In this section, I set out an example theory of HPSG principles derived from the grammar in PS94. It differs, of course, by the details of formalization, but more important, by the very different way I have carved up the theory. In the interest of space, I have only formulated a representative sample of HPSG principles.

The various kinds of constraint on interpretations that were discussed in the preceding section play very distinct parts in the following formalization. In each case where I use a kind of constraint for the first time, I point out what purpose constraints of that kind will play throughout the theory.

4.1 Sign Basics

Signs have two main "projections," one to a phonetic realization, the other to semantic content.

(1)
$$
sign : \begin{bmatrix} \text{PHON} & L[\text{phon-string}] \\ \text{CONTENT} & \text{content} \end{bmatrix}
$$

This vocabulary constraint, like all others in this section, simply introduce needed vocabulary. Informally, the constraint says "I am going to tell you about the sorts *sign*, *phon-string* and *content*, related by maps PHON and CONTENT. Vocabulary constraints are not exclusive. That is, elsewhere in the theory one may introduce other arrows relating *sign* to other sorts.

Signs decompose into two basic forms: words and phrases.

$$(2) \qquad \left(\begin{bmatrix} phrase & \text{PHRASE} \\ word & \text{WORD} \end{bmatrix} : sign, \emptyset \right)$$

This co-limit constraint characterizes the sort *sign* as decomposing into two (more basic) cases: *phrase* and *word*. In general, co-limit diagrams assert such decompositions, and thus take the place of subsort ordering.

4.2 The Head Feature Principle

Signs can be factored several different ways into cases. But for now, we are concerned only with the distinction between phrases with head daughters and all other signs.

$$(3) \qquad \left(\begin{bmatrix} hdd\text{-}phr & \text{HDD-PHR} \\ non\text{-}hdd\text{-}phr & \text{NON-HDD-PHR} \end{bmatrix} : sign, \emptyset \right)$$

Again, this is a decomposition of *sign* into two cases.

$$(4) \qquad hdd\text{-}phr : [\,\text{HD-DTR } sign\,]$$

$$(5) \qquad (\text{HDD-PHR} : hdd\text{-}phr \to sign) \succeq (\text{PHRASE} : phrase \to sign)$$

This constraint relates the decomposition of *sign* into *phrase* and *word* with the decomposition of *sign* into *hdd-phr* and *non-hdd-phr*. Informally it says, "the sort *hdd-phr* is part of the sort *phrase*." I could have proceeded differently, by decomposing *phrase* into two parts, but the part of the theory with which we are concerned right now has nothing to say about phrases without heads that distinguishes them from words. So this formulation seems more direct. The reader may wish to pursue this other path long enough to be convinced that the resulting theory will, in fact, be equivalent in the sense of Section 2.

Every sign has head characteristics,

$$(6) \qquad sign : [\,\text{HEAD } head\,]$$

that are shared between a headed phrase and its daughter

$$(7) \qquad \begin{array}{ccc} hdd\text{-}phr & \xrightarrow{\text{HD-DTR}} & sign \\ \text{HDD-PHR} \downarrow & & \downarrow \text{HEAD} \\ sign & \xrightarrow[\text{HEAD}]{} & head \end{array}$$

Here is the first example of a commutative diagram used as a constraint. This takes the place of the usual token identity characterization of the HFP in HPSG: the head feature of a headed phrase is token identical to the head feature of the phrase's head daughter. Informally, this reads "Whatever it is that we mean by *hdd-phr*, *sign*, etc., they relate in the following manner..."

4.3 The Subcategorization Principle

Signs also have certain characteristics that can be selected for in subcategorization, and a characteristic SUBCAT that lists selectional restrictions. Headed phrases have a list of complement daughters (which are also signs).

$$(8) \qquad sign : \begin{bmatrix} \text{SYNSEM } synsem \\ \text{SUBCAT } L[synsem] \end{bmatrix}$$

$$(9) \qquad hdd\text{-}phr : [\, \text{COMP-DTRS } L[sign]\,]$$

The Subcategorization Principle of HPSG claims that for every headed phrase, the subcategorization list of the head daughter is the concatenation of the phrase's subcategorization list and the list of selectional characteristics of the complement daughters.

Let p abbreviate $\langle \text{HDD-PHR}|\text{SUBCAT}, \text{COMP-DTRS}|\mathsf{map}[\text{SYNSEM}]\rangle$. Then the arrow $p : hdd\text{-}phr \to [L[synsem] \times L[synsem]]$ extracts from a headed phrase the pair consisting of the headed phrase's subcategorization list and the list of "synsems" of the complement daughters. So the Subcategorization Principle is

$$
(10) \qquad
\begin{array}{ccc}
hdd\text{-}phr & \xrightarrow{\ \ p\ \ } & [L[synsem] \times L[synsem]] \\
{\scriptstyle \text{HDD-PHR}}\big\downarrow & & \big\downarrow{\scriptstyle \text{CONCAT}} \\
sign & \xrightarrow[\text{SUBCAT}]{} & L[synsem]
\end{array}
$$

4.4 SYNSEM Depends on HEAD

Notice that the statements of the Subcategorization Principle (Constraint 10) and the Head Feature Principle (Constraint 7) are entirely independent of one another. That is, it is easy to construct models that satisfy one without the other. Nevertheless, the linguistic data suggest a relationship between HEAD and SYNSEM: it is possible to select complements based on head characteristics. Thus,

$$(11) \qquad (\text{SYNSEM} : sign \to synsem) \preceq (\text{HEAD} : sign \to head).$$

This left factor constraint is a typical use of this kind of constraint. It imposes certain dependencies between features. In this case, "head features are synsem features." Generally, left factor constraints can act as separate constraints governing the interactions of otherwise independent parts of the theory. In this case, the constraint governs the interaction of the Subcategorization Principle and the Head Feature Principle.

4.5   Some of the Theory of the Sort *head*

The sort *head* decomposes into *functional* and *substantive*:

$$(12) \qquad \left(\begin{bmatrix} functional & \text{FUNCTIONAL} \\ substantive & \text{SUBSTANTIVE} \end{bmatrix} : head, \emptyset \right).$$

Substantive heads decompose into parts of speech:

$$(13) \qquad \left(\begin{bmatrix} noun & \text{NOUN} \\ verb & \text{VERB} \\ adj & \text{ADJ} \\ prep & \text{PREP} \\ relativizer & \text{RELATIVIZER} \end{bmatrix} : substantive, \emptyset \right).$$

Verbs have a "form" characteristic, the values of which are "finite," "infinitive," "gerund," "base," "present-participle," "past-participle," and "passive-participle." They also have characteristics AUX and INV as follows.

$$(14) \qquad verb : \begin{bmatrix} \text{VFORM} & vform \\ \text{AUX} & bool \\ \text{INV} & bool \end{bmatrix}$$

$$(15) \qquad \left(\begin{bmatrix} 1 & \text{FIN} \\ 1 & \text{INF} \\ 1 & \text{GER} \\ 1 & \text{BASE} \\ 1 & \text{PRP} \\ 1 & \text{PSP} \\ 1 & \text{PAS} \end{bmatrix} : vform, \emptyset \right)$$

$$(16) \qquad \left(\begin{bmatrix} 1 & \text{TRUE} \\ 1 & \text{FALSE} \end{bmatrix} : bool, \emptyset \right)$$

Define *fin-verb*, *inf-verb*, etc., as the pullbacks of VFORM and the corresponding cases:

$$(17) \qquad \left(fin\text{-}verb : [\,\text{FIN-VERB } verb\,], \quad \begin{array}{c} 1 \\ \downarrow \text{FIN} \\ verb \xrightarrow[\text{VFORM}]{} vform \end{array} \right),$$

and similarly for *inf-verb*, *ger-verb*, and so on. Limit diagrams such as this characterize a sort as a kind of composition of other sorts. In this case, *fin-verb* is the composition of *verb* and 1 in such a way that, in the result, VFORM and FIN agree. Roughly, constraints of this sort take the place of definitions by set comprehension. In this case,

$$fin\text{-}verb = \{x \in verb \mid \text{VFORM}(x) = \text{FIN}\}.$$

4.6   The Trace Principle

The Trace Principle involves two definitions, one of traces and the other of substantive words, that are instructive to consider separately. Traces and substantive words, however defined, are signs. That is, we expect to have an arrow

$$(18) \qquad \begin{bmatrix} trace & \text{TRACE} \\ subst\text{-}wrd & \text{SUBST-WRD} \end{bmatrix} : sign$$

The Trace Principle requires that the SYNSEM value of any trace must be a member of the subcategorization list of a substantive word. So for each trace, we must produce a substantive word for which the trace's SYNSEM value appears on that substantive word's subcategorization list. Formally,

$$(19) \qquad trace : [\, \text{TRACE-WITNESS} \; [\mathsf{L}[synsem] \times [synsem \times \mathsf{L}[synsem]]]\,]$$

Here TRACE-WITNESS can be thought of as producing the (non-empty) subcategorization list of some substantive word. As the SYNSEM value of a trace is required to belong on this list,

$$(20) \qquad \begin{array}{ccc} & trace & \xrightarrow{\;\text{TRACE}\;} & sign \\ \text{TRACE-WITNESS} \downarrow & & \downarrow \text{SYNSEM} \\ [\mathsf{L}[synsem] \times [synsem \times \mathsf{L}[synsem]]] & \xrightarrow[\pi'|\pi]{} & synsem \end{array}$$

Roughly, this commutative diagram requires that the *synsem* of a trace be the lone *symsem* appearing between two lists that is singled out by TRACE-WITNESS.

Let p abbreviate

$$[\mathsf{id} \times \mathsf{cons}]|\mathsf{concat},$$

so that

$$p : [\mathsf{L}[synsem] \times [synsem \times \mathsf{L}[synsem]]] \to \mathsf{L}[synsem]$$

builds a non-empty list from a list, a *synsem* and a list. The Trace Principle is thus stated simply as

$$(\text{TRACE-WITNESS}|p : trace \to \mathsf{L}[synsem])$$
$$(21) \qquad \succeq \quad (\text{SUBST-WRD}|\text{SUBCAT} : subst\text{-}wrd \to \mathsf{L}[synsem]).$$

What remains to explain about the Trace Principle are the sorts *trace* and *subst-wrd*. According to PS94, a trace is a sign that satisfies the attribute-value matrix

$$
\begin{bmatrix}
\text{PHON} & \langle\rangle \\
\text{SYNSEM} & \begin{bmatrix}
\text{LOCAL} & \boxed{1} \\
\text{NONLOCAL} & \begin{bmatrix}
\text{INHER} & \begin{bmatrix}
\text{QUE} & \emptyset \\
\text{REL} & \emptyset \\
\text{SLASH} & \{\boxed{1}\}
\end{bmatrix} \\
\text{TO-BIND} & \begin{bmatrix}
\text{QUE} & \emptyset \\
\text{REL} & \emptyset \\
\text{SLASH} & \emptyset
\end{bmatrix}
\end{bmatrix}
\end{bmatrix}
\end{bmatrix} .
$$

To state this definition, independent of subcategorization, I use a "flat" feature geometry in which SYNSEM and NONLOCAL are removed. Then a trace is characterized by

$$
\begin{bmatrix}
\text{PHON} & \langle\rangle \\
\text{LOCAL} & \boxed{1} \\
\text{INHER} & \begin{bmatrix}
\text{QUE} & \emptyset \\
\text{REL} & \emptyset \\
\text{SLASH} & \{\boxed{1}\}
\end{bmatrix} \\
\text{TO-BIND} & \begin{bmatrix}
\text{QUE} & \emptyset \\
\text{REL} & \emptyset \\
\text{SLASH} & \emptyset
\end{bmatrix}
\end{bmatrix} .
$$

In words, a *trace* is a sign with empty PHON, whose QUE and REL values of both the INHER and TO-BIND features are empty, whose TO-BIND|SLASH feature is empty, and whose INHER|SLASH feature is a singleton consisting of the value of the sign's LOCAL feature.

This description can be represented as a certain finite diagram. Each feature appearing in the matrix produces an edge, labeled by the same feature. Each instance of a "constant" $\langle\rangle$ or $\emptyset$ produces an edge from a vertex labeled 1 to the vertex that is the target of the edge for the corresponding feature. For example, the appearance of $\langle\rangle$ in the above diagram translates into an edge

$$
\mathsf{nil} : 1 \to L[\textit{phon-string}].
$$

Finally, the index $\{\boxed{1}\}$ results in a extra edge labeled $\{_-\}$[4] from the vertex labeled LOCAL to the vertex that is the target of the path INHER|SLASH. Altogether, *trace* is described by the following limit diagram:

---

[4] Recall that $\{_-\}$ abbreviates $\Lambda[\mathsf{id}, \mathsf{id}]$. The arrows

$$
\emptyset : 1 \to \mathsf{P}[\sigma]
$$

which correspond to the empty relations are definable by limits.

$$(22) \quad \begin{pmatrix} trace : \begin{bmatrix} \text{TRACE} & sign \end{bmatrix}, \\[2em] \begin{array}{ccccccc} & & \text{nil} & & & & \emptyset \\ 1 & \longrightarrow & L[phon\text{-}string] & & P[local] & \longleftarrow & 1 \\ & & \text{PHON} \uparrow & & \text{SLASH} \uparrow & & \downarrow \emptyset \\ & \text{LOCAL} & & \text{TO-BIND} & & \text{REL} & \\ local & \longleftarrow & sign & \longrightarrow nonlocal & \longrightarrow & P[ref] \\ \{\_\} \downarrow & & \text{INHER} \downarrow & & \downarrow \text{QUE} & & \\ & \text{SLASH} & & \text{QUE} & & & \\ P[local] \longleftarrow & & nonlocal & \longrightarrow & P[npro] & & \\ & \text{REL} \downarrow & & & \uparrow \emptyset & & \\ & P[ref] & & \longleftarrow_{\emptyset} & 1 & & \end{array} \end{pmatrix} .$$

The point of this characterization of trace is that a trace is regarded as a sign that meets several additional criteria. That is, one expects to have an arrow of the form TRACE : $trace \to sign$ that codifies how the necessary criteria are met by *trace*.

The parochial (English) version of the Trace Principle in which the SYNSEM must be a *non-initial* element of the subcategorization list of a substantive word may be formulated as an additional constraint. That is, simply by adding the constraint

$$(23) \quad \begin{aligned} & \left(\text{TRACE-WITNESS} : trace \to \mathsf{L}^+[synsem]\right) \\ & \succeq \quad \left(q : \mathsf{L}^{++}[synsem] \to \mathsf{L}^+[synsem]\right) \end{aligned}$$

using the following abbreviations.

$$q \quad \text{abbreviates} \quad (\mathsf{cons} \times \mathsf{cons})|\mathsf{concat}$$
$$\mathsf{L}^+[\sigma] \quad \text{abbreviates} \quad [\mathsf{L}[\sigma] \times [\sigma \times \mathsf{L}[\sigma]]]$$
$$\mathsf{L}^{++}[\sigma] \quad \text{abbreviates} \quad [[\sigma \times \mathsf{L}[\sigma]] \times [\sigma \times \mathsf{L}[\sigma]]].$$

This added constraint requires that TRACE-WITNESS factor through q. As the rest of the formulation of the Trace Principle refers to a *synsem* embedded between two lists, the effect of this additional constraint is to ensure that the witness to a trace must appear as a non-initial member of a subcategorization list. Note the advantage of the current formulation over standard HPSG accounts. To wit, the parochial version is in fact merely a specialization of the general theory by addition of constraints, not by modification of constraints. Thus, one can envision a universal grammar T_0 with parochial specializations $T_{\text{English}} \supseteq T_0$, $T_{\text{German}} \supseteq T_0$, etc. corresponding to individual languages.

It appears that one can always translate an attribute-value matrix into an $\mathcal{H}$-diagram, though a precise meaning to this claim must await a clearer understanding of the roles that attribute-value matrices play in linguistic theory. In particular, attribute-value matrices in HPSG do not always mean the same thing. In the case of traces, the matrix is used to define traces as a limit: traces are *all signs* that fit certain criteria. In other cases, e.g., in a statement of the Head Feature Principle, an attribute-value matrix is used as a commutative diagram: whatever we mean by *sign* and *phrase*, certain facts hold of them. This difference is not well distinguished in current formalizations of HPSG.

A substantive word, by the way, is a word, the head value of which is substantive:

(24)
$$\left(\begin{array}{c} subst\text{-}wrd : \begin{bmatrix} \text{SUBST-WRD} & word \end{bmatrix}, \\[2ex] substantive \\ \downarrow \text{SUBSTANTIVE} \\[1ex] word \xrightarrow[\text{WORD|HEAD}]{} head \end{array} \right) .$$

4.7 The ID Principle

The sort *hdd-phr* decomposes into exactly four cases:

(25)
$$\left(\begin{bmatrix} hd\text{-}comp\text{-}phr & \text{HD-COMP-PHR} \\ hd\text{-}mrk\text{-}phr & \text{HD-MRK-PHR} \\ hd\text{-}adj\text{-}phr & \text{HD-ADJ-PHR} \\ hd\text{-}fllr\text{-}phr & \text{HD-FLLR-PHR} \end{bmatrix} : hdd\text{-}phr, \emptyset \right) .$$

4.7.1 The Head Marker Schema

Every sign has a "marking" characteristic.

(26) $\qquad sign : \begin{bmatrix} \text{MARKING} & marking \end{bmatrix}$

A head marker phrase has a distinguished daughter, which must be a word; this daughter is called the marker daughter.

(27) $\qquad hd\text{-}mrk\text{-}phr : \begin{bmatrix} \text{MRK-DTR} & sign \end{bmatrix}$

(28) $\qquad (\text{MKR-DTR} : hd\text{-}mrk\text{-}phr \rightarrow sign) \succeq (\text{WORD} : word \rightarrow sign)$

Also in a head marker phrase, the head daughter is a phrase and there are no complement daughters.

(29)
$$\begin{array}{c} (\text{HD-MRK-PHR|HD-DTR} : hd\text{-}mrk\text{-}phr \rightarrow sign) \\ \succeq (\text{PHRASE} : phrase \rightarrow sign) \end{array}$$

(30)
$$\begin{array}{c} (\text{HD-MRK-PHR|COMP-DRTS} : hd\text{-}mrk\text{-}phr \rightarrow L[sign]) \\ \succeq (\text{nil} : 1 \rightarrow L[sign]) \end{array}$$

In a head marker phrase, the phrase's marking characteristic is the same as that of the marker daughter.

(31)

$$
\begin{array}{ccc}
 & \text{HD-MRK-PHR}|\text{PHRASE} & \\
hd\text{-}mrk\text{-}phr & \longrightarrow & sign \\
\text{MRKR-DTR} \downarrow & & \downarrow \text{MARKER} \\
sign & \xrightarrow[\text{MARKER}]{} & sign
\end{array}
$$

Furthermore, in a non-marker head phrase, the phrase's marking characteristic is the same as that of the head daughter.

(32)

$$
\begin{array}{ccc}
 & \text{HD-COMP-PHR}|\text{PHRASE} & \\
hd\text{-}comp\text{-}phr & \longrightarrow & sign \\
p \downarrow & & \downarrow \text{MARKER} \\
sign & \xrightarrow[\text{MARKER}]{} & sign
\end{array}
$$

where p abbreviates the arrow

$$\text{HD-COMP-PHR}|\text{HD-DTR}.$$

The sorts $hd\text{-}adj\text{-}phr$ and $hd\text{-}fllr\text{-}phr$ have similar constraints.

4.7.2 The Head Adjunct Schema

A head adjunct phrase has a distinguished head adjunct daughter. A sign has a MODIFIER feature.

(33) $\qquad hd\text{-}adj\text{-}phr : \begin{bmatrix} \text{ADJUNCT-DTR} & sign \end{bmatrix}$

(34) $\qquad sign : \begin{bmatrix} \text{MOD} & synsem \end{bmatrix}$

The MOD of an adjunct daughter is the same as the SYNSEM of the head daughter.

(35)

$$
\begin{array}{ccc}
 & \text{HD-ADJ-PHR}|\text{HD-DTR} & \\
hd\text{-}adj\text{-}phr & \longrightarrow & sign \\
\text{ADJUNCT-DTR} \downarrow & & \downarrow \text{SYNSEM} \\
sign & \xrightarrow[\text{MOD}]{} & synsem
\end{array}
$$

4.7.3 The Filler Head Schema

A head filler phrase has a distinguished daughter, called the filler daughter:

(36) $\qquad hd\text{-}fllr\text{-}phr : \begin{bmatrix} \text{FLLR-DTR} & sign \end{bmatrix} .$

In a head filler phrase, the head daughter is a finite verb with an empty subcategorization list and an inherited slash value that contains the filler daughter's local value. Let p abbreviate HD-FLLR-PHR|HD-DTR and q abbreviate $\langle p|\text{HDD-PHR}|\text{INHERITED}|\text{SLASH}, \text{FLLR-DTR}|\text{LOCAL}\rangle$. Then

(37) $\quad (p|\text{HEAD} : hd\text{-}fllr\text{-}phr \to head) \succeq (\text{FIN-VERB} : fin\text{-}verb \to head)$

(38) $\quad (p|\text{SUBCAT} : hd\text{-}fllr\text{-}phr \to \mathsf{L}[synsem]) \succeq (\mathsf{nil} : 1 \to \mathsf{L}[synsem])$

(39)
$$
\begin{array}{ccc}
\textit{hd-fllr-phr} & \xrightarrow{\;p\;} & \textit{sign} \\
{\scriptstyle q}\Big\downarrow & & \Big\downarrow{\scriptstyle \text{INERITED}|\text{SLASH}} \\
[\text{P}[\textit{local}] \times \textit{local}] & \xrightarrow[{[\text{id}\times\{\_\}]|\cup}]{} & \text{P}[\textit{local}]
\end{array}
$$

4.7.4 The Complement Schemata

The sort *hd-comp-phr* decomposes into three cases:

(40)
$$
\left(
\begin{bmatrix}
\textit{hs-phr} & \text{HS-PHR} \\
\textit{hc-phr} & \text{HC-PHR} \\
\textit{hsc-phr} & \text{HSC-PHR}
\end{bmatrix}
: \textit{hd-comp-phr}, \emptyset
\right)
$$

corresponding to the Head-Subject Schema, the Head-Complement Schema and the Head-Subject-Complement Schema.

In the Head-Subject Schema, the subcategorization list is empty, the head daughter is a phrase, and there is exactly one complement daughter.

(41)
$$
\begin{array}{c}
(\text{HS-PHR}|\text{HD-COMP-PHR}|\text{HDD-PHR}|\text{SUBCAT} : \textit{hs-phr} \to \mathsf{L}[\textit{synsem}]) \\
\succeq (\text{nil} : 1 \to \mathsf{L}[\textit{synsem}])
\end{array}
$$

(42)
$$
\begin{array}{c}
(\text{HS-PHR}|\text{HD-COMP-PHR}|\text{HD-DTR} : \textit{hs-phr} \to \mathsf{L}[\textit{sign}]) \\
\succeq (\text{PHRASE} : \textit{phrase} \to \textit{sign})
\end{array}
$$

(43)
$$
\begin{array}{c}
(\text{HS-PHR}|\text{HD-COMP-PHR}|\text{COMP-DTRS} : \textit{hs-phr} \to \mathsf{L}[\textit{sign}]) \\
\succeq (\langle \text{id}, \Diamond|\text{nil}\rangle\,|\text{cons} : \textit{sign} \to \mathsf{L}[\textit{sign}])
\end{array}
$$

In the Head-Complement Schema, the subcategorization list is of length one and the head daughter is a word.

(44)
$$
\begin{array}{c}
(\text{HC-PHR}|\text{HD-COMP-PHR}|\text{COMP-DTRS} : \textit{hc-phr} \to \mathsf{L}[\textit{sign}]) \\
\succeq (\langle \text{id}, \Diamond|\text{nil}\rangle\,|\text{cons} : \textit{sign} \to \mathsf{L}[\textit{sign}])
\end{array}
$$

(45)
$$
\begin{array}{c}
(\text{HC-PHR}|\text{HD-COMP-PHR}|\text{HD-DTR} : \textit{hc-phr} \to \textit{sign}) \\
\succeq (\text{WORD} : \textit{word} \to \textit{sign})
\end{array}
$$

The Head-Subject-Complement Schema requires the subcategorization list to be empty and the head daughter to be a word.

(46)
$$
\begin{array}{c}
(\text{HSC-PHR}|\text{HD-COMP-PHR}|\text{COMP-DTRS} : \textit{hsc-phr} \to \mathsf{L}[\textit{sign}]) \\
\succeq (\text{nil} : 1 \to \mathsf{L}[\textit{sign}])
\end{array}
$$

(47)
$$
\begin{array}{c}
(\text{HSC-PHR}|\text{HD-COMP-PHR}|\text{HD-DTR} : \textit{hsc-phr} \to \textit{sign}) \\
\succeq (\text{WORD} : \textit{word} \to \textit{sign})
\end{array}
$$

4.8 Coordination

To formalize coordination, suppose that coordinate phrases are a distinct sort of phrase

(48)
$$
\begin{bmatrix} \textit{coord-phr} & \text{COORD-PHR} \end{bmatrix} : \textit{phrase}
$$

and that a coordinate phrase possesses a list of conjunct daughters

(49)
$$
\textit{coord-phr} : \begin{bmatrix} \text{CONJ-DTRS} & \mathsf{L}[\textit{sign}] \end{bmatrix}.
$$

Furthermore, suppose that every sign has a coordinate characteristic

(50) $\qquad sign: \begin{bmatrix} \text{COORD} & coord \end{bmatrix}$.

With these assumptions, a coordination principle can be formulated in analogy to the Head Feature Principle.

Let A, B and C be objects and $f : A \to B$ be an arrow in category $\mathcal{A}$ so that B and C have list objects L_B and L_C. Then it is possible, provided the necessary limits and universal relations exist, to define an arrow $r_f : A \times L_C \to L_B$ so that for all $g : D \to A$,

$$r_f \circ (g \times \mathsf{nil}) = \mathsf{nil} \circ \pi'$$
$$r_f \circ (g \times \mathsf{cons}) = \mathsf{cons} \circ (g \times r_f) \circ \langle \pi, \langle \pi, \pi' \circ \pi' \rangle \rangle$$

The idea is that r_f produces a list of the same length as its second argument, by duplicating its first argument. Because this is definable using only finite limits and universal relations, for every path $p : \sigma \to \rho$ in $\mathcal{H}$ and every interpretation I, the arrow $r_{I(p)}$ can be given a canonical name, say $\mathsf{rep}[p]$ in $\mathcal{H}$ so that $I(\mathsf{rep}[p]) = r_{I(p)}$. In the present formulation of $L(\mathcal{H})$, this entails introducing several arrows that are used only in the definition of $\mathsf{rep}[p]$. A richer language for $\mathcal{H}$ could eliminate the need for the extra arrows without increasing the logical strength of $L(\mathcal{H})$.

Now the Coordination Principle is

(51)
$$\begin{array}{ccc}
\text{coord-phr} & \xrightarrow{\ \ p\ \ } & [sign \times \mathsf{L}[sign]] \\
{\scriptstyle\text{COORD-DTRS}}\downarrow & & \downarrow{\scriptstyle\mathsf{rep}[\text{COORD}]} \\
\mathsf{L}[sign] & \xrightarrow[\mathsf{map}[\text{COORD}]]{} & \mathsf{L}[coord]
\end{array}$$

where p abbreviates $\langle \text{COORD-PHR}, \text{COORD-DTRS} \rangle$. This principle says simply that the coordinate characteristic of the whole phrase is duplicated in the coordinate characteristic of all conjuncts. Of course, this says nothing of the details of *coord*, just as the Head Feature Principle says nothing about the details of *head*. This, nevertheless, provides a similar framework for formalizing the interactions between a coordinate phrase and its daughters.

4.9 Other Principles

The other principles of HPSG, such as the Nonlocal Feature Principle, the SPEC Principle and so on, are also easily formulated in terms of well-formed constraints. Some of the more intricate conditions appear in the Binding Theory. For example, obliqueness can be formulated as a table consisting of two arrows LESS : *obliqueness* $\to$ *synsem* and MORE : *obliqueness* $\to$ *synsem*, which is obtained as a limit of a diagram similar to the diagram used in defining *trace* in that it employs a "witness" subcategorization list that must belong to some word.

O-command and o-binding are more difficult in that they require that the LOCAL values of two *synsem* values be distinct. This condition can also be stated precisely as the requirement that an initial object 0 (definable by an empty co-limit diagram) be the limit of

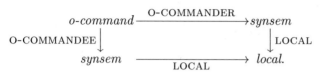

Then the table consisting of O-COMMANDER and O-COMMANDEE represents a relation on *synsem* in which two values are unrelated if their LOCAL values are the same. The other aspects of o-command are formulated by techniques used in the earlier sections.

5 Equivalent Theories

The theory presented in the previous section reflects many choices that seem to have no substantial bearing on linguistic claims. If the thesis of this paper is correct, that HPSG is essentially category-theoretic in nature, then the theories based on other choices should be equivalent. For example, in the Marking Schema, I chose to regard the arrow MKR-DTR as an arrow from *hd-mrk-phr* to *sign* (Constraint 27), rather than to *word*. This seems to be an inconsequential choice, as I then require that MKR-DTR factor through WORD (Constraint 28). Suppose that we replace these constraints by

$$hd\text{-}mrk\text{-}phr : \begin{bmatrix} \text{MKR-DTR} & word \end{bmatrix}$$

and then replace all other occurrences of MKR-DTR by MKR-DTR|WORD. If T denotes the $\mathcal{H}$-theory as presented above, and T' the modified $\mathcal{H}'$-theory (notice that the formal HPSG category changes as well), then it is easy to check that $\mathbf{Mod}_{\mathcal{H}}^{\mathcal{A}}(T)$ is equivalent to $\mathbf{Mod}_{\mathcal{H}'}^{\mathcal{A}}(T')$.

Similarly, any occurrence of

$$[\sigma \times [\rho \times \tau]]$$

may be replaced by

$$[\rho \times [\sigma \times \tau]]$$

or any other permutation without changing the resulting categories of models up to equivalence.

In the ID Principle, I assume that *hd-comp-phr* is one of the cases comprising *hdd-phr* and that *hd-comp-phr* is decomposed into hd-subject, hd-complement and hd-complement-subject. This more or less follows the exposition in PS94. But suppose it had never occurred to Pollard and Sag that the three cases of head complement phrases somehow constitute a natural subclass of headed phrases. Then I might as well have stated that

$$\left(\begin{bmatrix} hs\text{-}phr & \text{HS-PHR} \\ hc\text{-}phr & \text{HC-PHR} \\ hcs\text{-}phr & \text{HCS-PHR} \\ hd\text{-}mrk\text{-}phr & \text{HD-MRK-PHR} \\ hd\text{-}fllr\text{-}phr & \text{HD-FLLR-PHR} \\ hd\text{-}ajdunct\text{-}phr & \text{HD-ADJ-PHR} \end{bmatrix} : hdd\text{-}phr, \emptyset \right)$$

and written the complement schemata according to this different "geometry." Again, it is easy to check that the resulting theory has an equivalent category of models to the original theory.

In contrast, it is often thought that the choice between "features" and "sub-sorts" is inconsequential. But this is not always so. Consider

$$s : \begin{bmatrix} \text{F1} & t1 \\ \text{F2} & t2 \end{bmatrix}$$

and

$$\left(\begin{bmatrix} u1 & \text{U1} \\ u2 & \text{U2} \end{bmatrix} : t1, \emptyset \right).$$

In words, s has two features F1 and F2 and the values appropriate for F1 fall into two sub-sorts $u1$ and $u2$. One might suppose that the following is equivalent.

$$\left(\begin{bmatrix} s1 & \text{S1} \\ s2 & \text{S2} \end{bmatrix} : s, \emptyset \right),$$

$$s1 : \begin{bmatrix} \text{F1} & u1 \\ \text{F2} & \text{T2} \end{bmatrix}$$

and

$$s2 : \begin{bmatrix} \text{F1} & u2 \\ \text{F2} & \text{T2} \end{bmatrix}.$$

That is, one might suppose that it makes no difference whether (i) s is regarded as having two features, one of which decomposes as two cases, or (ii) s is regarded as decomposing into two cases, the first with features corresponding to the first case in (i) and the other with features corresponding to the second case if (i). But in fact, generally these two collections of constraints are not equivalent. If we take s in the first case to be a product of $t1$ and $t2$, then equivalence would require that a law of distributivity hold between products and co-products: $(A \times (B + C)) \cong (A \times B) + (A \times C)$. But no such law holds in a topos. Thus, a theory based on one analysis of s may have models that do not correspond to any model of the theory based on the other analysis.

From these examples, it is clear that some of the choices one makes that traditionally have come under the rubric of "feature geometry" are substantive, others not. What is important from the perspective of this paper, is that the distinction can be made on the grounds of category equivalence.

6   Conclusions

I have not written anything about a proof theory for $L(\mathcal{H})$, but of course a proof theory can be developed. Take $T \Rightarrow \theta$ for theory T and constraint θ to mean just what it usually means, θ holds in every model of T. This provides the conventional notion of semantic entailment. Immediately, one sees certain sound rules of inference based on the fact that limits and co-limits produce unique arrows under the right circumstances. So a sound proof system is quite easily formulated. The second thing to notice is that $\Rightarrow$ enjoys compactness: $T \Rightarrow \theta$ if and only if $T_0 \Rightarrow \theta$ for some finite $T_0 \subseteq T$. This fact is easily borrowed from first-order logic because the constraints can be stated in first-order. With compactness there is hope for a complete proof system, but I can only conjecture as to its existence. Certainly, elementary topos theory is undecidable, but the constraints that I allow are significantly weaker than all of topos theory. Thus, it seems quite plausible that a complete proof system for $\Rightarrow$ exists.

The relation between attribute-value matrices and limit constraints is an interesting one. The translation from the matrix describing traces in PS94 to the limit constraint used here was *ad hoc*. But the idea is quite simple at the intuitive level, and I am presently working on implementing a trans-lation algorithm from attribute-value matrices to limit constraints. The result will show clearly the role of attribute-value matrices as a descriptive mechanism within the category-theoretic perspective. Not all limit con-straints will arise as the result of a translated attribute-value matrix. So, this raises an empirical question for this research: are the limit constraints obtained from attribute-value matrices sufficient to formulate all of HPSG? If not, that fact would be a telling blow to current formalizations for HPSG. If so, then I would be interested to understand why.

I have not exploited the fact that models can be constructed in any topos, except as a way to verify my contention that HPSG is essentially category-theoretic. But models in toposes other than **Set** may prove to be useful tools for investigating the interactions of principles. For example, the product of a family of toposes is a topos. So one can check that a family of models of an $\mathcal{H}$-theory T is a model (in the product topos). This gives us the possibility of producing models of T in which specific con-straints fail, in analogy with classical model theory. In fact, toposes enjoy a construction similar to the ultra-product construction of classical model theory. And model-theoretic forcing (Freyd and Scedrov 1990) arguments are also available in toposes. To the extent that we actually believe that language universal principles are axioms of an empirical science, we should be very interested in these sorts of constructions.

In this paper, I have set out a radically different view of what constitutes a model of HPSG and, toward that end, have proposed a new formalization of HPSG. In contrast to other attempts at developing a model theory for HPSG, I do not assume feature structures to be fundamental. Rather I assume that the content of individual principles, viewed as independent axioms of a logical theory, is the main idea to be explicated by the model theory. Because feature-based model theory for HPSG relies on appropriateness conditions to fix a feature geometry, it is incapable of giving a reasonable account of individual principles. In the category-theoretic view taken here, the interactions between principles (the usual province of feature geometry) can be factored away from the statements of the principles themselves. This greatly increases the potential for a genuinely modular development of a grammar. So, I expect the investment in model theory that this paper represents to return benefits in the area of grammar engineering.

Acknowledgments

The editors, Patrick Blackburn and Maarten de Rijke, were exceptionally patient with me as I wrote this paper. Without their encouragement, I doubt that it would ever have seen the light of day. I cannot express my gratitude enough. Also, I wish to thank two anonymous reviewers for extremely helpful remarks regarding the presentation of this work, and for a kind assessment of the paper's worth. Needless to say, any remaining errors or clumsiness in arguments belong to me alone.

References

Aït-Kaci, Hassan, and R. Nasr. 1986. Logic and Inheritance. In *Proceedings of the 13th ACM Symposium on Principles of Programming Languages.*

Backofen, Rolf, and Gert Smolka. 1993. A Complete and Recursive Feature Theory. In 31st *Annual Meeting of the Association for Computational Linguistics*, 193–200.

Blackburn, Patrick. 1994. Structures, Language and Translations: The Structural Approach to Feature Logics. In *Constraints, Language and Computation*, ed. M. A. Rosner, C.J. Rupp, and R. L. Johnson. 1–27. Academic Press.

Carpenter, Bob. 1992. *The Logic of Typed Feature Structures with Applications to Unification-Based Grammars, Logic Programming and Constraint Resolution.* Cambridge Tracts in Theoretical Computer Science, Vol. 32. New York: Cambridge University Press.

Cohen, Paul J. 1966. *Set Theory and the Continuum Hypothesis.* Benjamin-Cummings.

Cooper, Richard. 1990. *Classification-Based Phrase Structure Grammar: An Extended Revised Version of HPSG.* Doctoral dissertation, University of Edinburgh.

Freyd, Peter J., and Andre Scedrov. 1990. *Categories, Allegories*. North-Holland.

Henschel, Renate. 1991. The Morphological Principle: A Proposal for Treating Russian Morphology Within an HPSG Framework. In *GWAI-91, 15. Fachtagung für künstliche Intelligenz*, ed. Th. Christaller, 116–125. Bonn.

Johnson, Mark. 1988. *Attribute-Value Logic and the Theory of Grammar*. CSLI Lecture Notes, No. 14. University of Chicago Press.

Kasper, Robert T., and William C. Rounds. 1990. The Logic of Feature Structures. *Linguistics and Philosophy* 13(1).

Keller, Frank. 1995. Towards an Account of Extraposition in HPSG. In *Proceedings of the Ninth Meeting of the European ACL*. Dublin. Association for Computational Linguistics.

King, Paul John. 1989. *A Logical Formalism for HPSG*. Doctoral dissertation, University of Manchester.

King, Paul John. 1994. An Expanded Logical Formalism for Head-Driven Phrase Structure Grammar. Technical report. Universität Stuttgart.

Moshier, M. Andrew. 1988. *Extensions to Unification Grammar for the Description of Programming Languages*. Doctoral dissertation, University of Michigan.

Moshier, M. Andrew, and Carl Pollard. 1994. The Domain of Set-Valued Feature Structures. *Linguistics and Philosophy* 17:607–631.

Pierce, Benjamin C. 1991. *Basic Category Theory for Computer Scientists*. MIT Press.

Pollard, Carl, and Ivan A. Sag. 1987. *Information-Based Syntax and Semantics, Vol. 1*. Lecture Notes, No. 13. Stanford University: CSLI Publications. Distributed by University of Chicago Press.

Pollard, Carl, and Ivan A. Sag. 1994. *Head-Driven Phrase Structure Grammar*. Chicago: University of Chicago Press.

Rentier, Gerrit. 1994. Dutch Cross Serial Dependencies in HPSG. In *Proceedings of Coling 94*. Kyoto.

6

On Descriptive Complexity, Language Complexity, and GB

JAMES ROGERS

ABSTRACT. We introduce $L^2_{K,P}$, a monadic second-order language for reasoning about trees which characterizes the strongly Context-Free Languages in the sense that a set of finite trees is definable in $L^2_{K,P}$ iff it is (modulo a projection) a Local Set — the set of derivation trees generated by a Context Free Grammar. This provides a flexible approach to establishing language-theoretic complexity results for formalisms that are based on systems of well-formedness constraints on trees. We demonstrate this technique by sketching two such results for Government and Binding Theory. First, we show that *free-indexation*, the mechanism assumed to mediate a variety of agreement and binding relationships in GB, is not definable in $L^2_{K,P}$ and therefore not enforcible by CFGs. Second, we show how, in spite of this limitation, a reasonably complete GB account of English D- and S-Structure can be defined in $L^2_{K,P}$. Consequently, the language licensed by that account is strongly context-free. We illustrate some of the issues involved in establishing this result by looking at the definition, in $L^2_{K,P}$, of chains. The limitations of this definition provide some insight into the types of natural linguistic principles that correspond to higher levels of language complexity. We close with some speculation on the possible significance of these results for generative linguistics.

1 Introduction

One of the more significant developments in generative linguistics over the last decade has been the development of *constraint-based* formalisms — grammar formalisms that define languages not in terms of the derivations of the strings in the language, but rather in terms of well-formedness conditions on the structures analyzing their syntax. Because traditional notions

Specifying Syntactic Structures
P. Blackburn and M. de Rijke, eds.
Copyright © 1997, CSLI Publications.

of language complexity are generally defined in terms of rewriting mechanisms complexity of the languages licensed by these formalisms can be difficult to determine.

A particular example, one that will be a focus of this paper, is Government and Binding Theory. While this is often modeled as a specific range of Transformational Grammars, the connection between the underlying grammar mechanism and the language a given GB theory licenses is quite weak. In an extreme view, one can take the underlying mechanism simply to generate the set of all finite trees (labeled with some alphabet of symbols)[1] while the grammatical theory is actually embodied in a set of principles that filter out the ill-formed analyses. As a result, it has been difficult to establish language complexity results for GB theories, even at the level of the recursive (Lapointe 1977, Berwick 1984) or context-sensitive (Berwick and Weinberg 1984) languages.

That language complexity results for GB should be difficult to come by is hardly surprising. The development of GB coincided with the abandonment, by GB theorists, of the presumption that the traditional language complexity classes would provide any useful characterization of the human languages. This followed, at least in part, from the recognition of the fact that the structural properties that characterize natural languages as a class may well not be those that can be distinguished by existing language complexity classes. There was a realization that the theory needed to be driven by the regularities identifiable in natural languages, rather than those suggested by abstract mechanisms. Berwick characterized this approach as aiming to "discover the properties of natural languages first, and then characterize them formally." (Berwick 1984, pg. 190)

But formal language theory still has much to offer to generative linguistics. Language complexity provides one of the most useful measures with which to compare languages and grammar formalisms. We have an array of results establishing the boundaries of these classes, and, while many of the results do not seem immediately germane to natural languages, even seemingly artificial diagnostics (like the copy language $\{ww \mid w \in (ab)^*\}$) can provide the basis for useful classification results (such as Shieber's argument for the non-context-freeness of Swiss-German (Shieber 1985)). More importantly, characterization results for language complexity classes tend to be in terms of the *structure* of languages, and the structure of natural language, while hazy, is something that can be studied more or less directly. Thus there is a realistic expectation of finding empirical evidence falsifying a given hypothesis. (Although such evidence may well be difficult to find, as witnessed by the history of less successful attempts to establish

---

[1]Or, following a strictly derivational approach, the set of all structures consisting of a triple of finite trees along with a representation of PF.

results such as Shieber's (Pullum and Gazdar 1982, Pullum 1984).) Further, language complexity classes characterize, along one dimension, the *types* of resources necessary to parse or recognize a language. Results of this type for the class of human languages, then, make specific predictions about the nature of the human language faculty, predictions that, at least in principle, can both inform and be informed by progress in uncovering the physical nature of that faculty.

In this paper we discuss a flexible and quite powerful approach to establishing language complexity results for formalisms based on systems of constraints on trees. In Section 2 we introduce a logical language, $L^2_{K,P}$, capable of encoding such constraints lucidly. The key merit of such an encoding is the fact that sets of trees are definable in $L^2_{K,P}$ if and only if they are strongly context-free. Thus definability in $L^2_{K,P}$ characterizes the strongly context-free languages. This is our primary result, and we develop it in Section 3.

We have used this technique to establish both inclusion and exclusion results for a variety of linguistic principles within the GB framework (Rogers 1994). In the remainder of the paper we demonstrate some of these. In Section 4 we sketch a proof of the non-definability of free-indexation, a mechanism that is nearly ubiquitous in GB theories. A consequence of this result is that languages that are licensed by theories that necessarily employ free-indexation are outside of the class of CFLs. Despite the unavailability of free-indexation, we are able to capture a mostly standard GB account of English D- and S-Structure within $L^2_{K,P}$. Thus we are able to show that the language licensed by this particular GB theory is strongly context-free. In Section 5 we illustrate some of the issues involved in establishing this result, particularly in light of the non-definability of free-indexation. We close, finally, with some speculation on the possible significance of these results for generative linguistics.

2 $L^2{}_{K,P}$

The idea of employing mathematical logic to provide a precise formalization of GB theories is a natural one. This has been done, for instance, by Johnson (1989) and Stabler (1992) using first-order logic (or the Horn-clause fragment of first-order logic) and by Kracht (1995) using a fragment of dynamic logic. What distinguishes the formalization we discuss is the fact that it is carried out in a language which can only define strongly context-free sets. The fact that the formalization is possible, then, establishes a relatively strong language complexity result for the theory we capture.

We have, therefore, two conflicting criteria for our language. It must be expressive enough to capture the relationships that define the trees licensed by the theory, but it must be restricted sufficiently to be no more expressive than Context-Free Grammars. In keeping with the first of these our language is intended to support, as transparently as possible, the kinds of reasoning about trees typical of linguistic applications. It includes binary predicates for the usual structural relationships between the nodes in the trees — parent (immediate domination), domination (reflexive), proper domination (irreflexive), left-of (linear precedence) and equality. In addition, it includes an arbitrary array of monadic predicate constants — constants naming specific subsets of the nodes in the tree. These can be thought of as atomic labels. The formula $NP(x)$, for instance, is true at every node labeled NP. It includes, also, a similar array of individual constants — constants naming specific individuals in the tree — although these prove to be of limited usefulness. There are two sorts of variables as well — those that range over nodes in the tree and those that range over arbitrary subsets of those nodes (thus this is a monadic second-order language). Crucially, though, this is all the language includes. By restricting ourselves to this language we restrict ourselves to working with properties that can be expressed in terms of these basic predicates.

To be precise, the actual language we use in a given situation depends on the sets of constants in use in that context. We are concerned then with a family of languages, parameterized by the sets of individual and set constants they employ.

Definition 2.1 For K a set of individual constant symbols, and P a set of propositional constant symbols, both countable, let $L^2_{K,P}$ be the language built up from K, P, a fixed countably infinite set of *ranked* variables $X = X^0 \cup X^1$, and the symbols:

$\lhd, \lhd^*, \lhd^+, \prec$ —

> two place predicates, *parent*, *domination*, *proper domination* and *left-of* respectively,

$\approx$ — equality predicate,

$\land, \lor, \neg, \ldots, \forall, \exists, (,), [,]$ —

> usual logical connectives, quantifiers, and grouping symbols.

We use infix notation for the fixed predicate constants $\lhd, \lhd^*, \lhd^+, \prec$, and $\approx$. We use lower-case for individual variables and constants, and upper-case for set variables and predicate constants. Further, we will say $X(x)$ to assert that the individual assigned to the variable x is included in the set assigned to the variable X. So, for instance,

$$(\forall y)[x \lhd^* y \to X(y)]$$

asserts that the set assigned to X includes every node dominated by the node assigned to x.

Truth, for these languages, is defined relative to a specific class of models. The basic models are just ordinary structures interpreting the individual and predicate constants.

Definition 2.2 *Models* for the language $L_{K,P}$ are tuples:

$$\langle \mathcal{U}, \mathcal{I}, \mathcal{P}, \mathcal{D}, \mathcal{L}, \mathcal{R}_p \rangle_{p \in P},$$

where: $\mathcal{U}$ is a non-empty universe,

$\mathcal{I}$ is a function from K to $\mathcal{U}$,

$\mathcal{P}$, $\mathcal{D}$, and $\mathcal{L}$ are binary relations over $\mathcal{U}$

    (interpreting $\lhd$, $\lhd^*$, and $\prec$ respectively),

for each $p \in P$, $\mathcal{R}_p$ is a subset of $\mathcal{U}$ interpreting p.

If the domain of $\mathcal{I}$ is empty (i.e., the model is for a language $L_{\emptyset,P}$) we will generally omit it. Models for $L_{\emptyset,\emptyset}$, then, are tuples $\langle \mathcal{U}, \mathcal{P}, \mathcal{D}, \mathcal{L} \rangle$.

The intended class of these models are, in essence, labeled *tree domains*. A tree domain is the set of node addresses generated by giving the address ϵ to the root and giving the children of the node at address w addresses (in order, left to right) $w \cdot 0, w \cdot 1, \ldots$, where the centered dot denotes concatenation.[2] Tree domains, then, are particular subsets of $\mathbb{N}^*$. ($\mathbb{N}$ is the set of natural numbers.)

Definition 2.3 A *tree domain* is a non-empty set $T \subseteq \mathbb{N}^*$, satisfying, for all $u, v \in \mathbb{N}^*$ and $i, j \in \mathbb{N}$, the conditions:

$\boldsymbol{TD1}$ $uv \in T \Rightarrow u \in T,$ $\boldsymbol{TD2}$ $ui \in T, \ j < i \Rightarrow uj \in T.$

Every tree domain has a natural interpretation as a model for $L_{\emptyset,\emptyset}$ (which interprets only the fixed predicate symbols).

Definition 2.4 The *natural interpretation* of a tree domain T is a model $T^\natural = \langle T, \mathcal{P}^T, \mathcal{D}^T, \mathcal{L}^T \rangle$, where:

$$
\begin{aligned}
\mathcal{P}^T &= \{\langle u, ui \rangle \in T \times T \mid u \in \mathbb{N}^*, i \in \mathbb{N} \}, \\
\mathcal{D}^T &= \{\langle u, uv \rangle \in T \times T \mid u, v \in \mathbb{N}^* \}, \\
\mathcal{L}^T &= \{\langle uiv, ujw \rangle \in T \times T \mid u, v, w \in \mathbb{N}^*, i < j \in \mathbb{N} \}.
\end{aligned}
$$

The structures of interest to us are just those models that are the natural interpretation of a tree domain, augmented with interpretations of additional individual and predicate constants.[3]

In general, satisfaction is relative to an assignment mapping each individual variable into a member of $\mathcal{U}$ and each predicate variable into a subset of $\mathcal{U}$. We use

$$M \models \phi\,[s]$$

to denote that a model M satisfies a formula ϕ with an assignment s. The notation

$$M \models \phi$$

---

[2] We will usually dispense with the dot and denote concatenation by juxtaposition.

[3] A partial axiomatization of this class of models is given in Rogers (1994).

asserts that M models ϕ with any assignment. When ϕ is a sentence (has no unbound variables) we will usually use this form.

Proper domination is a defined predicate:

$$M \models x \triangleleft^+ y\,[s] \Leftrightarrow M \models x \triangleleft^* y, x \not\approx y\,[s].$$

2.1 Definability in $L^2{}_{K,P}$

We are interested in the subsets of the class of intended models which are definable in $L^2_{K,P}$ using any sets K and P. If Φ is a set of sentences in a language $L^2_{K,P}$, we will use the notation **Mod**(Φ) to denote the set of *trees*, i.e., intended models, that satisfy all of the sentences in Φ. We are interested, then, in the sets of trees that are **Mod**(Φ) for some such Φ. In developing our definitions we can use individual and monadic predicates freely (since K and P can always be taken to be the sets that actually occur in our definitions) and we can quantify over individuals and sets of individuals. We will also use non-monadic predicates and even higher-order predicates, e.g., properties of subsets, but only those that can be *explicitly* defined, that is, those which can be eliminated by a simple syntactic replacement of the predicate by its definition.

This use of explicitly defined predicates is crucial to the transparency of definitions in $L^2_{K,P}$. We might, for instance, define a simplified version of government in three steps:

$$
\begin{aligned}
\text{Branches}(x) \quad &\leftrightarrow \quad (\exists y, z)[x \triangleleft y \wedge x \triangleleft z \wedge y \not\approx z] \\
\text{C-Command}(x,y) \quad &\equiv \quad \neg x \triangleleft^* y \wedge \neg y \triangleleft^* x \wedge \\
&\qquad (\forall z)[(z \triangleleft^+ x \wedge \text{Branches}(z)) \to z \triangleleft^+ y] \\
\text{Governs}(x,y) \quad &\equiv \quad \text{C-Commands}(x,y) \wedge \\
&\qquad \neg(\exists z)[\text{Barrier}(z) \wedge z \triangleleft^+ y \wedge \neg z \triangleleft^+ x],
\end{aligned}
$$

in words, x governs y iff it c-commands y and no barrier intervenes between them. It c-commands y iff neither x nor y dominates the other and every branching node that properly dominates x also properly dominates y. Branches(x) is just a monadic predicate; it is within the language of $L^2_{K,P}$ (for suitable P) and its definition is simply a biconditional $L^2_{K,P}$ formula. In contrast, C-Command and Governs are non-monadic and do not occur in $L^2_{K,P}$. Their definitions, however, are ultimately in terms of monadic predicates and the fixed predicates (parent, etc.) only. One can replace each of their occurrences in a formula with the right hand side of their definitions and eventually derive a formula that *is* in $L^2_{K,P}$. We will reserve the use of $\equiv$ (in contrast to $\leftrightarrow$) for explicit definitions of non-monadic predicates.

Definitions can also use predicates expressing properties of sets and relations between sets, as long as those properties can be explicitly defined.

The subset relation, for instance can be defined:

$$\text{Subset}(X, Y) \equiv (\forall x)[X(x) \rightarrow Y(x)].$$

We can also capture the stronger notion of one set being partitioned by a collection of others:

$$\text{Partition}(\vec{X}, Y) \equiv$$
$$(\forall x) \left[\left(Y(x) \leftrightarrow \bigvee_{X \in \vec{X}} X(x) \right) \wedge \bigwedge_{X \in \vec{X}} \left[X(x) \rightarrow \bigwedge_{Z \in \vec{X} \setminus \{X\}} \neg Z(x) \right] \right].$$

Here $\vec{X}$ is a some sequence of set variables and $\bigvee_{X \in \vec{X}} X(x)$ is shorthand for the disjunction $X_0(x) \vee X_1(x) \cdots$ for all X_i in $\vec{X}$, etc. There is a distinct instance of Partiton for each sequence $\vec{X}$, although we can ignore distinctions between sequences of the same length. Finally, we note that finiteness is a definable property of subsets in our intended models. This follows from the fact that these models are linearly ordered by the *lexicographic order* relation:

$$x \preceq y \equiv x \vartriangleleft^* y \vee x \prec y.$$

and that every non-empty subset of such a model has a least element with respect to that order. A set of nodes, then, is finite iff each of its non-empty subsets has an upper-bound with respect to lexicographic order as well.

$$\text{Finite}(X) \equiv$$
$$(\forall Y) \left[(\text{Subset}(Y, X) \wedge (\exists x)[Y(x)]) \rightarrow (\exists x) \left[Y(x) \wedge (\forall y)[Y(y) \rightarrow y \preceq x] \right] \right].$$

These three second-order relations will play a role in the next section.

3   Characterizing the Local Sets

We can now give an example of a class of sets of trees that is definable in $L^2_{K,P}$ — the local sets (i.e., the sets of derivation trees generated by Context-Free Grammars). The idea behind the definition is simple. Given an arbitrary Context-Free Grammar, we can treat its terminal and non-terminal symbols as monadic predicate constants. The productions of the grammar, then, relate the label of a node to the number and labels of its children. If the set of productions for a non-terminal A, for instance, is

$$A \longrightarrow BC \mid AB \mid D$$

we can translate this as

$$(\forall x)[A(x) \rightarrow \quad ((\exists y_1, y_2)[\text{Children}(x, y_1, y_2) \wedge B(y_1) \wedge C(y_2)] \vee$$
$$(\exists y_1, y_2)[\text{Children}(x, y_1, y_2) \wedge A(y_1) \wedge B(y_2)] \vee$$
$$(\exists y_1)[\text{Children}(x, y_1) \wedge D(y_1)] \qquad)],$$

where

$$\text{Children}(x, y_1, \ldots, y_n) \equiv \bigwedge_{i \leq n}[x \vartriangleleft y_i] \wedge \bigwedge_{i < j \leq n}[y_i \prec y_j] \wedge$$
$$(\forall z)[x \vartriangleleft z \rightarrow \bigvee_{i \leq n}[z \approx y_i]].$$

We can collect such translations of all the productions of the grammar together with sentences requiring nodes labeled with terminal symbols to have no children, requiring the root to be labeled with the start symbol, requiring the sets of nodes labeled with the terminal and non-terminal symbols to partition the set of all nodes in the tree, and requiring that set of nodes to be finite. It is easy to show that the models of this set of sentences are all and only the derivation trees of the grammar.[4] In this way we get the first half of our characterization of the local sets.

Theorem 3.1 *The set of derivation trees generated by an arbitrary Context-Free Grammar is definable in $L^2_{K,P}$.*

It is, perhaps, not surprising that we can define the local sets with $L^2_{K,P}$. This is superficially quite a powerful language, allowing, as it does, a certain amount of second-order quantification. It is maybe more remarkable that, modulo a projection, the *only* sets of finite trees (with bounded branching) that are definable in $L^2_{K,P}$ are the local sets.

Theorem 3.2 *Every set of finite trees with bounded branching that is definable in $L^2_{K,P}$ is the projection of a set of trees generated by a finite set of Context-Free (string) Grammars.*

The proof hinges on the fact that one can translate formulae in $L^2_{K,P}$ into the language of SnS — the monadic second-order theory of multiple successor functions. This is the monadic second-order theory of the structure:

$$\mathcal{N}_n \stackrel{\text{def}}{=} \langle T_n, \lhd^*, \preceq, r_i \rangle_{i<n},$$

a generalization of the natural numbers with successor and less-than. The universe, T_n, is the complete n-branching tree domain. The relation $\lhd^*$ is domination, $\preceq$ is lexicographic order, and the functions r_i are the successor functions, each taking nodes into their i^{th} child ($w \mapsto wi$). Rabin (1969) showed that SnS is decidable for any $n \leq \omega$. One way of understanding his proof is via the observation that satisfying assignments for a formula $\phi(\vec{X})$, with free variables[5] among $\vec{X}$ can be understood as trees labeled with (subsets of) the variables in $\vec{X}$. A node is in the set assigned to X_i in $\vec{X}$ iff it is labeled with X_i. Rabin showed that, for any $\phi(\vec{X})$ in the language of SnS, the set of trees encoding the satisfying assignments for $\phi(\vec{X})$ in $\mathcal{N}_n$ is accepted by a particular type of finite-state automaton on infinite trees. We say that the set is *Rabin recognizable*. He goes on to show that emptiness of these sets is decidable. It follows that satisfiability of these formulae, and hence the theory SnS, is decidable.

---

[4] A more complete proof is given in Rogers (1994).

[5] We will assume, for simplicity, that only set variables occur free. Since individual variables can be re-interpreted as variables ranging over singleton sets, this is without loss of generality.

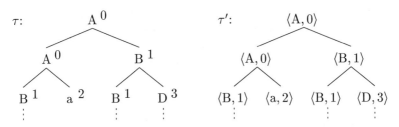

FIGURE 1 Proof of Theorem 3.2

For us, the key point is the fact that the sets encoding satisfying assignments are Rabin recognizable. It is not difficult to exhibit a syntactic transformation which, given any $\psi(\vec{X})$ in $L^2_{K,P}$, produces a formula $\phi(X_U, \vec{X}_P, \vec{X})$ in the language of SnS, where X_U is a new variable and $\vec{X}_P$ is a sequence of new variables (one for each of the finitely many predicates in P that occur in ψ) such that,

$$\mathcal{N}_n \models \phi[A_U, \vec{A}_P, \vec{A}]$$

iff

$$\left\langle A_U, \mathcal{P}^{A_U}, \mathcal{D}^{A_U}, \mathcal{L}^{A_U}, \vec{A}_P \right\rangle \models \psi[\vec{A}],$$

that is, the set A_U and the sequences of sets $\vec{A}_P$ and $\vec{A}$ form a satisfying assignment for ϕ in $\mathcal{N}_n$ iff the structure consisting of the universe A_U along with the natural interpretation of $\lhd$, $\lhd^*$, and $\prec$ on A_U, and the sets $\vec{A}_P$, satisfies ψ with the assignment taking $\vec{X}$ into $\vec{A}$. It follows that a set of trees is definable in $L^2_{K,P}$ iff they are Rabin recognizable.

If we restrict our attention to sets of finite trees, we can take Rabin's automata to be ordinary finite-state automata over finite trees (Gécseg and Steinby 1984), that is, the sets of finite trees that are definable in $L^2_{K,P}$ are simply *recognizable*. One can think of these automata as traversing the tree, top down, assigning states to the children of a node on the basis of a transition function that depends on the state of the node, its label, and the position of the child among its siblings. A tree is accepted if it can be labeled by the automaton in such a way that the root is labeled with a start state and the set of states labeling the leaves is one of a set of accepting sets of states. Every set of trees that is accepted in this way is the projection of a local set. To see this,[6] suppose that τ is a tree accepted by a tree automaton. Then there is some assignment of states to the nodes in τ that witnesses this fact. Suppose, for instance, τ is the tree of Figure 1, labeled as shown. Consider the tree τ' in which each node is labeled with a pair consisting of the label from τ and the state assigned to that node. It is easy

---

[6]This proof is evidently originally due to Thatcher (1967). In addition, Theorem 3.2 is implicit in the proof of a related theorem due to Doner (1970).

to show that, given a recognizable set of trees, one can construct a CFG to generate the corresponding set of trees labeled with pairs as in τ'. In the example, for instance, this would include, among others, the productions

$$\langle A,0 \rangle \longrightarrow \langle A,0 \rangle \langle B,1 \rangle \mid \langle B,1 \rangle \langle a,2 \rangle \mid \cdots$$
$$\langle B,1 \rangle \longrightarrow \langle B,1 \rangle \langle D,3 \rangle \mid \cdots$$
$$\vdots$$

The original set of trees is then the first projection of the set generated by this CFG.

Together, these two theorems give us our primary result.

Corollary 3.3 *A set of finite trees with bounded branching is local (modulo projection) iff it is definable in $L^2_{K,P}$.*

4 Non-Definability of Free Indexation

This characterization provides us with a powerful tool for establishing strong context-freeness of classes of languages that are defined by constraints on the structure of the trees analyzing the strings in the language. If one can show that the constraints defining such a set, or perhaps that any constraints in the class employed by a given formalism, can be defined within $L^2_{K,P}$ then the corresponding language or class of languages is strongly context-free. Much of the value of standard language complexity classes, on the other hand, comes from results that allow one to show that a given language or class of languages is not included in a particular complexity class. Such results are available here as well, in the form of non-definability results for $L^2_{K,P}$. One relatively easy way of establishing such results is by employing the contrapositive of Theorem 3.2. If one can show that a given predicate, when added to $L^2_{K,P}$ allows definition of known non-CF languages, then clearly that predicate properly extends the power of the language and cannot be definable. In this way, one can show that the predicate $\text{YieldsEq}_P(x,y)$ which holds between two nodes iff the yields of the subtrees rooted at those nodes are labeled identically w.r.t. P is not definable in $L^2_{K,P}$, for if it were one could define the copy language $\{ww \mid w \in (ab)^*\}$.

In this section we will explore an approach that is more difficult but is one of the most general — reduction from the monadic second-order theory of the grid — and will use it to demonstrate non-definability of free-indexation — a mechanism which shows up in a number of modules of GB.

The grid is the structure $G = \langle \mathbb{N}^2, O, r_0, r_1 \rangle$ where

$$O = \langle 0,0 \rangle$$
$$r_0(\langle x,y \rangle) = \langle x+1,y \rangle$$

$$r_1(\langle x, y \rangle) = \langle x, y+1 \rangle.$$

This is the structure of the (discrete) first quadrant. Note the similarity to $\mathcal{N}_2$, the structure of two successor functions. The key distinction is the fact that G satisfies the property

$$(\forall x)[r_0(r_1(x)) = r_1(r_0(x))],$$

that is, the horizontal successor of the vertical successor of a point is the same as the vertical successor of its horizontal successor. Let $\mathbf{Th}_2(G)$ be the monadic second-order theory of G. Lewis (1979) showed that this theory is undecidable by showing how one could define the set of terminating computations of an arbitrary Turing machine within it.

Now, the monadic second-order theory of any of our intended structures is decidable (by reduction to SnS), as is the monadic second-order theory of any of our intended structures augmented with any predicate that is definable in $L^2_{K,P}$ (since we can reduce this to the theory of the original structure via that definition). Our approach to showing that a predicate is not definable in $L^2_{K,P}$ is to show that the theory of one of our structures augmented with that predicate is not decidable. In particular, we will show that the theory of such a structure includes an undecidable fragment of the monadic second-order theory of the grid.

Our focus, in this section, is the mechanism known as *free-indexation*. In the Government and Binding Theory framework this is the mechanism that is generally assumed to mediate issues like agreement, co-reference of nominals, and identification of moved elements with their traces. In its most general form this operates by assigning indices to the nodes of the tree randomly and then filtering out those assignments that do not meet various constraints on agreement, co-reference, etc. In essence, the indexation is an equivalence relation, one that distinguishes unboundedly many equivalence classes among the nodes of the tree. That is, each value of the index identifies an equivalence class and there is no a priori bound on its maximum value. Free-indexation views constraints on the indexation as a filter that admits only those equivalence relations that meet specific conditions on the relationships between the individuals in these classes.

To see that we cannot define such equivalence relations in $L^2_{K,P}$, consider the class of structures

$$\mathcal{T}_{\mathrm{CI}} = \langle T_2, \mathcal{P}_2, \mathcal{D}_2, \mathcal{L}_2, \mathrm{CI} \rangle,$$

where T_2 is the complete binary-branching tree domain, $\mathcal{P}_2$, $\mathcal{D}_2$, and $\mathcal{L}_2$ are the natural interpretations of parent, domination, and left-of on that domain, and CI is any arbitrary equivalence relation. Let S2S+CI be the monadic second-order theory of this class of structures. Our claim is that this is an undecidable theory.[7]

---

[7]Since the property of being an equivalence relation — being reflexive, symmetric, and

Theorem 4.1 *S2S+CI is not decidable.*

Lewis's proof of the non-decidability of $\mathbf{Th}_2(G)$ is based on a construction that takes any given Turning Machine M into a formula $\phi_M(\vec{P})$ such that $G \models (\exists \vec{P})[\phi_M(\vec{P})]$ iff M halts (when started, say, on the empty tape). The idea behind our proof of the non-decidability of S2S+CI is that there is a natural correspondence between points in T_2 and those in $\mathbb{N}^2$ that is induced by interpreting node addresses in T_2 as paths (non-decreasing in both x and y) from the origin in $\mathbb{N}^2$. Of course, in general, there will be many points in T_2 that correspond to the same point in $\mathbb{N}^2$, but we can restrict the interpretation of CI in such a way that all points in T_2 that correspond to the same point in $\mathbb{N}^2$ will be co-indexed. We then restrict the interpretation of the variables in $\vec{P}$ in such a way that it does not break the classes of CI. In more typically linguistic terms, we require co-indexed nodes to agree on the features in $\vec{P}$.

The formula $\phi_M(\vec{P})$ of Lewis' proof involves only the constant O, the successor functions r_0 and r_1, some set of (bound) individual variables, the (free) monadic predicate variables in $\vec{P}$, and the logical connectives.

Let

$$\begin{aligned}
O(x) &\leftrightarrow (\forall y)[y \triangleleft^* x \rightarrow y \approx x] \\
r_0(x,y) &\equiv x \triangleleft y \wedge (\forall z)[x \triangleleft z \rightarrow z \not\prec y] \\
r_1(x,y) &\equiv x \triangleleft y \wedge (\forall z)[x \triangleleft z \rightarrow y \not\prec z].
\end{aligned}$$

Then $O(x)$ is true only at the root, $r_0(x,y)$ is true iff y is the leftmost child of x and $r_1(x,y)$ is true iff y is the rightmost child of x. These translations are sufficient for us to translate $\phi_M(\vec{P})$ into a formula $\psi_M(\vec{P})$ that, when combined with an axiom $\Phi_G(\vec{P})$ constraining the interpretation of CI and $\vec{P}$ as sketched above, will be satisfiable by a model in the class $\mathcal{T}_{\text{CI}}$ iff $\phi_M(\vec{P})$ is satisfied by G. That is:

There exists $T \in \mathcal{T}_{\text{CI}}$ such that $T \models (\exists \vec{P})[\psi_M(\vec{P}) \wedge \Phi_G(\vec{P})]$

iff

$$G \models (\exists \vec{P})[\phi_M(\vec{P})].$$

This in turn implies that

$$(\exists \vec{P})[\phi_M(\vec{P})] \in \mathbf{Th}_2(G) \quad \text{iff} \quad \neg(\exists \vec{P})[\psi_M(\vec{P}) \wedge \Phi_G(\vec{P})] \notin \text{S2S} + \text{CI}.$$

Decidability of S2S+CI, then, would imply decidability of the halting problem.

It remains only to define $\Phi_G(\vec{P})$.

---

transitive — is definable in $L^2_{K,P}$, our result is one way of showing that $\mathcal{N}_2$ augmented with a single arbitrary binary relation has a non-decidable monadic second-order theory.

Let:

$$\Phi_G(\vec{P}) \equiv$$
$$(\forall x, y)[\ \ \mathrm{CI}(x, y) \leftarrow ($$

$x \approx y \quad \vee$
— **x and y are equal or**
$(\exists x_0, y_0)[\ \mathrm{CI}(x_0, y_0) \wedge$
$(\ (\mathrm{r}_0(x_0, x) \wedge \mathrm{r}_0(y_0, y)) \vee$
$(\mathrm{r}_1(x_0, x) \wedge \mathrm{r}_1(y_0, y))\ )]\quad \vee$
— **x and y are both left-children or**
both right-children of co-indexed
nodes or
$(\exists x_0, y_0, x_1, y_1)[\ \mathrm{CI}(x_0, y_0) \wedge$
$\mathrm{r}_0(x_0, x_1) \wedge \mathrm{r}_1(x_1, x) \wedge$
$\mathrm{r}_1(y_0, y_1) \wedge \mathrm{r}_0(y_1, y)\ ]$
— **x is the right-child of the left-child**
and y is the left-child of the right-
child of co-indexed nodes, or v.v.
$)\ \wedge$

$$\mathrm{CI}(x, y) \to \mathrm{Agree}_{\vec{P}}(x, y)\ ],$$

where

$$\mathrm{Agree}_{\vec{P}}(x, y) \equiv \bigwedge_{P \in \vec{P}} (P(x) \leftrightarrow P(y)).$$

This requires that every node is co-indexed with itself, that the left children of co-indexed nodes are co-indexed as are the right children of co-indexed nodes, and that the left child of the right child and right child of the left child of co-indexed nodes are co-indexed. Finally all co-indexed nodes are forced by $\mathrm{Agree}_{\vec{P}}$ to agree on all predicates in $\vec{P}$. That this is sufficient to carry the reduction of the halting problem to membership in S2S ∣ CI depends on the fact that $\Phi_G(\vec{P})$ forces all points in T_2 equivalent in the sense that they correspond to the same point in G as sketched above, to agree on the predicates in $\vec{P}$. Thus we (roughly) can take the quotient with respect to this equivalence without affecting satisfiability of $\psi_M(\vec{P})$. The resulting structure is isomorphic to G and satisfies $(\exists \vec{P})[\psi_M(\vec{P})]$ iff G satisfies $(\exists \vec{P})[\phi_M(\vec{P})]$. The proof is carried out in detail in Rogers (1994).

The non-definability of free-indexation is a significant obstacle to capturing GB accounts of language in $L^2_{K,P}$. As it turns out, other constraints employed in GB theories are not generally difficult to define. Our ability to capture these accounts, then, depends directly on the degree to which they necessarily employ free-indexation. The common practice, in GB, is to simply assume co-indexation almost whenever there is a need to identify components of the tree in some way. Unfortunately, we cannot capture directly accounts that are defined in these terms, but rather are compelled to restate them without reference to indices. On the other hand, it is not at all clear that accounts that appeal to free-indexation actually require so general a mechanism. On the contrary, it seems that indices are frequently only a conceptually simple way of encoding more complicated, but less general relationships. There has been a tendency, in the more recent GB literature, to avoid free-indexation in favor of these more specific relationships. Chomsky, for instance, comments:

> A theoretical apparatus that takes indices seriously as entities...is questionable on more general grounds. Indices are basically the expression of a relationship, not entities in their own right. They should be replaceable without loss by a structural account of the relation they annotate. (Chomsky 1993, pg. 49, note 52)

This quote comes in the context of a suggestion for a re-interpretation of the standard account of Binding Theory in a manner that avoids use of indices. Rizzi (1990) motivated by an examination of a wide variety of extraction phenomena, offers a re-interpretation of the Empty Category Principle and the theory of chains that restricts the role of indices to a relatively small class of movements. As we will see in the next section, Rizzi's theory provides us with the foundation we need to capture a largely complete GB account of English D- and S-Structure in $L^2_{K,P}$. We thus establish that this account licenses a strongly context-free language. It seems noteworthy that GB theorists have been led, by purely linguistic considerations, to precisely the kind of re-interpretation of the theory we require in order to establish our language-theoretic results.

5 Defining Chains

We turn now to an example that is particularly relevant to the issue of capturing a Government and Binding Theory account of English in $L^2_{K,P}$, and in particular capturing it without use of indices. This is our definition of *chains* — the core notion in contemporary GB accounts of movement. Our exposition is intended to be accessible without prior familiarity with GB, although possibly mysterious in some of its details. It will necessarily be somewhat meager both in the details of the definition and in the details of the underlying theory. A more complete treatment can be found in Rogers (1994).

5.1 Identifying Antecedents of Traces

Government and Binding Theory analyzes sentences with four distinct syntactic representations which are related by the general transformation *move-α*. These are *D-Structure* — corresponding to the deep-structure of earlier transformational theories, *S-Structure* — roughly corresponding to

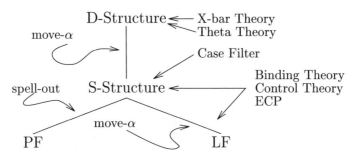

FIGURE 2   Levels of representation.

the surface-structure of those theories, *Phonetic Form* — the actual phonetic structure of the sentence, and *Logical Form* — a more or less direct representation of the sentence's semantic content. The principles embodying a GB theory of language are collected into modules which apply at various levels of this analysis. The principles we capture include basic X-bar Theory, Theta Theory, the Case Filter, Binding Theory, Control Theory and various constraints on movement, in particular the Empty Category Principle. In this section we focus on the Empty Category Principle and the definition of *chains*.

As we noted in the introduction, we prefer to regard GB theories as a set of constraints on structures rather than a mechanism for constructing them. We take this a step further by assuming that those constraints apply to a single tree which includes S-Structure and D-Structure as submodels,[8] rather than having some constraints apply to one structure, others to the other, and others still to the relationship between them. In this view, D-Structure and move-α are best understood as perspicuous means of stating constraints which are obscured in a single-level representation (see, for instance, Koster 1987 and Brody 1993).[9] One argument against such a view is that in some cases (such as head-raising) chains formed by one movement can be disrupted by subsequent movement. Indeed, representational accounts, such as ours, frequently appeal to a notion of *reconstruction* — effectively derivation in reverse — to resolve such difficulties. In fact, at least if one can employ indices to identify the elements of chains, there is no need for such a retreat. Even limiting oneself to the language of $L^2_{K,P}$, if one restricts attention to languages, like English, in which head-movement is strictly limited, it is possible to get a purely declarative (and reasonably

---

[8]While we don't treat Logical Form, there is no obvious reason this cannot be incorporated into our structures in much the same way.

[9]It is interesting that Johnson (1989) initially defines all four levels of structure, but then, through a series of standard program transformations, optimizes away everything except PF and LF.

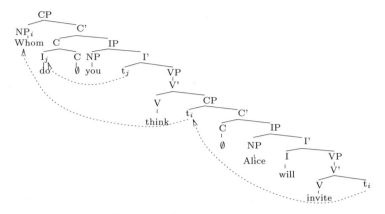

FIGURE 3 Extraction from the object, S-Structure.

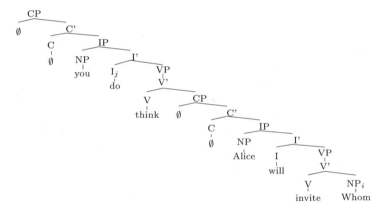

FIGURE 4 Extraction from the object, D-Structure.

clear) account of the issues usually treated by reconstruction. Details of such an account are given in Rogers (1994).

Figure 3 gives the S-Structure of a more or less typical GB analysis of the sentence:

(1)   Whom do you think Alice will invite.

In the D-Structure (Figure 4) the element carrying the inflection is positioned between the subject and the predicate and *Whom* is in its standard position as the object of *invite*. Move-α transforms this structure by cutting out the subtrees rooted at I$_j$ and NP$_i$, leaving phonetically empty traces (t$_j$ and t$_i$), and re-attaching them a higher positions in the tree. In the case of *Whom* the movement occurs in two steps, with traces being left at each intermediate position. The original position of the moved element is referred to as the *base* position, and its final resting place is the *target* position. The moved element is identified with its traces by co-indexation. Together, an element and the traces co-indexed with it form a *chain*. Chains can be broken up into a sequence of *links* each consisting of a trace and its *antecedent* — the next higher element of the chain.

The fundamental issue we must address in defining chains within $L^2_{K,P}$ is how to identify the antecedent of a trace without reference to indices. Our key idea is that, if we can limit the portion of the tree in which an antecedent can occur, then we can possibly bound the number of potential antecedents a trace may have. Such a bound would suffice since, while we cannot capture indexations with an unbounded range of index, we can capture any indexation in which there is a constant bound on the total number of distinct indices.

In the standard GB account of movement, that of Barriers (Chomsky 1986), there are two principles that tend to bound the length of links. The first is *n-subjacency* which, roughly, limits the number of phrasal boundaries that a link can cross. This is exactly the kind of constraint we need. Unfortunately it is responsible only for weak effects; there are many sentences that violate *n*-subjacency that are only of degraded acceptability rather than outright ungrammatical. The second principle that might do is the *Empty Category Principle*. This puts specific constraints on the structural relationship between a trace and its antecedent. Indices, however, play a significant role in Chomsky's formulation of this principle.

There is a formulation of ECP, due to Rizzi and based on his notion of *Relativized Minimality* (Rizzi 1990), in which the role of indexation is largely eliminated. In Rizzi's theory, ECP is a conjunctive principle with two components — a Formal Licensing requirement and an Identification requirement:

ECP (Rizzi):

- A non-pronominal empty category must be properly head-governed. (Formal Licensing)
- Operators must be identified with their variables. (Identification)

We are interested in the identification requirement, which, incidentally, is responsible for most of the effects attributed to ECP in the Barriers account. This constraint requires every trace (variable) to be identified with its target (operator). This can be done in one of two ways, either by a particular class of index, the referential indices, or by a sequence of *antecedent-government* links. In the latter case the role of indices in identifying chains can be taken over by the antecedent-government relation.

To a first approximation, government is simply a relation between an element and those elements occurring in a specifically limited region of the

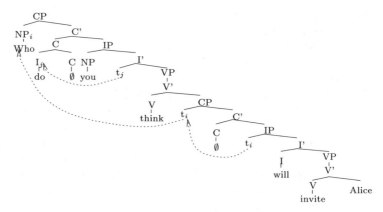

FIGURE 5 Extraction from the subject.

tree dominated by the phrase in which that element (the governor) occurs. Its definition has three components. First, for the class of government relations we are considering here, the governor must c-command the elements it governs, that is, those elements must be dominated by a sibling of the governor. Second, there must be no intervening barrier. For Rizzi, the notion of barrier is much weaker than it is in the Barriers account. Here, this constraint simply forbids the government relation from crossing certain phrasal boundaries (in particular specifiers, adjuncts and complements of nouns or prepositions). The final component of the government relation requires a governor to be the minimal potential governor of the elements it governs, that is, no potential governor can fall properly between a governor and the elements it governs. There are a range of types of government relations that fall under this general category. In Rizzi's theory only potential governors of the same type count for the minimality requirement. (This is the relativized aspect of his theory.) For antecedent-government there is an additional requirement that the governor be co-indexed with the trace.

Definition 5.1 x *antecedent-governs* y iff

- x c-commands y.
- No barrier falls between x and y.
- Minimality is respected.
- x and y are co-indexed.

As we will see, we can drop the co-indexation requirement on the grounds that, when it exists, the antecedent-governor is unique.

As an example of these relationships, consider, in Figure 5, the trace in the *specifier* of the lower IP, that is, the trace of *Who* falling immediately under the IP. The elements c-commanding this trace include the (empty)

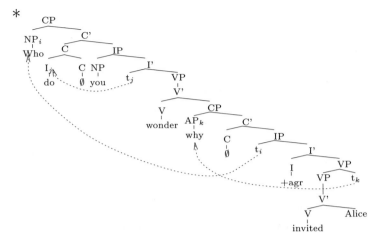

FIGURE 6 An ECP violation.

C, the t_i in the specifier of CP, the V, etc. This is a *Wh-Trace* which means that, by the principles of Binding Theory, its antecedent must fall in a *non-argument* position. In the example, the non-argument positions c-commanding the trace are just the specifiers of the CPs. By minimality, no potential antecedent of the trace beyond the closest specifier of a CP can govern it. Thus the only possible antecedent-governor of the trace in question is the trace in the specifier of the lower CP, which is, in fact, its antecedent.

In contrast, if we fill that position with a moved adverbial, as in the example of Figure 6, there is a problem. The element *why* cannot be the antecedent of the trace in the specifier of the lower IP, but it blocks government by all other potential antecedents. Thus the trace t_i cannot be identified with its antecedent, and the sentence is ruled ungrammatical on the grounds that it violates ECP.

In this way, minimality suffices to pick out the unique antecedent of traces in chains that are identified by antecedent-government. But under Rizzi's criteria chains can also be identified by referential indices. These are just indices assigned to elements that receive what are termed *referential* Theta roles. Again to a first approximation, we can take these simply to be elements that are the objects of verbs. In Figure 6 *Who* is extracted from the embedded subject. If we return to our original example, in which we extract from the object, we find that filling the specifier of the lower CP with a moved adverbial (Figure 7) has a less dramatic effect. While antecedent government of the trace in the complement of the lower VP is blocked, that trace can now be identified with its target by the referential index they share. The fact that this example is not judged to be as bad as

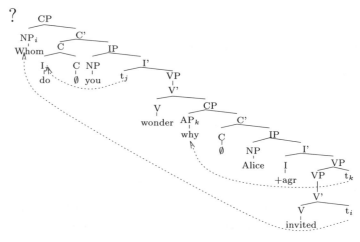

FIGURE 7 A 1-subjacency violation.

the example from Figure 6 is attributed, then, to the fact that it is only a 1-subjacency violation rather than an ECP violation.

In general, we could be forced to resort to a mechanism equivalent to indexation in order to distinguish such referential chains. It turns out, however, in English at least, that chains of this type do not overlap. Manzini (1992), in fact, argues for an account of $\overline{A}$-movement (movements, like these we have been considering, to non-argument positions) which implies that no more than two such chains — one referential and one non-referential — may ever overlap. Thus, we need to identify only a single referential antecedent in any single context.

5.2 Defining Antecedent-Government, Links, and Chains

Relativized Minimality theory distinguishes a number of distinct varieties of antecedent-government, one for each class of movement. We look at one representative case $\overline{A}$-antecedent-government. This is defined, in $L^2_{K,P}$ as follows:

$\overline{A}$-Antecedent-Governs$(x,y) \equiv$

$\qquad \neg A\text{-pos}(x) \wedge C\text{-Commands}(x,y) \wedge T.\text{Eq}(x,y) \wedge$

$\qquad\qquad$ — x **is a potential antecedent in an** $\overline{A}$**-position**

$\qquad \neg(\exists z)[\text{Intervening-Barrier}(z,x,y)] \wedge$

$\qquad\qquad$ — **no barrier intervenes**

$\qquad \neg(\exists z)[\text{Spec}(z) \wedge \neg A\text{-pos}(z) \wedge$

$\qquad\qquad C\text{-Commands}(z,x) \wedge \text{Intervenes}(z,x,y)]$

$\qquad\qquad$ — **minimality is respected**

In words, this says simply that x is an $\overline{\text{A}}$-antecedent-governor of y iff x is in a non-argument ($\overline{\text{A}}$) position, it c-commands y, no barrier intervenes between x and y, and no non-argument specifier falls between x and y. The actual definitions of A-Pos, T.Eq, Intervening-Barrier, Spec, and Intervenes is unimportant here. The predicate T.Eq is used to check the compatibility of the features of the trace with those of its antecedent.

Using this, we can define the link relation.

$\overline{\text{A}}$-$\overline{\text{Ref}}$-Link$(x, y) \equiv$

   $\overline{\text{A}}$-Antecedent-Governs$(x, y) \wedge \neg\text{Ref}(x) \wedge \neg\text{Ref}(y) \wedge$

   Bar2$(x) \wedge (\neg\text{Target}(x) \vee \text{Spec}(x)) \wedge$

   — x **is an XP and is a specifier if it is the target**

   $\neg\text{Base}(x) \wedge \text{Trace}(y) \wedge -\text{anaphor}(y) \wedge -\text{pronominal}(y)$

   — y **is an $\overline{\text{A}}$-trace, x is not in Base position**

This is just antecedent-government with certain additional configurational requirements. We can extend the notion of links based on Rizzi's antecedent-government to include antecedents and traces that Rizzi identifies with a referential index (which we refer to as $\overline{\text{A}}$-referential links), and links formed by rightward movement. This gives us five distinct link relations. As they are mutually exclusive, we can take their disjunction to form a single link relation which must be satisfied by every trace and its antecedent.

$$\text{Link}(x, y) \equiv \text{A-Link}(x, y) \vee \overline{\text{A}}\text{-}\overline{\text{Ref}}\text{-Link}(x, y) \vee$$
$$\overline{\text{A}}\text{-Ref-Link}(x, y) \vee \text{X}^0\text{-Link}(x, y) \vee$$
$$\text{Right-Link}(x, y)$$

The idea, now, is to define chains as any set of nodes that are linearly ordered by Link. Before we can do this, though, we have one more issue to resolve. The problem is that, while we can identify a unique antecedent for each trace, nothing assures us that there will be a unique trace for each antecedent, that is, nothing prevents us from identifying the same node as the antecedent of more than one trace. As an example, we might license the tree in Figure 8. This is the conflation of two sentences:

(2)   a. Who$_i$ has t$_i$ told you Alice invited him.
      b. Who$_i$ has Alice told you t$_i$ t$_i$ invited him.

In the first we have extracted *Who* from the subject of the matrix clause and in the second we have extracted it from the subject of the embedded clause. We can find a link relation between *Who* and the trace in the specifier of the matrix IP and a link relation between *Who* and the trace in the specifier of the embedded CP, but clearly it cannot have moved from both positions.

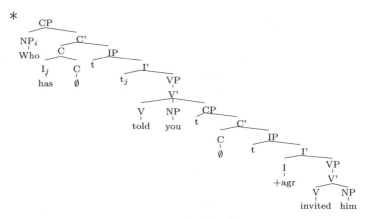

FIGURE 8 Conflated chains.

We rule out such structures by requiring that chains not only be linearly ordered by Link, but that they are also closed under the link relation, that is, every chain includes every node that is related by Link to any node in the chain. Trees like the the one in Figure 8 are ruled out on the grounds that any chain that contains either of the traces in question must include both of them, and will therefore not be linearly ordered.

Formalizing this, we get:

Chain$(X) \equiv$

$\quad (\exists!x)[X(x) \wedge \text{Target}(x)] \wedge (\exists!x)[X(x) \wedge \text{Base}(x)] \wedge$

$\quad\quad$ — X **contains exactly one Target and one Base**

$\quad (\forall x)[X(x) \wedge \neg\text{Target}(x) \rightarrow (\exists!y)[X(y) \wedge \text{Link}(y,x)]] \quad \wedge$

$\quad\quad$ — **All non-Target have a unique antecedent in** X

$\quad (\forall x)[X(x) \wedge \neg\text{Base}(x) \rightarrow (\exists!y)[X(y) \wedge \text{Link}(x,y)]] \quad \wedge$

$\quad\quad$ — **All non-Base have a unique successor in** X

$\quad (\forall x,y)[X(x) \wedge (\text{Link}(x,y) \vee \text{Link}(y,x)) \rightarrow X(y)]$

$\quad\quad$ — X **is closed wrt the Link relation.**

5.3 Defining the ECP

We can now capture Rizzi's version of the Empty Category Principle:

Licensing

$\quad (\forall x)[\text{Trace}(x) \rightarrow (\text{Bar0}(x) \vee (\exists y)[\text{Proper-Head-Governs}(y,x)])]$

Identification

$\quad\quad (\forall x)[\text{Trace}(x) \rightarrow (\exists X)[\text{Chain}(X) \wedge X(x)]]$

Note, in particular, that in our definition the identification requirement is reduced simply to a requirement that every trace is a member of some well-formed chain. As we admit the notion of *trivial* chains — chains with a single element, formed by zero movements — we can generalize this to a global requirement that every element of the tree is a member of a (possibly trivial) well-formed chain.

Identification (Generalized)

$$(\forall x)(\exists X)[\text{Chain}(X) \land X(x)].$$

Recall that identification is the component of Rizzi's definition that accounts for most of the effects attributed to ECP in the Barrier's account of movement. Thus we have reduced a variety of effects to a single simple global principle. Of course we have paid for this with a complex definition of chains, but much of this complexity lies in the definition of antecedent-government and Rizzi argues, on linguistic grounds, for essentially this definition in any case. It is satisfying that we can recover its added complexity in the form of a greatly simplified ECP.

5.4 Limits of the Definition

The fact that we can exhibit a definition in $L^2_{K,P}$ of the class of trees licensed by a specific GB account of English provides a strong complexity result for that class of trees — it is strongly context-free. We don't, on the other hand, expect this formalization to work for GB theories in general, and, in particular we don't expect it to work for a GB account of Universal Grammar. A more or less typical account of head-raising in Dutch, for instance, is given in Figure 9. This is the type of movement presumed to be responsible for the cross-serial dependencies that form the basis of Shieber's claim that Swiss-German is non-context-free (Shieber 1985). Bresnan, et al., (1982) have pointed out that analyses such as these form a non-recognizable set. Consequently, it cannot be possible to capture this account within $L^2_{K,P}$, and, in fact, the definition we give fails to license these structures. Examining why this is the case provides some insight into the kinds of natural properties of linguistic structures that correspond to increased language-theoretic complexity.

In order to rule out the possibility of "forking" chains — of some nodes participating in the licensing of multiple gaps — we have required chains to be maximal in the sense that they include every node that is related by link to any node in the chain. Consequently, we can license overlapping chains only if they are distinguished in some way. The account works for English because we can classify chains in English into a bounded set of types in such a way that no two chains of the same type ever cross. (This fact depends to a great extent on the minimality requirement in the antecedent-government relation.)

This property can be stated as a principle:

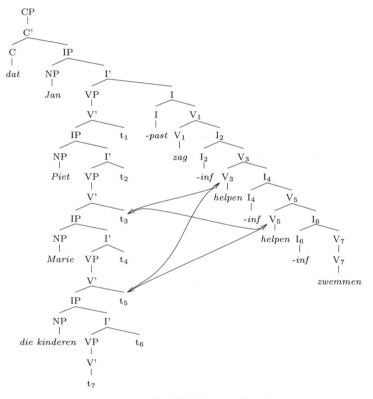

FIGURE 9 Head-Raising in Dutch

The number of chains which overlap at any single position in the tree is bounded by a constant.

Our approach to chains will work for any account of language that satisfies this principle. Once again, the linguistics literature provides arguments that such bounds exist, at least in some cases. As we have already noted, Manzini's *Locality Theory* (Manzini 1992) implies that no more than two Ā-chains ever overlap. Stabler (1994) makes the stronger claim that such bounds exist for all linguistically relevant relationships in all languages.

Leaving aside the possibility that it may be possible to account for cross-serial dependencies in Dutch in other ways, we can note that accounts employing structures such as the one in Figure 9 fail to meet the bound on overlapping chains. This is despite the fact that, if one orders the movements bottom-up, each movement meets the strictest conceivable locality constraint — each head moves to the closest possible position (often stated as the *Head Movement Constraint*). The problem is that, even if the movements are ordered in this way, each movement carries the target positions of the prior movements along with it. Thus, in the final structure all chains of head-movement overlap. Given that the number of heads participating in these structures is arbitrary, there can be no *a priori* bound on the number of overlapping chains. Note that in the example the two *helpen* chains ($[V_3, t_3]$ and $[V_5, t_5]$) are indistinguishable. Any attempt to form a chain including any of these nodes will be required to include all four and the result will not be linearly ordered.

6 Conclusion

In this paper we have introduced a kind of descriptive complexity result for the strongly Context-Free Languages — a language is strongly context-free iff the set of trees analyzing the syntax of its strings is definable in $L^2_{K,P}$ (modulo a projection). Using this result we have sketched a couple of language complexity results relevant to GB, namely, that free-indexation cannot, in general, be enforced by CFGs, and that a specific GB account of English licenses a strongly context-free language. The first of these results is not likely to come as a surprise to the GB community. The appropriateness of free-indexation as a fundamental component in linguistic theories has been questioned in the more recent GB literature on purely linguistic (rather than complexity theoretic) grounds.

The second result is more surprising. We don't expect it to extend to the whole range of human languages, that is, to any theory of Universal Grammar. Shieber (1985) and Miller (1991) (to cite two examples) give fairly strong evidence that there are constructions that occur in human languages that are beyond the CFLs, and hence not possible to capture in $L^2_{K,P}$. As expected, our definitions fail for these constructions. The fact that the definition works for English is a consequence of the fact that, in the account of English we capture, it is possible to classify chains into finitely many categories in such a way that no two chains from a given category ever overlap. GB-style analyses of the constructions studied by Shieber and by Miller include positions in which an unbounded number of chains can overlap. Our definition will fail to identify well-formed chains including these positions; indeed, there is unlikely to be any way to distinguish these chains without the equivalent of unbounded indices.

As it stands, this result speaks only of the particular account of English we capture. The fact that this is context-free says nothing about the nature of human language faculty, since the principle it depends upon is unlikely to be a principle of Universal Grammar. It does, however, raise the prospect of wider results. Extensions of this descriptive complexity result to larger language complexity classes could provide formal restrictions on the principles employed by GB theories that would be sufficient to provide non-trivial generative capacity results for those theories without losing the ability to capture the full range of human language. With such extended characterizations one might establish upper bounds on the complexity of human language in general. The possibility that such results might be obtainable is suggested by the fact that we find numerous cases in which the issues arising in our studies for definability reasons, and ultimately for language complexity reasons, have parallels that arise in the GB literature motivated by more purely linguistic concerns. This suggests that the regularities of human languages that are the focus of the linguistic studies are perhaps reflections of properties of the human language faculty that can be characterized, at least to some extent, by language complexity classes.

References

Berwick, Robert C. 1984. Strong Generative Capacity, Weak Generative Capacity, and Modern Linguistic Theories. *Computational Linguistics* 10:189–202.

Berwick, Robert C., and Amy S. Weinberg. 1984. *The Grammatical Basis of Linguistic Performance*. MIT Press.

Bresnan, Joan, Ronald M. Kaplan, Stanley Peters, and Annie Zaenen. 1982. Cross-Serial Dependencies in Dutch. *Linguistic Inquiry* 13:613–635.

Brody, Michael. 1993. Θ-Theory and Arguments. *Linguistic Inquiry* 24(1):1–23.

Chomsky, Noam. 1986. *Barriers*. MIT Press.

Chomsky, Noam. 1993. A Minimalist Program for Linguistic Theory. In *The View from Building 20*. 1–52. MIT Press.

Doner, John. 1970. Tree Acceptors and Some of Their Applications. *Journal of Computer and System Sciences* 4:406–451.

Gécseg, Ferenc, and Magnus Steinby. 1984. *Tree Automata*. Budapest: Akadémiai Kiadó.

Johnson, Mark. 1989. The Use of Knowledge of Language. *Journal of Psycholinguistic Research* 18(1):105–128.

Koster, Jan. 1987. *Domains and Dynasties*. Dordrecht, Holland: Foris Publications.

Kracht, Marcus. 1995. Syntactic Codes and Grammar Refinement. *Journal of Logic, Language, and Information* 4:41–60.

Lapointe, Steven G. 1977. Recursiveness and Deletion. *Linguistic Analysis* 3(3):227–265.

Lewis, Harry R. 1979. *Unsolvable Classes of Quantificational Formulas*. Addison-Wesley.

Manzini, Maria Rita. 1992. *Locality: A Theory and Some of Its Empirical Consequences*. Cambridge, Ma: MIT Press.

Miller, Philip H. 1991. Scandinavian Extraction Phenomena Revisited: Weak and Strong Generative Capacity. *Linguistics and Philosophy* 14:101–113.

Pullum, Geoffery K. 1984. On Two Recent Attempts to Show that English Is Not a CFL. *Computational Linguistics* 10:182–188.

Pullum, Geoffrey K., and Gerald Gazdar. 1982. Natural Language and Context-Free Languages. *Linguistics and Philosophy* 4:471–504.

Rabin, Michael O. 1969. Decidability of Second-Order Theories and Automata on Infinite Trees. *Transactions of the American Mathematical Society* 141:1–35.

Rizzi, Luigi. 1990. *Relativized Minimality*. MIT Press.

Rogers, James. 1994. *Studies in the Logic of Trees with Applications to Grammar Formalisms*. Ph.D. dissertation, Univ. of Delaware.

Shieber, Stuart M. 1985. Evidence Against the Context-Freeness of Natural Language. *Linguistics and Philosophy* 8:333–343.

Stabler, Jr., Edward P. 1994. The Finite Connectivity of Linguistic Structure. In *Perspectives on Sentence Processing*, ed. C. Clifton, L. Frazier, and K. Rayner. Chap. 13, 303–336. Hillsdale, NJ: Lawrence Erlbaum.

Stabler, Jr., Edward P. 1992. *The Logical Approach to Syntax*. Bradford.

Thatcher, J. W. 1967. Characterizing Derivation Trees of Context-Free Grammars through a Generalization of Finite Automata Theory. *Journal of Computer and System Sciences* 1:317–322.

7

Feature Trees over Arbitrary Structures

RALF TREINEN

ABSTRACT. This paper presents a family of first order feature tree theories, indexed by the theory of the feature labels used to build the trees. A given feature label theory, which is required to carry an appropriate notion of sets, is conservatively extended to a theory of feature trees with the predicates $x[t]y$ (feature t leads from the root of tree x to the tree y, where we require t to be a ground term) and $xt{\downarrow}$ (feature t is defined at the root of tree x; t may be a variable). We present a quantifier elimination procedure to reduce any sentence of the feature tree theory to an equivalent sentence of the feature label theory. Hence, if the feature label theory is decidable, the feature tree theory is too.

If the feature label theory is the theory of infinitely many constants and finite sets over infinitely many constants, we obtain an extension of the feature theory CFT, giving first-class status to arities. As another application, we obtain decidability of the theory of feature trees, where the feature labels are words, and where the language includes the successor function on words, lexical comparison of words and first-class status of arities.

1 Introduction

Feature trees have been introduced as record-like data structures in constraint (logic) programming (Aït-Kaci et al. 1994, Smolka and Treinen 1994), and as models of feature descriptions in computational linguistics (Backofen 1994b, 1994a). The use of record-like structures in logic programming languages, in the form of so-called ψ-terms (Aït-Kaci 1986), was pioneered by the languages LOGIN (Aït-Kaci and Nasr 1986) and LIFE (Aït-Kaci and Podelski 1991). More recently, Oz (Henz et al. 1995, Smolka 1995) uses a feature constraint system, the semantics of which is directly

Specifying Syntactic Structures
P. Blackburn and M. de Rijke, eds.
Copyright © 1997, CSLI Publications.

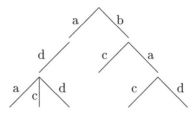

FIGURE 1 A Feature Tree

based on feature trees. In computational linguistics, feature structures have a long history in the field of unification grammars (as described by Smolka 1992).

In both areas, first order predicate logic has been recognized as a powerful description language for feature trees. For the first area, this is clear from the role constraints play in constraint logic programming (Jaffar and Lassez 1987) and in concurrent constrained-based languages (Smolka 1995), and, although in the second area various approaches have been proposed, Smolka and Aït-Kaci 1989, Johnson 1988 and Smolka 1992 have all advocated the use of predicate logic as feature description languages. Moreover, Backofen 1994a argues that predicate logic is the right language to express phenomena in both fields, and that feature trees constitute the canonical semantical model.

Feature trees (Aït-Kaci et al. 1994) are possibly infinite, finitely branching trees, where the edges carry labels taken from some given set of feature symbols. Features are functional, that is all edges departing from the same node have different labels. In contrast to the usual definition from the literature, we will omit in this paper the labeling of nodes by so-called sort symbols.

Different first order languages for feature trees have been studied. The most basic class of predicate symbols, which is contained in any first order feature language, consists of binary relation symbols $x[f]y$ for every feature symbol f. In the standard model of feature trees, the denotation of this predicate is "*y is the direct subtree of x under edge f*". The feature theory FT (Aït-Kaci et al. 1994) is an axiomatization of feature trees based on this language together with equality and sort predicates. The feature theory CFT (Smolka and Treinen 1994) uses a much more expressive language which extends FT by so-called arity constraints $x\{f_1, \ldots, f_n\}$. The denotation of such a constraint in the standard model is "*x has exactly edges labeled by $f_1, \ldots, f_n$ departing from its root*". Furthermore, regular path expressions (which contain an implicit existential quantification over feature paths, Backofen 1994b), and subsumption ordering constraints (Dörre and Rounds 1992, Dörre 1994) have been considered. Finally, the language F (Treinen 1993) contains a ternary feature predicate $x[y]z$. Using quantification over features, all other feature theories can be embedded in the theory F (Treinen 1993, Backofen 1994a).

With the establishment of first order logic as feature description language, various concrete problems concerning logical theories of feature trees were attacked. Much of this works treats the decision problems for various syntactically characterized fragments of the theory of feature trees. Satisfiability of existentially quantified conjunctions of atomic constraints (so-called basic constraints) and entailment between basic constraints is efficiently decidable for the languages FT (Aït-Kaci et al. 1994) and CFT (Smolka and Treinen 1994), and satisfiability of regular path constraints (Backofen 1994b) and weak subsumption constraints (Dörre 1994) is decidable, while it is undecidable for subsumption constraints (Dörre 1993). Such results lead to a more general question: whether or not the full first order theories of these languages is decidable. An affirmative answer was given for the case of FT (Backofen and Smolka 1995) and CFT (Backofen and Treinen 1994, Backofen 1995). Not surprisingly, however, the full first order theory of feature trees over F is undecidable, although the existential fragment of the theory is NP-complete, even with arity constraints as additional primitive notions (Treinen 1993).

The reason for the undecidability of F is the fact that it allows one to quantify over the direct subtrees of a tree. Taking $x \prec y$ ("x is a direct subtree of y") as abbreviation of $\exists f\, y[f]x$, we can define for trees x with only finitely many different subtrees (rational trees) the predicate "x is a subtree of y" by

$$\forall z \left(y \prec z \wedge \forall y_1, y_2\, (y_1 \prec y_2 \prec z \to y_1 \prec z) \to x \prec z \right).$$

Here, the idea is to "abuse" feature trees as sets, taking the direct subtrees of a tree as the elements of a set. Note that z fulfills the hypothesis in the above formula exactly if the "set" z contains y and is transitive, and that hence the transitive closure of y is the smallest z which satisfies the hypothesis.

Thus, we can easily show (for example, with the method of Treinen 1992) the undecidability of the theory of feature trees in the language of F. Consequently, in order to get a decidable sub-theory of F, we have to restrict the use of quantification over features.

The first contribution of this paper is the formulation of a decidable theory of feature trees which lies between CFT and F. The idea is to allow quantification over features only in order to state which features are defined, but not to quantify over the direct subtrees of a tree. More precisely, we will define the *restricted theory* of feature trees as the set of formulae where t

in $x[t]y$ is always a ground term, but where atomic constraints $xf\downarrow$ ("f is defined on x"), where f may be a variable, are still allowed. This situation is similar to that in Process Logic, where unrestricted quantification over path and state variables lead immediately to an undecidable validity problem, while a syntactic restriction leads to a decidable sub-logic (Parikh 1978).

In spite of these restrictions, the resulting theory is an essential extension of CFT. As a first example, note that we can encode a CFT arity constraint $x\{f_1, \ldots, f_n\}$ as $\forall f (xf\downarrow \leftrightarrow \bigvee_{i=1}^{n} f \doteq f_i)$. Once this is observed, we can move beyond the expressivity of CFT. We can make statements about the arities of trees; for example, we can say that the arity of x is contained in the arity of y by

$$\forall f (xf\downarrow \rightarrow yf\downarrow).$$

As a second example, the following formula expresses that x has exactly three features:

$$\exists f_1, f_2, f_3 \left(f_1 \not\doteq f_2 \wedge f_2 \not\doteq f_3 \wedge f_1 \not\doteq f_3 \wedge \forall g(xg\downarrow \leftrightarrow [g \doteq f_1 \vee g \doteq f_2 \vee g \doteq f_3]) \right).$$

From these examples, one gets the idea that the theory of sets of feature symbols is hidden in our restricted theory of feature trees. This leads to the second contribution of our approach, which we now explain in three steps.

The first step is to realize that, in order to decide the validity of first order sentences over feature trees, we can save some work if we employ an existing decision algorithm for the theory of finite sets over infinitely many constants. Since this theory is easily encoded in the theory WS1S, the weak second order monadic theory of one successor function, the existence of such an algorithm follows immediately from Büchi's result on the decidability of WS1S (Büchi 1960)[1].

The following examples give an idea why logical statements involving feature trees can be reduced to logical statements on sets of features. Let x, y, z denote variables ranging over feature trees, f, g, h range over features and F, G, H range over sets of features. First, the formula

$$\exists x, y \left(\forall f (xf\downarrow \rightarrow yf\downarrow) \wedge \neg\forall g (yg\downarrow \rightarrow xg\downarrow) \right)$$

does not involve any tree construction. This formula is just about the sets of features defined at the roots of x and y, and hence can be translated to:

$$\exists F, G \left(\forall f (f \dot\in F \rightarrow f \dot\in G) \wedge \neg\forall g (g \dot\in G \rightarrow g \dot\in F) \right).$$

---

[1]The reader shouldn't be confused by the fact that we are apparently mixing first and second order structures. A second order structure can always be considered as a two-sorted first order structure, with one sort for the elements, and another sort for the sets. Only in the context of *classes of* structures does it really make sense to distinguish first order from second order structures.

Formulae like the above subformula ($\forall f \, (x f \downarrow \ldots)$), where the feature tree x is only used as a set of features, will be called primitive formulae.

The formula

$$(1) \qquad \exists x \, (x[a]x \wedge x[b]y \wedge \neg x h \downarrow)$$

where a and b are two different constants, is clearly satisfiable if we can find a set which contains a and b, but not h. Hence, (1) can be reduced to

$$(2) \qquad \exists F \, (a \stackrel{.}{\in} F \wedge b \stackrel{.}{\in} F \wedge \neg h \stackrel{.}{\in} F).$$

In the setting we have defined so far, this is equivalent to $a \stackrel{.}{\neq} h \wedge b \stackrel{.}{\neq} h$.

The next step is to generalize this idea to the situation where we have *some* structure of feature symbols and finite sets of feature symbols given, and to build the feature trees with the feature labels we find in the given feature label structure. Hence, we now obtain a family of feature tree structures, indexed by the feature label structures. This is a well-known situation, for instance in constraint domains for programming languages (Smolka 1995), where feature constraints are not isolated but come in combination with other constraint domains like numbers and words.

Hence, our decision procedure now decides the validity of a sentence of the feature tree theory *relative* to the theory of the feature labels. As a consequence, our feature tree theory is decidable if the feature label theory is. Relatively little needs to be done to adapt the reduction procedure to this more general case. The only problem is that two different ground terms, like the constants a and b in example (1) above, need not necessarily denote semantically different elements. This means that we have to consider the two cases $a \stackrel{.}{=} b$ and $a \stackrel{.}{\neq} b$. In the first case, $a \stackrel{.}{=} b$ and the functionality of features yield $x \stackrel{.}{=} y$. Hence, we can eliminate x, and obtain for the first case

$$a \stackrel{.}{=} b \wedge y[a]y \wedge y[b]y \wedge \neg y h \downarrow.$$

In the second case, we get the same reduction as before:

$$a \stackrel{.}{\neq} b \wedge \exists F \, (a \stackrel{.}{\in} F \wedge b \stackrel{.}{\in} F \wedge \neg h \stackrel{.}{\in} F).$$

The feature label structure may be equipped with operations and predicate symbols of their own, which of course can be used in the feature tree structure as well. We could for instance take as feature label structure WS2S, that is the structure of words over the alphabet $\{a, b\}$, finite sets of words, and successor functions for every symbol of the alphabet. Since the membership predicate in any regular language is definable in the theory of this structure, we can express in this feature tree theory for any regular language L that the arity of some x is contained in L.

So far, feature trees have been finitely branching trees; that is, we took as possible arities all finite sets of features. The third step is to generalize this to an arbitrary notion of arities. That is, we assume that the feature label structure comes with a notion of sets, where we only require that there are at least two different sets. From this, we construct the feature trees such that the arities of the trees are always sets of the given feature label structure. For instance, we get as before the *finitely branching* feature trees if the feature label structure contains all the *finite* sets of feature trees. If we take as feature label structure natural numbers and all the initial segments of the natural numbers, that is sets of the form $\{1, \ldots, n\}$, we get a structure of feature trees where at every node the edges are consecutively numbered. In example (1) above, this has the consequence that we cannot reduce (2) to $a \not\doteq h \wedge b \not\doteq h$. Instead, the satisfiability of (3) depends on the theory of the feature label structure.

As another example, consider

$$(3) \qquad \exists x, y \, (x[f]x \wedge y[f]y \wedge x \not\doteq y).$$

Here, we will make a case distinction: Either both x and y have the arity $\{f\}$, that is f is the only feature defined, or at least one of them has a greater arity. In the first case both variables are called tight, in the second case a variable with arity greater than $\{f\}$ is called sloppy. Intuitively, a sloppy variable has features for which there are no constraints. For the case that both variables are tight, the formula can not be satisfied. This is a consequence of the fact that the formula $x[f]x \wedge \text{arity}(x, \{f\})$, a so-called *determinant* (Smolka and Treinen 1994), has a *unique* solution. In the other case, the formula is clearly satisfied, since we can use the unconstrained features of x, respectively y, to make both values different. Hence, we can translate (3) to the formula which states that this other case is indeed possible:

$$(4) \qquad \exists F, g \, (f \dot\in F \wedge \neg g \dot\in F).$$

Up to now, we have been talking about the feature tree structures defined upon some feature label structure. The quantifier elimination procedure we are going to present will be based on an axiomatization FX only; no other properties of the structures will be used for the justification of the procedure. The axiomatization is not subject to the syntactic restriction we imposed on the input formulae to the procedure, that is the axioms may contain subformulae $x[t]y$ where t is non-ground.

The quantifier elimination procedure proposed in this paper takes another road than the quantifier eliminations which have been given for the feature theories FT (Backofen and Smolka 1995) and CFT (Backofen 1995). We believe that, in the case of FT and CFT, our procedure is simpler than the existing ones for these theories. The difference lies in the way the procedure deals with the fact that these feature theories themselves do not have the property of quantifier elimination. A theory T is defined to have the *property of quantifier elimination* (Hodges 1993), if for every variable x and atomic formulae $\phi_1, \ldots, \phi_n$ there is a quantifier-free formula ψ such that $T \models \exists x \, (\phi_1 \wedge \ldots \wedge \phi_n) \leftrightarrow \psi$. An effective procedure to compute this ψ

yields immediately a decision procedure for T, provided ψ does not contain new free variables, and provided *True* and *False* are the only quantifier-free formulae. A simple counterexample, showing that for instance FT does not have the property of quantifier elimination, is

(5) $$\exists x \, (y[l]x \wedge xk\!\downarrow).$$

We can not simply eliminate x, since we need it to express a property of the free variable y, which we must not drop.

The classical way to solve this problem is to extend the language, such that non-reducible formulae like (5) become atomic formulae in the extended language. In our example, this means that we have to add so-called *path-constraints* like $y(lk)\!\downarrow$ to the language. This solution was chosen by Backofen and Smolka 1995 and Backofen 1995.

We will use another idea: we exploit the functionality of features to trade an existential quantifier, in the above situation, for a universal quantifier, and transform (5) into:

$$yl\!\downarrow \wedge \forall x \, (y[l]x \rightarrow xk\!\downarrow).$$

We can benefit from this quantifier-switching if we consider the elimination of *blocks* of quantifiers of the same kind. This idea has already been used, for instance by Malc'ev 1971 and Comon and Lescanne 1989. We will consider formulae in prenex normal form, for instance

$$\exists \cdots \exists \forall \cdots \forall \exists \cdots \exists \phi.$$

where ϕ is quantifier-free. If we can transform $\exists \cdots \exists \phi$ into a formula of the form $\forall \cdots \forall \psi$ for some quantifier-free ψ, then we have reduced the number of *quantifier alternations* from 2 to 1, although the total number of quantifiers might have increased.

The rest of the paper is organized as follows: Section 2 fixes the necessary notions from predicate logic. In Section 3, we define by an axiom the class of feature label structures, which will be called *admissible parameter structures* in the rest of the paper. In Section 4 we construct the standard model of feature trees over some arbitrary admissible parameter structure, present the axiomatization FX and show that the feature tree structure is a model of FX. Some basic properties of the axiomatization FX are stated in Section 5. The overall structure of the quantifier elimination procedure is presented in Section 6, the details are given in Section 7.

2   Preliminaries

We consider many-sorted predicate logic with equality. We use a number of standard shortcuts from predicate logic. We write $\overset{\sim}{\forall} \phi$ for the universal closure of ϕ. We write $\exists \bar{x} \, \phi$, where $\bar{x} = (x_1, \ldots, x_n)$ is a list of variables, for $\exists x_1 \ldots \exists x_n \, \phi$ ($\forall \bar{x} \, \phi$ is defined analogously). We sometimes use the notation $\exists X \, \phi$, where X is a finite set of variables, for $\exists \bar{x} \, \phi$, where $\bar{x}$ is some linear arrangement of X. Instead of writing the sort with every quantified variable, as in "$\forall x \in S \ldots$", we will introduce naming conventions which allow us to directly read off the sort of a variable. As usual, variables may be decorated with sub-and superscripts. Lists of variables will be denoted with an overstrike as in $\bar{x}$.

The connectives $\wedge, \vee$ take precedence over (bind tighter than) $\leftrightarrow, \rightarrow$. Negation $\neg$ and quantifiers bind tightest. It is understood that conjunction is commutative and associative. Consequently, we identify a conjunction of formulae with the multiset of its conjuncts. We use notions like $\psi \in \phi$ or $\psi \subseteq \phi$, where ϕ is a conjunction, accordingly.

We write the negation of $x \doteq y$ as $x \not\doteq y$. We consider equality as symmetrical, that is we identify $x \doteq y$ with $y \doteq x$ (and hence, $x \not\doteq y$ with $y \not\doteq x$). The reader should be aware, that $x \doteq y$ and $x \not\doteq y$ are formulae of our object logic, while $x = y$, respectively $x \neq y$, is a mathematical statement, expressing that the two variables x, y are syntactically identical, respectively, distinct.

We write $\mathtt{fr}(\phi)$ for the set of free variables of ϕ, and $\phi[y/x]$ denotes the formula that is obtained from ϕ by replacing every occurrence of x by y, after possibly renaming bound variables to avoid capture.

An assignment α is a X-update of an assignment α', where X is a set of variables, if $\alpha(x) = \alpha'(x)$ for all variables $x \notin X$. We write $\alpha[x_1 \mapsto a_1, \ldots, x_n \mapsto a_n]$ for the $\{x_1, \ldots, x_n\}$-update of α which assigns a_i to x_i, respectively.

3 Admissible Parameter Structures

In this section, we specify the class of parameter structures which we want to allow as a basis for the construction of feature trees.

Definition 3.1 (Admissible parameter signature) The signature $\Sigma = \langle S_\Sigma, F_\Sigma, R_\Sigma \rangle$ is an *admissible parameter signature*, if S_Σ contains at least the two sorts Feat and Set, and R_Σ contains at least the relational symbol Feat $\dot{\in}$ Set, that is the binary infix relation symbol $\dot{\in}$ of profile Feat, Set.

The sort Feat is intended to denote the features, and the sort Set is intended to denote the sets of features. In this sense, $\dot{\in}$ can be thought of as the usual membership relation.

Small letters from the middle of the alphabet $f, g, h, \ldots$ are variables of sort Feat, and capital letters from the middle of the alphabet $F, G, H, \ldots$ are variables of sort Set.

The only requirement on the class of admissible parameter structures is that they contain at least two (observationally) different sets:

$$(\text{S2}) \qquad \exists F, G, f \; (f \dot{\in} F \wedge \neg f \dot{\in} G)$$

Definition 3.2 (Admissible parameter structure) Let Σ be an admissible parameter signature. We call a Σ-structure $\mathcal{B}$ an *admissible parameter structure*, if $\mathcal{B} \models (S2)$.

This is in two respects weaker than what is usually required by axioms systems of second order logic (Andrews 1986). First, we don't require extensionality; that is, two different sets may have the same elements. Second, axiom (S2) is much weaker than the usual comprehension axiom of second order logic which states that every formula denotes a set. Note that, as a consequence of (S2), every admissible parameter structure contains at least one element of sort Feat.

Examples of admissible parameter signatures and algebras are

1. The signature Σ_C consists of an infinite set C of Feat-constants and the $\in$ predicate symbol. The algebra $\mathcal{B}_C$ assigns C to Feat, every constant of C to itself, the powerset over C to Set, and the membership relation to $\in$.

2. Σ_F and $\mathcal{B}_F$ are defined as above with the only difference that Set is interpreted as the class of *finite* sets over C.

3. The signature Σ_N contains the constant 1 of sort Feat, the unary function symbol *succ* of profile Feat $\rightarrow$ Feat, and $\in$. The algebra $\mathcal{B}_N$ assigns the set of natural numbers to Feat, the number 1 to the constant 1 and the successor function to *succ*. Set denotes the class of initial segments of natural numbers (that is, sets of the form $\{1, \ldots, n\}$), and $\in$ denotes membership.

4. The signature Σ_S contains the constant ϵ of sort Feat, finitely many function symbols $succ_i$, $1 \le i \le n$, of profile Feat $\rightarrow$ Feat, two predicate symbols $\le_{pre}$ and $\le_{lex}$, and $\in$. The algebra $\mathcal{B}_S$ assigns the set $\{1, \ldots, n\}^*$ to Feat, the empty word to ϵ, the function $\lambda x.xn$ to $succ_n$, the prefix (respectively lexical) ordering to $\le_{pre}$, respectively $\le_{lex}$, the powerset of $\{1, \ldots, n\}^*$ to Set, and membership to $\in$.

4 Feature Tree Structures

In this section we give the definition of a standard model of features trees over some given admissible parameter structure. We also present a set of axioms for feature trees, and prove that the standard model of feature trees is indeed a model of this axiomatization. No other properties of the feature tree model than the axiomatization will be used for the justification of the quantifier elimination procedure to be presented in the next sections.

Definition 4.1 (Tree signature) For a given admissible parameter signature Σ, we define the *tree signature* $\Sigma^\dagger = \langle S_{\Sigma^\dagger}, F_{\Sigma^\dagger}, R_{\Sigma^\dagger} \rangle$ by

$$S_{\Sigma^\dagger} = S_\Sigma \stackrel{+}{\cup} \{\mathsf{Tree}\}$$

$$F_{\Sigma^\dagger} = F_\Sigma$$

$$R_{\Sigma^\dagger} = R_\Sigma \stackrel{+}{\cup} \{\mathsf{Tree}[\mathsf{Feat}]\mathsf{Tree}, \mathsf{Tree}\,\mathsf{Feat}{\downarrow}\}$$

In the standard model to be defined below, the sort symbol Tree denotes a set of trees. Small letters at the end of the alphabet ($x, y, z \ldots$) denote Tree-variables. Note that the only Tree-terms are the Tree-variables, and that any $\Sigma^\dagger$-formula without Tree-variables is in fact a Σ-formula. We write the negation of $xt{\downarrow}$ as $xt{\uparrow}$.

Definition 4.2 (Tree) For a set M, a set $\tau \subseteq M^*$ of finite M-words is called a *tree over* M if it is prefix-closed, that is if $vw \in \tau$ implies $v \in \tau$ for all $v, w \in M^*$. $\mathcal{T}(M)$ denotes the set of trees over M.

Note that every tree contains the empty word ϵ and hence is non-empty, and that a tree may be infinite. This is of course the usual definition of trees — the tree in Figure 1, for instance, is

$$\{\epsilon, a, b, ad, bc, ba, ada, adc, add, bac, bad\}.$$

Definition 4.3 (Admissible tree) For an admissible parameter structure $\mathcal{B}$, an *admissible tree over* $\mathsf{Feat}^\mathcal{B}$ is a tree $\tau \in \mathcal{T}(\mathsf{Feat}^\mathcal{B})$, such that

$$\text{for all } v \in \tau \text{ exists } M \in \mathsf{Set}^\mathcal{B} \text{ with:} \quad \beta \in {}^\mathcal{B} M \Leftrightarrow v\beta \in \tau.$$

$\mathcal{AT}(\mathsf{Feat}^\mathcal{B})$ denotes the set of admissible trees over $\mathsf{Feat}^\mathcal{B}$.

Intuitively, this means that the set of features defined at some node of an admissible tree must be licensed by the denotation of Set in the admissible parameter structure $\mathcal{B}$. If we take, for example, an admissible structure $\mathcal{B}$ where $\mathsf{Set}^\mathcal{B}$ is the class of finite subsets of $\mathsf{Feat}^\mathcal{B}$, then $\mathcal{AT}(\mathsf{Feat}^\mathcal{B})$ contains exactly the finitely branching trees over $\mathsf{Feat}^\mathcal{B}$.

Definition 4.4 (Feature tree structure) For any admissible Σ-structure B, we define the $\Sigma^\dagger$-structure $B^\dagger$ by

1. $\mathcal{B}^\dagger \mid_\Sigma = \mathcal{B}$,
2. $\mathsf{Tree}^{\mathcal{B}^\dagger} = \mathcal{AT}(\mathsf{Feat}^\mathcal{B})$,
3. $\tau[\beta]^{\mathcal{B}^\dagger}\sigma$ iff $\sigma = \{v \mid \beta v \in \tau\}$,
4. $\tau\beta{\downarrow}^{\mathcal{B}^\dagger}$ iff $\beta \in \tau$.

Hence, $\mathcal{B}^\dagger$ is a conservative extension of $\mathcal{B}$.

The first axiom gives an explicit definition for the $\cdot\,\cdot\,{\downarrow}$ predicate:

($\downarrow$)	$\forall x, f\ (xf{\downarrow} \leftrightarrow \exists y\ x[f]y)$

The next axiom scheme expresses that every feature is functional:

(F)	$\forall x, y, z\ (x[t]y \wedge x[t]z \rightarrow y \doteq z)$	where t is ground.

Syntactic Convention. $\text{arity}(x, F) := \forall f\, (xf{\downarrow} \leftrightarrow f \dot{\in} F)$

If $\bar{x} = (x_1, \ldots, x_n)$ and $\bar{F} = (F_1, \ldots, F_n)$, we write $\text{arity}(\bar{x}, \bar{F})$ for $\bigwedge_{i=1}^{n} \text{arity}(x_i, F_i)$.

The next axiom states that every tree has an arity, and hence reflects the fact that we consider admissible trees only.

> (A) $\forall x\, \exists F\, \text{arity}(x, F)$

By construction, we immediately get:

Proposition 4.5 *For any admissible Σ-structure $\mathcal{B}$, we have that $\mathcal{B}^\dagger \models$ $(\downarrow), (F), (A)$.*

The next axiom scheme asserts that certain formulae indeed have a solution in the domain of feature trees.

Definition 4.6 (Graph, Constrained variable) A conjunction γ of formulae of the form $x[t]y$ is a called a *graph*. For a graph γ, let $\text{co}(\gamma) := \{x \mid x[t]y \in \gamma \text{ for some } t \text{ and } y\}$ be the set of variables *constrained* by γ.

Syntactic Convention.   For a graph γ and variable x, we define

$$F_\gamma^x := \{t \mid x[t]y \in \gamma \text{ for some variable } y\}$$
$$\Delta_\gamma := \{t \neq s \mid \text{ there are } x[t]y, x[s]z \in \gamma \text{ where } t \neq s \text{ or } y \neq z\}$$

For instance,

$$\gamma := x[a(f)]y \wedge x[b(g, a(f))]z \wedge y[a(a(f))]x \wedge y[a(a(f))]y$$

is a graph with $\text{co}(\gamma) = \{x, y\}$, $F_\gamma^x = \{a(f), b(g, a(f))\}$, $F_\gamma^y = \{a(a(f))\}$, $F_\gamma^z = \emptyset$, and $\Delta_\gamma = a(f) \neq b(g, a(f))$.

> (E) $\tilde{\forall} \left[\left(\Delta_\gamma \wedge \bigwedge_{i=1}^{n} \bigwedge_{a \in F_\gamma^{x_i}} a \dot{\in} F_i \right) \to \exists \text{co}(\gamma) \left(\gamma \wedge \bigwedge_{i=1}^{n} \text{arity}(x_i, F_i) \right) \right]$
>
> where γ is a graph with $\text{co}(\gamma) = \{x_1, \ldots, x_n\}$.

An example of axiom scheme (E) is

(6) $\forall z, f_1, f_2, g, F, G\, (f_1 \neq f_2 \wedge f_1 \dot{\in} F \wedge f_2 \dot{\in} F \wedge g \dot{\in} G$
$\to \exists x_1, x_2\, (x_1[f_1]x_2 \wedge x_1[f_2]z \wedge x_2[g]x_1 \wedge$
$\text{arity}(x_1, F) \wedge \text{arity}(x_2, G)))$

Proposition 4.7 $\mathcal{T}(M)$ *with the subset relation is a cpo.*

(See, for example, Gunter and Scott 1990 for a definition and basic properties of cpos). Note, that in general $\mathcal{AT}(\mathcal{M})$ does not constitute a sub-cpo of $\mathcal{T}(M)$. Obviously, the set of compact elements of $\mathcal{T}(M)$ are exactly the finite sets in $\mathcal{T}(M)$, and $\mathcal{T}(M)$ is an algebraic cpo.

Lemma 4.8 *For any admissible Σ-structure $\mathcal{B}$, we have $\mathcal{B}^\dagger \models (E)$.*

Proof. (Sketch) Let γ be a graph, $\mathsf{co}(\gamma) = \{x_1, \ldots, x_n\}$, and $\mathcal{B}^\dagger, \alpha \models \Delta_\gamma \wedge \bigwedge_{i=1}^n \bigwedge_{a \in F_\gamma^{x_i}} a \in F_i$. We construct $\tau_1, \ldots, \tau_n \in \mathcal{AT}(\mathsf{Feat}^\mathcal{B})$, such that

$$(7) \qquad \mathcal{B}^\dagger, \alpha[x_1 \mapsto \tau_1, \ldots, x_n \mapsto \tau_n] \models \gamma \wedge \bigwedge_{i=1}^n \mathrm{arity}(x_i, F_i).$$

We define the operator $\Phi \colon (\mathcal{T}(\mathsf{Feat}^\mathcal{B}))^n \to (\mathcal{T}(\mathsf{Feat}^\mathcal{B}))^n$ by its n components $pr_i \circ \Phi$. For given i, let $\{x_i[t_1]z_1, \ldots, x_i[t_m]z_m\}$ be the set of atoms in γ which constrain x_i.

$$pr_i \circ \Phi(\nu_1, \ldots, \nu_n) = \{\epsilon\} \cup \beta_1\sigma_1 \cup \ldots \cup \beta_m\sigma_m \cup \{\beta \in \mathsf{Feat}^\mathcal{B} \mid \beta \dot{\in}^\mathcal{B} \alpha(F_i)\}$$

where β_j is the evaluation of t_j in $\mathcal{B}, \alpha$, and where we define $\sigma_j := \nu_k$ if $z_j = x_k$ for some $1 \le k \le n$, and otherwise $\sigma_j := \alpha(z_j)$. As usual $\beta_j\sigma_j$ is an abbreviation for $\{\beta_j v \mid v \in \sigma_j\}$.

Φ is obviously continuous, hence we can define $(\tau_1, \ldots, \tau_n)$ as the least fixed point of Φ. By construction, $\tau_i \in \mathcal{AT}(\mathsf{Feat}^\mathcal{B})$ for all i. Since $\mathcal{B}^\dagger, \alpha \models \Delta_\gamma$, all β_j for given i are different. Hence, (7) holds. $\square$

As an example of this construction, consider the formula (6). Let $\alpha(z) = \{\epsilon, e, ee\}$, $\alpha(f_1) = a$, $\alpha(f_2) = b$, $\alpha(g) = c$, $\alpha(F) = \{a, b\}$ and $\alpha(G) = \{c, d\}$. In this case, we define Φ by

$$
\begin{aligned}
pr_1 \circ \Phi(\nu_1, \nu_2) &= \{\epsilon\} \cup a\nu_2 \cup b\{\epsilon, e, ee\} \cup \{a, b\} \\
&= \{\epsilon, b, be, bee\} \cup a\nu_2 \\
pr_2 \circ \Phi(\nu_1, \nu_2) &= \{\epsilon\} \cup c\nu_1 \cup \{c, d\} \\
&= \{\epsilon, d\} \cup c\nu_1.
\end{aligned}
$$

The least fixed point of Φ is (L_1, L_2), where L_1 is the prefix-closure of $(ac)^*(bee \cup ad)$, and L_2 is the prefix-closure of $(ca)^*(d \cup cbee)$.

Syntactic Convention. Let M be a finite set of Feat-terms.

$$\mathrm{arity}(x, M) := \forall f \, (xf{\downarrow} \leftrightarrow \bigvee_{a \in M} f \dot{=} a).$$

As above, this notion generalizes to $\mathrm{arity}(\bar{x}, \bar{M})$.

Definition 4.9 A *determinant* δ is a formula

$$\gamma \wedge \bigwedge_{x \in \mathsf{co}(\gamma)} \mathrm{arity}(x, F_\gamma^x)$$

where γ is a graph and has only free variables of sort Tree.

In other words, for every constraint $x[t]y$ in a determinant, the term t must be ground.

For instance, of the following three formulae

$$x[a(c)]y \wedge x[d]z \wedge y[a(d))]x \wedge \mathrm{arity}(x, \{a(c), d\}) \wedge \mathrm{arity}(y, \{a(d)\})$$
$$x[a(f)]y \wedge \mathrm{arity}(x, \{a(f)\})$$
$$x[a(c)]y \wedge x[b(d, a(c))]z \wedge \mathrm{arity}(x, \{a(c)\})$$

only the first one is a determinant (since f denotes a variable).

The last axiom scheme expresses that determinants have at most one solution in the constrained variables.

Syntactic Convention. $\exists^{\leq 1}\bar{x}\,\phi$ is an abbreviation for

$$\forall \bar{x}, \bar{y}\,(\phi(\bar{x}) \wedge \phi(\bar{y}) \to \bar{x} \doteq \bar{y}),$$

where $\bar{y}$ is some list of distinct variables as long as $\bar{x}$, and disjoint to $\mathtt{fr}(\phi)$.

$\exists^{\leq 1}\bar{x}\,\phi$ reads "there is at most one tuple $\bar{x}$, such that ϕ".

(U)	$\tilde{\forall}\,(\Delta_\gamma \to \exists^{\leq 1}\mathrm{co}(\delta)\,\delta)$	where δ is a determinant.

An example of (U) is

$$\forall z\,(a_1 \not\doteq a_2 \to \exists^{\leq 1}x, y\,(x[a_1]y \wedge x[a_2]z \wedge y[b]x$$
$$\wedge \mathrm{arity}(x, \{a_1, a_2\}) \wedge \mathrm{arity}(y, \{b\})))$$

Note, that (U) does not state that a determinant always has a solution. In the above example, it might be the case that, for example, the "set" $\{b\}$ does not exist, that is that $\exists F\,\forall x\,(x \in F \leftrightarrow x \doteq b)$ does not hold in the parameter structure. In this case, the determinant does not have a solution due to axiom (A).

Lemma 4.10 *For any admissible Σ-structure $\mathcal{B}$, we have $\mathcal{B}^\dagger \models (U)$.*

Proof. (Sketch) We split the determinant δ into $\gamma \wedge \rho$, where γ is a graph and ρ is a conjunction of arities. As in the proof of Lemma 4.8, let $\mathcal{B}^\dagger, \alpha \models \Delta_\delta$, and let Φ be the operator defined by γ. By the construction given in the proof of Lemma 4.8, $\mathcal{B}^\dagger, \alpha[x_1 \mapsto \tau_1, \ldots, x_n \mapsto \tau_n] \models \delta$ iff $(\tau_1, \ldots, \tau_n)$ is a fixed point of Φ.

We show, that Φ has only one fixed point. Let $(\tau_1, \ldots, \tau_n), (\sigma_1, \ldots, \sigma_n)$ be two fixed points of Φ. Define $\tau_i^j := \{v \in \tau_i \mid length(v) = j\}$ for any $j \geq 0$, and analogously for σ_i^j. One shows easily by induction on j that $\tau_i^j = \sigma_i^j$ for all i, j. Taking the limits of the two chains, the claim follows immediately. $\square$

Definition 4.11 The axiom system FX consists of the axioms (S2), ($\downarrow$), (F), (A), (E) and (U).

Corollary 4.12 *For every admissible parameter structure $\mathcal{B}$, we have that $\mathcal{B}^\dagger \models FX$.*

5 Some Properties of FX

5.1 Determinants

As an immediate consequence of (U) and the definition of $\exists^{\leq 1}$, we get

Proposition 5.1 *For every formula ψ and determinant δ, we have*

$$FX \models \tilde{\forall}\,(\Delta_\delta \wedge \exists\mathsf{co}(\delta)\,(\delta \wedge \psi) \to \forall\mathsf{co}(\delta)\,(\delta \to \psi)).$$

This prominent role of determinants is the heart of the entailment check for the feature theory CFT (Smolka and Treinen 1994).

5.2 Primitive Formulae

Definition 5.2 The set of *primitive formulae* is defined by the grammar

$$p ::= \sigma \mid xt{\downarrow} \mid p \wedge p \mid p \vee p \mid \neg p \mid \forall\chi\,p \mid \exists\chi\,p,$$

where σ denotes an arbitrary Σ-formula, and where χ denotes a variable not of sort Tree.

In other words, a primitive formula is a $\Sigma^\dagger$-formula that does not contain a Tree-quantifier, and does not contain an atom of the form $x \doteq y$ or $x[t]y$. A primitive formula without free Tree-variables is in fact a Σ-formula. Intuitively, in a primitive formula, the sort Tree is only used to express statements that could be as well expressed using sets. The following definition makes this intuition formal:

Definition 5.3 We define inductively $\phi[F /\!/ x]$, the replacement of a Tree-variable x by a Set-variable F in a primitive formula ϕ.

$$
\begin{aligned}
xt{\downarrow}[F /\!/ x] &= t \dot{\in} F \\
a[F /\!/ x] &= a \qquad \text{if } a \text{ is an atomic formula} \\
&\qquad\qquad \text{different from } xt{\downarrow} \text{ for all } t \\
(\neg\phi)[F /\!/ x] &= \neg(\phi[F /\!/ x]) \\
(\phi_1 \wedge \phi_2)[F /\!/ x] &= \phi_1[F /\!/ x] \wedge \phi_2[F /\!/ x] \\
(\exists\chi\,\phi)[F /\!/ x] &= \exists\chi\,(\phi[F /\!/ x]) \qquad \text{if } F \neq \chi \\
(\exists F\,\phi)[F /\!/ x] &= \exists G\,((\phi[G/F])[F /\!/ x]) \qquad \text{if } G \notin \mathtt{fr}(\phi)
\end{aligned}
$$

and similarly for the derived logical operations.

Intuitively, $\phi[F /\!/ x]$ abstracts the feature tree x in ϕ to a set F. This operation is an abstraction since it "drops" all the subtrees of a feature tree and just keeps the information about the features defined at the root. Again, this notation generalizes to simultaneous replacement $\gamma[\bar{F} /\!/ \bar{x}]$. For instance, $\phi := xa(f){\downarrow} \wedge \forall g\,(xa(g){\downarrow} \to xb(g){\downarrow})$ is a primitive formula, and

$$\phi[F /\!/ x] = a(f) \dot{\in} F \wedge \forall g(a(g) \dot{\in} F \to b(g) \dot{\subset} F).$$

The following lemma expresses that the definition of $\phi[F /\!/ x]$ meets the intuition of replacing a Tree-variable x by a Set-variable F.

Proposition 5.4 *Let ϕ be a primitive formula. Then*

$$\models \tilde{\forall} \left(\text{arity}(\bar{x}, \bar{F}) \to (\phi \leftrightarrow \phi[\bar{F}/\!/\bar{x}]) \right)$$

It would be possible to extend the definition of a primitive formula and of $\phi[F/\!/x]$ to allow also for Tree-quantifiers. The definition given here is sufficient for the quantifier elimination as described below.

6 The Main Theorem

We first define the class of *restricted formulae*, which is the class of input formulae for our quantifier elimination procedure.

Definition 6.1 (Restricted formula) A $\Sigma^\dagger$-formula is called a *restricted formula*, if in every subformula $x[t]y$ the term t is ground.

In the following, we will also speak of restricted sentences, the restricted theory of a $\Sigma^\dagger$-structure, and so on.

Theorem 6.2 (Main Theorem) *There is an algorithm which computes for every restricted $\Sigma^\dagger$-sentence σ a Σ-sentence γ with $FX \models \sigma \leftrightarrow \gamma$.*

Before we can discuss the top-level structure of the proof we need some additional concepts which describe the intermediate results we get during the quantifier elimination.

Definition 6.3 (Molecule) The set of *molecules* is defined by the following grammar:

$$m ::= x \doteq y \mid x \not\doteq y \mid x[t]y \mid \neg x[t]y \mid p.$$

where p is a primitive formula, and where t is a ground term.

Hence, any molecule without free Tree-variables is in fact a primitive formula without free Tree-variables, and hence a Σ-formula.

Definition 6.4 (Basic formula) A *basic formula* is a $\Sigma^\dagger$-formula of the form

$$\exists \bar{x} \, (m_1 \wedge \ldots \wedge m_n),$$

where $m_1, \ldots, m_n$ are molecules. A variable is *local* to a basic formula $\exists \bar{x} \, \phi$ if it occurs in $\bar{x}$, and *global* otherwise.

Let $\exists \bar{x} \, \phi$ be a basic formula, and let γ be the greatest graph contained in ϕ. That is, γ is the set of all molecules of the form $x[t]y$ contained in ϕ. Then we define $F_\phi^x = F_\gamma^x$.

Theorem 6.2 follows from the following lemma:

Lemma 6.5 (Main Lemma) *There is an algorithm which computes for every basic formula ϕ a universally quantified Boolean combination ψ of molecules, such that*

1. $FX \models \tilde{\forall} \, (\phi \leftrightarrow \psi)$
2. $\text{fr}(\psi) \subseteq \text{fr}(\phi)$

3. *if* $\mathtt{fr}(\phi) = \emptyset$, *then* ψ *is a boolean combination of molecules.*

We borrow the technique of proving Theorem 6.2 from Lemma 6.5 from Malc'ev 1971 and Comon and Lescanne 1989.

Proof of Theorem 6.2. It is sufficient to consider only sentences σ in a weak prenex normal form, where the matrix is just required to be boolean combination of molecules (instead of a boolean combination of atoms). We proceed by induction on the number n of quantifier blocks in the quantifier prefix.

If $n = 0$, then since σ is a sentence, it does not contain any Tree-variables and hence is a Σ-sentence.

Let $n \geq 1$ and $\sigma = Q \exists \bar{x}\ \phi$, where Q is a (possibly empty) string of quantifiers, not ending with $\exists$, and ϕ is a Boolean combination of molecules. We transform ϕ into disjunctive normal form and obtain an equivalent formula

$$Q \exists \bar{x}\ (\phi_1 \vee \ldots \vee \phi_n),$$

where every ϕ is a conjunction of molecules. This is equivalent to

$$Q(\exists \bar{x}\ \phi_1 \vee \ldots \vee \exists \bar{x}\ \phi_n),$$

where every $\exists \bar{x}\ \phi_i$ is a basic formula. Using (1) of Lemma 6.5, we can transform this equivalently into

$$Q(\forall \bar{y}_1\ \psi_1 \vee \ldots \vee \forall \bar{y}_n\ \psi_n),$$

where every ψ_i is a Boolean combination of molecules, and where all $\bar{y}_i$ are empty if Q is the empty string (because of (3) in Lemma 6.5). After possibly renaming bound variables, this can be transformed into the sentence $Q \forall \bar{x}\ \psi$, where ψ is Boolean combination of molecules. By condition (2) of Lemma 6.5, $Q \forall \bar{z}\ \psi$ is again a sentence. Since the number of quantifier alternations in $Q \forall \bar{x}\ \psi$ is $n - 1$, we can now apply the induction hypothesis.

If the innermost block of quantifiers consists of universal quantifiers, we consider the negation $\neg\sigma$ of the sentence (which now has an existential innermost block of quantifiers) and transform it into a restricted sentence γ. Consequently, $FX \models \sigma \leftrightarrow \neg\gamma$. $\square$

Corollary 6.6 *If B is an admissible Σ-structure, then the restricted theory of $B^\dagger$ is decidable relative to the theory of B.*

Note that all four admissible parameter structures introduced at the end of Section 3 have a decidable first-order theory.

1. We can interpret the theory of $\mathcal{B}_C$ in *S1S*, the monadic second order theory of natural numbers with successor. The decidability of the theory of $\mathcal{B}_C$ follows from Büchi's result (Büchi 1960) on the decidability of *S1S*.

2. Analogously, the decidability of the theory of $\mathcal{B}_F$ follows from the decidability of *WS1S*, the weak monadic second order theory of the

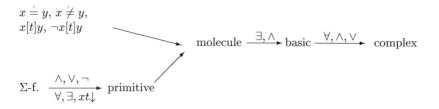

FIGURE 2 Classes of formulae

natural numbers with successor. The decidability of *WS1S* is an easy corollary of Büchi 1960, since the finite sets are definable in *S1S*.

3. Decidability of the theory of $\mathcal{B}_N$ follows again from Büchi 1960, since the initial fragments of natural numbers are definable in *S1S*.

4. Definability of the theory of $\mathcal{B}_S$ follows from Rabin's celebrated result (Rabin 1969) on the decidability of *S2S*, the monadic second order theory of two successor functions. Note that the prefix relation and the lexical ordering can be defined in *S2S* (Thomas 1990).

Corollary 6.7 *The restricted theory of* $B^\dagger$, *where* B *is one of* $\mathcal{B}_C$, $\mathcal{B}_F$, $\mathcal{B}_N$, $\mathcal{B}_S$, *is decidable.*

7 The Reduction

We now prove Lemma 6.5. Our goal is to eliminate, by equivalence transformations with respect to FX, all the quantifiers of sort Tree, taking care not to introduce new variables. This will be achieved by transformation rules which transform basic formulae into combinations of basic formulae. To make this formal, we introduce the class of *complex formulae* (see Figure 2 for an overview of the different syntactic classes of formulae):

Definition 7.1 (Complex formula) The set of *complex formulae* is defined by the following grammar:

$$F ::= \forall x\, F \mid F \wedge F \mid F \vee F \mid \langle \textit{basic formula} \rangle.$$

Note that this fragment, by closure of the set of molecules under negation, also contains constructions like

$$\textit{molecule}_1 \wedge \ldots \wedge \textit{molecule}_n \to \textit{basic formula}.$$

The transformation rules always have a basic formula in the hypothesis. Such a rule can be applied to any maximal basic formula occurring in a complex formula. The maximality condition means here, that we have to use the complete existential quantifier prefix. If a complex formula does not contain any existential quantifier then it can be easily transformed into a universally quantified boolean combination of molecules by moving universal quantifiers outside.

$$(\text{Sc}) \quad \frac{\exists \bar{x}\,(m \wedge \phi)}{m \wedge \exists \bar{x}\,\phi} \qquad \mathbf{fr}(m) \cap \bar{x} = \emptyset,\ m \text{ is not a primitive formula}$$

$$(\text{E1}) \quad \frac{\exists \bar{x}, x\,(x \doteq y \wedge \phi)}{\exists \bar{x}\,\phi[y/x]} \qquad y \neq x$$

$$(\text{E2}) \quad \frac{\exists \bar{x}\,(x \doteq x \wedge \phi)}{\exists \bar{x}\,\phi}$$

$$(\text{IE1}) \quad \frac{\exists \bar{x}\,(x \not\doteq x \wedge \phi)}{\bot}$$

$$(\text{UD}) \quad \frac{\exists \bar{x}\,(\neg x[t]y \wedge \phi)}{\exists \bar{x}\,(xt{\uparrow} \wedge \phi) \atop \vee\ \exists \bar{x}, z\,(x[t]z \wedge z \not\doteq y \wedge \phi)} \qquad z \text{ new}$$

$$(\text{FD}) \quad \frac{\exists \bar{x}\,(x[t]y \wedge x[t]z \wedge \phi)}{\exists \bar{x}\,(x[t]y \wedge y \doteq z \wedge \phi)}$$

$$(\text{FI}) \quad \frac{\exists \bar{x}\,\phi}{s \doteq t \wedge \exists \bar{x}\,\phi[t/s] \atop \vee\ \exists \bar{x}\,(s \not\doteq t \wedge \phi)} \qquad \begin{array}{l}\text{the ground terms } s,\ t \text{ occur in } \phi, \\ s \neq t\end{array}$$

$$(\text{FQ}) \quad \frac{\exists \bar{x}, x\,(y[t]x \wedge \phi)}{yt{\downarrow} \wedge \forall z\,(y[t]z \to \exists \bar{x}\,\phi[z/x])} \qquad y \notin \bar{x}, z \text{ new}$$

FIGURE 3 The rule set (QSF) for quasi-solved forms.

Definition 7.2 (Quasi-solved from) A basic formula $\exists \bar{x}\,\gamma$ is a *quasi-solved form*, if

1. γ does not contain a molecule $x \doteq y$ or $\neg x[t]y$,
2. if $x \not\doteq y \in \gamma$, then $x \neq y$, and $x \in \bar{x}$ or $y \in \bar{x}$.
3. if $x[t]y \in \gamma$, then $x \in \bar{x}$,
4. if $x[t]y \wedge x[t]z \subseteq \gamma$, then $y = z$.
5. if the ground Feat-terms t, s occur in γ and $t \neq s$, then $t \not\doteq s \in \gamma$.
6. if $x \in \bar{x}$, then $\text{arity}(x, F^x_\phi) \in \gamma$ or $\neg\text{arity}(x, F^x_\phi) \in \gamma$.

7.1 Transformation into Quasi-solved Form

The goal of the rules in Figure 3 is to have only basic formulae which are quasi-solved forms.

Proposition 7.3 *The rules described by (SC), (E1), (E2), (IE1), (FI) are equivalence transformations in every structure.*

Lemma 7.4 *(UD) describes an equivalence transformation in every model of the axioms schemes ($\uparrow$), (F).*

Proof. Axiom scheme (F) is equivalent to

$$\forall x, y \left(x[t]y \leftrightarrow \exists z\, x[t]z \wedge \forall z\, (x[t]z \to z \doteq y) \right),$$

which can be transformed equivalently, using axiom ($\downarrow$), into

$$\forall x, y \left(\neg x[t]y \leftrightarrow xt{\uparrow} \vee \exists z\, (x[t]z \wedge z \not\doteq y) \right).$$

As a consequence, we have for every formula ϕ with $z \notin \mathbf{fr}(\phi)$:

$$(\uparrow), (F) \models \tilde{\forall} \left(\neg x[t]y \wedge \phi \leftrightarrow (xt{\uparrow} \wedge \phi) \vee \exists z\, (x[t]z \wedge z \not\doteq y \wedge \phi) \right),$$

and hence

$$(\uparrow), (F) \models \tilde{\forall} \left(\exists \bar{x}\, (\neg x[t]y \wedge \phi) \leftrightarrow \exists \bar{x}\, (xt{\uparrow} \wedge \phi) \vee \exists \bar{x}, z\, (x[t]z \wedge z \not\doteq y \wedge \phi) \right). \quad \Box$$

Lemma 7.5 *(FD) describes an equivalence transformation in every model of the axiom scheme (F).*

Lemma 7.6 *(FQ) describes an equivalence transformation in every model of the axiom scheme (F).*

Proof. We have for any formula ψ with $z \notin \mathbf{fr}(\psi)$

$$(F) \models \tilde{\forall} \left(\exists x\, (y[t]x \wedge \psi) \leftrightarrow yt{\downarrow} \wedge \forall z\, (y[t]z \to \psi[z/x]) \right).$$

Choose ψ to be the formula $\exists \bar{x}\, \phi$. Since $y \notin \bar{x}$, the antecedent of the rule is equivalent to $\exists x\, (y[t]x \wedge \exists \bar{x}\, \phi)$, and the claim follows immediately. $\quad \Box$

For this rule it is essential that t is ground.

Lemma 7.7 *The rule system (QSF) is terminating.*

Proof. We define a measure on basic formulae and show, that for every rule application the measure of every single basic formula generated is smaller than the measure of the basic formula being replaced. Termination then follows by a standard multiset argument. We assign a basic formula γ the tuple $(\alpha_1, \alpha_2, \alpha_3, \alpha_4)$, where

1. α_1 is the number of $\neg x[t]y$ molecules in γ,
2. α_2 is the number of $x[t]y$ molecules in γ,
3. α_3 is the number of pairs (t, s) of **Feat**-ground terms, where both t and s occur in γ, but $t \not\doteq s$ does not occur in γ,
4. α_4 is the total length of γ.

It is now easily checked that the lexicographic ordering on these measures is strictly decreased by every application of a rule. The side condition of rule (Sc) guarantees that no formula of the form $t \not\doteq s$, $\mathrm{arity}(x, F_\phi^x)$ or $\neg\mathrm{arity}(x, F_\phi^x)$ is moved out of a basic formula. $\quad \Box$

Corollary 7.8 *There is an algorithm, which transforms any basic formula into a FX-equivalent complex formula, in which all basic formulae are quasi-solved forms.*

Proof. We compute a normal-from with respect to the rule set (QSF), and from this compute a normal form with respect to the following rule:

$$\text{(ST)} \quad \frac{\exists \bar{x}, x \; \phi}{\begin{array}{c} \exists \bar{x}, x \; (\phi \wedge \text{arity}(x, F_\phi^x)) \\ \vee \; \exists \bar{x}, x \; (\phi \wedge \neg\text{arity}(x, F_\phi^x)). \end{array}} \quad \text{arity}(x, F_\phi^x), \neg\text{arity}(x, F_\phi^x) \notin \phi \qquad \square$$

7.2 Eliminating Quasi-Solved Forms with Sloppy Inequations

In this section, we show how to eliminate quasi-solved forms with only benign inequations, in a sense to be explained soon. In the next subsection, we will explain how to get rid of nasty inequations.

Definition 7.9 (Sloppy and tight variables) Let $\exists \bar{x} \; \gamma$ be a basic formula. We call a local variable $x \in \bar{x}$ *tight (in $\exists \bar{x} \; \gamma$)* if $\text{arity}(x, F_\gamma^x) \in \gamma$, and otherwise *sloppy*.

By the definition of a quasi-solved form, $\neg\text{arity}(x, F_\phi^x) \in \gamma$ for every sloppy variable x.

Definition 7.10 (Closure) For a graph γ, we define for every feature path π of Feat-terms the relation $\leadsto_\gamma^\pi$ as the smallest relation on $\text{fr}(\gamma)$ with

$$x \leadsto_\gamma^\epsilon x \quad \text{if } x \in \text{fr}(\gamma)$$

$$\text{if } x \leadsto_\gamma^\pi y \text{ and } y[t]z \in \gamma, \text{ then } x \leadsto_\gamma^{\pi t} z$$

We write $x \leadsto_\gamma y$ if $x \leadsto_\gamma^\pi y$ for some π.

For a graph γ and variables x, y, we define the *closure* of (x, y)

$$\langle x, y \rangle_\gamma := \{(u, v) \in \text{fr}(\gamma)^2 \mid x \leadsto_\gamma^\pi u \text{ and } y \leadsto_\gamma^\pi v \text{ for some } \pi\}.$$

In Backofen 1995, the variable y with $x \leadsto_\gamma^\pi y$ has been called the *value* $|x\pi|_\gamma$ of the rooted path $x\pi$ in γ. Obviously, $\langle x, y \rangle_\gamma$ can be computed in finitely many steps.

Proposition 7.11 *For every graph γ, variables x, y and $(u, v) \in \langle x, y \rangle_\gamma$ we have*

$$(F) \models (\gamma \wedge u \neq v \to x \neq y).$$

Definition 7.12 (Sloppy and tight inequations) Let $\exists \bar{x} \; \gamma$ be a basic formula. We call an inequation $x \neq y$ *sloppy (in $\exists \bar{x} \; \gamma$)*, if there is a $(u, v) \in \langle x, y \rangle_\gamma$ with $x \neq y$, where at least one of u and v is sloppy. Otherwise, the inequation is called *tight*.

The benign inequations handled in this section are the sloppy ones. The idea is that for sloppy variables, we have enough freedom to make them all different.

In the following, we assume a partition of a quasi-solved form as $\exists \bar{x} (\gamma \wedge \iota \wedge \rho)$, where γ denotes a graph, ι denotes a conjunction of inequations between Tree-variables, and ρ denotes a primitive formula. Note that in this case, by the definition of quasi-solved forms, $\mathtt{co}(\gamma) \subseteq \bar{x}$, $\Delta_\gamma \subseteq \rho$, and ι contains only non-trivial inequations which use at least one local variable. For a graph γ, we denote by $\tilde{\gamma}$ the formula obtained by replacing every atom $x[t]y$ by $xt{\downarrow}$.

Lemma 7.13 *Let $\exists \bar{x} (\gamma \wedge \rho)$ be a quasi solved form without inequations. Then*

$$FX \models \tilde{\forall} \Big(\exists \bar{x} (\gamma \wedge \rho) \to \exists \bar{F} ((\tilde{\gamma} \wedge \rho)[\bar{F}/\!/\bar{x}]) \Big),$$

where $\bar{F}$ is disjoint with $\mathtt{fr}(\rho)$.

Proof. Let $\mathcal{A} \models FX$ and α be a valuation with $\mathcal{A}, \alpha \models \exists \bar{x} (\gamma \wedge \rho)$. Since $\models \gamma \to \tilde{\gamma}$, we get $\mathcal{A}, \alpha \models \exists \bar{x} (\tilde{\gamma} \wedge \rho)$. Together with axiom (A), this means since $\bar{F}$ is disjoint with $\mathtt{fr}(\rho)$, that $\mathcal{A}, \alpha \models \exists \bar{x}, \bar{F} (\mathrm{arity}(\bar{x}, \bar{F}) \wedge \tilde{\gamma} \wedge \rho)$. With Proposition 5.4, we get

$$\mathcal{A}, \alpha \models \exists \bar{F} ((\tilde{\gamma} \wedge \rho)[\bar{F}/\!/\bar{x}]),$$

since $\bar{x}$ is disjoint with $\mathtt{fr}((\tilde{\gamma} \wedge \rho)[\bar{F}/\!/\bar{x}])$. $\quad\square$

Lemma 7.14 *Let $\exists \bar{x} (\gamma \wedge \iota \wedge \rho)$ be a quasi solved form, where $\bar{F}$ is disjoint with $\mathtt{fr}(\rho)$ and ι consists of sloppy inequations only. Then*

$$FX \models \tilde{\forall} \Big(\exists \bar{F} ((\tilde{\gamma} \wedge \rho)[\bar{F}/\!/\bar{x}]) \to \exists \bar{x} (\gamma \wedge \iota \wedge \rho) \Big).$$

Proof. Let $\mathcal{A} \models FX$ and α be a valuation with $\mathcal{A}, \alpha \models \exists \bar{F} (\tilde{\gamma} \wedge \rho)[\bar{F}/\!/\bar{x}]$. Let β be an $\bar{F}$-update of α, such that $\mathcal{A}, \beta \models (\tilde{\gamma} \wedge \rho)[\bar{F}/\!/\bar{x}]$. Let Sl be the set of sloppy variables of $\gamma \wedge \rho$. Let f, F be new variables, and for every $x \in Sl$, let $n_x \geq 0$, and $f_x, x^0, \ldots, x^{n_x}$ be variables not occurring in $\gamma \wedge \rho$. Let $Slf = \{f_x \mid x \in Sl\}$, and $Slx = \{x^i \mid x \in Sl, 0 \leq i \leq n_x\}$. We define an extension ξ of γ by

$$\xi := \gamma \wedge \bigwedge_{x \in Sl} (x[f_x]x^0 \wedge x^0[f]x^1 \wedge \ldots x^{n_x - 1}[f]x^{n_x} \wedge \mathrm{arity}(x^{n_x}, F)).$$

Hence, $\models \xi \to \gamma$. By axiom (S2), there are $a \in \mathrm{Feat}^{\mathcal{A}}$ and $A, B \in \mathrm{Set}^{\mathcal{A}}$ with $a \in^{\mathcal{A}} A$ and $a \notin^{\mathcal{A}} B$. We denote by $\bar{\bar{x}}$ the extension of $\bar{x}$ by Slx, and by $\bar{\bar{F}}$ an according extension of $\bar{F}$. Hence, by definition of sloppiness, there is a $Slf \cup Slx \cup \{f, F\}$-update β' of β such that

$$\mathcal{A}, \beta' \models \Delta_\xi \wedge (\tilde{\xi} \wedge \rho)[\bar{\bar{F}}/\!/\bar{\bar{x}}].$$

Especially, $\beta'(f) = a$, $\beta'(F^i) = A$ if F corresponds to some x^i with $i \leq n_x$, and $\beta'(F^i) = B$ if F corresponds to some x^{n_x}. Note, that Δ_ξ extends

$\Delta_\gamma \subseteq \rho$ just by stating that f_x is assigned a value different from all (ground) terms in F_γ^x. By construction, $\mathcal{A}, \beta' \models \bigwedge_{i=1}^n \bigwedge_{a \in F_\xi^{x_i}} a \in F_i$. Hence, by axiom (E), there is an $\bar{\bar{x}}$-update β'' of β', such that

$$\mathcal{A}, \beta'' \models \xi \wedge \mathrm{arity}(\bar{\bar{x}}, \bar{\bar{F}}).$$

Let $\alpha'(x) = \beta''(x)$ if $x \in \bar{x}$, and $\alpha'(x) = \alpha(x)$ otherwise. Hence, $\mathcal{A}, \alpha' \models \gamma$. By Proposition 5.4 and since $\bar{F}$ is disjoint with $\mathrm{fr}(\rho)$, $\mathcal{A}, \alpha' \models \rho$.

Since there are infinitely many choices of n_x for every $x \in Sl$, we can easily find values n_x such that $\beta''(x) \neq \beta''(y)$ for every variable $y \in \mathrm{fr}(\gamma \wedge \iota \wedge \rho)$ with $y \neq x$. Hence, by Proposition 7.11, $\mathcal{A}, \alpha' \models \iota$. □

We are now ready to give the elimination rule for quasi-solved forms with benign inequations:

(IE2) $$\frac{\exists \bar{x}\,(\gamma \wedge \iota \wedge \rho)}{\exists \bar{F}\,((\tilde{\gamma} \wedge \rho)[\bar{F}/\!/\bar{x}])} \qquad \begin{array}{l} \text{if } \iota \text{ contains only sloppy inequations} \\ \bar{F} \cap \mathrm{fr}(\rho) = \emptyset \end{array}$$

As an example of rule (IE2), consider

$$\frac{\exists x, y, u\,(\ x[s]y \wedge u[s]v \wedge y[t]y \wedge x \not\doteq u \wedge \mathrm{arity}(x, \{s\}) \wedge}{\exists F, G, H\,(\ s \doteq F \wedge s \in G \wedge t \in H \wedge \forall \nu\,(\nu \in F \leftrightarrow \nu \doteq s) \wedge}$$
$$\frac{\mathrm{arity}(u, \{s\}) \wedge \neg\mathrm{arity}(y, \{t\})))}{\forall \nu\,(\nu \in G \leftrightarrow \nu \doteq s) \wedge \neg\forall \nu\,(\nu \in F \leftrightarrow \nu \doteq s))}$$

Here, $x \not\doteq u$ is a sloppy inequation since y is a sloppy variable.

From Lemma 7.14 and Lemma 7.13, we get immediately

Lemma 7.15 *The rule (IE2) describes an equivalence transformation in every model of FX.*

Corollary 7.16 *There is an algorithm, which transforms any complex formula, in which all basic formulae are quasi-solved forms containing only sloppy inequations, into a FX-equivalent universally quantified boolean combination of molecules.*

7.3 Eliminating Tight Inequations

In the closure of tight inequations, there are only inequations of type *tight* $\neq$ *tight* or *tight* $\neq$ *global*. We first show how to transform the quasi-solved form such that the only tight inequations are of type *tight* $\neq$ *global*. Then, we show how to get rid of the *tight* $\neq$ *global* inequations.

(IE3) $$\frac{\exists \bar{x}\,(\gamma \wedge \iota \wedge x \not\doteq y \wedge \rho)}{\exists \bar{x}\,(\gamma \wedge \iota \wedge \rho)} \qquad \begin{array}{l} \text{there are tight variables } u, v \text{ with} \\ (u, v) \in \langle x, y \rangle_\gamma \text{ and } F_\gamma^u \neq F_\gamma^v. \end{array}$$

From Proposition 7.11, we get

Proposition 7.17 *The rule (IE3) describes an equivalence transformation on quasi-solved forms in every model of FX.*

Proof. This is a consequence of condition (5) in the definition of a quasi-solved form. □

We say that the set η of equations is *closed* under a graph γ, if whenever $x \doteq y \in \gamma$ and $(u, v) \in \langle x, y \rangle_\gamma$, then $u \doteq v \in \gamma$.

Proposition 7.18 *Let δ be a determinant and η a set of equations which is closed under δ. If $\mathtt{fr}(\eta) \subseteq \mathtt{co}(\delta)$ and $F_\delta^x = F_\delta^y$ for every equation $x \doteq y \in \eta$, then*

$$FX \models \tilde{\forall}\,(\Delta_\delta \to (\delta \to \eta)).$$

Proof. Let $\mathcal{A}, \alpha \models \Delta_\delta$. By Proposition 5.1, we have to show that

(8) $$\mathcal{A}, \alpha \models \exists \mathtt{co}(\delta)(\delta \wedge \eta)$$

Let θ be an idempotent substitution equivalent to η. Then

$$
\begin{aligned}
(8) \quad &\Leftrightarrow \quad \mathcal{A}, \alpha \models \exists \mathtt{co}(\delta)(\delta \wedge \theta) \\
&\Leftrightarrow \quad \mathcal{A}, \alpha \models \exists \mathtt{co}(\delta)(\theta\delta \wedge \theta) \\
(9) \quad &\Leftrightarrow \quad \mathcal{A}, \alpha \models \exists \mathtt{co}(\delta)(\theta\delta) \qquad \text{since } \mathtt{fr}(\theta) \subseteq \mathtt{co}(\delta)
\end{aligned}
$$

By construction, $\theta\delta$ is again a determinant, with $\mathtt{co}(\theta) \subseteq \mathtt{co}(\delta)$, and $\Delta_{\theta\delta} = \Delta_\delta$. Hence, (9) follows from axiom (E). □

A similar lemma, in the context of CFT, was presented in Smolka and Treinen 1994.

Proposition 7.19 *Let δ be a determinant and η, η' be sets of equations such that $\eta \wedge \eta'$ is closed under δ. If $\mathtt{fr}(\eta) \subseteq \mathtt{co}(\delta)$ and $F_\delta^x = F_\delta^y$ for every equation $x \doteq y \in \eta$, then*

$$FX \models \Delta_\delta \to \tilde{\forall}\,(\delta \to (\eta' \leftrightarrow \eta \wedge \eta')).$$

Proof. We have to show that

(10) $$FX \models \tilde{\forall}\,(\Delta_\delta \wedge \delta \wedge \eta' \to \eta).$$

Let θ' be an idempotent substitution equivalent to η'. Then (10) is equivalent to

(11) $$FX \models \tilde{\forall}\,(\Delta_\delta \wedge \theta'\delta \to \theta'\eta),$$

since $\theta'\Delta_\delta = \Delta_\delta$. Observe, that $\Delta_\delta = \Delta_{\theta'\delta}$, $\mathtt{fr}(\theta'\eta) \subseteq \mathtt{co}(\theta'\delta)$, $\theta'\eta$ is closed under $\theta'\delta$, and that $F_{\theta'\delta}^x = F_{\theta'\delta}^y$ for every equation $x \doteq y \in \gamma$. Hence, (11) follows from Proposition 7.18. □

We can now give the rule which reduces the *tight $\neq$ tight* inequations to *tight $\neq$ global* inequations:

(IE4) $\quad\dfrac{\exists \bar{x}\,(\gamma \wedge \iota \wedge x \not\doteq y \wedge \rho)}{\displaystyle\bigvee_{(u,v)\in I} \exists \bar{x}\,(\gamma \wedge \iota \wedge u \not\doteq v \wedge \rho)}\qquad \begin{array}{l} x \not\doteq y \text{ tight, (IE3) does not apply,} \\ I = \{(u,v) \in \langle x,y\rangle_\gamma \mid \{u,v\} \not\subseteq \\ \bar{x}\} \end{array}$

As an example of rule (IE4), consider

$$\dfrac{\begin{array}{l}\exists x,y,v\ (\ x[s]v \wedge x[t]v' \wedge y[s]w \wedge y[t]w' \wedge s \not\doteq t \wedge \\ \qquad \text{arity}(x,\{s,t\}) \wedge \text{arity}(y,\{s,t\}) \wedge \text{arity}(v,\{\}) \wedge x \not\doteq y)\end{array}}{\begin{array}{l}\quad\ \exists x,y,v\ (\ x[s]v \wedge x[t]v' \wedge y[s]w \wedge y[t]w' \wedge s \not\doteq t \wedge \\ \qquad \text{arity}(x,\{s,t\}) \wedge \text{arity}(y,\{s,t\}) \wedge \text{arity}(v,\{\}) \wedge v \not\doteq w) \\ \vee\ \ \exists x,y,v\ (\ x[s]v \wedge x[t]v' \wedge y[s]w \wedge y[t]w' \wedge s \not\doteq t \wedge \\ \qquad \text{arity}(x,\{s,t\}) \wedge \text{arity}(y,\{s,t\}) \wedge \text{arity}(v,\{\}) \wedge v' \not\doteq w')\end{array}}$$

Lemma 7.20 *The rule (IE4) describes an equivalence transformation in every model of FX.*

Proof. This follows immediately from Proposition 7.19. $\square$

Finally, we give the rule to eliminate *tight $\not\doteq$ global* inequations.

Definition 7.21 (Generated subformula) For a conjunction ϕ of molecules and variable x, the *subformula ϕ_x of ϕ generated by x* is defined as

$$\phi_x := \{u[t]v, \text{arity}(u,M) \in \phi \mid x \leadsto_\phi u\}.$$

Note that, if $x \not\doteq y$ is tight in the quasi-solved form $\exists \bar{x}\,\phi$, then ϕ_x is a determinant.

(IE5) $\quad\dfrac{\exists \bar{x}, x\,(\phi \wedge x \not\doteq y)}{\exists \bar{x}, x\,\phi \wedge \forall \text{co}(\phi_x)\,(\phi_x \to x \not\doteq y)}\qquad y \notin \bar{x}, y \not\doteq x, x \text{ tight}$

As an example of rule (IE5), consider

$$\dfrac{\exists x,x'\,(x[s]x \wedge x[t]y \wedge x'[t]x' \wedge s \not\doteq t \wedge \text{arity}(x,\{f\}) \wedge x \not\doteq y)}{\begin{array}{l}\exists x,x'\,(x[s]x \wedge x[t]y \wedge x'[t]x' \wedge s \not\doteq t \wedge \text{arity}(x,\{f\})) \wedge \\ \forall x\,(x[s]x \wedge x[t]y \wedge \text{arity}(x,\{f\}) \to x \not\doteq y)\end{array}}$$

Lemma 7.22 *The rule (IE5) describes an equivalence transformation in every model of FX.*

Proof. First note that $\text{co}(\phi_x) \subseteq \bar{x} \cup \{x\}$. Since $\models \phi \to \phi_x$, the conclusion implies the hypothesis.

The hypothesis obviously implies the first part of the conclusion. By Proposition 5.1, it also implies the second part (note that $\Delta_{\phi_x} \subseteq \phi$, since ϕ is a quasi-solved form). $\square$

Corollary 7.23 *There is an algorithm, which transform any complex formula in which all basic formulae are quasi-solved forms, into a FX-*

equivalent complex formula, in which all basic formulae are quasi-solved forms containing only sloppy inequations.

Hence, we obtain the proof of Lemma 6.5 by composing the Corollaries 7.8, 7.16 and 7.23.

Acknowledgments. David Israel pointed out the analogy to the situation in process logic. Rolf Backofen, Patrick Blackburn, Andreas Podelski and Gert Smolka provided helpful criticism and remarks.

This work has been partially supported by the Bundesminister für Bildung, Wissenschaft, Forschung und Technologie (Hydra, ITW 9105), the Human Capital and Mobiliy Programme of the European Union (SOL, CHRX-CT92-0053 and CONSOLE, CHRX-CT91-0195), the Esprit Basic Research Project ACCLAIM (EP 7195) and the Esprit Working Group CCL (EP 6028).

References

Aït-Kaci, Hassan. 1986. An Algebraic Semantics Approach to the Effective Resolution of Type Equations. *Theoretical Computer Science* 45:293–351.

Aït-Kaci, Hassan, and Roger Nasr. 1986. LOGIN: A Logic Programming Language with Built-In Inheritance. *Journal of Logic Programming* 3:185–215.

Aït-Kaci, Hassan, and Andreas Podelski. 1991. Towards a Meaning of LIFE. In *3rd International Symposium on Programming Language Implementation and Logic Programming*, ed. Jan Maluszyński and Martin Wirsing, 255–274. Lecture Notes in Computer Science, vol. 528. Springer-Verlag.

Aït-Kaci, Hassan, Andreas Podelski, and Gert Smolka. 1994. A Feature-based Constraint System for Logic Programming with Entailment. *Theoretical Computer Science* 122(1–2):263–283.

Andrews, Peter B. 1986. *An Introduction to Mathematical Logic and Type Theory: To Truth through Proof.* Computer Science and Applied Mathematics. Academic Press.

Backofen, Rolf. 1994a. *Expressivity and Decidability of First-Order Theories over Feature Trees.* Doctoral dissertation, Technische Fakultät der Universität des Saarlandes, Saarbrücken, Germany.

Backofen, Rolf. 1994b. Regular Path Expressions in Feature Logic. *Journal of Symbolic Computation* 17:421–455.

Backofen, Rolf. 1995. A Complete Axiomatization of a Theory with Feature and Arity Constraints. *Journal of Logic Programming* 24(1–2):37–71.

Backofen, Rolf, and Gert Smolka. 1995. A Complete and Recursive Feature Theory. *Theoretical Computer Science* 146(1–2):243–268.

Backofen, Rolf, and Ralf Treinen. 1994. How to Win a Game with Features. In *1st International Conference on Constraints in Computational Logics*, ed. Jean-Pierre Jouannaud. Lecture Notes in Computer Science, vol. 845. München, Germany. Springer-Verlag. Extended Version accepted for publication in *Information and Control*, special issue on CCL'94.

Büchi, J. R. 1960. On a Decision Method in Restricted Second Order Arithmetic. In *International Congr. on Logic, Methodology and Philosophy of Science*, ed. E. Nagel et. al., 1–11. Stanford University Press.

Comon, Hubert, and Pierre Lescanne. 1989. Equational Problems and Disunification. *Journal of Symbolic Computation* 7(3,4):371–425.

Dörre, Jochen. 1993. *Feature-Logik und Semiunfikation*. Doctoral dissertation, Philosophische Fakultät der Universität Stuttgart. In German.

Dörre, Jochen. 1994. Feature-Logic with Weak Subsumption Constraints. In *Constraints, Language and Computation*, ed. M. A. Rosner C. J. Rupp and R. L. Johnson. Chap. 7, 187–203. Academic Press.

Dörre, Jochen, and William C. Rounds. 1992. On Subsumption and Semiunification in Feature Algebras. *Journal of Symbolic Computation* 13(4):441–461.

Gunter, C. A., and D. S. Scott. 1990. Semantic Domains. In van Leeuwen 1990, Chap. 12, 633–674.

Henz, Martin, Gert Smolka, and Jörg Würtz. 1995. Object-oriented Concurrent Constraint Programming in Oz. In *Principles and Practice of Constraint Programming*, ed. V. Saraswat and P. Van Hentenryck. Chap. 2, 27–48. Cambridge, MA: MIT Press.

Hodges, Wilfrid. 1993. *Model Theory*. Encyclopedia of Mathematics and its Applications 42. Cambridge University Press.

Jaffar, Joxan, and Jean-Louis Lassez. 1987. Constraint Logic Programming. In *Proceedings of the 14th ACM Conference on Principles of Programming Languages*, 111–119. Munich, Germany. ACM.

Johnson, Mark. 1988. *Attribute-Value Logic and the Theory of Grammar*. CSLI Lecture Notes 16. Stanford University, CA: Center for the Study of Language and Information.

Malc'ev, Anatolií Ivanovič. 1971. Axiomatizable Classes of Locally Free Algebras of Various Type. In *The Metamathematics of Algebraic Systems: Collected Papers 1936–1967*, ed. III Benjamin Franklin Wells. Chap. 23, 262–281. North Holland.

Parikh, Rohit. 1978. A Decidability Result for a Second Order Process Logic. In *19th Annual Symposion on Foundations of Computer Science*, 177–183. Ann Arbor, Michigan. IEEE.

Rabin, Michael O. 1969. Decidability of Second-Order Theories and Automata on Infinite Trees. *Transactions of the American Mathematical Society* 141:1–35.

Rounds, William C., and Robert Kasper. 1986. A Complete Logical Calculus for Record Structures Representing Linguistic Information. In *Proceedings of the First Symposium on Logic in Computer Science*, 38–43. Cambridge, MA, June. IEEE Computer Society.

Smolka, Gert. 1992. Feature Constraint Logics for Unification Grammars. *Journal of Logic Programming* 12:51–87.

Smolka, Gert. 1995. The Oz Programming Model. In *Current Trends in Computer Science*, ed. Jan van Leeuwen. 324–343. Lecture Notes in Computer Science, vol. 1000. Berlin, Heidelberg, New York: Springer-Verlag.

Smolka, Gert, and Hassan Aït-Kaci. 1989. Inheritance Hierarchies: Semantics and Unification. *Journal of Symbolic Computation* 7:343–370.

Smolka, Gert, and Ralf Treinen. 1994. Records for Logic Programming. *Journal of Logic Programming* 18(3):229–258.

Thomas, Wolfgang. 1990. Automata on Infinite Objects. In van Leeuwen 1990, Chap. 4, 133–191.

Treinen, Ralf. 1992. A New Method for Undecidability Proofs of First Order Theories. *Journal of Symbolic Computation* 14(5):437–457.

Treinen, Ralf. 1993. Feature Constraints with First-Class Features. In *Mathematical Foundations of Computer Science*, ed. Andrzej M. Borzyszkowski and Stefan Sokołowski, 734–743. Lecture Notes in Computer Science, vol. 711. Springer-Verlag.

van Leeuwen, Jan (ed.). 1990. *Handbook of Theoretical Computer Science*. Elsevier Science Publishers and The MIT Press.

8

Dutch Verb Clustering without Verb Clusters

GERTJAN VAN NOORD AND GOSSE BOUMA

ABSTRACT. We propose an analysis of Dutch cross-serial dependencies and related constructions based on minimal assumptions about phrase structure. We argue that there is no need to assume the existence of a constituent containing a "verb cluster" or "verbal complex". Furthermore, in clauses with normal (non-extraposed and non-topicalized) word order there are no (full or partial) VP's. Instead, all elements of a cross-serial dependency construction are directly dominated by S. The analysis is formulated in terms of Head-driven Phrase Structure Grammar (Pollard and Sag 1987, 1994), and makes crucial use of argument inheritance (Hinrichs and Nakazawa 1994). We demonstrate that our analysis not only accounts for the basic word order in cross-serial dependency constructions, but also for instances of partial extraposition and partial topicalization of VP's. We also show that a recent version of the HPSG binding theory is fully compatible with our analysis. Finally, we demonstrate how verb sequences in which the strictly cross-serial word order is not obeyed can be accounted for.

1 Introduction

1.1 The Cross-Serial Dependency Construction

Dutch subordinate clauses are verb-final. Furthermore, if the clause is headed by a modal, an auxiliary, or a verb such as *horen* (*to hear*), *proberen* (*to try*), *helpen* (to help) or *laten* (*to let*) (these are the so-called "verb-raising" verbs), the head of its non-finite VP-complement must occur right of the head of the main clause. This is illustrated in (1a, b). As the head of the non-finite VP can be a verb-raising verb itself, the construction can (in principle) lead to an arbitrary number of crossing dependencies between pre-verbal complements and verbs subcategorizing for these complements.

Specifying Syntactic Structures
P. Blackburn and M. de Rijke, eds.
Copyright © 1997, CSLI Publications.

This is illustrated in (1c), where subscripts are used to make the dependencies explicit.

(1) a. dat   Jan   het boek   *wil*   lezen
         that John   the book wants   read
         that John wants to read the book

     b. dat   Jan   Marie het boek   *laat* lezen
         that John   Mary   the book   lets   read
         that John lets Mary read the book

     c. dat Jan_1 $Marie_2$ het $boek_3$ wil_1 $laten_2$ $lezen_3$
         that John   Mary   the book   wants   let   read
         that John wants to let Mary read the book

In the remainder of this introduction, we review previous non-transformational accounts of the cross-serial dependency construction. In particular, we argue that in categorial and HPSG accounts, characterizing what counts as a verb-cluster is problematic. Next, we argue that there is little evidence for the existence of partial VP's in clauses with normal (i.e., non-topicalized and non-extraposed) word order. We conclude that our analysis, in which the verb cluster is not a constituent and partial VP's are not derivable in clauses with normal word order is an attractive alternative.

1.2   Problems with Verb-Clusters

There are numerous non-transformational accounts of the cross-serial dependency construction.[1] All these accounts assume that the clause-final sequence of verbs is a constituent (the "verb cluster" or "verbal complex"). Furthermore, with the exception of Kroch and Santorini 1987, who argue for a left-branching verb cluster, it is assumed that this cluster has a right-branching structure, as illustrated in (2).

(2)   dat Jan Marie het boek [wil [laten lezen]]

The assumption that the verb cluster is right-branching is problematic for categorial accounts as well as for HPSG accounts using argument inheritance.

Within Categorial Grammar, it has been proposed to derive verb clusters by means of (disharmonic versions of) composition or division. Composition can be used to combine a functor with its argument, even if this argument is "unsaturated". Division derives a category $(A/C)/(B/C)$ (or $(C\backslash A)/(C\backslash B)$ if used disharmonically) from a category A/B. The effect of such a rule is that a functor "inherits" the arguments of its argument. Us-

---

[1] See Bresnan et al. 1983 and Johnson 1988 for an account in terms of Lexical Functional grammar, Kroch and Santorini 1987 for an account in terms of Tree Adjoining Grammar, and Houtman 1984, Steedman 1985, Moortgat 1988, and Hoeksema 1991 for categorial accounts.

ing disharmonic division, one can for instance derive the verb cluster in (2) as follows:

(3)

$$
\begin{array}{ccc}
\textit{wil} & \textit{laten} & \textit{lezen} \\
\text{VP}/\text{VP} & (\text{NP}\backslash\text{VP})/\text{VP} & \text{NP}\backslash\text{VP} \\
\Downarrow & \Downarrow & \\
(\text{NP}\backslash\text{VP})/(\text{NP}\backslash\text{VP}) & \dfrac{(\text{NP}\backslash(\text{NP}\backslash\text{VP}))/(\text{NP}\backslash\text{VP})}{\text{NP}\backslash(\text{NP}\backslash\text{VP})} \\
\Downarrow & \\
\dfrac{(\text{NP}\backslash(\text{NP}\backslash\text{VP}))/(\text{NP}\backslash(\text{NP}\backslash\text{VP}))}{\text{NP}\backslash\text{NP}\backslash\text{VP}}
\end{array}
$$

A problem for categorial accounts has been the fact that cross-serial word order is obligatory, that is, if the governing verb is a verb-raising verb, it must be followed by the governed verb and may not be followed by any of the non-verbal arguments of the governed VP. Sequences in which the governed verb is followed by a full or partial VP including non-verbal complements are ungrammatical:

(4) a. * dat Jan *wil* het boek lezen
      that John wants the book read

  b. * dat Jan Marie *laat* het boek lezen
      that John Mary lets the book read

In a categorial grammar, such word orders are derived quite easily, however, using application instead of division or composition:

(5) ... *Jan* *wil* *het boek* *lezen*

$$
\begin{array}{cccc}
\text{NP} & \text{VP}/\text{VP} & \text{NP} & \text{NP}\backslash\text{VP} \\
& & \multicolumn{2}{c}{\overline{\hspace{2cm}}} \\
& & \multicolumn{2}{c}{\text{VP}} \\
\multicolumn{4}{c}{\overline{\hspace{4cm}}} \\
\multicolumn{4}{c}{\text{VP}}
\end{array}
$$

To eliminate these ungrammatical derivations, it has been proposed that the verbal argument of a verb-raising verb must be "lexical". However, example (2) illustrates that under the assumption that verb clusters are right-branching, the proper requirement cannot be that the verbal argument must be a single verb. Rather, complex phrases consisting of a sequence of verbs must be allowed as arguments, whereas phrases containing one or more non-verbal complements must be excluded. As such information cannot be read off the categories of the constituents involved, this implies that the categorial formalism needs to be extended with a feature distinguishing "verbal complexes" from other verbal constituents and a method for assigning this feature to derived constituents. Although such a system can be designed (see Bouma and van Noord 1994, for instance), the result remains unsatisfactory as it requires an ad-hoc system of feature passing, which cannot be subsumed by general methods such as head-feature passing.

The problem is not restricted to CG, but surfaces in HPSG accounts as well. Hinrichs and Nakazawa 1994, for instance, use an argument-inheritance mechanism, which lets the SUBCAT-list of a modal or auxiliary be determined in part by the SUBCAT-list of its verbal complement. Essentially, this is a restatement of the categorial rule of division as a constraint on SUBCAT-lists. They account for "auxiliary-flip" in German by assuming that an auxiliary may either follow or precede a verbal complex. The latter case gives rise to "flipped" word order (note that this order is the standard situation in Dutch). To avoid spurious ambiguity and ungrammatical word orders, they must introduce a feature NPCOMP, distinguishing phrases containing NP-complements from phrases not containing such complements. That is, as in categorial accounts, NPCOMP must distinguish between verb clusters and other verbal constituents. The percolation of NPCOMP does not follow from general principles of feature-percolation, but instead is stipulated in the relevant rule schemata.[2]

In this paper, we argue that the problem of characterizing verb clusters can be avoided if one assumes that clause-final verb sequences do not constitute a constituent.

1.3 Problems with Partial VPs

While early transformational accounts of the Dutch cross-serial dependency construction assumed that the clause-initial complements of the verbs present in the verb-cluster are sisters (after a "pruning" transformation had eliminated VP-nodes whose head had been V-raised to a clause-final position (Evers 1975)), non-transformational accounts have assumed that the initial part of the clause, preceding the verb cluster, has considerable internal structure. However, there is little theory-independent motivation for postulating the existence of several verbal projections dominating the non-verbal arguments in the clause.

For German, it has been argued that the phenomenon of "partial fronting" (6) requires the existence of partial (or "contoured") VP's in the "Mittelfeld".

(6)   a. *Das Buch lesen* wird er   schon können
         the book   read   will he   already can
         He'll surely be able to read the book
      b. *lesen können* wird er das Buch schon
      c. er wird das Buch schon lesen können

Given the un-controversial assumption that the fronted material in (6a,b) is a constituent, it seems at first sight that at least two different ways of

---

[2]In Rentier 1994, the analysis of Hinrichs and Nakazawa 1994 is used to account for Dutch cross-serial dependencies. The feature NPCOMP is replaced by LEX, whose distribution is again governed by the same rule-specific stipulations.

analyzing (6c) must exist, even-though it is semantically unambiguous. Accounts of partial VP-fronting using contoured VP's (Nerbonne 1986, Johnson 1986) have indeed made this assumption. The disadvantage of such an analysis is not only that it introduces spurious ambiguity, but also that it makes crucial use of this fact to account for the data.

An interesting alternative is provided in Nerbonne 1994, who argues that the fact that partial VP's can be fronted not necessarily implies that such constituents exist within the "Mittelfeld". His analysis assumes that the normal clause structure contains a "flat" VP and that partial VP's can only be derived in fronted position. This eliminates the spurious ambiguity problem and furthermore has the advantage that one does not have to motivate the existence of partial VP's in the Mittelfeld.

1.4 An Alternative Analysis

Postulating a verb-complex requires ad-hoc methods for characterizing what distinguishes a verb-complex from other verbal projections. Postulating partial VP's to account for partial fronting of VP's introduces the spurious ambiguity problem. The alternative we propose below assumes that the constituent structure for the cross-serial dependency construction does not contain a verb-cluster and does not contain partial VP's. Instead, all verbs and all non-verbal complements are directly dominated by S. We demonstrate that this not only accounts for cross-serial word order, but also that it is compatible with the analysis of a number of constructions that appear to be problematic for a flat analysis.

Note that the "flat" analysis that we propose is different from analyses based on sequence union (Reape 1990, 1994) or similar non-concatenative operations (Kathol 1995). In those analyses only the derived structure is flat. In contrast, our analysis assumes that both the derived structure and the derivation structure is flat.

After briefly introducing our version of HPSG in the next section, we present the basic rule of the grammar in Section 3 and demonstrate how it accounts for cross-serial word order. In Section 4 we discuss two constructions in Dutch involving partial VP's. In Section 5, we give an account of anaphoric binding that is largely independent of clause structure. In Section 6, we demonstrate how verb-sequences with inverted word order and verb-sequences containing particles can be accounted for.

2 Preliminaries

The version of HPSG that will be used throughout this paper is introduced in this section.

2.1 Features and Types

For expository purposes the feature declarations that we will assume will be somewhat simpler than for example found in the HPSG book (Pollard and Sag 1994). Signs will generally contain the following attributes, given here with their types:

$$
(7) \quad
\begin{bmatrix}
\text{HEAD} & noun \lor verb \lor \ldots \\
\text{SUBCAT} & list\_of\_sign \\
\text{ARG-S} & list\_of\_sign \\
\text{DIR} & left \lor right \\
\text{SLASH\_INHER} & list\_of\_sign \\
\text{SLASH\_TOBIND} & list\_of\_sign \\
\text{PFX} & boolean
\end{bmatrix}_{sign}
$$

The type *sign* has two subtypes, *word* and *phrase*. The type of the feature HEAD encodes the syntactic category of the sign. For type *verb*, the feature VFORM (which can have values such *inf*, *fin* or *prt*) is appropriate. For type *noun*, the feature CASE (with values such as *nom* or *acc*) is appropriate. The feature SUBCAT encodes the syntactic valence information of the sign. Following recent work in HPSG we assume that the feature ARG-S encodes the argument structure. This is the level at which e.g., binding theory applies, and where control relations are established. This feature will be motivated in Section 5. The feature DIR encodes the direction in which a head selects its argument (cf. Section 3.3). The features SLASH_INHER, SLASH_TOBIND are used in the analysis of non-local dependencies. The type *sign* itself has two subtypes, *word* and *phrase*. In Section 6 we introduce the features VR (which is appropriate for verbs) and PFX (which is appropriate for signs).

We use the following abbreviations. NP will be used for a nominal sign with an empty subcat list. S stands for a finite verbal sign with an empty SUBCAT list. VP will be used for a verbal sign with an empty subcat list. V will be used for lexical verbal signs. Finally PVP (partial VP) will be used for anything that is verbal.

2.2 Rules

The rule schemata that will be defined in this paper are instantiations of the following general schema:

(8) $M \rightarrow L^*\ H\ R^*$ COMBINATION-SCHEMA

This rule states that a mother node dominates a head daughter H, with an arbitrary number of daughters to the left of H and an arbitrary number of daughters to the right of H.[3]

The following constraints are attached to this rule schema:

(9) **Head-feature principle:** The HEAD and ARG-S features of the mother node M and the head daughter H are identical.

Subcat principle: The subcategorization list of the mother node consists of the elements of the subcategorization list of the head node, minus the signs left and right of the head.

Nonlocal feature principle: The nonlocal features (SLASH_INHE-RITED and SLASH_TOBIND) are propagated as usual (Pollard and Sag 1994).

Directionality principle: All elements left of the head have the value *left* for the DIR feature, whereas the elements right of the head have *right*.

Note that the first three constraints are standard in HPSG. The fourth constraint will be motivated in Section 3.3.

We consider the rules that will be defined in the remainder of this article as (more specific) sub-types of (8) and (9).

3 Dutch Verb-Raisers in HPSG

3.1 Lexical Entries

We assume that Dutch modals, auxiliaries and certain raising and equi-verbs select for a list of complements that consists of a verb and the complements selected by that verb. Perception verbs, as well as the causative *laten* and the verb *helpen* (to help) select for a verb, the complements of that verb, and an object NP. Sample lexical entries are given below.

(10) a. willen *(to want)* $\mapsto$ $\begin{bmatrix} \text{HEAD} & verb[inf] \\ \text{SUBCAT} & \boxed{1} \oplus \left\langle \begin{bmatrix} \text{HEAD} & verb[inf] \\ \text{SUBCAT} & \boxed{1} \end{bmatrix}_{word} \right\rangle \end{bmatrix}$

b. hebben *(to have)* $\mapsto$ $\begin{bmatrix} \text{HEAD} & verb[inf] \\ \text{SUBCAT} & \boxed{1} \oplus \left\langle \begin{bmatrix} \text{HEAD} & verb[prt] \\ \text{SUBCAT} & \boxed{1} \end{bmatrix}_{word} \right\rangle \end{bmatrix}$

---

[3]We disallow the use of this rule if both L and R are both instantiated as the empty list. Thus, there is no place for unary rules in our grammar.

c. $\begin{array}{c} \text{laten} \\ \text{(to let)} \end{array} \mapsto \begin{bmatrix} \text{HEAD} & verb[inf] \\ \\ \text{SUBCAT} & \left\langle \text{NP}[acc] \right\rangle \oplus \boxed{1} \oplus \left\langle {}_{wd}\begin{bmatrix} \text{HEAD } v[inf] \\ \text{SUBCAT } \boxed{1} \end{bmatrix} \right\rangle \end{bmatrix}$

We assume that finite forms are derived from a non-inflected root form by means of a lexical rule, which, among other things, prefixes a subject to the SUBCAT-list, and requires that this subject has nominative case. Thus, the finite (singular present tense) form of *willen* is:

(11) wil $\mapsto \begin{bmatrix} \text{HEAD} & verb[fin] \\ \\ \text{SUBCAT} & \left\langle \text{NP}[nom] \right\rangle \oplus \boxed{1} \oplus \left\langle {}_{word}\begin{bmatrix} \text{HEAD } verb[inf] \\ \text{SUBCAT } \boxed{1} \end{bmatrix} \right\rangle \end{bmatrix}$

3.2 The Head-Complement Schema

The most important innovation of our analysis is the fact that we assume that only one rule is needed to derive subordinate clauses. The rule is an instance of the head-complement-schema given in (12).

(12) HEAD-COMPLEMENT-SCHEMA

$${}_{phrase}\begin{bmatrix} \text{SUBCAT} & \boxed{1} \end{bmatrix} \rightarrow L^* \quad {}_{word}\begin{bmatrix} \text{SUBCAT} & \boxed{1} \oplus \left\langle \ldots \right\rangle \end{bmatrix} R^*$$

This schema inherits from the rule schema given in (8). Therefore, the head-feature principle, subcategorization principle, nonlocal feature principle, and the directionality principle hold for this rule. The subcategorization principle together with the information in (12) implies that the non-head daughters that are selected by the head in this rule form a suffix of the SUBCAT list of the head. The remaining SUBCAT elements of the head form the subcategorization requirements of the mother node. Thus, this schema can be used to form both partial and saturated verb-phrases. In the first case only a subset of the SUBCAT elements are selected (and hence the SUBCAT list of the mother is non-empty). In the latter case all SUBCAT elements are selected (and hence the SUBCAT list of the mother is empty).

The HEAD-COMPLEMENT schema assigns a "flat" clausal structure to phrases containing a clause-final verb sequence. As an example we give a derivation for (13) in (14).

(13) (dat) Jan Marie het boek wil laten lezen
(that) Jan Marie the book wants to let to read
that Jan wants to let Marie read the book

(14)

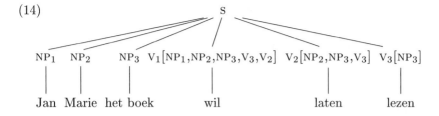

This example can best be understood by looking at the verb *lezen* first. This ordinary transitive verb subcategorizes for an (accusative) noun phrase NP$_3$. The verb *laten* is a typical verb-raiser. It selects a verb, all subcat elements of this verb (in this case NP$_3$) and an accusative noun phrase of its own, NP$_2$. This verb in turn is selected by the finite modal *wil*. This modal subcategorizes for *laten*, all subcat elements of *laten* and a nominative subject NP$_1$. Because *wil* is the head of the rule it is the subcat list of *wil* that will effectively be used by the rule.

The HEAD-COMPLEMENT schema does not require that all complements must be selected. No "spurious ambiguity" results from this liberal formulation, as (12) requires that its head must be lexical (i.e., of type *word*), whereas the mother is non-lexical (i.e., of type *phrase*). This prevents a complex phrase licensed by (12) to be the head of another phrase licensed by (12), and thus "contoured" VP's cannot be derived.

This should be compared with analyses in which a verb cluster is assumed, such as the analysis of Hinrichs and Nakazawa 1994. As explained in the introduction, in such analyses it is difficult to account for the fact that raising is obligatory; those accounts need ad-hoc feature-passing mechanisms.

By not imposing any constraint on the length of SUBCAT of the mother in (12), we do allow unsaturated, partial, VP's. Such phrases do play a role in the discussion below.

Since we assume that subjects are part of the SUBCAT list of finite verbs, there is no need for a separate schema to combine a head with a subject.

3.3 Word-Order

The directionality feature. Remember that the directionality principle makes sure that arguments that are marked [DIR *left*] are selected to the left of the head, and that arguments that are marked [DIR *right*] are selected to the right of the verb. This is similar to the order feature of UCG (Zeevat et al. 1987).

Encoding word order by making reference to a separate feature has the advantage that it is possible to formulate word order constraints, while at the same time lexical entries can specify an exceptional word order. As will be explained in Section 6, such exceptions do exist.

Word-order in verb raising constructions. The unmarked word order in verb raising constructions is one in which the "governing" verb precedes the "governed" verb. Furthermore, (NP-) complements of a "governing" verb precede those of the "governed" verb. This gives rise to so-called "cross-serial" dependencies. These ordering constraints are implemented as follows.

The default values for DIR (for verbal heads) are *right* for verbal complements and *left* for all other complements. That is, verbal complements normally occur right of the head, whereas NP's and other non-verbal complements occur left of the head.

The value of SUBCAT is an ordered list, and thus, the order of complements on SUBCAT is significant. We assume that complements are ordered in terms of "obliqueness", with the least oblique elements occurring first on the list, and with the most oblique elements occurring last. This notion of obliqueness is important for our account of word order, since we assume that word order in Dutch is determined by the obliqueness ordering. In particular, we require that more oblique complements appear closer to the head.

In order to implement this observation we assume the following rule, which is an instantiation of the HEAD-COMPLEMENT schema (12).

(15) RULE 1

Rule 1 is an instance of the head-complement-schema such that for all left daughters l_1, l_2: l_1 precedes l_2 iff l_1 precedes l_2 on the SUBCAT list of the head. And similarly, for all right daughters of the rule r_1, r_2: r_1 precedes r_2 iff r_1 occurs after r_2 on the SUBCAT list of the head.

Note that the word-order in (14) is the only possible word-order that can be derived by this rule.

Thus, the obligatory cross-serial dependency word-order is obtained by assigning a flat structure (by the requirement that the verbal argument of a verb-raiser is *lexical*); furthermore all arguments of a head are ordered in terms of obliqueness: the more oblique elements occur closer to the head.

In Section 6 we discuss a number of exceptions to the word-order generalizations given above, and we show how the analysis can be extended to treat these exceptions. In Bouma and van Noord 1996 our analysis of word-order in verb-clustering constructions is extended and applied to German as well.

4 Partial VPs

Even though our analysis is based on a flat structure for verb phrases, partial verb-phrases can be formed without any problem. In the grammar of Dutch such partial verb-phrases are only allowed in a few environments, in particular in the partial extraposition construction (also known as "the third construction"), and in topicalization.

4.1 Extraposition and Partial Extraposition

4.1.1 Extraposition

Some verbs subcategorize for a saturated verbal complement (sometimes marked with the infinitival complementizer *om*), as the following examples illustrate.

(16) a. dat   Jan heeft geprobeerd [(om)   het boek te lezen]
         that Jan has   tried   [(COMPL) the book to read]
         that Jan has tried to read the book

     b. dat   Jan Piet heeft gedwongen [(om)   het boek te lezen]
         that Jan Piet has   forced   [(COMPL) the book to read]
         that Jan has forced Piet to read the book

It is not entirely clear whether we should analyse such examples as involving extraposition (the standard transformational point of view), or rather as straightforward selection to the right (Hoeksema 1991). Here we will assume that such verbal constituents to the right of the verb-cluster are simply analyzed as arguments that need to be selected to the right, using the feature DIR introduced earlier.

Verbs that only allow extraposition of saturated verb-phrases (such as the verbs *beloven* (to promise) en *dreigen* (to threaten) in their non-modal reading) will not inherit the arguments of their verbal argument, but simply require that the verbal argument is saturated:

$$
(17) \quad beloven \mapsto \begin{bmatrix} \text{HEAD} & verb \\ \text{SUBCAT} & \left\langle \text{NP}[acc], \begin{bmatrix} \text{HEAD} & verb[te \lor om] \\ \text{SUBCAT} & \langle\rangle \\ \text{DIR} & right \end{bmatrix} \right\rangle \end{bmatrix}
$$

The word *om* is analyzed as a verbal element (with VFORM *om*) that subcategorizes for a saturated verb-phrase with VFORM *te*:

$$
(18) \quad om \mapsto \begin{bmatrix} \text{HEAD} & verb[om] \\ \text{SUBCAT} & \left\langle \begin{bmatrix} \text{HEAD} & verb[te] \\ \text{SUBCAT} & \langle\rangle \\ \text{DIR} & right \end{bmatrix} \right\rangle \end{bmatrix}
$$

The disjunctive specification of the VFORM feature of the verbal argument thus accounts for the optionality of *om*. Verbs which do subcategorize for a VP, but do not allow this complement to be headed by *om* (such as *menen* (*to believe/suppose*)), simply select a complement whose head is *verb[te]*.

The main difference between extraposition and raising constructions is that extraposition verbs require that their verbal argument is saturated. A verb raiser, on the other hand, requires that its verbal argument is lexical— and inherits the arguments of this verbal argument.

Another difference between the verb raising construction and the extraposition construction is the *infinitivus pro participio* (IPP) effect. The verb *hebben* ordinarily requires that its verbal argument is headed by a participle. However, if this verbal argument is a verb-raiser then an infinitive is required:

(19) a. dat Jan de vrouwen heeft zien   slapen
        that Jan the women   has   see (INF) sleep
        that Jan saw the women sleep

    b. * dat Jan de vrouwen heeft gezien   slapen
          that Jan the women   has   seen (PRT) sleep
          that Jan saw the women sleep

The IPP effect can be used to distinguish between the verb-raising and the extraposition construction.

(20) a. dat Jan Piet heeft zien   slapen
        that Jan Piet has   see (INF) sleep
        that Jan saw Piet sleep

    b. dat Jan Piet heeft gedwongen   te slapen
        that Jan Piet has   forced (PRT) to sleep
        that Jan forced Piet to sleep

4.1.2 Partial Extraposition

The interesting thing about extraposition in relation with verb clusters is the occurrence of partial verb-phrases that seem to mix the properties of ordinary extraposition on the one hand and verb-raising on the other hand (den Besten and Rutten 1989). Thus we get sentences such as:

(21) a. dat Jan *de trainer van zijn gelijk* heeft gemeend *te overtuigen*
        that John the trainer of his right has   believed to convince
        that John has believed to convince the trainer that he was right

    b. dat Jan heeft gemeend *de trainer van zijn gelijk te overtuigen*

    c. dat Jan *de trainer* heeft gemeend *van zijn gelijk te overtuigen*

Verbs that allow partial extraposition mix properties of ordinary extraposition verbs with the properties of raising verbs. On the one hand, partial extraposition verbs also inherit the remaining arguments on the SUBCAT list of a verbal argument that is selected to the right. But unlike raising verbs this argument need not be lexical. Furthermore the VFORM *om* (cf. below) is never allowed in case arguments are inherited. Finally the IPP effect does not occur in partial extraposition constructions.

In our analysis partial extraposition verbs do not specify a lexicality requirement on their verbal argument. Furthermore, unexpressed elements from the SUBCAT list are inherited by the head. Thus partial extraposition verbs are similar to verb-raising verbs in the sense that they inherit subcategorization information from their verbal argument. For example, the participle *gemeend* will have the lexical specification given in (22). The derivation for (21c) is given in (23).

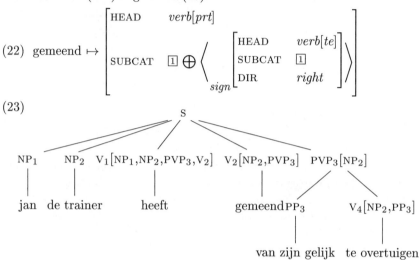

$$(22) \quad gemeend \mapsto \begin{bmatrix} \text{HEAD} & verb[prt] \\ \\ \text{SUBCAT} & \boxed{1} \oplus \left\langle \begin{bmatrix} \text{HEAD} & verb[te] \\ \text{SUBCAT} & \boxed{1} \\ \text{DIR} & right \end{bmatrix}_{sign} \right/ \right\rangle \end{bmatrix}$$

(23)

Our analysis correctly predicts that *om* can never occur with partial extraposition. As indicated above, the complementizer *om* only combines with a saturated verb-phrase:

(24) a. dat Jan de vrouwen heeft geprobeerd te kussen
         that Jan de vrouwen has   try   to kiss
         that John has tried to kiss the women
     b. * dat Jan de vrouwen heeft geprobeerd om te kussen
     c.   dat Jan heeft geprobeerd om de vrouwen te kussen

Note that the following sentence is ungrammatical:

(25) * dat Jan *van zijn gelijk* heeft gemeend *de trainer te overtuigen*

The contrast between this sentence and (21c) is explained by our assumption that only a suffix of the subcategorization elements can be selected by Rule 1 (12). Thus the VP *de trainer te overtuigen* cannot be built (with the relevant reading of *overtuigen*).

A difference between partial extraposition and verb-raising is the IPP effect: this effect only occurs with verb-raising constructions but not in (partial) extraposition constructions. There is a class of verbs (including *proberen* (to try)) that allow both verb-raising and (partial) extraposition. Our analysis predicts that these verbs can occur both in their infinitival form and in their participle form, when they are selected by the auxiliary *hebben*. This prediction is correct:

(26) a. dat   Jan   de vrouwen   heeft   proberen   te kussen
        that   Jan   the women   has   try (INF)   to kiss
        that John has tried to kiss the women

   b.   dat   Jan   de vrouwen   heeft   geprobeerd   te kussen
        that   Jan   the women   has   tried (PRT)   to kiss
        that John has tried to kiss the women

   c. * dat   Jan   heeft   proberen   de vrouwen   te kussen
        that   Jan   has   try (INF)   the women   to kiss
        that John has tried to kiss the women

   d.   dat   Jan   heeft   geprobeerd   de vrouwen   te kussen
        that   Jan   has   tried (PRT)   the women   to kiss
        that Jan has tried to kiss the women

The first example is the verb-raising variant of *probeer*, the second example is the partial extraposition variant of *probeer* in which the extraposed argument happens to be lexical too. The third example shows that verb-raising is obligatory if the IPP effect is present. The subcategorization requirements of *hebben* are discussed in Section 6.

4.2   Partial VP Fronting

There is another set of examples in which partial VP's occur. Examples of Dutch partial VP topicalization are (sometimes only marginally) acceptable:

(27) a. [$_{pvp}$ bezocht]   heeft   Jan   dat congres   nog nooit
        visited   has   Jan   that conference   not yet
        Jan hasn't visited that conference yet

   b.   [$_{pvp}$ bezoeken]   zou   Jan   dat congres   niet   willen
        to visit   would   Jan   that conference   not   want
        Jan wouldn't want to visit that conference

   c.   [$_{pvp}$ willen   bezoeken]   heeft   Jan   dat congres   nooit
        want   to visit   has   Jan   that conference   never
        Jan has never wanted to visit that conference

Our analysis of such partial VP topicalizations is based on the analysis of Nerbonne 1994 for German, but improves upon that analysis because we do not need a special rule to build partial verb-phrases in topic position.

Following Nerbonne's analysis, we assume a lexical complement extraction rule for verbs, which moves a complement from SUBCAT to SLASH. The rule differs from the standard complement extraction rule in that the extracted complement and the element added on SLASH only structure-share the value of their features (HEAD and SUBCAT in particular):

$$
(28) \quad
\begin{bmatrix}
\text{HEAD} & verb \\[4pt]
\text{SUBCAT} & \boxed{1} \oplus \left\langle \begin{bmatrix} \text{HEAD} & \boxed{3} \\ \text{SUBCAT} & \boxed{4} \end{bmatrix} \right\rangle_{sign} \oplus \boxed{2} \\[10pt]
\text{SLASH\_INHER} & \boxed{5}
\end{bmatrix}
$$

$$\Downarrow$$

$$
\begin{bmatrix}
\text{HEAD} & verb \\
\text{SUBCAT} & \boxed{1} \oplus \boxed{2} \\[8pt]
\text{SLASH\_INHER} & \left\langle \begin{bmatrix} \text{HEAD} & \boxed{3} \\ \text{SUBCAT} & \boxed{4} \end{bmatrix} \right\rangle_{sign} \oplus \boxed{5}
\end{bmatrix}
$$

Thus, if a verb subcategorizes for a complement of type *word*, this requirement will not be present once the element has been moved to SLASH_INHER. Consequently, a verb-raiser which ordinarily requires that its argument is lexical (i.e., of type *word*) may allow for a non-lexical verbal projection (of type *phrase*) in topic position. Everything else remains the same: as before, unexpressed SUBCAT elements are inherited by the verb-raiser.

Apart from this lexical rule Nerbonne 1994 needs a special mechanism to construct partial VP's. In order to prevent spurious ambiguities (of the kind discussed in Pollard 1990) this rule is supposed to build such VP's only in topic position. For this reason the binary feature FOCUS is introduced. In the current analysis this gymnastics is not needed at all: our Rule 1 introduced in (12) also creates partial VP's. On the other hand, we do not get spurious ambiguities because of the lexicality specifications on the head and the mother of Rule 1. Consider for example the relevant lexical specification of the verb *heeft* in (27a) (leaving the adjunct out of the discussion — for an analysis of adjuncts that is compatible with the analysis given here, see van Noord and Bouma 1994). This specification (30) is output of the lexical rule given above and is produced on the basis of (29).

$$
(29) \quad heeft \mapsto
\begin{bmatrix}
\text{HEAD} & verb[\text{fin}] \\[4pt]
\text{SUBCAT} & \left\langle \boxed{1}\, NP[nom] \right\rangle \oplus \boxed{3} \oplus \left\langle \begin{bmatrix} \text{HEAD} & verb[prt] \\ \text{SUBCAT} & \boxed{3} \end{bmatrix} \right\rangle_{word} \\[10pt]
\text{SLASH\_INHER} & \langle\,\rangle
\end{bmatrix}
$$

$$(30) \quad \text{heeft} \mapsto \begin{bmatrix} \text{HEAD} & verb[\mathit{fin}] \\ \text{SUBCAT} & \left\langle \boxed{1}\ \text{NP}[\mathit{nom}] \right\rangle \oplus \boxed{3} \\ \text{SLASH\_INHER} & \left\langle \begin{bmatrix} \text{HEAD} & verb[\mathit{prt}] \\ \text{SUBCAT} & \boxed{3} \end{bmatrix}_{sign} \right\rangle \end{bmatrix}$$

The derivation of (27a) is illustrated in (31). It is assumed here that verb-fronting is analyzed by a rule that is also an instance of the head-complement-schema (12), in which word-order is the same as in rule 1 except that the finite verb precedes everything else. Furthermore the topic is selected by a filler-gap rule of the kind that is standard in HPSG.

(31)

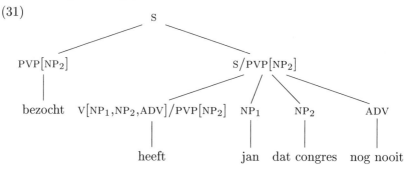

This section illustrated how the "flat" analysis is compatible with the occurrence of partial VP's. We have shown that the fact that partial VP's can be topicalized and extraposed need not imply that such partial VP's occur in the verb-cluster. Furthermore such partial VP's do not need to give rise to the spurious ambiguities of Pollard 1990, and neither require the *ad-hoc* rule of Nerbonne 1994.

5 Verb Clusters and Binding

The HPSG treatment of binding in Pollard and Sag 1994 uses the notion o-command. This notion is defined in terms of the SUBCAT list. In this section we show that the subcategorization lists that surface in inheritance-based accounts are not the appropriate structures for the binding theory. We present an alternative account of binding to account for Dutch binding phenomena in verb raising constructions, on the basis of the feature ARG-S introduced by Iida et al. 1994.

5.1 Binding Constraints

The binding constraints we assume are essentially those found in chapter 6.4 of Pollard and Sag 1994:

(32) **principle A.** A locally o-commanded anaphor must be locally o-bound.

principle B. A personal pronoun must be locally o-free.

principle C. A non-pronoun must be o-free.

In Pollard and Sag 1994 the notion o-command is defined in terms of the SUBCAT list: a referential sign X locally o-commands Y iff X precedes Y on SUBCAT. The general notion o-command then holds between X and Y iff X locally o-commands a Z, and Z dominates Y.

The fact that arguments can be shared in SUBCAT lists raises the question how we should interpret the principles of binding. For example, principle B can be understood at least in two ways:

- A personal pronoun must be locally o-free *in all* SUBCAT *lists it is a member of*
- A personal pronoun must be locally o-free *in at least one* SUBCAT *list it is a member of*

We show that if the binding constraints are defined with respect to SUBCAT lists then both interpretations give rise to problems. As an alternative we will then use the feature ARG-S introduced in Iida et al. 1994 to account for the binding data from Dutch.

5.2   Some Linguistic Data

It is typically assumed (Model 1991) that verb-cluster constructions do not witness clause-union effects as far as binding phenomena are concerned. This should imply that sentences of the kind *dat* NP NP NP *ziet wassen* witness the same binding facts as sentences of the kind *dat* NP *ziet dat* NP NP *wast*, where *ziet* (sees) is a verb-raiser and *wassen/wast* (to wash/washes) is an ordinary transitive verb. This is not true. Consider the following examples:[4]

(33) a.   dat   Jan   Piet$_i$ zichzelf$_i$ ziet   wassen
that   Jan   Pict$_i$ himself$_i$ sees   wash
that Jan sees Piet$_i$ wash himself$_i$

b. * dat   Jan   Piet$_i$ hem$_i$ ziet   wassen
that   Jan   Piet$_i$ him$_i$ sees   wash
that Jan sees Piet$_i$ wash him$_i$

c. * dat   Jan$_i$ Piet   zichzelf$_i$ ziet   wassen
that Jan$_i$ sees Piet wash himself$_i$

---

[4]Note that we will not discuss the Dutch reflexive *zich* which has some peculiar properties. The current analysis (Bredenkamp 1994, Koster 1986) of this reflexive assumes that it needs to be bound by the subject of the minimal finite domain. Given that verb-clusters at best introduce non-finite domains the distribution of *zich* does not shed any new light on the structure of verb-cluster constructions.

    d.   dat Jan_i Piet hem_i ziet wassen
        that Jan_i sees Piet wash him_i

    e. * dat Jan $zichzelf_i$ $Piet_i$ ziet wassen
        that Jan sees $himself_i$ wash $Piet_i$

    f. * dat Jan hem_i $Piet_i$ ziet wassen
        that Jan sees him_i wash $Piet_i$

    g.   dat Jan_i $zichzelf_i$ Piet ziet wassen
        that Jan_i sees $himself_i$ wash Piet

    h. * dat Jan_i hem_i Piet ziet wassen
        that Jan_i sees him_i wash Piet

In these examples, the impossibility of (33h) illustrates a clause-union effect:

(34) dat Jan_i ziet dat hij_i Piet wast
       that Jan_i sees that he_i Piet washes
       that Jan_i sees that he_i washes Piet

Let us attempt to analyse the sentences above solely in terms of SUBCAT. Since we are assuming that non-finite verbs do not contain a subject on their SUBCAT list, such an account is utterly impossible. However, we will illustrate that problems remain, even if we tentatively assume that subjects are present on the subcat list of non-finite verbs.

In (33a–d) there are two relevant SUBCAT lists: the matrix one essentially is a list containing three noun phrases, the most oblique one being the anaphor: $\langle Jan, Piet, pro \rangle$; and the embedded one which is similar except that the (matrix) subject is not there: $\langle Piet, pro \rangle$.

Example (33a) is predicted to be grammatical: principle A is satisfied (in both lists). Example (33b) is ruled out, because principle B is violated (in both lists). In order to properly rule out (33c) we must assume that principle A holds universally because only in the embedded SUBCAT list principle A is violated. In (33d) we must assume that principle B applies in an existential way: in the embedded SUBCAT list the pronoun is locally free.

In (33e–h) the two SUBCAT lists are $\langle Jan, pro, Piet \rangle$ and $\langle pro, Piet \rangle$, respectively. Examples (33e) and (33f) are ungrammatical (principle C violation). Example (33g) is allowed in both a universal and existential interpretation of the binding constraints. Finally (33h) can only be ruled out under a universal interpretation of principle B.

Thus we have constructed a paradox concerning principle B. Example (33d) requires an existential interpretation of principle B, but (33h) requires a universal interpretation. Note that principle A requires a universal interpretation.

5.3 Binding Constraints on ARG-S

The previous examples indicate that binding constraints cannot be expressed in terms of SUBCAT, if the grammar makes use of argument inheritance. As an alternative account we use the feature ARG-S ("argument-structure") Iida et al. 1994, Manning and Sag 1995.

The feature ARG-S will be the focus of control and binding. Typically the value of ARG-S is a list of syntactic dependents, ordered with the least oblique element (often the subject) left.

Note that in our analysis only finite verbs contain a subject on the SUBCAT list. This is in line with our assumption that control relations are established on the value of ARG-S. In (35) the verb *kussen* has a SUBCAT list only containing its accusative object. The verb *probeert* has a SUBCAT list containing a VP and its nominative subject. Hence control cannot be established on SUBCAT.

(35) dat   Jan probeert om   Marie te kussen
     that Jan tries   COMPL Marie to kiss
     that Jan tries to kiss Marie

The value of ARG-S can be used, as can be seen from the lexical specifications of the two verbs:

$$(36)\ \text{a. kussen} \mapsto \begin{bmatrix} \text{HEAD} & verb[\textit{inf}] \\ \text{SUBCAT} & \langle \boxed{1} \rangle \\ \text{ARG-S} & \langle \text{NP}, \boxed{1}\ \text{NP} \rangle \end{bmatrix}$$

$$\text{b. probeert} \mapsto \begin{bmatrix} \text{HEAD} & verb[\textit{fin}] \\ \text{SUBCAT} & \langle \boxed{1}\ \text{NP}[\textit{nom}], \boxed{2}\ \text{VP}[\textit{om}] \rangle \\ \text{ARG-S} & \langle \boxed{1}, \boxed{2} \rangle \end{bmatrix}$$

Control theory should establish that the index of the nominative subject of *proberen* is structure-shared with the first element on the ARG-S list of its VP-complement.

Note that the value of ARG-S of verbs generally must contain a subject. Even subject-raising verbs have to contain a subject on ARG-S because otherwise control relations cannot be established in examples such as:

(37) dat   Jan belooft   om   Marie te zullen kussen
     that Jan promises COMPL Marie to will   to kiss
     that Jan promises that he will kiss Marie

Here the subject-raiser *zullen* has a subject on its ARG-S even though it does not assign a semantic role to that noun-phrase.

We can then define o-command in terms of the structure of ARG-S; i.e., a referential sign X locally o-commands Y iff X precedes Y on ARG-S.

The general notion o-command then holds between X and Y iff X locally o-commands a Z, and Z dominates Y.[5]

Let us now return to the examples (33). As we will explain below, it is necessary to assume a subject-to-object raising analysis for the ARG-S value of verbs such as *zien*. The value of ARG-S of the verb *ziet* is therefore as follows for the first four examples of (33).

$$(38) \quad \begin{bmatrix} \text{HEAD} & verb \\ \text{ARG-S} & \left\langle \text{NP}_{jan} \,,\, \boxed{1}\ \text{NP}_{piet} \,,\, \begin{bmatrix} \text{HEAD} & verb \\ \text{ARG-S} & \left\langle \boxed{1} \,,\, \text{NP}_{pro} \right\rangle \end{bmatrix} \right\rangle \end{bmatrix}$$

The embedded ARG-S value is in these cases the relevant binding domain both for principle A as for principle B. (33a) is well-formed because the reflexive is locally bound. Example (33b) is ruled out because the pronominal is not locally free. In (33c) the reflexive is locally o-commanded but not locally bound, hence (33c) is ruled out. Example (33d) is fine because the pronominal is not locally bound.

If the anaphor is the raised object (33e–h) then the ARG-S of the verb *ziet* will be:

$$(39) \quad \begin{bmatrix} \text{HEAD} & verb \\ \text{ARG-S} & \left\langle \text{NP}_{jan} \,,\, \boxed{1}\ \text{NP}_{pro} \,,\, \begin{bmatrix} \text{HEAD} & verb \\ \text{ARG-S} & \left\langle \boxed{1} \,,\, \text{NP}_{piet} \right\rangle \end{bmatrix} \right\rangle \end{bmatrix}$$

Examples (33e–f) are ruled out because the nonpronoun *Piet* is not o-free. The remaining two examples are more interesting, and form the motivation for the raising-to-object structure of the value of ARG-S. Given such an analysis, the reflexive in (33g) is not o-commanded in the embedded ARG-S structure, hence it need not be o-bound there. It is locally o-commanded in the topmost ARG-S structure, and it indeed is o-bound there. In (33h) the pronominal is not locally free in the topmost ARG-S structure. Note that the structure of ARG-S is similar to the functional structures advocated in LFG for English raising-to-object verbs, cf. for example Dalrymple 1993.

However, note that we now still have to face the question whether the binding constraints are interpreted existentially or universally, because on ARG-S we also have (a limited form of) structure-sharing. We argue (against Iida et al. 1994) for the universal interpretation. The universal interpretation seems to be the formally most attractive assumption because it allows for a "local" check (binding constraints can be implemented as constraints on argument structures). In the existential interpretation this can only be

---

[5]For the moment we will assume that "dominates" is defined in terms of the ARG-S feature rather than the DTRS feature.

done in relation with global information of all other argument structures that a pronoun might appear in.

The universal interpretation is also forced by sentence (33h). This sentence should be ruled out. Note though that the pronominal occurs both in the argument structure of the matrix verb and in the argument structure of the embedded verb. The sentence is ruled out in the universal interpretation, because the pronoun is not free in the argument structure of the matrix verb. The existential interpretation, on the other hand, predicts that the sentence is well-formed, because the pronoun is free in the argument structure of the embedded verb.

The universal interpretation is also necessary in order to rule out anaphors in the subject-to-object-raising position that don't find an antecedent:

(40) * dat   Jan$_i$ zichzelf$_j$ Piet$_k$ ziet wassen
      that Jan$_i$ himself$_j$ Piet$_k$ sees to wash
      that Jan$_i$ sees himself$_j$ wash Piet$_k$

In an existential interpretation this sentence would be accepted because the anaphor is not o-commanded in the embedded ARG-S hence principle A is satisfied in the embedded ARG-S.

If we follow the suggestion in Pollard and Sag 1994, chapter 6.8.3 that local o-command should include subjects of embedded (infinite) VP's then we could adopt an analysis for raising-to-object verbs in which there is no structure-sharing on ARG-S. This would complicate the definition of (local) o-command, but it would avoid the choice between the existential and universal interpretation of binding constraints.

It is interesting to compare the current analysis to the LFG analysis of Dalrymple 1993. As indicated above the functional structures she assumes are similar to our ARG-S. Anaphors and pronouns lexically constrain the (functional) environment in which they are allowed to occur. In such an approach it is quite natural to assume that constraints that are expressed in a positive way ("my environment should contain ...") need only be satisfied once. On the other hand, constraints that are expressed in a negative way ("my environment should not contain ...") will get a kind of universal interpretation. Dalrymple's analysis predicts the set of facts given above. However, in order to be able to give such a lexical account of binding she needs a special type of functional uncertainty ("inside-out functional uncertainty"). Even if functional uncertainty were added to the formal machinery of HPSG it would be unclear how the "inside-out" type of functional uncertainty could be expressed in HPSG (Bredenkamp 1994).

6 Word Order Variation in the Verb Sequence

The standard word order for clauses containing one or more verb-raising verbs is the one that gives rise to a pattern of strictly cross-serial dependencies. There are at least two important exceptions to this pattern, however. With a governing modal or auxiliary, word orders in which the governed verb precedes the governor are possible. Second, verbs selecting a "separable verb prefix" give rise to word orders in which the prefix may occur in a number of positions within the clause-final verb sequence. An account of these constructions is given below.

6.1 Inversion

Modals do allow the head of their infinitival complement to occur either right or left of the head:

(41) a. dat   Jan   het boek   *wil*   lezen
        that   John   the book   wants   read
        that John wants to read the book
     b. dat Jan het boek lezen *wil*

Example (41a) illustrates normal word order, while (41b) illustrates the construction in which the governed infinitive occurs right of the head. Word orders in which the head of a verbal complement precedes its governor are usually referred to as instances of "inversion".

At first blush, we can account for inversions by simply allowing a modal verb to select for its verbal complement either to the right or to the left (that is, the DIR feature is left uninstantiated). We need to impose additional constraints on the [DIR *left*] option, however, as the possibility of inversion is not always available.

First of all, it is restricted to *finite* modal governors:

(42) a.   dat   Jan   het boek   zou   *moeten*   lezen
        that   John   the book   would(FIN)   must(INF)   read
        that John should read the book
     b. * dat Jan het boek zou lezen *moeten*
     c. * dat Jan het boek lezen zou *moeten*

Second, inversion is possible only if the governed verb is not itself a verb-raiser. This is illustrated for modals, perception verbs, and auxiliaries, in the examples below. Note the difference between (42b, c), in which the most deeply embedded verb occurs left of its (infinitival) governor, and (43a, b), in which governed modal occurs left of its (finite) governor.

(43) a. * dat Jan het boek moeten lezen *zou*
     b. * dat Jan het boek moeten *zou* lezen
     c.   dat   Jan   Marie   *kan*   horen   zingen
        that   John   Mary   can(FIN)   hear   sing
        that John can hear Mary sing

d. * dat Jan Marie horen zingen *kan*

e. * dat Jan Marie horen *kan* zingen

f. dat Jan dit boek *moet* hebben gelezen
    that John this book must have read
    that John must have read this book

g. * dat Jan dit boek hebben gelezen *moet*

h. * dat Jan dit boek hebben *moet* gelezen

The second constraint on inversion implies that somehow a distinction between "verb raisers" and other verbs must be made. To this end, we introduce the (boolean) feature VR (comparable to the feature AUX in the grammar of English), which has a positive value only if a verb is a "verb raiser".

We can now account for modal inversion by adding the following type of lexical entry for finite modals:

$$
(44) \quad \text{wil} \mapsto
\begin{bmatrix}
\text{HEAD} & verb[\mathit{fin}] \\[1em]
\text{SUBCAT} & \left\langle \boxed{1}\,\text{NP}[nom] \right\rangle \oplus \boxed{2} \oplus \left\langle \underset{word}{\boxed{3}}\begin{bmatrix} \text{HEAD} & verb[\mathit{inf},\text{-}vr] \\ \text{SUBCAT} & \boxed{2} \\ \text{DIR} & \mathit{left} \end{bmatrix} \right\rangle \\[1em]
\text{ARG-S} & \left\langle \boxed{1}\,,\,\boxed{3} \right\rangle
\end{bmatrix}
$$

One can either consider the lexical entry in (44) as stipulated, or else, if these finite forms are derived by means of a lexical rule from an un-inflected root (as are the regular finite forms), one can attach a constraint to the lexical entries of modal roots. The constraint is a disjunction, saying that the last element on SUBCAT is [DIR *right*], or else the last element is [DIR *left*,-VR] and the sign itself is [VFORM *fin*].

Auxiliaries allow for the same type of inversion as modals, that is, the participle of an auxiliary may often occur either to the right or to the left of the auxiliary.

(45) a. dat Jan het boek heeft gelezen
      that John the book has read
      that John has read the book

    b. dat Jan het boek gelezen heeft

Auxiliaries differ from modals, however, in that the possibility of inversion exists with non-finite auxiliaries as well:

(46) a. dat Jan het boek moet hebben gelezen
       that John the book must have read
       that John must have read the book

    b. dat Jan het boek gelezen moet hebben

    c. ?* dat Jan het boek moet gelezen hebben

Note that in these complex inversion cases, the participle has to occur as the first element of the verb sequence, and (normally) cannot occur left-adjacent to the governing auxiliary, as in (46c).[6]

Auxiliaries are like modals, in that inversion is excluded if the governed verb is a verb-raiser:

(47) a. dat   Jan   Marie heeft   horen   zingen
that John Mary has(FIN) hear(INF) sing
that John has heard Mary sing

b. * dat Jan Marie horen zingen heeft

c. * dat Jan Marie horen heeft zingen

d. dat   Jan   dit boek   heeft   moeten   lezen
that John this book has(FIN) must(INF) read
that John has had to read this book

e. * dat Jan dit boek moeten lezen heeft

f. * dat Jan dit boek moeten heeft lezen

Note that the (47) illustrates IPP (*infinitivus pro participio*, see also Section 4), i.e., the governed verb-raiser appears not as a participle but in its infinitival form.

We can account for inversion with a governing auxiliary as follows. First of all, we account for the IPP-effect by simply stipulating two different entries for *hebben*, one selecting -VR participles, and one selecting +VR infinitives. As inversion is possible for governed participles, but not for governed infinitives, the DIR-value of the last argument can remain unspecified in the first entry, but must be *right* for the second:

$$
(48)\ a.\ \text{hebben}_1 \mapsto
\begin{bmatrix}
\text{HEAD} & verb[inf] \\
\text{SUBCAT} & \boxed{1} \oplus \left\langle \underset{word}{\boxed{2}}\begin{bmatrix} \text{HEAD} & verb[prt,\ -vr] \\ \text{SUBCAT} & \boxed{1} \end{bmatrix} \right\rangle \\
\text{ARG-S} & \left\langle \text{NP},\ \boxed{2} \right\rangle
\end{bmatrix}
$$

$$
b.\ \text{hebben}_2 \mapsto
\begin{bmatrix}
\text{HEAD} & verb[inf] \\
\text{SUBCAT} & \boxed{1} \oplus \left\langle \underset{word}{\boxed{2}}\begin{bmatrix} \text{HEAD} & verb[inf,\ +vr] \\ \text{SUBCAT} & \boxed{1} \\ \text{DIR} & \text{RIGHT} \end{bmatrix} \right\rangle \\
\text{ARG-S} & \left\langle \text{NP},\ \boxed{2} \right\rangle
\end{bmatrix}
$$

The possibility of inversion with participles now follows if we instantiate DIR as *left* in (48a). Note that there is no need to restrict this option to finite

---

[6]Some speakers accept the word order in (46c) . We come back to this issue at the end of Section 6.2.

forms only. As with modals, one might consider the possibility of merging both lexical entries into one entry, subject to a disjunctive constraint.

The interesting aspect of this analysis is that it immediately accounts for the dubious status of (46c). As, under a flat analysis, the participle (including an unspecified value for DIR) is an inherited argument of the finite verb (*moet* in (46)), the participle must occur either to the right of *moet* (in which case it must also be right of the auxiliary because of the obliqueness constraint on word order) or to its left. The possibility that *gelezen* occurs right of the modal but left of the auxiliary is ruled out. Under a binary-branching analysis of the verb-cluster, this fact appears to be much harder to account for. One might pursue the possibility of using the feature FLIP (used by Hinrichs and Nakazawa 1994 to account for German AUX-flip) to allow participles to occur left instead of right of the head. Note however, that a binary rule which allows a participle to combine with a following verbal head will also produce the dubious (46c).[7]

6.2 Separable Verb Prefixes

Certain verbs in Dutch subcategorize for a so-called "separable prefix". These particle-like elements appear as part of the verb in subordinate clauses, but appear in clause-final position if their governor heads a main clause:

(49) a. dat   Jan   Marie   *aan*spreekt
      that   John   Mary   PRT speaks
      that John speaks to Mary
  b. Jan spreekt Marie aan

In complex verb-sequences, the prefix can appear not only as part of its governor, but also in positions further to the left:

(50) a. dat   Jan   Marie   zou   hebben   *aan*gesproken
      that   John   Mary   would   have   PRT spoken
      that John would have spoken to Mary
  b. dat Jan Marie zou *aan* hebben gesproken
  c. dat Jan Marie *aan* zou hebben gesproken

In the analysis below, we assume that separable prefixes are selected as complements, and thus appear on the SUBCAT-list of the verbs introducing them (51). Such an analysis immediately accounts for example (50c). The phrase structure for this example is given in (52).

---

[7]A way out for the binary-branching analysis would be the ensure somehow that combinations of a "flipped" participle and a verbal head are not marked as verb-clusters (see Bouma and van Noord 1994).

(51) gesproken $\mapsto$ $\begin{bmatrix} \text{HEAD} & verb[prt] \\ \text{SUBCAT} & \left\langle \boxed{1}\ \text{NP}, \begin{bmatrix} \text{HEAD} & particle \\ \text{DIR} & left \end{bmatrix} \right\rangle \\ \text{ARG-S} & \left\langle \text{NP}, \boxed{1} \right\rangle \end{bmatrix}$

(52)

```
                          S
         _____/_____
        /  ___/___/___/    /          \              \
NP₁    NP₂    PRT  V₁[NP₁,NP₂,PRT,V₃,V₂]  V₂[NP₂,PRT,V₃]  V₃[NP₂,PRT]
 |      |      |          |                   |                |
Jan   Marie   aan        zou                hebben         gesproken
```

Cases in which the prefix is adjacent to its governor, or placed in some intermediate position, require a different analysis. When the prefix is adjacent to its governor, it is often assumed that the prefix has been incorporated by its governor. If we believe that this suggestion is on the right track, we could introduce a new rule schema to deal with this kind of "incorporation":[8]

(53) RULE 2: $\begin{bmatrix} \ \\ \ \end{bmatrix}_{word} \rightarrow \begin{bmatrix} \text{PFX} & + \end{bmatrix}, \begin{bmatrix} \text{HEAD} & verb[\neg fin] \end{bmatrix}_{head \wedge word}$

Rule 2 instantiates the general rule schema presented in Section 2, and thus the Head-feature, Subcategorization, Nonlocal feature, and Directionality principle apply.[9]

The rule can be used to combine a non-finite head with a prefix, and gives rise to a complex constituent that is lexical instead of phrasal. The distinction between complements that can be prefixed and other comple-

---

[8] For a different analysis of separable prefixes refer to Bouma and van Noord 1996.

[9] Let us take a moment to summarize the rules and rule schemata used in this paper:

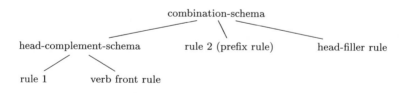

```
                    combination-schema
           _____/              _____
          /                                     \
head-complement-schema        rule 2 (prefix rule)    head-filler rule
       /          \
    rule 1    verb front rule
```

The combination-schema is defined in (8) and (9). The head-complement-schema is defined in (12). Rule 1 is an instantiation of that schema, with the ordering constraint (15) added.

ments is implemented using the boolean feature PFX. The default will be that elements of SUBCAT are -PFX, but that separable prefixes are +PFX.

Rule 2 is restricted to non-finite verbs for two reasons. First of all, this restriction prevents a spurious derivation of cases such as (50c), where the prefix can be considered to be an ordinary complement. Second, we must prevent the rule from applying in main clauses (49). If Rule 2 could apply on finite verbs (which may head main clauses) the ungrammatical (54) would be derivable.

(54) *Jan   *aan*spreekt Marie
       John   PRT speaks   Mary
       John speaks to Mary

The following word order constraint holds for Rule 2:

(55) The non-head daughter must be the most oblique element marked
      [DIR *left*] on the SUBCAT-list of the head.

This constraint not only orders prefixes left of the head, but also introduces a limited amount of ordering freedom. In particular, prefixes are not only allowed to precede the verbs that introduce them (see (56)), but are also allowed to precede governors which "inherit" the prefix as argument (57).

(56)

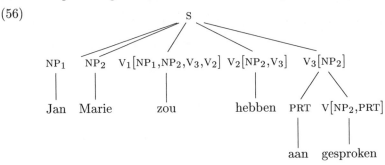

(57)

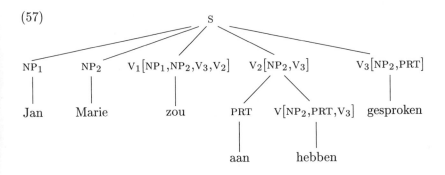

While the word order constraint imposed on Rule 2 allows a prefix to appear in a number of positions within the verb cluster, at the same time, an important restriction on the position of "inherited" prefixes is obeyed. The restriction is illustrated in the examples below, in which inversion applies to participles selecting a prefix:

(58) a.   dat   Jan   Marie   *aan*gesproken   zou   hebben
         that   John   Mary   PRT spoken   would   have
         that John would have spoken to Mary

     b.   * dat Jan Marie gesproken zou aan hebben

     c.   * dat Jan Marie gesproken aan zou hebben

The derivation of the ungrammatical (58b) is excluded, as the prefix is not the most oblique [DIR *left*] element on SUBCAT of *hebben* (59), and thus Rule 2 cannot license *aan hebben* as a complex lexical element. For the same reason, Rule 2 does not license *aan zou* as a lexical element in (58c). Note also that a derivation of the latter example by means of Rule 1 is excluded, as this would imply a violation of the word order constraint for Rule 1, which says that if two complements occur left of the head, the most oblique complement should be closest to the head.

(59)   hebben $\mapsto$

$$
\begin{bmatrix}
\text{HEAD} & verb[inf] \\
\\
\text{SUBCAT} & \boxed{1} \left\langle \text{NP}, \begin{bmatrix} \text{HEAD} & particle \\ \text{DIR} & left \end{bmatrix} \right\rangle \oplus \underset{word}{\left\langle \boxed{2} \begin{bmatrix} \text{HEAD} & verb[prt,\ -vr] \\ \text{SUBCAT} & \boxed{1} \\ \text{DIR} & left \end{bmatrix} \right\rangle} \\
\\
\text{ARG-S} & \left\langle \text{NP}, \boxed{2} \right\rangle
\end{bmatrix}
$$

The word order constraint on Rule 2 has deliberately been formulated to allow prefixes to precede verbs which only "inherit" this prefix. Some speakers of Dutch, however, are reluctant to accept sentences in which a prefix appears in intermediate positions in the verb cluster. Such speakers do accept examples in which the prefix is adjacent to the verb introducing it, and also examples in which the prefix appears left of the finite verb, but they do not accept the word order in (60b)

(60) a.   dat   Jan   Marie   zou   hebben   *aan*gesproken
         that   John   Mary   would   have   PRT spoken
         that John would have spoken to Mary

     b.   ?* dat Jan Marie zou *aan* hebben gesproken

     c.   dat Jan Marie *aan* zou hebben gesproken

This dialect can be described by imposing a more restrictive word order constraint on Rule 2. As it stands, the word order constraint requires that the selected prefix must be the most oblique [DIR *left*] element on SUBCAT.

If the prefix is simply required to be the most oblique (i.e., the last) element on SUBCAT, Rule 2 can only apply to verbs which introduce the prefix. Remember that if a verb subcategorizes for a prefix via inheritance, the prefix can never be the last element on SUBCAT, and thus the ungrammaticality (in the restrictive dialect) of (60b) would be accounted for.

Finally, we come back to inversion with auxiliaries. Some speakers of Dutch accept not only instances of inversion with a governing auxiliary in which the governed participle occurs as the first element of the verb sequence, but also instances in which the participle occurs in intermediate positions left of the auxiliary. That is, such speakers also accept the word order in (61c).

(61) a. dat   Jan   het boek   moet   hebben   gelezen
         that John the book   must   have   read
         that John must have read the book
     b. dat Jan het boek gelezen moet hebben
     c. ?* dat Jan het boek moet gelezen hebben

As we pointed out above, a flat analysis of the verb cluster makes it easy to account for the dialect in which only (61a) and (61b) are grammatical.

In dialects in which (61c) is grammatical as well, the position of participles in inverted word orders is highly similar to that of prefixes (in the standard dialect that accepts these in intermediate positions). Our suggestion is therefore that for dialects that accept the word order in (61c), participles are marked +PFX as well.

References

Bouma, Gosse, and Gertjan van Noord. 1994. A lexicalist account of the Dutch verb cluster. In *CLIN 1993, Papers from the fourth CLIN Meeting 1993*, 19–34.

Bouma, Gosse, and Gertjan van Noord. 1996. Word Order Constraints on Germanic Verb Clusters. Manuscript available from http://www.let. rug.nl/~vannoord/papers/. Rijksuniversiteit Groningen.

Bredenkamp, Andrew. 1994. Binding Constraints in HPSG. Paper presented at the 1994 HPSG Conference. Copenhagen.

Bresnan, Joan W., Ronald M. Kaplan, Stanley Peters, and Annie Zaenen. 1983. Cross-serial dependencies in Dutch. *Linguistic Inquiry* 13.

Dalrymple, Mary. 1993. *The Syntax of Anaphoric Binding*. Stanford: CSLI Lecture Notes.

den Besten, Hans, and Jean Rutten. 1989. On Verb Raising, Extraposition, and Free Word Order in Dutch. In *Sentential Complementation and the Lexicon*, ed. D. Jaspars, W. Klooster, Y. Putseys, and P. Seuren. Dordrecht: Foris.

Evers, Arnold. 1975. *The Transformational Cycle in Dutch and German*. Doctoral dissertation, Rijksuniversiteit Utrecht.

Hinrichs, Erhard, and Tsuneko Nakazawa. 1994. Linearizing AUXs in German Verbal Complexes. In *German in Head-driven Phrase Structure Grammar*, ed. John Nerbonne, Klaus Netter, and Carl Pollard. 11–38. Lecture Note Series. Stanford: CSLI.

Hoeksema, Jack. 1991. A Categorial Theory of Reanalysis Phenomena. ms. RUG Groningen.

Houtman, Joop. 1984. Een kategoriale beschrijving van het Nederlands. *TABU* 14(1):1–27.

Iida, Masayo, Christopher Manning, Patrick O'Neill, and Ivan Sag. 1994. The Lexical Integrity of Japanese Causatives. Paper presented at the LSA 1994 Annual Meeting.

Johnson, Mark. 1986. A GPSG account of VP structure in German. *Linguistics* 24-25(285):871–82.

Johnson, Mark. 1988. *Attribute Value Logic and the Theory of Grammar*. Center for the Study of Language and Information Stanford.

Kathol, Andreas. 1995. *Linearization-based German Syntax*. Doctoral dissertation, Ohio State University.

Koster, Jan. 1986. *Domains and Dynasties: the Radical Autonomy of Syntax*. Foris Dordrecht.

Kroch, Anthony S., and Beatrice Santorini. 1987. The Derived Constituent Structure of the West Germanic Verb Raising Construction. In *Proceedings of the Princeton Workshop on Comparative Grammar*. MIT Cambridge Mass.

Manning, Christopher, and Ivan Sag. 1995. Dissociations between Argument Structure and Grammatical Relations. Draft.

Model, Jan. 1991. *Grammatische Analyse. Syntactische verschijnselen van het Nederlands en Engels*. Dordrecht Netherlands: ICG Publications.

Moortgat, Michael. 1988. *Categorial Investigations*. Doctoral dissertation, University of Amsterdam.

Nerbonne, John. 1986. "Phantoms" and German fronting: Poltergeist constituents? *Linguistics* 24-25(285):857–70.

Nerbonne, John. 1994. Partial Verb Phrases and Spurious Ambiguities. In *German Grammar in HPSG*, ed. John Nerbonne, Klaus Netter, and Carl Pollard. 109–149. Lecture Note Series. Stanford: CSLI.

Pollard, Carl. 1990. On Head Non-Movement. In *Appendix to the Proceedings of the Symposium on Discontinuous Constituency*. ITK Tilburg.

Pollard, Carl, and Ivan Sag. 1987. *Information Based Syntax and Semantics, Volume 1*. Center for the Study of Language and Information Stanford.

Pollard, Carl, and Ivan Sag. 1994. *Head-driven Phrase Structure Grammar*. Center for the Study of Language and Information Stanford.

Reape, Mike. 1990. Getting Things in Order. In *Proceedings of the Symposium on Discontinuous Constituency*. ITK Tilburg.

Reape, Mike. 1994. Domain Union and Word-Order Variation in German. In *German in Head-Driven Phrase Structure Grammar*, ed. John Nerbonne, Klaus Netter, and Carl Pollard. 151–198. CSLI Stanford.

Rentier, Gerrit. 1994. Dutch Cross Serial Dependencies in HPSG. In *Proceedings of the 15th International Conference on Computational Linguistics (COLING)*. Kyoto.

Steedman, Mark. 1985. Dependency and Coordination in the Grammar of Dutch and English. *Language* 61:523–68.

van Noord, Gertjan, and Gosse Bouma. 1994. Adjuncts and the Processing of Lexical Rules. In *Proceedings of the 15th International Conference on Computational Linguistics (COLING)*. Kyoto.

Zeevat, Henk, Ewan Klein, and Jo Calder. 1987. Unification Categorial Grammar. In *Categorial Grammar, Unification Grammar and Parsing*, ed. Nicholas Haddock, Ewan Klein, and Glyn Morrill. University of Edinburgh: Centre for Cognitive Science. Volume 1 of Working Papers in Cognitive Science.

9

Approaches to Unification in Grammar: A Brief Survey

Jürgen Wedekind

ABSTRACT. This paper gives an informal survey of several prominent approaches to the formal modeling of unification-based theories of grammar. We concentrate exclusively on the lattice-theoretic
notion of unification, which assigns to two feature structures their
least upper bound. We sketch equivalent reconstructions of this notion based on graphs, ψ-terms, feature descriptions, Kasper-Rounds
logic, and first-order terms.

1 Introduction

Over the last 25 years a whole family of grammatical theories, commonly
called *unification-based*, has been developed. Among them are: Functional
Unification Grammar (FUG) (Kay 1979), Lexical Functional Grammar
(LFG) (Kaplan and Bresnan 1982), Generalized Phrase Structure Grammar (GPSG) (Gazdar et al. 1985), Categorial Unification Grammar (CUG)
(Uszkoreit 1986), Unification Categorial Grammar (UCG) (Zeevat et al.
1987) and Head-Driven Phrase Structure Grammar (HPSG) (Pollard and
Sag 1987). Although these theories differ in many respects, they share one
important property: they all use, in various ways, the same type of data
structures, namely *feature structures*, to represent linguistic information;
moreover they all employ — sometimes rather implicitly — *unification* as
the basic operation for combining feature structures.

Since the mechanisms underlying these approaches proved appropriate
for computational implementation, the development of the various theories
was accompanied by research on their formal and computational foundations. This foundational research yielded results of two different types.
On the one hand, implementations of new formalisms (notably PATR-II
(Shieber et al. 1983)) were carried out which covered most of the expres-

Specifying Syntactic Structures
P. Blackburn and M. de Rijke, eds.
Copyright © 1997, CSLI Publications.

sive devices of at least some unification-based theories. Typically, a (more or less explicitly elaborated) methodology of how to translate the expressible parts of the various theories into the new formalisms (see, for example, Shieber 1988) was also provided. Such developments facilitated the use of different unification-based theories within natural language systems. On the other hand, reformalizations of parts of the (underlying and newly developed) formalisms were given in mathematical frameworks such as universal algebra and first-order logic. Although this type of research was not primarily intended to result in implementations, it provided new insights into formal properties (such as computational complexity) of the original systems.

However this research activity also had a less desirable result: today we find a variety of formalisms and reformalizations whose relationships are still not entirely clear. (This situation may also be partially ascribable to the interdisciplinary character of computational linguistics. The various approaches were influenced by a number of independent fields such as graph or automata theory, knowledge representation, logic programming, and logic.) Whatever its origins, this diversity makes it rather difficult to give an introduction to unification-based formalisms which elucidates the relations between the different approaches and covers some of the more prominent ones. Nonetheless, it seems worthwhile to make an attempt, and we shall do so in this survey by concentrating exclusively on the truly common core of these theories.

What is this common core? In this survey we take it to be formal models of feature structures and their combining operation "unification". This core is "lattice-theoretic"; the set of feature structures forms a join semilattice under a binary relation called subsumption, whose join operation is unification. Many models are mutually reducible with respect to this core. That is, it is possible to specify a translation between the different models of feature structures which reveals a metalevel equivalence between those parts of the formalisms comprising this hard core. The mutual reducibility permits a clear and precise explicative reinterpretation of the notion "unification-based grammar theory/formalism": a grammar theory or formalism is classified as unification-based if there is a restriction (of its underlying formalism) which allows a reduction to this lattice-theoretic core.

So that the reader can judge the success of our explication, we begin our paper by introducing the explicandum: that is, we give an informal description of the lattice-theoretic core shared by the models considered here. We then give formal models of this core which are prototypical for each of five important approaches: we reconstruct feature structures in terms of graphs, ψ-terms, feature descriptions, Kasper-Rounds logic, and first-order terms. Furthermore, we specify functions which allow us to translate the different formal models of feature structures into each other in a manner that respects lattice-theoretic properties.

To examine the different approaches in a way that reveals metalevel equivalences seems of particular importance in an introductory survey such as this. On the one hand it facilitates a comparison of the different approaches, since the translations make clear not only which concepts correspond to each other, but also which algorithms correspond. (It becomes evident, for example, how term unification, or an algorithm for testing satisfiability in a feature logic, can be used for the implementation of a formalism defined over graphs.) On the other hand it provides a basis for investigating whether (and how) extensions to the common core which are natural for one approach can be integrated into others.

The order of presentation in this paper is motivated by the simplicity of the equivalence proofs and not by historical or other systematic considerations. In the interest of finding simple, prototypical modelings of the common core, we have sometimes simplified the original proposals. The reader is urged to supplement this survey with a reading of the original literature.

2 The Explicandum

Unification-based grammars assign to sentences a special data structure called a *feature structure*. The feature structure associated with a sentence encodes information that corresponds to a (partial) linguistic analysis of that sentence. Depending on the theory, and perhaps on the particular application, the encoded information may range from phonological to pragmatic information.

An example will be helpful. When unification-based approaches were first developed, feature structures were mainly used to encode the underlying predicate-argument structure of sentences. This is illustrated by the (simplified) feature structure which could be assigned to the sentence

(1) John promised to come

by a unification grammar of English. The structure is shown in Figure 1 in each of the two most common representations of feature structures: as matrices and as graphs.

The encoding of information is based on a system of *attributes* (or *features*) and atomic *values*. Labels of the arcs are attributes (in the example: PRED, TENSE, XCOMP and SUBJ), while (instantiated) terminal nodes are atomic values (PROMISE, PAST, JOHN and COME). Substructures rooted by other nodes constitute *complex values*.

The graph representation is clearly not a tree, for it contains *reentrant paths*. Such reentrant paths play an important role in encoding linguis-

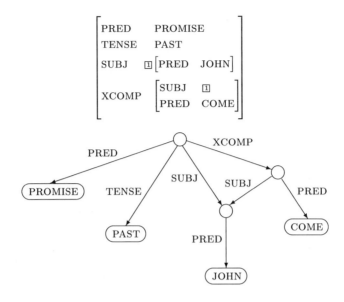

FIGURE 1 A feature structure in matrix and graph representation.

tic information. In matrix notation the reentrancy of paths in graphs is expressed by coindexing substructures.[1]

The information encoded in a feature structure can be read off rather easily. For instance, the information encoded in the structure of Figure 1 can be expressed as follows: *the* PRED*icate of the sentence is* PROMISE, *its* TENSE *is* PAST, *its* SUBJ*ect's* PRED*icate is* JOHN, *its* XCOMP*lement's* SUBJ *is equal to its* SUBJ*ect and its* XCOMP*lement's* PRED*icate is* COME. That is, making some necessary concessions to English syntax, we simply read the attributes in the lines of the matrix from left to right until we reach an atomic value or an index. Sequences which lead to an atomic value are said to have that value, while sequences which lead to the same index are said to be equal.[2]

At a rather early stage of their development, feature structures were

---

[1]In LFG, connecting lines instead of indices are used to indicate path reentrancies in matrix notation. Using this method, the graph depicted in Figure 1 would have the following matrix representation.

$$\begin{bmatrix} \text{PRED} & \text{PROMISE} \\ \text{TENSE} & \text{PAST} \\ \text{SUBJ} & \begin{bmatrix} \text{PRED} & \text{JOHN} \end{bmatrix} \\ \text{XCOMP} & \begin{bmatrix} \text{SUBJ} \\ \text{PRED} & \text{COME} \end{bmatrix} \end{bmatrix}$$

[2]Sometimes feature structures have terminal nodes which are not atomic-valued. Se-

FIGURE 2   The information contributed by the VP- (left) and
NP-constituent (right) of sentence (1).

— in graph-theoretical terms — conceived as labeled directed finite graphs
fulfilling four additional conditions. It was required that:

(C) (0) the graph be connected and rooted,
   (1) the graph be acyclic,
   (2) an atomic value have no outgoing arcs, and
   (3) the outgoing arcs of a node lead to a unique value for each at-
        tribute.

These conditions don't have equal status, and conditions (C0, 1) were oc-
casionally abandoned in later work. But (C2, 3) are crucial, since they
express the *uniqueness* condition: each attribute occurring in a feature
structure or its subsidiary structures has exactly one value. In this article
we shall assume that all four conditions hold.

During this early period, *unification* was regarded as the basic operation for combining the partial information contributed by the constituents
of a sentence; ultimately this operation yielded the feature structure corresponding to the entire sentence. For example, the two structures in Figure 2 (which might be assumed to comprise the information contributed
by the VP- and NP-constituent of our sentence (1)) can be combined by
unification, yielding the structure given in Figure 1.

Intuitively, this is the *least* structure containing all the information encoded in the two structures of Figure 2. As this choice of words already
suggests, unification is here regarded as a lattice-theoretic operation based
on some sort of information ordering. In this survey we will call this ordering the "extension relation".[3] Intuitively, the extension relation holds
between two feature structures if the information encoded in one structure
can also be read off the other. For the most part, intuition is a sufficient
guide to this relation — but a little more care is needed when the information corresponding to reentrancies is discussed. Note, for example, that

---

quences which lead to those nodes are read existentially. That is, they assert that some
node is reachable by following the sequence.

[3]This relation is usually called "subsumption" in the literature. We use "extension" to
avoid confusion with the subsumption relation on first-order terms.

$$\begin{bmatrix} \text{SUBJ} & \boxed{1}\begin{bmatrix}\text{PRED} & \text{JOHN}\end{bmatrix} \\ \text{XCOMP} & \begin{bmatrix}\text{SUBJ} & \boxed{1} \\ \text{PRED} & \text{COME}\end{bmatrix} \end{bmatrix} \qquad \begin{bmatrix} \text{XCOMP} & \begin{bmatrix}\text{SUBJ} & \begin{bmatrix}\text{PRED} & \text{MARY}\end{bmatrix}\end{bmatrix}\end{bmatrix}$$

FIGURE 3 Feature structures which are not unifiable.

the information encoded in the structure of Figure 1 cannot be read off the following (linguistically rather unmotivated) structure,

$$\begin{bmatrix} \text{PRED} & \text{PROMISE} \\ \text{TENSE} & \text{PAST} \\ \text{SUBJ} & \begin{bmatrix}\text{PRED} & \text{JOHN}\end{bmatrix} \\ \text{XCOMP} & \begin{bmatrix}\text{SUBJ} & \begin{bmatrix}\text{PRED} & \text{JOHN}\end{bmatrix} \\ \text{PRED} & \text{COME}\end{bmatrix} \end{bmatrix}$$

since the SUBJ and the XCOMP SUBJ values are (only) identical but not coindexed. Coindexed values (called *token identities*) are assumed to be more informative than the corresponding *type identical* values, since token identical (but not type identical values) are forced to be identical.

It should now be easy to see that the structure in Figure 1 extends both structures of Figure 2. Since some information encoded in the structures of Figure 2 cannot be read off any more if any part of the structure in Figure 1 is eliminated, this structure is the least or smallest structure which extends the structures in Figure 2.

Unification fails if there is no well-formed structure which extends the information encoded in two given structures. For example, all extensions of the structures in Figure 3 would violate condition (C3). There is no well-formed structure whose XCOMPlement's SUBJject's PREDicate is both JOHN and MARY. As is so often the case, however, it is convenient to be able to treat partial operations as total operations. Thus, it is common to introduce a "value for unification failure" by stipulation. A distinct additional element (usually denoted by a possibly indexed ⊥ symbol) is added to the set of feature structures, and is given the role of the *greatest element* in the information ordering. Intuitively, this element contains far too much information — inconsistent information — and failed attempts at unification denote this entity.

After this short introduction of the explicandum we can now turn to the different reconstructions. We assume that they all make reference to a fixed attribute-value system $\langle A, V \rangle$ consisting of two finite disjoint sets: the attributes A and the atomic values V.

3   Feature Graphs

Perhaps the most down to earth approach to reconstructing the concept of unification in grammar is the one based on automata or graph theory. The type of automata we will take as our starting point is the kind used as models for Kasper-Rounds logic (Kasper and Rounds 1990), which we will be discussing later. This class of automata $(\mathcal{D})$ consists of deterministic finite automata[4]

$$D = \langle Q, A, \delta, q_0, F \rangle,$$

whose final states are elements of the set of atomic values V ($F \subseteq V$).

Example 3.1 An automaton appropriate for the reconstruction of the structure in Figure 1 is $D = \langle Q, A, \delta, q_0, F \rangle$, with

$$
\begin{array}{rclcrcl}
Q & = & \{q_0, q_1, q_2\} \cup F, \\
F & = & \{\text{PROMISE}, \text{PAST}, \text{JOHN}, \text{COME}\}, \\
\delta(q_0, \text{PRED}) & = & \text{PROMISE}, & \delta(q_2, \text{PRED}) & = & \text{COME}, \\
\delta(q_0, \text{TENSE}) & = & \text{PAST}, & \delta(q_2, \text{SUBJ}) & = & q_1, \\
\delta(q_0, \text{SUBJ}) & = & q_1, & \delta(q_1, \text{PRED}) & = & \text{JOHN}, \\
\delta(q_0, \text{XCOMP}) & = & q_2.
\end{array}
$$

The *transition graph* for this automaton can be represented as follows:

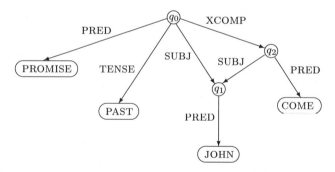

Since δ assigns to each labeled arc of the graph a unique value, only the adequacy conditions (C0–2) have to be covered by additional defining conditions. Thus, the appropriate automata are also rooted and connected (D0), acyclic (D1) and have no transitions from the final states (D2):

(D) (0) $\forall q \in Q \, \exists p \in A^* (\delta^*(q_0, p) = q)$,
    (1) $\forall p \in A^* \, \forall p' \in A^+ (\delta^*(q_0, p) \neq \delta^*(q_0, pp'))$,
    (2) $\forall a \in F \, \forall f \in A(\langle a, f \rangle \notin Dom(\delta))$.

---

[4]The concepts of automata theory that we use are introduced in Appendix A.

(Here A^* denotes the set of strings over A, A^+ is A^* without the empty string and δ^* is the extension of δ to strings.)

But it is not the automata themselves that will be used to model feature structures; rather, we shall view feature structures as *equivalence classes of isomorphic automata*. That is, automata that are "mathematically the same" (identical up to biunique renaming of the non-final states) are lumped together in one class, and this class is taken to represent a feature structure. As a first step towards defining automata isomorphism, we introduce the notion of *homomorphic extension*, that establishes a 2-place reflexive, transitive relation on $\mathcal{D}$ (see also Kasper and Rounds 1990).

An automaton $D = \langle Q, A, \delta, q_0, F \rangle$ is a *homomorphic extension* of $D' = \langle Q', A, \delta', q_0', F' \rangle$ ($D' \preceq D$) iff there is a function h in $[Q' \mapsto Q]$ (the set of all functions from Q' to Q), such that for all $\langle q_0', p \rangle$ in $Dom(\delta'^*)$ and a in F':

$$h(\delta'^*(q_0', p)) = \delta^*(q_0, p),$$
$$h(a) = a.^5$$

Example 3.2 As can easily be verified by the transition graphs and the graphical representation of the function h, the automaton D of Example 3.1 is an extension of the automaton $D' = \langle Q', A, \delta', q_0', F' \rangle$, with

$$
\begin{aligned}
Q' &= \{q_0', q_1', \text{COME}\}, \\
F' &= \{\text{COME}\}, \\
\delta'(q_0', \text{XCOMP}) &= q_1', \\
\delta'(q_1', \text{PRED}) &= \text{COME}.
\end{aligned}
$$

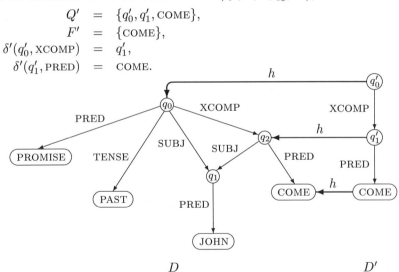

$$D \qquad\qquad\qquad\qquad D'$$

Within the world of concrete automata, the homomorphic extension relation captures exactly our intuitive conception of extension. If D is an

---

[5] Actually, it's unnecessary to stipulate the root to root correspondence $h(q_0') = q_0$ explicitly, for it follows as a special case from the first clause of the definiens, with p set to λ (the empty string).

extension of D' then the definiens ensures that the atomic-valued path information encoded in D' by $\delta'^*(q_0', p) = a$ can be read off D by $\delta^*(q_0, p) = a$ as well. Similarly, paths in D' which lead to non-atomic-valued terminal nodes have to exist in D as well. Furthermore, for each identity in D' encoded by a path congruence $\delta'^*(q_0', p) = \delta'^*(q_0', p')$ in D', there must be a corresponding path congruence $\delta^*(q_0, p) = \delta^*(q_0, p')$ in D, since h is a function.

Defining two automata D and D' to be *isomorphic* ($D \simeq D'$) iff both $D \preceq D'$ and $D' \preceq D$ hold, we get with $\simeq$ an equivalence relation that captures exactly our intuitive individuation criterion on automata: isomorphic automata are essentially the same, and we will regard the set of all equivalence classes of $\simeq$ on $\mathcal{D}$ (written $\mathcal{D}/\simeq$) as a mathematical reconstruction of the collection of feature structures. For example, the structure in Figure 1 would be represented automata-theoretically by the equivalence class $[D]_\simeq$.[6]

Only one small step remains. Recall that it is usual to turn the unification operation into a total function by adding a greatest element (here denoted by '$\perp_\mathcal{G}$') to the set of feature structures. Thus, we define the set of feature structures to be

$$\mathcal{G} = \mathcal{D}/\simeq \,\cup \{\perp_\mathcal{G}\},$$

and we say that G is an *extension* of G' ($G' \sqsubseteq_\mathcal{G} G$; $G', G \in \mathcal{G}$) iff either $G = \perp_\mathcal{G}$, or

$$D' \preceq D, \text{ for } G' = [D'] \text{ and } G = [D].$$

Apart from the role assigned to $\perp_\mathcal{G}$, $\sqsubseteq_\mathcal{G}$ is simply the relation which is induced by $\preceq$ on the equivalence classes. It can easily be verified that $\mathcal{G}$ and $\sqsubseteq_\mathcal{G}$ constitute a partial order with greatest element in which any pair of elements G_1 and G_2 has a least upper bound (LUB). This least upper bound of two graphs can then be identified with their unification:

$$G_1 \sqcup_\mathcal{G} G_2 =_{df} \text{LUB}(G_1, G_2).$$

4 ψ-Terms

Approaches influenced by work in Artificial Intelligence tend to reconstruct feature structures as special data structures called ψ-terms (Aït-Kaci 1984). A class of ψ-terms Ψ adequate for the feature structures considered here consists of a distinct element $\perp_\Psi$ (which will be stipulated to be the greatest element) together with complex terms of the form

$$t_\psi = \langle P, \mu, l \rangle.$$

These terms consist of a prefix-closed set P of strings over A, the so-called *term domain*, a right invariant (see Appendix A) equivalence relation μ on

---

[6]If it is clear from the context we omit the index of the equivalence classes in the following.

P with finite index, and a partial biunique labeling function $l \in [P/\mu \mapsto V]$ which assigns atomic values to some of the equivalence classes in P/μ.

In the ψ-term approach, feature structures are reconstructed by complete descriptions of their paths and path congruences.

Example 4.1 The feature structure in Figure 1 is represented by the ψ-term $\langle P, \mu, l \rangle$, with

$$P = \left\{ \begin{array}{c} \lambda, \text{PRED}, \text{TENSE}, \text{SUBJ}, \text{SUBJ.PRED}, \text{XCOMP}, \\ \text{XCOMP.PRED}, \text{XCOMP.SUBJ}, \text{XCOMP.SUBJ.PRED} \end{array} \right\},$$

$$\mu = \left\{ \begin{array}{c} \langle \lambda, \lambda \rangle, \langle \text{PRED}, \text{PRED} \rangle, \langle \text{TENSE}, \text{TENSE} \rangle, \langle \text{SUBJ}, \text{SUBJ} \rangle, \\ \langle \text{SUBJ.PRED}, \text{SUBJ.PRED} \rangle, \langle \text{XCOMP}, \text{XCOMP} \rangle, \\ \langle \text{XCOMP.PRED}, \text{XCOMP.PRED} \rangle, \langle \text{XCOMP.SUBJ}, \text{XCOMP.SUBJ} \rangle, \\ \langle \text{XCOMP.SUBJ.PRED}, \text{XCOMP.SUBJ.PRED} \rangle, \\ \langle \text{SUBJ}, \text{XCOMP.SUBJ} \rangle, \langle \text{XCOMP.SUBJ}, \text{SUBJ} \rangle, \\ \langle \text{SUBJ.PRED}, \text{XCOMP.SUBJ.PRED} \rangle, \\ \langle \text{XCOMP.SUBJ.PRED}, \text{SUBJ.PRED} \rangle \end{array} \right\},$$

$$
\begin{array}{rcl}
l([\text{PRED}]) & = & \text{PROMISE}, \\
l([\text{TENSE}]) & = & \text{PAST}, \\
l([\text{SUBJ.PRED}]) & = & \text{JOHN}, \\
l([\text{XCOMP.PRED}]) & = & \text{COME}.^7
\end{array}
$$

However, if ψ-terms are to fully capture our pretheoretic intuitions about feature structures, we must ensure that (C0), (C1), (C2) and (C3) hold. Clearly (C0) and (C3) hold, and by imposing two further requirements on ψ-terms, we can ensure that (C1) and (C2) hold as well. In fact, all we have to do is ensure that all ψ-terms are acyclic, and that only equivalence classes whose paths have no proper prolongation in P can be labeled. More precisely, from now on we are going to demand that ψ-terms satisfy the following conditions:

(Ψ) (1) $\forall p \in A^* \, \forall p' \in A^+ (\langle p, pp' \rangle \notin \mu)$,

(2) $\forall p \in P \, \forall f \in A([p] \in Dom(l) \rightarrow pf \notin P)$.

What is the information ordering on ψ-terms? We define this as follows. A ψ-term t_ψ is an *extension* of t'_ψ ($t'_\psi \sqsubseteq_\Psi t_\psi$) iff either $t_\psi = \bot_\Psi$, or $t'_\psi = \langle P', \mu', l' \rangle$, $t_\psi = \langle P, \mu, l \rangle$ and

$$\mu' \subseteq \mu, \text{ and}$$
$$l'([p]_{\mu'}) = l([p]_\mu), \text{ for each } p \in P'.$$

It follows directly from the definition that Ψ and $\sqsubseteq_\Psi$ form a partial order with greatest element $\bot_\Psi$.

---

[7] If we have to deal with strings of attributes and the attributes themselves are strings (as in most of the examples), we use concatenation (denoted by '.') explicitly.

The unification of two ψ-terms t^1_ψ, t^2_ψ ($t^1_\psi \sqcup_\Psi t^2_\psi$) is defined as follows. If t^1_ψ or t^2_ψ is equal to $\bot_\Psi$, then their unification is also equal to $\bot_\Psi$. Now assume that t^1_ψ and t^2_ψ are the complex terms $\langle P_1, \mu_1, l_1 \rangle$ and $\langle P_2, \mu_2, l_2 \rangle$. If the symmetric, transitive and right invariant closure of $\mu_1 \cup \mu_2 \cup \{\langle p, p' \rangle \mid l_1([p]_{\mu_1}) = l_2([p']_{\mu_2})\}$ is acyclic, then this closure (μ) gives us the least acyclic right invariant equivalence relation on $P = P_1 \cup P_2$ that includes $\mu_1 \cup \mu_2 \cup \{\langle p, p' \rangle \mid l_1([p]_{\mu_1}) = l_2([p']_{\mu_2})\}$.[8] If, in addition, also

$$l = \{\langle [p]_\mu, a \rangle \mid \langle [p]_{\mu_1}, a \rangle \in l_1 \vee \langle [p]_{\mu_2}, a \rangle \in l_2\}$$

is a function satisfying ($\Psi 2$), the term $\langle P, \mu, l \rangle$ is the unification of t^1_ψ and t^2_ψ;[9] in all other cases we set $t^1_\psi \sqcup_\Psi t^2_\psi = \bot_\Psi$.

It follows immediately from the definitions that the unification of two ψ-terms is their least upper bound in Ψ. That is,

$$t^1_\psi \sqcup_\Psi t^2_\psi = \mathrm{LUB}(t^1_\psi, t^2_\psi)$$

is provable.

Equivalence with the Graph-Theoretical Reconstruction

What is the relationship between the ψ-term account of feature structures and the automata theoretic? In fact, the reconstructions are equivalent. As we shall now see, $\langle \mathcal{G}, \sqsubseteq_\mathcal{G} \rangle$ and $\langle \Psi, \sqsubseteq_\Psi \rangle$ are in fact *isomorphic* (similar) orders and therefore order-theoretically indistinguishable.

The transition from the equivalence classes of isomorphic automata $\mathcal{G}$ to the ψ-terms follows from the fact that all automata in an equivalence class $[D]$ are uniquely described by their path set $P(D)$ and Nerode relation $\mathcal{N}_D$ (see Appendix A). Since $P(D)$ is a finite, prefix-closed set and $\mathcal{N}_D$ is a right invariant, acyclic equivalence relation on $P(D)$, the transition from graphs to ψ-terms is achieved by the following function $\mathcal{G}_\Psi$:

$$\mathcal{G}_\Psi(\bot_\mathcal{G}) = \bot_\Psi,$$
$$\mathcal{G}_\Psi([D]) = \langle P(D), \mathcal{N}_D, l \rangle, \text{ with}$$
$$l = \{\langle [p]_{\mathcal{N}_D}, a \rangle \mid \delta^*(q_0, p) = a \wedge a \in V\}.$$

It can easily be verified from the given definitions that $\mathcal{G}_\Psi$ is an injective function with range Ψ. Moreover, $\mathcal{G}_\Psi$ carries an extension relation between two equivalence classes $[D']$ and $[D]$ ($[D'] \sqsubseteq_\mathcal{G} [D]$) over to their homomorphic images in Ψ ($\mathcal{G}_\Psi([D']) \sqsubseteq_\Psi \mathcal{G}_\Psi([D])$). That is, $\mathcal{G}_\Psi$ is a lattice homomorphism.

---

[8]The closure can be constructed, for example, by closing the symmetric, transitive closure of $\mu_1 \cup \mu_2 \cup \{\langle p, p' \rangle \mid l_1([p]_{\mu_1}) = l_2([p']_{\mu_2})\}$ under right invariance in an inductive construction which terminates as soon as a cycle is derived. In fact, the construction terminates in any case.

[9]Although the symmetric, transitive, right invariant closure of $\mu_1 \cup \mu_2$ would give us the least right invariant equivalence relation on $P_1 \cup P_2$ that includes $\mu_1 \cup \mu_2$, we have to add $\{\langle p, p' \rangle \mid l_1([p]_{\mu_1}) = l_2([p']_{\mu_2})\}$ in order to ensure the biuniqueness of l.

On the other hand, each complex ψ-term induces a canonical representative of an equivalence class in $\mathcal{G}$ whose non-final states are the (unlabeled) equivalence classes in P/μ. Thus, the transition from Ψ to $\mathcal{G}$ can be established by the function $\Psi_{\mathcal{G}}$ which is defined as follows:

$$\Psi_{\mathcal{G}}(\perp_{\Psi}) = \perp_{\mathcal{G}},$$
$$\Psi_{\mathcal{G}}(\langle P, \mu, l \rangle) = [\langle Q, A, \delta, q_0, F \rangle], \text{ with}$$

$$q_0 = \begin{cases} [\lambda]_{\mu} & \text{if } [\lambda]_{\mu} \notin Dom(l) \\ l([\lambda]_{\mu}) & \text{otherwise,} \end{cases}$$

$$\delta([p]_{\mu}, f) = \begin{cases} [pf]_{\mu} & \text{if } [pf]_{\mu} \notin Dom(l) \\ l([pf]_{\mu}) & \text{if } [pf]_{\mu} \in Dom(l) \\ \text{undefined} & \text{otherwise,} \end{cases}$$

$$Q = \{q_0\} \cup Ran(\delta),$$
$$F = Ran(l).$$

Note that $\Psi_{\mathcal{G}}$ is not only a homomorphism from $\langle \Psi, \sqsubseteq_{\Psi} \rangle$ to $\langle \mathcal{G}, \sqsubseteq_{\mathcal{G}} \rangle$, it is actually the inverse of $\mathcal{G}_{\Psi}$, since it assigns to a term t_{ψ} exactly the equivalence class that $\mathcal{G}_{\Psi}$ maps to t_{ψ}. This proves also the bijectivity of $\mathcal{G}_{\Psi}$ and thus the similarity of the orders.

5   Feature Descriptions

Our next reconstruction of the feature structure concept is an intrinsically *logical* one. That is, we proceed not by defining some concrete model of feature structures, but by considering how feature structures are described. Our starting point will be those unification-based theories and formalisms which make explicit use of a description language for feature structures, for example LFG and PATR-II (Kaplan and Bresnan 1982, Shieber et al. 1983). In these systems, descriptions of feature structures (henceforth *feature descriptions*) are constructed by means of equations which annotate the context-free rules and lexical entries.

A simple example, reminiscent of LFG, is given by the following grammar. This allows us to derive sentence (1) (*John promised to come*) with the structure in Figure 1.

(2) S $\rightarrow$ NP   VP   John: NP, PRED↑ ≈ JOHN
$\quad$ SUBJ↑ ≈ ↓ ↑ ≈ ↓
$\qquad\qquad\qquad\qquad\qquad\qquad$ promised: V, PRED↑ ≈ PROMISE
$\quad$ VP $\rightarrow$ V   VP′   TENSE↑ ≈ PAST
$\quad\quad$ ↑ ≈ ↓ XCOMP↑ ≈ ↓   SUBJ↑ ≈ SUBJ XCOMP↑

$\quad$ VP′ $\rightarrow$ to   V   come: V, PRED↑ ≈ COME
$\quad\quad\quad\quad$ ↑ ≈ ↓

Here, the attributes are regarded as unary partial function symbols and the

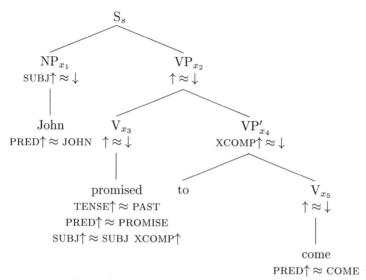

FIGURE 4   The annotated constituent structure which is derivable
with the grammar in (2) for sentence (1).

values as individual constants.[10] The arrows '↑' and '↓' are usually called
metavariables, and refer to the annotated node (↓) or its mother node (↑)
respectively. For a given sentence, the feature description is constructed
by instantiating the metavariables in constants or variables on the nodes
of its phrase structure tree.

Let's consider an example. One possible reconstruction of the concept
of feature descriptions ensues if we suppose that there is a distinct constant
s for the root, and a distinct variable x_i for each other node in the phrase
structure tree.[11] This is done in the phrase structure tree for (1), given
in Figure 4. The feature description is then constructed by closing the
conjunction of all instantiated annotations existentially. The description
for the constituent structure in Figure 4 is shown in (3) below.

(3) $\exists x_1 \exists x_2 \exists x_3 \exists x_4 \exists x_5 (\text{SUBJ}.s \approx x_1$ & $\text{PRED}.x_1 \approx \text{JOHN}$ & $s \approx x_2$ &
      $x_2 \approx x_3$ & $\text{SUBJ}.x_3 \approx \text{SUBJ}.\text{XCOMP}.x_3$ &
      $\text{TENSE}.x_3 \approx \text{PAST}$ & $\text{PRED}.x_3 \approx \text{PROMISE}$ &
      $\text{XCOMP}.x_2 \approx x_4$ & $x_4 \approx x_5$ & $\text{PRED}.x_5 \approx \text{COME})$

---

[10]Compared to the standard literature, this results in a "mirror imaged" term structure.
Note that the terms are formed without using brackets. (Since all function symbols are
unary, the introduction of brackets would not improve readability anyway.) In order
to preserve a certain similarity with the notation in the standard literature, we will
dispense with explicit representation of the concatenation for the time being.
[11]Smolka (1989) gives a similar reconstruction of PATR-II grammars.

In such feature description approaches, a string is accepted as grammatical if the grammar assigns to it a feature description which is *satisfiable* by those models which are considered to be admissible. Note that this definition of grammaticality is a *logical* one: it is formulated in terms of the satisfiability of descriptions. Logical approaches sometimes speak of the feature structure assigned to a string. Intuitively, this is the graphical representation of the (up to isomorphism) unique minimal model of its (satisfiable) feature description.

Let's look a little closer at the mechanisms underlying these approaches, and see what sort of feature description languages can be abstracted from them.

In early feature description formalisms, all feature structures had to satisfy condition (C0), so the annotations of the rules and lexical entries were subject to restrictions. In particular, each daughter node of the local tree introduced by a context-free rule had to be annotated with at least one *function assigning* equation of the form $\sigma\uparrow \approx \downarrow$ (σ a sequence of attributes), and in the lexical entries only the metavariable $\uparrow$ could be used. This guaranteed that all quantifiers and variables in the $\exists$-prenex conjunctions of atomic equations could be eliminated by substitution.[12] For example, this trivial quantifier elimination procedure turns the formula (3) into the logically equivalent set of equations depicted in (4).

$$(4) \qquad E \;=\; \left\{ \begin{array}{l} \text{PRED.SUBJ}.s \approx \text{JOHN}, \\ \text{TENSE}.s \approx \text{PAST}, \\ \text{PRED}.s \approx \text{PROMISE}, \\ \text{SUBJ}.s \approx \text{SUBJ.XCOMP}.s, \\ \text{PRED.XCOMP}.s \approx \text{COME} \end{array} \right\}$$

Since it can be ensured by the eliminability of the quantifiers that at least the minimal model of an $\exists$-prenex conjunction is connected and rooted, the first logic-oriented reconstructions made use of feature descriptions like (4) where (C0) is guaranteed on purely syntactical grounds.

As is obvious from the feature description in (4), the expressive power of the underlying description language is quite limited. The nonlogical vocabulary consists of A, V and a distinct constant s. The set of *terms* is

$$\{\sigma a \mid a \in V \cup \{s\} \wedge \sigma \in A^*\}.$$

For the description of feature structures, only descriptions of the following form may be used:

$$(5) \qquad \begin{array}{l} \sigma s \approx c \\ \sigma s \approx \sigma' s, \end{array}$$

with $\sigma, \sigma' \in A^*; c \in V$.

---

[12]This follows from a corollary of the equality theorem (Shoenfield 1967, p. 36).

A feature description is meant to be a description of a feature structure. One describes a congruence of the automata in a class $[D]$

$$\langle f_1 \ldots f_n, g_1 \ldots g_m \rangle \in \mathcal{N}_D \ (\in \mu) \text{ by } f_n \ldots f_1 s \approx g_m \ldots g_1 s,$$

and a transition to an atomic value

$$\delta^*(q_0, f_1 \ldots f_n) = a \ (l([f_1 \ldots f_n]_\mu) = a) \text{ by } f_n \ldots f_1 s \approx a.$$

The path described by a term σs is simply the mirrored functor sequence, in the following denoted by $\vec{\sigma}$. In addition, we need a description of the greatest feature structure; we use $\perp$ (*false*) for this purpose.

Since the restriction to formulas of the form (5) ensures by purely syntactical means that only connected structures with a unique root can be described, one needs, aside from a logical axiom for $\perp$, three classes of non-logical axioms for capturing the linguistically motivated well-formedness conditions (C1–3) on feature structures:

(L) (1) $\vdash \sigma' \sigma s \not\approx \sigma s$, for all $\sigma' \in A^+$ and $\sigma \in A^*$,

    (2) $\vdash fa \not\approx fa$, for all $a \in V$ and $f \in A$,

    (3) $\vdash a \not\approx b$, for all $a, b \in V$, with $a \neq b$,

    (4) $\vdash \sim\perp$.

Note that the set of axioms under (L2) and (L3) is finite, whereas the set of acyclicity axioms (L1) is not. Further, note that the axioms under (L1) and (L2) are obvious analogs of the requirements ($\Psi 1$) and ($\Psi 2$) for ψ-terms. Finally, note that the axioms (L3) really are required, for from a purely logical point of view a set of equations like $\{\sigma s \approx a, \sigma s \approx b\}$ is consistent, but the structure it describes does not fit our intuitive concept of feature structures.

Apart from the fact that one has to allow that everything follows from an inconsistency, the consequence relation between feature-structure-describing sets of equations is captured precisely by those inference rules which enable us to construct completely *deductively closed* descriptions from a given description. Moreover, in order to get such rules, one can simply translate the closure properties of ψ-terms into inference rules for equation sets. Besides the rules for symmetry and transitivity we need a substitution rule to capture the right invariance of μ and the rule for subterm reflexivity to capture the reflexivity of μ on the prefix-closed set P. The biuniqueness of l ($l([\vec{\sigma}]_\mu) = l([\vec{\sigma}']_\mu)$ implies $\langle \vec{\sigma}, \vec{\sigma}' \rangle \in \mu$) does not need any special attention, since the rules allow us to derive $\sigma s \approx \sigma' s$ from $\sigma s \approx a \ (= l([\vec{\sigma}]_\mu))$ and $\sigma' s \approx a$. The required inference rules are:

$\sigma \tau \approx \tau' \vdash \tau \approx \tau$ (*Subterm Reflexivity*),

$\tau_1 \approx \tau_2 \vdash \tau_2 \approx \tau_1$ (*Symmetry*),

$\tau_1 \approx \tau_2, \tau_2 \approx \tau_3 \vdash \tau_1 \approx \tau_3$ (*Transitivity*),

$\sigma \tau_1 \approx \tau, \tau_1 \approx \tau_2 \vdash \sigma \tau_2 \approx \tau$ (*Substitutivity*),

$\tau_1 \approx \tau_2, \tau_1 \not\approx \tau_2 \vdash \perp,$

$\perp \vdash \tau_1 \approx \tau_2.$

The consistency of a given finite set of equations E of the form (5) can be tested very easily by closing it deductively. Here is one simple way of doing so, which is guaranteed to terminate. First, one adds to E all of the axioms under (L2) and (L3) (a finite set) together with some finite subset of the axioms under (L1) sufficient for testing the consistency of E. One such subset is determined as follows. A cyclic but otherwise well-formed feature structure $[D]$ ($\langle P, \mu, l \rangle$) must contain at least one path congruence $\delta^*(q_0, pp') = \delta^*(q_0, p)$ with $p' \in A^+$ ($\langle pp', p \rangle \in \mu$) for which $|pp'| \leq |Q|$ ($\leq |P/\mu|$) holds. Since in each feature description E of this structure there must be for each node at least one subterm referring to it, one needs only those axioms of the form $\sigma'\sigma s \not\approx \sigma s$ ($\sigma' \in A^+$) where the length of $\sigma'\sigma s$ does not exceed the cardinality of the set of all subterms occurring in E. If this augmented set is closed inductively under subterm reflexivity, symmetry, transitivity and substitutivity, then either an explicit contradiction is derived after a finite number of steps or the construction terminates with a finite set of atomic formulas.

Here is an example. For the set E given in (4) the construction yields (aside from the negations) the set in (6).

(6)
$$\left\{ \begin{array}{c}
s \approx s, \text{PRED}.s \approx \text{PRED}.s, \text{TENSE}.s \approx \text{TENSE}.s, \\
\text{SUBJ}.s \approx \text{SUBJ}.s, \text{XCOMP}.s \approx \text{XCOMP}.s, \\
\text{PRED.SUBJ}.s \approx \text{PRED.SUBJ}.s, \text{PRED.XCOMP}.s \approx \text{PRED.XCOMP}.s, \\
\text{SUBJ.XCOMP}.s \approx \text{SUBJ.XCOMP}.s, \\
\text{PRED.SUBJ.XCOMP}.s \approx \text{PRED.SUBJ.XCOMP}.s, \\
\text{JOHN} \approx \text{JOHN}, \text{PAST} \approx \text{PAST}, \\
\text{PROMISE} \approx \text{PROMISE}, \text{COME} \approx \text{COME}, \\
\text{SUBJ}.s \approx \text{SUBJ.XCOMP}.s, \text{SUBJ.XCOMP}.s \approx \text{SUBJ}.s, \\
\text{PRED.SUBJ.XCOMP}.s \approx \text{PRED.SUBJ}.s, \\
\text{PRED}.s \approx \text{PROMISE}, \\
\text{PROMISE} \approx \text{PRED}.s, \text{TENSE}.s \approx \text{PAST}, \\
\text{PAST} \approx \text{TENSE}.s, \text{PRED.SUBJ}.s \approx \text{JOHN}, \\
\text{JOHN} \approx \text{PRED.SUBJ}.s, \text{PRED.SUBJ.XCOMP}.s \approx \text{JOHN}, \\
\text{JOHN} \approx \text{PRED.SUBJ.XCOMP}.s, \text{PRED.XCOMP}.s \approx \text{COME}, \\
\text{COME} \approx \text{PRED.XCOMP}.s
\end{array} \right\}$$

If the construction terminates without yielding an explicit contradiction, the expanded set defines a (minimal) term model which establishes the consistency of the original equation set. The universe of such a model consists of the set of equivalence classes which is induced by $\approx$ on the terms occurring in the equations of the constructed set. Each constant is interpreted by the equivalence class containing it. (If there is no such equivalence class the constant remains uninterpreted.) Each function symbol f is interpreted by the partial function $\Im(f)$ that maps every equivalence class $[\tau]$ to the class $[f\tau]$, if this class exists; otherwise the function is undefined for $[\tau]$.

Note that this means that we are taking the interpretation function itself to be a partial function. This is natural: a total function would have to interpret constants which do *not* occur in a given feature description. (In the minimal model for the feature description (4) given in the following example, the value MARY $\in V$ would have to be interpreted as well, and the graph representing the minimal model would contain nodes not occurring in the graph-theoretical reconstruction.)

Example 5.1 The minimal term model constructed on the basis of the deductive closure in (6) for the feature description (4) consists of the universe that contains the following equivalence classes:

$$
\begin{aligned}
[s] &= \{s\}, & [4] &= \left\{ \begin{array}{l} \text{SUBJ}.s, \\ \text{SUBJ.XCOMP}.s \end{array} \right\}, \\
[1] &= \left\{ \begin{array}{l} \text{PRED}.s, \\ \text{PROMISE} \end{array} \right\}, & [5] &= \left\{ \begin{array}{l} \text{PRED.XCOMP}.s, \\ \text{COME} \end{array} \right\}, \\
[2] &= \left\{ \begin{array}{l} \text{TENSE}.s, \\ \text{PAST} \end{array} \right\}, & [6] &= \left\{ \begin{array}{l} \text{PRED.SUBJ}.s, \\ \text{PRED.SUBJ.XCOMP}.s, \\ \text{JOHN} \end{array} \right\}. \\
[3] &= \{\text{XCOMP}.s\},
\end{aligned}
$$

The constants and function symbols are interpreted by individuals and partial functions as follows:

$$
\begin{aligned}
\Im(\text{PROMISE}) &= [1], \\
\Im(\text{PAST}) &= [2], \\
\Im(\text{JOHN}) &= [6], \\
\Im(\text{COME}) &= [5], \\
\Im(\text{PRED}) &= \left\{ \begin{array}{l} \langle[s],[1]\rangle, \\ \langle[4],[6]\rangle, \\ \langle[3],[5]\rangle \end{array} \right\}, \\
\Im(\text{TENSE}) &= \left\{ \langle[s],[2]\rangle \right\}, \\
\Im(\text{SUBJ}) &= \left\{ \begin{array}{l} \langle[s],[4]\rangle, \\ \langle[3],[4]\rangle \end{array} \right\}, \\
\Im(\text{XCOMP}) &= \left\{ \langle[s],[3]\rangle \right\}.
\end{aligned}
$$

If $\langle x, y \rangle \in \Im(f)$ is represented by an f-labeled arc from x to y, then the graph of $\Im$ is given by the following structure.

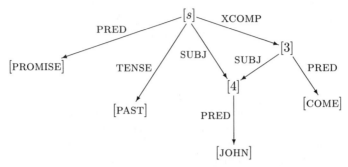

Such (up to isomorphism) unique minimal models of (consistent) feature descriptions represent exactly the feature structures which are assigned to sentences by the grammar — and here a general point emerges that is well worth emphasizing: *to construct this model, we didn't have to explicitly use a unification operation.* This is characteristic of logical approaches: testing for satisfiability, not explicitly unifying structures, is the key concept. If a string is well-formed its feature structure falls out as the (up to isomorphism) unique minimal model — it's not something built up by unification.

Of course, it is possible to go one additional step and re-establish within logical reconstructions the ideas of information ordering and unification. One way to do this is to re-create the feature structures as entities on the *syntactic* level.[13] Such syntactic reconstructions go back to Pereira and Shieber (1984). A feature structure is simply identified with the deductive closure ($E_{\vdash}$) of any of its descriptions (E). Thereby one gets on a syntactic level not only biunique representations for the classes of isomorphic minimal models, but with $\{\bot\}_{\vdash}$ also a possible greatest element.

More precisely, the set of feature structures $\mathcal{E}$ consists of the deductive closures of all finite sets of equations of the form (5) plus $\{\bot\}_{\vdash}$. Note that the extension relation between deductively closed sets of equations reduces completely to the subset relation, since not only the congruences ($\mu' \subseteq \mu$) have to be contained in an extension but also the equations describing transitions to atomic values. So, if we define the *extension* relation $E'_{\vdash} \sqsubseteq_{\mathcal{E}} E_{\vdash}$ by

$$E'_{\vdash} \subseteq E_{\vdash},$$

then we have a partial order with $\{\bot\}_{\vdash}$ as greatest element. Note that $E'_{\vdash} \subseteq E_{\vdash}$ iff $E \vdash E'$; that is, this information ordering corresponds to the

---

[13] Another approach would be to regard specific classes of isomorphic models (namely the ones that are actually describable) as feature structures. Such a semantic reconstruction would give us — analogously to the graph-theoretical reconstruction — via the notion of homomorphic extension an information ordering, though one with no greatest element.

relation of logical deducibility. It is easy to show that the *unification*

$$E^1_\vdash \sqcup_{\mathcal{E}} E^2_\vdash =_{\mathrm{df}} (E^1_\vdash \cup E^2_\vdash)_\vdash$$

assigns to any pair of deductively closed sets of equations their least upper bound.

Equivalence with the ψ-Term-Reconstruction

The proof that $\langle \Psi, \sqsubseteq_\Psi \rangle$ and the partial order induced by $\sqsubseteq_{\mathcal{E}}$ on the deductively closed sets of equations are equivalent is even easier than the equivalence of $\langle \mathcal{G}, \sqsubseteq_{\mathcal{G}} \rangle$ and $\langle \Psi, \sqsubseteq_\Psi \rangle$, for apart from the axioms the two reconstructions differ only notationally. One gets from the terms σs to the paths of a term domain simply by mirroring the functor sequences ($\vec{\sigma}$). So, for the transition from the deductively closed sets of equations to the ψ-terms a homomorphism $\mathcal{E}_\Psi$ is defined by:

$$\mathcal{E}_\Psi(\{\perp\}_\vdash) = \perp_\Psi,$$
$$\mathcal{E}_\Psi(E_\vdash) = \langle P, \mu, l \rangle, \text{ for each consistent set } E_\vdash, \text{ with}$$
$$P = \{\vec{\sigma} \mid \sigma s \approx \sigma s \in E_\vdash\},$$
$$\mu = \{\langle \vec{\sigma}, \vec{\sigma}' \rangle \mid \sigma s \approx \sigma' s \in E_\vdash\},$$
$$l = \{\langle [\vec{\sigma}]_\mu, a \rangle \mid \sigma s \approx a \in E_\vdash\}.$$

$\approx$ induces on the mirror imaged strings thus obtained an equivalence relation μ whose right invariance is due to the fact that $E_\vdash$ is closed under substitutivity. The function property of l is ensured by the axioms (L3). The biuniqueness of l follows, since $\sigma s \approx \sigma' s$ must be element of $E_\vdash$ if $\sigma s \approx a, \sigma' s \approx a \in E_\vdash$. That the orders $\langle \mathcal{E}, \sqsubseteq_{\mathcal{E}} \rangle$ and $\langle \Psi, \sqsubseteq_\Psi \rangle$ are homomorphic then follows directly from their definitions.

For the proof of the other direction one proceeds in reverse. With the homomorphism $\Psi_{\mathcal{E}}$

$$\Psi_{\mathcal{E}}(\perp_\Psi) = \{\perp\}_\vdash,$$

$$\Psi_{\mathcal{E}}(\langle P, \mu, l \rangle) = \begin{pmatrix} \{\vec{\sigma} s \approx \vec{\sigma}' s \mid \langle \sigma, \sigma' \rangle \in \mu\} \cup \\ \{\vec{\sigma} s \approx a \mid l([\sigma]_\mu) = a\} \end{pmatrix}_\vdash$$

one can prove not only the homomorphy, but (as $\Psi_{\mathcal{E}} = \mathcal{E}_\Psi{}^{-1}$) also the isomorphy of the orders.

6 A Rudimentary Kasper-Rounds Logic as an Example of a Mixed Form

We now develop a rudimentary Kasper-Rounds logic (in the sequel abbreviated to KR-logic) which allows a reconstruction of the notion of unification which is equivalent to the approaches sketched so far.[14] We call this ap-

---

[14] Our version is rudimentary, since we assume complete "path expansion" and dispense with the explicit introduction of conjunction and the notational convenience of referring to "non-local path values".

proach a *mixed form*, since on the one hand its "deductive" apparatus can be derived from our feature logic by translating the equalities back into ψ-term congruences and path values. On the other hand, since the resulting apparatus operates on descriptions of automata, its semantics can be obtained by taking automata as models and reinterpreting the ordinary satisfaction definition.[15]

Besides TOP, the description language consists of formulas describing atomic-valued paths and path congruences. For all $p, p_1, \ldots, p_n \in A^*$ and $a \in V$ the following expressions are formulas:

TOP,

$p{:}a,$

$[\![\langle p_1 \rangle, \ldots, \langle p_n \rangle]\!].$

The meaning of the formulas is determined by the following satisfiability relation whose definition is based on automata $D \in \mathcal{D}$ now acting as models:

$D \not\models \text{TOP},$

$D \models p{:}a \leftrightarrow \delta^*(q_0, p) = a,$

$D \models [\![\langle p_1 \rangle, \ldots, \langle p_n \rangle]\!] \leftrightarrow \exists X \in P(D)/\mathcal{N}_D(\{p_1, \ldots, p_n\} \subseteq X).$

A KR-*description* is simply a finite set of formulas K not containing TOP. An automaton D *satisfies* a KR-description K, if D satisfies all formulas in K. A KR-description is *satisfiable* if there exists an automaton which satisfies it.

Since the relationship between feature descriptions and automata is now sufficiently known through the various isomorphisms, we can specify the intuitively obvious relation between feature descriptions E and KR-descriptions K by two translation functions Ω and $\mho$. If the path sets in the KR-logic are denoted by — possibly indexed — C's, we can define these functions on the basis of the functions Ω' and $\mho'$ which translate atomic equations into KR-formulas and atomic KR-formulas into atomic equations or sets of atomic equations:

$$\Omega'(\sigma s \approx a) = \vec{\sigma}{:}a \qquad \mho'(p{:}a) = \vec{p}s \approx a$$
$$\Omega'(\sigma s \approx \sigma' s) = [\![\langle \vec{\sigma} \rangle, \langle \vec{\sigma}' \rangle]\!] \qquad \mho'(C) = \{\vec{p}s \approx \vec{p}'s \mid \langle p \rangle, \langle p' \rangle \in C\}.$$

Then we define

$$\Omega(E) = \{\Omega'(\phi) \mid \phi \in E\}$$

and

$$\mho(K) = \{\mho'(p{:}a) \mid p{:}a \in K\} \cup \bigcup \{\mho'(C) \mid C \in K\}.$$

From the feature description in (4) we then get the KR-description in (7)

---

[15]If we had integrated negation and disjunction in our feature logic (see, for example, Wedekind 1994), this would, of course, hold also for the full KR-logic.

below.

$$(7) \qquad \Omega(E) \;=\; \left\{ \begin{array}{c} \text{SUBJ:PRED:JOHN,} \\ \text{TENSE:PAST,} \\ \text{PRED:PROMISE,} \\ \text{XCOMP:PRED:COME,} \\ [\![\langle \text{SUBJ} \rangle, \langle \text{XCOMP:SUBJ} \rangle]\!] \end{array} \right\}$$

Testing satisfiability can be reduced to applying semantic equivalences. These equivalences state on the one hand (KR1–3) the unsatisfiability of those formulas which *obviously* do not describe well-formed structures in the sense of our conditions (C1–3). In addition, they recapitulate that the satisfiability of a KR-description is invariant under prefix closure and closure under right invariance and transitivity. In order to get full substitutivity we had to add (KR10) which is not in the set of equivalences in Kasper and Rounds 1990. With ϕ an arbitrary formula, $p, w, u \in A^*$, $p' \in A^+$, $f \in A$ and $a, b \in V$, the following equivalences are used:

(KR) I. *Failure*:

$$[\![\dots \langle p \rangle \dots \langle p{:}p' \rangle \dots]\!] \;\Leftrightarrow\; \text{TOP} \tag{1}$$

$$p{:}a \wedge [\![\dots \langle p{:}f \rangle \dots]\!] \;\Leftrightarrow\; \text{TOP} \tag{2}$$

$$p{:}a \wedge p{:}b \;\Leftrightarrow\; \text{TOP} \tag{3}$$

$$\phi \wedge \text{TOP} \;\Leftrightarrow\; \text{TOP} \tag{4}$$

II. *Path Equivalences*:

 Prefix Closure:

$$C \;\Leftrightarrow\; C \wedge \bigwedge \{ [\![\langle p \rangle]\!] \mid \langle p{:}w \rangle \in C \} \tag{5}$$

$$p{:}a \;\Leftrightarrow\; p{:}a \wedge \bigwedge \{ [\![\langle u \rangle]\!] \mid p = u{:}w \} \tag{6}$$

 Right Invariance:

$$C \wedge C' \;\Leftrightarrow\; C \wedge (C' \cup \{ \langle p{:}w \rangle \mid p \in C \}) \tag{7}$$
$$\text{for any } w \text{ such that}$$
$$\exists u \in C(\langle u{:}w \rangle \in C')$$

$$C \wedge p{:}w{:}a \;\Leftrightarrow\; C \wedge \bigwedge \{ u{:}w{:}a \mid \langle u \rangle \in C \}, \text{ if } \langle p \rangle \in C \tag{8}$$

 Transitivity:

$$C \wedge C' \;\Leftrightarrow\; C \cup C', \text{ if } C \cap C' \neq \emptyset \tag{9}$$

 Atomic Coreference:

$$p{:}a \wedge w{:}a \;\Leftrightarrow\; p{:}a \wedge w{:}a \wedge [\![\langle p \rangle, \langle w \rangle]\!]. \tag{10}$$

To test for satisfiability, these equivalences are used as "rewrite rules" in the direction "left to right". So, if a description K contains, for example, the sets C and C' and the sets are not disjoint, then by (KR9) we can replace these two sets in K by $C \cup C'$ and end up with a description which is semantically equivalent with K.[16] Without (KR10) the set of equivalences is incomplete, since for two KR-descriptions which are satisfied by the same models (for example $\{f_1{:}f_2{:}a, g_1{:}g_2{:}a\}$ and $\{[\![\langle f_1{:}f_2\rangle, \langle g_1{:}g_2\rangle]\!], f_1{:}f_2{:}a\}$ with f_1, f_2, g_1, g_2 in A and pairwise distinct) it is in general not possible to "derive" one from the other by rewriting. The incompleteness of the original system would not allow us to establish a one-to-one correspondence between sets of equivalent KR-descriptions and sets of isomorphic models, and would thus block the proof of the isomorphy with the previous approaches.

For deciding satisfiability of a KR-description K, a KR-description in *normal form* K_η is constructed using the algorithm sketched below. First, K is closed under the rules which correspond to the schemata (KR5, 6). The resulting prefix-closed KR-description is then expanded by the instances of (KR7–10) until a rule corresponding to (KR1–3) can be applied. After applying the respective rule, the KR-description which then contains TOP is successively reduced to {TOP} by the instances of (KR4).

This construction terminates after a finite number of steps with a set K_η which is equivalent to K. K_η is either equal to {TOP} or a set in *Nerode normal form*, that is, a set which is closed under (KR5–10).

The construction is adequate because it can be shown that a KR-description K is satisfiable iff $K_\eta \neq$ {TOP} holds. Since K is equivalent with K_η and $K_\eta =$ {TOP} implies $\not\models K_\eta$, to prove adequacy it suffices to construct a model by which the satisfiability of a KR-description K_η in Nerode normal form $(K_\eta \neq$ {TOP}$)$ can be shown.

However, let us approach this result in a somewhat less orthodox way, by taking advantage of the results on the relationships between the various reconstructions. First, we change the model space by switching from automata to equivalence classes of isomorphic automata $\mathcal{D}/{\simeq}$. (This transition is unproblematic: since a formula is satisfied by an automaton D iff it is also satisfied by the automata isomorphic to D, we can leave the defining conditions of the satisfiability relation as they were.) Then, using the isomorphism between ψ-terms and classes of isomorphic automata, we can change the model space yet again. The satisfiability relation has now to be defined as follows:

$\langle P, \mu, l\rangle \not\models \text{TOP},$

$\langle P, \mu, l\rangle \models p{:}a \leftrightarrow l([p]_\mu) = a,$

$\langle P, \mu, l\rangle \models [\![\langle p_1\rangle, \ldots, \langle p_n\rangle]\!] \leftrightarrow \exists X \in P/\mu(\{p_1, \ldots, p_n\} \subseteq X).$

That $[D]$ satisfies a formula ϕ iff ϕ is satisfied by $\mathcal{G}_\Psi([D])$ follows immediately from the definition of our isomorphism.

---

[16]Note that the equivalences are formulated by using the conjunction ($\wedge$) of the *meta-language*, which is not part of our rudimentary object language.

Now suppose that $\mathcal{K}$ denotes the set of all KR-descriptions in Nerode normal form plus $\{\text{TOP}\}$. We can now make more precise the intuitively clear relations between ψ-terms and KR-descriptions K_η with the help of the following two functions κ_Ψ and $\Psi_\mathcal{K}$. The transition to the ψ-terms is achieved by the function κ_Ψ

$$\kappa_\Psi(\{\text{TOP}\}) = \perp_\Psi,$$
$$\kappa_\Psi(K_\eta) = \langle P, \mu, l \rangle, \text{ for each consistent set } K_\eta, \text{ with}$$
$$P/\mu = \{C \mid C \in K_\eta\},$$
$$l = \{\langle [p]_\mu, a \rangle \mid p{:}a \in K_\eta\},$$

and the transition from the ψ-terms to the canonical KR-descriptions by the function $\Psi_\mathcal{K}$

$$\Psi_\mathcal{K}(\perp_\Psi) = \{\text{TOP}\},$$
$$\Psi_\mathcal{K}(\langle P, \mu, l \rangle) = P/\mu \cup \{p{:}a \mid l([p]_\mu) = a\},$$

which is, as can be easily verified, the inverse of κ_Ψ.

On the basis of the modified satisfiability relation, it follows by the definition of κ_Ψ that if K_η $(K_\eta \neq \{\text{TOP}\})$ is a KR-description in Nerode normal form, then $\kappa_\Psi(K_\eta)$ is the unique minimal model which satisfies K_η with respect to the extension ordering $\langle \Psi, \sqsubseteq_\Psi \rangle$. According to our original definition of the satisfiability relation each automaton in $\Psi_G(\kappa_\Psi(K_\eta))$ has then to be — up to isomorphism — a unique minimal model for K_η. This completes the proof.

Since we have committed ourselves already with respect to the transition functions, it is also obvious how the extension relation has to be defined in order to prove similarity: a KR-description in normal form K_η is called an *extension* of K'_η $(K'_\eta \sqsubseteq_\mathcal{K} K_\eta)$ iff either $K_\eta = \{\text{TOP}\}$, or

$$\forall C' \in K'_\eta \, \exists C \in K_\eta (C' \subseteq C) \text{ and}$$
$$\forall p{:}a \in K'_\eta (p{:}a \in K_\eta).$$

Then we get a partial order of KR-descriptions in normal form with $\{\text{TOP}\}$ as greatest element which is isomorphic to $\langle \Psi, \sqsubseteq_\Psi \rangle$. Hence, the set of feature structures is given by the set of KR-descriptions in normal form and *unification* is (analogously to the logical reconstruction) the operation which assigns to two KR-descriptions in normal form their least upper bound:

$$K^1_\eta \sqcup_\mathcal{K} K^2_\eta =_{\text{df}} (K^1_\eta \cup K^2_\eta)_\eta.$$

But there are further similarities between feature descriptions and KR-logic which go beyond the order-theoretic isomorphy of their respective reconstructions of the concept of feature structures. The clear relationship between deductively closed sets of equations and KR-descriptions in normal form can be made more precise even at the level of feature descriptions, since it can be shown that our intuitively justified translation functions are in fact correct. In order to show this, we make use of ψ-terms as an *interlingua*, assigning to a feature description E as its meaning the ψ-term $\varepsilon_\Psi(E_\vdash)$ and to a KR-description K the ψ-term $\kappa_\Psi(K_\eta)$. That our translation functions are in fact correct then follows simply from the provability of

$$\varepsilon_\Psi(E_\vdash) = \kappa_\Psi((\Omega(E))_\eta)$$

and

$$\kappa_\Psi(K_\eta) = \varepsilon_\Psi((\mho(K))_\vdash).$$

From their intertranslatability it follows immediately that both approaches are notational variants. Indeed, they are even variants which use the same procedure for testing satisfiability, namely an unrestricted (deductive) closure construction.

7 Term and Graph Unification

Feature structures can be represented as (special) expressions of a first-order language. This kind of representation, which seems to be possible only on the basis of the restrictions (C0–3), allows us to use first-order unification as the combining operation. Thus, the whole unification problem of feature structures can be tackled using resolution in a first-order calculus without equality.

The simplest (and most commonly used) method of representing feature structures as first-order terms assumes a distinct function symbol f whose arity is identical to the number of attributes and whose argument positions are typed in a biunique way with the attributes. (We will modify these representations a little bit later on in order to ensure the isomorphy of the approaches.) A term representation of a structure $[D]$ can then be constructed by induction on the complexity of the values, that is, bottom-up. First, the atomic-valued terminal nodes ($q \in V$) are represented by the atomic values (constants) themselves and all other terminal nodes are represented by distinct variables. Then the non-terminal nodes are represented successively bottom-up by $|A|$-place terms of the form $f(\tau_1, \ldots, \tau_{|A|})$ which contain in each (typed) argument position either the representation of the corresponding attribute value (if it exists) or a new variable if the attribute has no value for the given non-terminal node.

If $|A| = n$, we need (in addition to the n-place function f and a denumerable set of variables $\mathcal{V}$ (with $Q\backslash V \subseteq \mathcal{V}$)) a function I which types biuniquely the argument positions of f with attributes:[17]

$$I \in [\{1, \ldots, n\} \mapsto A]_b.$$

The successive bottom-up translation of a representative of a graph $[D]$ is then achieved by the following inductive construction.

---

[17] A set of bijective functions is b-indexed in the following.

Suppose that m is the length of the longest path of D, that is,

$$m = max\{|p| \mid p \in P(D)\}.$$

We then order the nodes according to the complexity of the substructures which they dominate; that is, we define for each $i = 0, \ldots, m$ a complexity class Q_i consisting of those nodes which dominate substructures whose maximal number of embeddings (that is, whose longest path) is less or equal to i:

$$Q_i = \{q \in Q \mid max\{|p| \mid \delta^*(q,p) \notin Proj_1(Dom(\delta))\} \le i\}.$$

For the term construction we define by induction on $i = 0, \ldots, m$ a function $\hbar_i^D$ from Q_i to first-order terms. For the terminal nodes Q_0 we set

$$\hbar_0^D(q) = q.$$

In this case q is either a constant or it is $q \notin V$ and q is regarded as a variable. If $\hbar_i^D$ is defined, we first define $\hbar_{i+1}^D$ for each $q \in Q_i \, (= Dom(\hbar_i^D))$ as $\hbar_i^D$:

$$\hbar_{i+1}^D(q) = \hbar_i^D(q), \text{ for each } q \in Q_i.$$

For each $q \in Q_{i+1} \backslash Q_i$ we then set

$$\hbar_{i+1}^D(q) = f(\tau_1, \ldots, \tau_n), \text{ with } \tau_j = \begin{cases} \hbar_i^D(\delta(q, I_j)) & \text{if } \langle q, I_j \rangle \in Dom(\delta) \\ q_j \in V & \text{otherwise,} \end{cases}$$

for each $j = 1, \ldots, n$.

With the unary predicate FS and the term representation of the root ($\hbar_m^D(q_0)$) as the argument we then construct by $FS(\hbar_m^D(q_0))$ an ordinary formula of first-order predicate calculus without equality.

Example 7.1 If $I = \{\langle 1, \text{PRED} \rangle, \langle 2, \text{TENSE} \rangle, \langle 3, \text{XCOMP} \rangle, \langle 4, \text{SUBJ} \rangle\}$, then the automaton of Example 3.1 is represented by the following formula:[18]

$$FS(f(\text{PROMISE},$$
$$\text{PAST},$$
$$f(\text{COME}, x_2, x_3, f(\text{JOHN}, y_2, y_3, y_4)),$$
$$f(\text{JOHN}, y_2, y_3, y_4))).$$

Although it still remains to make this construction invariant against biunique renaming of the variables, it will become obvious that our present (and, as we will see later, actually useful) reconstruction is *not* adequate if we want to ensure its isomorphy with the other approaches we have discussed. On the basis of $\hbar$ it is not possible to define an isomorphism, since we lose information on

(i) path congruences, and on

(ii) non-atomic-valued terminal nodes.

To see (i), consider the graphs induced by the automata given in Figure 5.

---

[18] In order to avoid double indices, we sometimes rename the variables biuniquely.

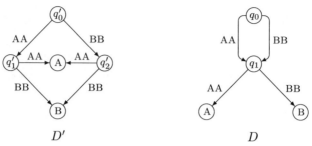

FIGURE 5 The distinction between *type* (D') and
token identity (D) of values in graphs.

Here $\hbar$ would yield for $A = \{\text{AA}, \text{BB}\}$ and $I_1 = \text{AA}, I_2 = \text{BB}$ in both cases $f(f(\text{A}, \text{B}), f(\text{A}, \text{B}))$. That is, the term representation via $\hbar$ does not preserve the type/token distinction.

Information on token identities of non-terminal nodes (we treat token identities of terminal nodes shortly) can be easily encoded by assigning to each non-terminal node an $n+1$-place term $f(\tau_1, \ldots, \tau_{n+1})$ (instead of an n-place term) which contains in the $n+1st$ argument position a variable which stands for the node. We then inductively define (analogously to $\hbar_i^D$) for each graph $[D]$ a function k_i^D:

$$k_{i+1}^D(q) = f(\tau_1, \ldots, \tau_n, q).$$

If we used for k the same induction base as for $\hbar$, k would yield for the graphs in Figure 5

$$f(f(\text{A}, \text{B}, q_1'), f(\text{A}, \text{B}, q_2'), q_0') \text{ and } f(f(\text{A}, \text{B}, q_1), f(\text{A}, \text{B}, q_1), q_0)$$

and the token identity would remain identifiable.

That we can lose information also on terminal nodes that are not atomic-valued is illustrated by the following automata D and D'

which are regarded as representatives of different graphs. However, if we used for k the induction base of $\hbar$, k would give us terms

$$f(\text{A}, x, q_0') \text{ and } f(\text{A}, q_1, q_0)$$

identical up to biunique renaming of the variables.

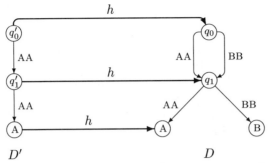

FIGURE 6 Homomorphic extension between automata having
only atomic-valued terminal nodes.

The simplest way to preserve this information is achieved by constructing, for each non-atomic-valued terminal node q, a complex term of the
form $f(q_1, \ldots, q_n, q)$ with $q_i, q \in \mathcal{V}$. But this possibility has consequences
for the representation of the atomic-valued terminal nodes, at least if we
want to define the extension relation between term representations on the
basis of the classical *subsumption* relation between terms. In order to as-
sess these consequences, let us assume for the moment that the domain
consists of graphs with only atomic-valued terminal nodes and that k is
defined as above. These assumptions ensure that the terms assigned to
the elements of $[D]$ are identical up to renaming of the variables and that
the term thus associated with each class is biunique. These properties of
k already provide a good basis for the definition of isomorphic orders. In
order to get the right extension relation between the term representations
(for this domain) we have to next figure out how the term translations are
related if one automaton is — as in Figure 6 — a homomorphic extension
of the other. If we abbreviate in the following $k_{m'}^{D'}$ and k_m^D by $k^{D'}$ and k^D,
respectively, then the term translations of D' and D in Figure 6 are given
by

$$k^{D'}(q_0') = f(f(\textsc{a}, x, q_1'), y, q_0') \text{ and } k^D(q_0) = f(f(\textsc{a}, \textsc{b}, q_1), f(\textsc{a}, \textsc{b}, q_1), q_0).$$

A partial mapping θ from the variables to first-order terms $(\mathcal{T})$ is called
a *substitution* and $\phi[\theta]$ is used to designate the expression obtained from ϕ
by replacing *all* variables x_i in ϕ *simultaneously* by $\theta(x_i)$. For a homomorphic extension $D' \preceq D$ as in Figure 6, it is then easy to see by induction on
the complexity classes Q_i' $(i = 0, \ldots, m')$ that we can find a substitution θ
which makes $k^{D'}(q_0')$ identical to $k^D(q_0)$ (that is, we can show: if $D' \preceq D$
then $\exists \theta(k^{D'}(q_0')[\theta] = k^D(q_0)))$. According to the standard terminology, we
have in this case the classical subsumption relation between $k^{D'}(q_0')$ and
$k^D(q_0)$ ($k^{D'}(q_0')$ subsumes $k^D(q_0)$). This relation is defined for arbitrary ex-

pressions as follows. An expression ϕ' *subsumes* an expression ϕ iff there is a substitution θ for which $\phi'[\theta] = \phi$ holds.

In order to illustrate how we can verify our claim, let h be the homomorphism from D' to D of Figure 6. We can then define a substitution θ such that $k^{D'}(q')[\theta] = k^D(h(q'))$ for each $q' \in Q'_i$ by induction on $i = 0, \ldots, m'$. For the atomic value $\text{A} \in Q'_0$ we need the empty subset of θ, since $h(\text{A}) = \text{A}$ and $k^{D'}(\text{A}) = k^D(\text{A}) = \text{A}$. For the inductive step, consider $q'_1 \in Q'_1$ and the term translations $k^{D'}(q'_1) = f(\text{A}, x, q'_1)$, $k^D(h(q'_1)) = f(\text{A}, \text{B}, q_1)$. If θ assigns to each jth variable argument τ'_j of $k^{D'}(q'_1)$ the jth argument τ_j of $k^D(h(q'_1))$ we get $\{\langle x, \text{B}\rangle, \langle q'_1, q_1\rangle\} \subseteq \theta.$[19] We then have:

$$k^{D'}(q'_1)[\theta] = f(\text{A}, x, q'_1)[\theta] = f(\text{A}[\theta], x[\theta], q'_1[\theta]) = f(\text{A}, \text{B}, q_1) = k^D(h(q'_1)).$$

(For the variable arguments of $k^{D'}(q'_1)$ this follows by the definition of θ. For the other arguments this follows because $h(\delta'(q'_1, \text{AA})) = \delta(h(q'_1), \text{AA})$ by the inductive hypothesis.) So, we get the right substitution by setting for each $q' \in Q'$ with $k^{D'}(q') = f(\tau'_1, \ldots, \tau'_{n+1})$ and $k^D(h(q')) = f(\tau_1, \ldots, \tau_{n+1})$

$$\theta(\tau'_j) = \tau_j,$$

for every $\tau'_j \in \mathcal{V}$. The complete substitution for our example is then given by

$$\theta = \{\langle x, \text{B}\rangle, \langle q'_1, q_1\rangle, \langle y, f(\text{A}, \text{B}, q_1)\rangle, \langle q'_0, q_0\rangle\}.$$

Now suppose — for the other direction — that we have a subsumption relation $k^{D'}(q'_0)[\theta] = k^D(q_0)$. We can then show $D' \preceq D$, since we get a homomorphism by the function h which is defined for each constant and each complex subterm τ' of $k^{D'}(q'_0)$ by $h(k^{D'-1}(\tau')) = k^{D-1}(\tau'[\theta])$. We can show for h first that $h(\delta'^*(q'_0, p)) = \delta^*(q_0, p)$, by induction on the length of p. In our example this is trivial for $|p| = 0$. It follows for AA.AA, since we get $\delta'^*(q'_0, \text{AA}) = k^{D'-1}(f(\text{A}, x, q'_1))$ and

$$h(\delta'^*(q'_0, \text{AA})) = h(k^{D'-1}(f(\text{A}, x, q'_1))) = k^{D-1}(f(\text{A}, x, q'_1)[\theta]) = \delta^*(q_0, \text{AA})$$

by inductive hypothesis. Because of $f(\text{A}, x, q'_1)[\theta] = f(\text{A}[\theta], x[\theta], q'_1[\theta])$ we get

$$\begin{aligned}
h(k^{D'-1}(\text{A})) &= h(\delta'(k^{D'-1}(f(\text{A}, x, q'_1)), \text{AA})) \\
&= \delta(k^{D-1}(f(\text{A}, x, q'_1)[\theta]), \text{AA}) = k^{D-1}(\text{A}[\theta])
\end{aligned}$$

by the definition of k and h and then

$$h(\delta'(\delta'^*(q'_0, \text{AA}), \text{AA})) = \delta(\delta^*(q_0, \text{AA}), \text{AA}).$$

This step also illustrates that $h(\text{A}) = \text{A}$ follows for the constants due to $\text{A} = \text{A}[\theta]$.

---

[19]The function property results, of course, from the fact that for all q'_i, q'_j with $q'_i \neq q'_j$ the variable arguments in $k^{D'}(q'_i)$ and $k^{D'}(q'_j)$ are pairwise distinct according to our construction.

After this excursion on subsumption we can solve our original problem quite easily. Let us consider two automata D' and D with $D' \preceq D$, and a non-atomic terminal node q' of D' which is (according to our last suggestion) now represented by the complex term $f(q'_1, \ldots, q'_n, q')$. If $h(q')$ is a non-atomic terminal node or a non-terminal node, we get our θ without problems by the construction given above. But if $h(q') = a$ is an atomic terminal node, the construction fails, since the term representation of q' is complex, whereas the one of $h(q')$ is atomic. We can easily repair this failure, if we *raise* the representation of $h(q')$ as well. So, if we construct by k for atomic nodes a complex $n + 1$-place terms $f(a, \ldots, a)$, we obtain according to our construction again a θ for which $k^D(q')[\theta] = k^D(h(q'))$ holds.

To sum up: for an adequate transition we have to define for each automaton D by induction on $i = 0, \ldots, m = max\{|p| \mid p \in P(D)\}$ a function k_i^D from Q_i in $\mathcal{T}$ as follows. For the terminal nodes we set

$$k_0^D(q) = \begin{cases} f(q_1, \ldots, q_n, q) & \text{if } q \notin V \\ f(q, \ldots, q, q) & \text{if } q \in V, \end{cases}$$

and in the induction step

$$k_{i+1}^D(q) = \begin{cases} k_i^D(q) & \text{if } q \in Q_i; \text{ otherwise} \\ f(\tau_1, \ldots, \tau_n, q), \text{ with } \tau_j = \begin{cases} k_i^D(\delta(q, I_j)) & \text{if } \langle q, I_j \rangle \in Dom(\delta) \\ q_j \in V & \text{otherwise,} \end{cases} \end{cases}$$

for every $j = 1, \ldots, n$. By $FS(k_m^D(q_0))$ we get again a formula of first-order predicate logic without equality.

Example 7.2 If we assume the typing I of Example 7.1 and abbreviate PROMISE by PR, PAST by PA, COME by C and JOHN by J, then the following formulas correspond to the feature structures given in Figure 2:

$$\begin{aligned} FS(f(&f(\text{PR}, \text{PR}, \text{PR}, \text{PR}, \text{PR}), \\ &f(\text{PA}, \text{PA}, \text{PA}, \text{PA}, \text{PA}), \\ &f(f(\text{C}, \text{C}, \text{C}, \text{C}, \text{C}), x_2, x_3, f(y_1, y_2, y_3, y_4, y), x), \\ &f(y_1, y_2, y_3, y_4, y), \\ &z)), \\ FS(f(&u_1, u_2, u_3, f(f(\text{J}, \text{J}, \text{J}, \text{J}, \text{J}), v_2, v_3, v_4, v), u)). \end{aligned}$$

Since term representations of isomorphic automata are identical up to biunique renaming of the variables, we map feature structures $[D]$ (classes of isomorphic automata) onto classes of representations which are identical in exactly this sense. Let $\perp_\Theta$ be an additional distinct element which will again be determined as the greatest element and

$$[\phi]_{\rightleftarrows} = \{\psi \mid \exists \theta \in [V \mapsto V]_b (\psi = \phi[\theta])\},$$

then the adequate transition is achieved by the function g_Θ defined by

$$g_\Theta(\bot_\mathcal{G}) = \bot_\Theta, \text{ and } g_\Theta([D]) = [FS(k_m^D(q_0))].$$

Within our new domain $\Theta = Ran(g_\Theta)$ a class $g_\Theta(G)$ is an *extension* of $g_\Theta(G')$ $(g_\Theta(G') \sqsubseteq_\Theta g_\Theta(G); G, G' \in \mathcal{G})$ iff either $g_\Theta(G) = \bot_\Theta$ or $G' = [D']$, $G = [D]$ and

$$\exists \theta \in [\mathcal{V} \mapsto \mathcal{T}](FS(k^{D'}(q_0'))[\theta] = FS(k^D(q_0))).$$

We then get with $\langle \Theta, \sqsubseteq_\Theta \rangle$ a partial order with greatest element which is isomorphic to $\langle \mathcal{G}, \sqsubseteq_\mathcal{G} \rangle$ due to the bijectivity of g_Θ. This fact, which we have tried to illustrate by examples, is shown in more detail in Appendix B.

In principle we could stop this excursion now, since we already know on the basis of the isomorphy that $\langle \Theta, \sqsubseteq_\Theta \rangle$ constitutes a semilattice. But the computation of LUB's would then only be possible by resort to the other approaches, and the relationship between graph and term unification would not be fully clear. So, let us conclude by sketching the procedure for computing LUB's which is typical of this approach. This will fully clarify the correlations.

In general a set $S = \{\phi_1, \phi_2\}$ of two (quantifier-free) expressions of first-order predicate logic without equality is called *unifiable* iff there is a substitution θ with $\phi_1[\theta] = \phi_2[\theta]$. That is, the set $\{\phi_1[\theta], \phi_2[\theta]\}$, which is henceforth written as $S[\theta]$, is a singleton set. Let us assume for the rest of the paper that we choose from two first-order translations $[\phi_1]$ and $[\phi_2]$ a set of representatives $\{\phi_1, \phi_2\}$ such that ϕ_1 and ϕ_2 have no variables in common. It is then easy to verify that two reconstructions $[\phi_1]$ and $[\phi_2]$ have an upper bound $[\phi]$ (not equal to $\bot_\Theta$) iff there is a unifier θ of $\{\phi_1, \phi_2\}$ and $\phi = \phi_1[\theta]$. For the right-to-left direction we get this, since $[\phi_1], [\phi_2] \sqsubseteq_\Theta [\phi_1[\theta]]$ holds for a unifier on the basis of the definition of the extension relation. For the other direction our assumption on the disjointness of the variables is crucial, since it allows us to get a unifier from $\phi_1[\theta_1] = \phi$ and $\phi_2[\theta_2] = \phi$ by $\theta_1 \cup \theta_2$. (Otherwise we would not be able to get, for example, a unifier for the formulas $FS(f(u_1, u_2, u_3, u_4, u))$ and $FS(f(f(u_1, u_2, u_3, u_4, u), v_2, v_3, v_4, v))$, although the corresponding equivalence classes have common upper bounds not equal to $\bot_\Theta$.)

That there is always a least upper bound follows from the fact (see below) that if S is unifiable there always is a *most general unifier* (*mgu*) of S. Let the *composition* of two substitutions θ and θ' be given by

$$\theta\theta' = \{\langle x, \tau \rangle \mid x \in Dom(\theta \cup \theta') \wedge \tau = (x[\theta])[\theta']\}.$$

A unifier θ_S is called the *most general unifier* of S, if for all unifiers θ of S there is a substitution ϑ with $\theta = \theta_S \vartheta$. If there are for two reconstructions $[\phi_1]$ and $[\phi_2]$ upper bounds not equal to $\bot_\Theta$, the *mgu* θ_S of $S = \{\phi_1, \phi_2\}$ gives us with $[\phi_1[\theta_S]]$ a unique least upper bound (up to biunique renaming of the variables), since by definition there is for each unifier θ of S a substitution ϑ with $(\phi_1[\theta_S])[\vartheta] = \phi_1[\theta]$ and thus it follows that

$$[\phi_1], [\phi_2] \sqsubseteq_\Theta [\phi_1[\theta_S]] \sqsubseteq_\Theta [\phi_1[\theta]].$$

To define an algorithm which tests whether a set S of two atomic formulas is unifiable, and which returns an *mgu* of S if S is in fact unifiable, we make use of a partial function *diff*$_1$ assigning to two atomic formulas a substitution which unifies the leftmost disagreeing argument position in the two expressions (if this is possible). If S is a set of atomic formulas $(1 \leq |S| \leq 2)$ and p, w and w' are strings, then

$$diff_1(S) = \begin{cases} \{\langle v, \tau \rangle\} & \text{if } S = \{pvw, p\tau w'\}, v \in \mathcal{V}, \tau \in \mathcal{T} \\ & \text{and } v \text{ is not subterm of } \tau \\ \text{undefined} & \text{otherwise.} \end{cases}$$

This substitution must evidently exist if the set S is unifiable.

The unification algorithm consists of a successive adjustment of the disagreeing argument positions. Since each *diff*$_1$-value $\{\langle v, \tau \rangle\}$ is *mgu* of $\{v, \tau\}$, one only needs to compose successively the *diff*$_1$-values in parallel to obtain an *mgu* of S (if S is unifiable). So, we construct for a set of two atomic formulas S a sequence of pairs $\langle S_i, \theta_i \rangle$ $(i \geq 0)$ by induction

$$\langle S_0, \theta_0 \rangle = \langle S, \emptyset \rangle,$$

$$\langle S_{i+1}, \theta_{i+1} \rangle = \begin{cases} \langle S_i[diff_1(S_i)], \theta_i \, diff_1(S_i) \rangle & \text{if } diff_1(S_i) \text{ is defined} \\ \langle S_i, \theta_i \rangle & \text{otherwise,} \end{cases}$$

for which $S_i = S[\theta_i]$ holds according to the construction of θ_i.

Since in each step with $S_i \neq S_{i+1}$ at least one variable is eliminated from the expressions, the construction must terminate after a finite number of steps with a pair $\langle S_j, \theta_j \rangle$ with $j = min\{i \mid \langle S_i, \theta_i \rangle = \langle S_{i+1}, \theta_{i+1} \rangle\}$ (the maximum is, of course, the number of distinct variables occurring in S).

Example 7.3 For the set consisting of the two expressions given in Example 7.2 the construction terminates after 9 steps, for example, with the *mgu*

$$\left\{ \begin{array}{l} \langle u_1, f(\text{PR}, \text{PR}, \text{PR}, \text{PR}, \text{PR}) \rangle, \\ \langle u_2, f(\text{PA}, \text{PA}, \text{PA}, \text{PA}, \text{PA}) \rangle, \\ \langle u_3, f(f(\text{C}, \text{C}, \text{C}, \text{C}, \text{C}), x_2, x_3, f(f(\text{J}, \text{J}, \text{J}, \text{J}, \text{J}), v_2, v_3, v_4, v), x) \rangle, \\ \langle y_1, f(\text{J}, \text{J}, \text{J}, \text{J}, \text{J}) \rangle, \\ \langle y_2, v_2 \rangle, \\ \langle y_3, v_3 \rangle, \\ \langle y_4, v_4 \rangle, \\ \langle y, v \rangle, \\ \langle z, u \rangle \end{array} \right\}$$

that applied to both expressions yields

$$FS(f(f(\text{PR}, \text{PR}, \text{PR}, \text{PR}, \text{PR}),$$
$$f(\text{PA}, \text{PA}, \text{PA}, \text{PA}, \text{PA}),$$
$$f(f(\text{C}, \text{C}, \text{C}, \text{C}, \text{C}), x_2, x_3, f(f(\text{J}, \text{J}, \text{J}, \text{J}, \text{J}), v_2, v_3, v_4, v), x),$$
$$f(f(\text{J}, \text{J}, \text{J}, \text{J}, \text{J}), v_2, v_3, v_4, v),$$
$$u)),$$

a representative of the class representing the feature structure of Figure 1.

The correctness of the algorithm can be established with help of the following *unification theorem* (see, for example, Robinson 1965, 1979 and Loveland 1978).

Theorem 7.4 (Unification Theorem (Robinson)) *If S is a set of two atomic formulas and $j = min\{i \mid \langle S_i, \theta_i \rangle = \langle S_{i+1}, \theta_{i+1} \rangle\}$ then*

(i) S is unifiable iff S_j is a singleton; moreover

(ii) $\theta_S = \theta_j$ is an mgu of S, if $|S_j| = 1$.

Now that we have our algorithm, we define the unification of feature structures by *mgu*'s as follows

$$\mathcal{G}_\Theta(G) \sqcup_\Theta \mathcal{G}_\Theta(G') = \begin{cases} [FS(k^D(q_0))[\theta_S]] & \text{if } G = [D], G' = [D'], \\ & S = \{FS(k^D(q_0)), FS(k^D(q'_0))\} \\ & \text{and } S \text{ is unifiable} \\ \bot_\Theta & \text{otherwise,} \end{cases}$$

and — as already sketched above — we get

$$\text{LUB}(\mathcal{G}_\Theta(G), \mathcal{G}_\Theta(G')) = \mathcal{G}_\Theta(G) \sqcup_\Theta \mathcal{G}_\Theta(G').$$

8 Conclusion

In this paper, we tried to survey the most prominent formal modelings of the notion of unification in grammar. We restricted our overview to the basic lattice-theoretic notion of unification which allowed us to give equivalent treatments of the different modelings fairly straightforwardly. The elementary relations between the various approaches should now be clear. A metatheoretical comparison of the more expressive unification-based grammar formalisms is a natural subject for further investigations.

Acknowledgments

I would like to thank Tim Fernando, Josef van Genabith, Hans Kamp, Ron Kaplan, Paul King, Steve Pulman, Ede Zimmermann, an anonymous reviewer and especially Patrick Blackburn for their comments on earlier versions of this paper. All remaining errors are, of course, my own.

Appendix

A Deterministic Finite Automata

A *deterministic finite automaton* (or *DFA*) D is a quintuple $\langle Q, \Sigma, \delta, q_0, F \rangle$, consisting of a finite nonempty set of states (Q), a finite, possibly empty vocabulary (Σ), a transition function $(\delta \in [(Q \times \Sigma) \mapsto Q])$ (here $[X \mapsto Y]$ denotes the set of all partial functions from X to Y), a distinct initial state $(q_0 \in Q)$ and a distinct subset of final states $(F \subseteq Q)$.

The extension of δ to sequences over Σ is a partial transition function δ^* $(\delta^* \in [(Q \times \Sigma^*) \mapsto Q])$ which is defined for all states q, the empty string λ and all strings pa $(p \in \Sigma^*, a \in \Sigma)$ by:

$\delta^*(q, \lambda) = q$, and

$$\delta^*(q, pa) = \begin{cases} \delta(\delta^*(q, p), a) & \text{if } \delta^*(q, p) = q' \text{ and } \delta \text{ is defined for } \langle q', a \rangle \\ \text{undefined} & \text{otherwise.} \end{cases}$$

A *DFA accepts* a string p, if $\delta^*(q_0, p) \in F$. The *language* accepted by a *DFA* D (abbreviation: $L(D)$) is the set of all strings accepted by D, that is:

$$L(D) = \{p \in \Sigma^* \mid \delta^*(q_0, p) \in F\}.$$

The set of *paths* of a *DFA* D (abbreviation: $P(D)$) is the set of all strings for which δ^* leads from the initial state to some other state:

$$P(D) = \{p \in \Sigma^* \mid \delta^*(q_0, p) \text{ is defined}\}.$$

In general a subset L of Σ^* is called *prefix-closed* if it contains for each element p also every prefix u of p $(uw = p; u, w \in \Sigma^*)$. It is clear that the path set of a *DFA* is prefix-closed. Note that if a *DFA* contains a loop which is reachable from the initial state, then its path set is infinite. If there is no such loop, the path set is finite.

The relation which holds for two paths p, p' of a *DFA* iff they lead to the same state $(p\mathcal{N}_D p')$, is called the *Nerode relation*:

$$p\mathcal{N}_D p' \leftrightarrow \delta^*(q_0, p) = \delta^*(q_0, p').$$

It follows immediately from the definition that the Nerode relation is an equivalence relation on the path set. Furthermore, the Nerode relation is *right invariant* with respect to concatenation. An equivalence relation R over a set of strings L is commonly called right invariant (with respect to concatenation), if $pwRp'w$ follows from pRp' and $pw \in L$. That is, R is *right invariant* on L iff

$$\forall p, p', w \in \Sigma^* (p, p', pw \in L \wedge pRp' \to pwRp'w).$$

B   The Similarity of $\langle \mathcal{G}, \sqsubseteq_{\mathcal{G}} \rangle$ and $\langle \Theta, \sqsubseteq_{\Theta} \rangle$

Since $\mathcal{G}_{\Theta}$ is bijective, to prove that $\langle \mathcal{G}, \sqsubseteq_{\mathcal{G}} \rangle$ and $\langle \Theta, \sqsubseteq_{\Theta} \rangle$ are isomorphic we must first show that if $G' \sqsubseteq_{\mathcal{G}} G$ then $\mathcal{G}_{\Theta}(G') \sqsubseteq_{\Theta} \mathcal{G}_{\Theta}(G)$.

For the case $G = \perp_{\mathcal{G}}$ this holds by definition of $\mathcal{G}_\Theta$ and $\sqsubseteq_\Theta$. If $G = [D]$ and $G' = [D']$, D has to be a homomorphic extension of D' according to the definition of $\sqsubseteq_{\mathcal{G}}$. Let h be this homomorphism and let θ be the substitution which is given by[20]

$$\left\{ \langle \tau'_j, \tau_j \rangle \mid \exists q' \in Q' \left(\begin{array}{l} k^{D'}(q') = f(\ldots, \tau'_j, \ldots) \wedge \\ k^D(h(q')) = f(\ldots, \tau_j, \ldots) \wedge \tau'_j \in \mathcal{V}. \end{array} \right) \right\}.$$

Then for θ we have that

$$FS(k^{D'}(q'_0))[\theta] = FS(k^D(q_0)),$$

since we can show by induction on $i = 0, \ldots, m'$ ($= max\{|p| \mid p \in P(D')\}$) for each $q' \in Q'_i$

$$k^{D'}(q')[\theta] = k^D(h(q')).$$

The base step ($q' \in Q'_0$) follows for $q' \in V$ because $q' = h(q')$, and for $q' \notin V$ immediately by definition of k and θ. For the inductive step let q' be in $Q_{i+1} \backslash Q_i$, $k^{D'}(q') = f(\tau'_1, \ldots, \tau'_{n+1})$ and $k^D(h(q')) = f(\tau_1, \ldots, \tau_{n+1})$. For each j with $\langle q', I_j \rangle$ in $Dom(\delta')$ we get because of $h(\delta'(q', I_j)) = \delta(h(q'), I_j)$

$$k^{D'}(\delta'(q', I_j))[\theta] = k^D(h(\delta'(q', I_j)))$$

by inductive hypothesis and for each j with $\langle q', I_j \rangle \notin Dom(\delta')$: $\tau'_j \in \mathcal{V}$ and $\langle \tau'_j, \tau_j \rangle \in \theta$. Hence we have

$$f(\tau'_1[\theta], \ldots, \tau'_{n+1}[\theta]) = f(\tau'_1, \ldots, \tau'_{n+1})[\theta] = f(\tau_1, \ldots, \tau_{n+1})$$

and thus

$$k^{D'}(q'_0)[\theta] = k^D(h(q'_0)) = k^D(q_0)$$

which completes the proof of $\mathcal{G}_\Theta([D']) \sqsubseteq_\Theta \mathcal{G}_\Theta([D])$.

Second, we must show that $\mathcal{G}_\Theta(G') \sqsubseteq_\Theta \mathcal{G}_\Theta(G)$ implies $G' \sqsubseteq_{\mathcal{G}} G$. This follows for $G = \perp_{\mathcal{G}}$ by the definition of $\sqsubseteq_{\mathcal{G}}$. If $G = [D]$ and $G' = [D']$, by definition of $\sqsubseteq_\Theta$ there is a substitution θ with

$$FS(k^{D'}(q'_0))[\theta] = FS(k^D(q_0)).$$

If we define a function h for each complex subterm $f(\tau'_1, \ldots, \tau'_{n+1})$ of $k^{D'}(q'_0)$ by

$$h(k^{D'-1}(f(\tau'_1, \ldots, \tau'_{n+1}))) = k^{D-1}(f(\tau'_1, \ldots, \tau'_{n+1})[\theta]),$$

then we obtain a homomorphism from D' to D.[21] Suppose for the proof $\mathcal{G}_\Theta([D']) = [FS(\tau')]$ and $\mathcal{G}_\Theta([D]) = [FS(\tau)]$. On the basis of $q'_0 = k^{D'-1}(\tau')$ and

$$h(q'_0) = h(k^{D'-1}(\tau')) = k^{D-1}(\tau'[\theta]) = k^{D-1}(\tau) = q_0 \text{ (induction base)}$$

---

[20]The function property of θ follows immediately from the function property of h and the fact that distinct nodes are represented by terms whose variable arguments are pairwise distinct.

[21]The function property of h follows immediately, since the substitution result $\tau[\theta]$ is unique for each term τ.

we can show $h(\delta'^*(q_0',p)) = \delta^*(q_0,p)$ for each $p \in P(D')$ by induction on $|p|$. Thus, suppose by inductive hypothesis $\delta'^*(q_0',p) = k^{D'-1}(f(\tau_1',\ldots,\tau_{n+1}'))$,

$$
\begin{aligned}
h(\delta'^*(q_0',p)) &= h(k^{D'-1}(f(\tau_1',\ldots,\tau_{n+1}'))) \\
&= k^{D-1}(f(\tau_1',\ldots,\tau_{n+1}')[\theta]) \\
&= \delta^*(q_0,p)
\end{aligned}
$$

and that $\delta'(\delta'^*(q_0',p),I_j)$ is defined. Then τ_j' has to be complex and due to $f(\tau_1',\ldots,\tau_{n+1}')[\theta] = f(\tau_1'[\theta],\ldots,\tau_{n+1}'[\theta])$ it must be the case that

$$
h(\delta'^*(q_0',p.I_j)) = k^{D-1}(\tau_j'[\theta]) = \delta(k^{D-1}(f(\tau_1',\ldots,\tau_{n+1}')[\theta]),I_j)
$$

by definition of h and k, and hence also

$$
h(\delta'^*(q_0',p.I_j)) = \delta(\delta^*(q_0,p),I_j) = \delta^*(q_0,p.I_j).
$$

Since $h(a) = a$ follows for each $a \in V$ immediately from the definition of h and k, D is a homomorphic extension of D' and thus $[D'] \sqsubseteq_{\mathcal{G}} [D]$.

One final remark. On the basis of the excursion on first-order unification and on the isomorphy of the orders it is now easier to see why our original construction is in fact useful. On the one hand, it is now easy to verify by induction on the construction of an *mgu* of $\{FS(\hbar^D(q_0)),FS(\hbar^{D'}(q_0'))\}$ that $\{FS(k^D(q_0)),FS(k^{D'}(q_0'))\}$ is unifiable, if $\{FS(\hbar^D(q_0)),FS(\hbar^{D'}(q_0'))\}$ is. Since we can also show that there must be at least a homomorphism from $\langle\mathcal{G},\sqsubseteq_{\mathcal{G}}\rangle$ in the order induced by our original construction, we get $\mathrm{LUB}([FS(\hbar^D(q_0))],[FS(\hbar^{D'}(q_0'))]) \neq \bot_\Theta$ iff $\mathrm{LUB}([FS(k^D(q_0))],[FS(k^{D'}(q_0'))]) \neq \bot_\Theta$. In short, the original construction can be used for testing unifiability of feature structures.

References

Aït-Kaci, Hassan. 1984. *A Lattice Theoretic Approach to Computation Based on a Calculus of Partially Ordered Type Structures*. Doctoral dissertation, University of Pennsylvania.

Gazdar, Gerald, Ewan Klein, Geoffrey Pullum, and Ivan Sag. 1985. *Generalized Phrase Structure Grammar*. Oxford: Basil Blackwell.

Kaplan, Ronald M., and Joan Bresnan. 1982. Lexical-Functional Grammar: A Formal System for Grammatical Representation. In *The Mental Representation of Grammatical Relations*, ed. Joan Bresnan. 173–281. Cambridge, MA: The MIT Press.

Kasper, Robert T., and William C. Rounds. 1990. The Logic of Unification in Grammar. *Linguistics and Philosophy* 13:35–58.

Kay, Martin. 1979. Functional Grammar. In *Proceedings of the 5th Annual Meeting of the Berkeley Linguistics Society*, 142–158. Berkeley. University of California.

Loveland, Donald W. 1978. *Automated Theorem Proving: A Logical Basis*. Amsterdam: North-Holland.

Pereira, Fernando C. N., and Stuart M. Shieber. 1984. The Semantics of Grammar Formalisms Seen as Computer Languages. In *Proceedings of the 10th International Conference on Computational Linguistics*, 123–129. Stanford University.

Pollard, Carl, and Ivan Sag. 1987. *Information-Based Syntax and Semantics.* CSLI Lecture Notes Number 13. Stanford: CSLI Publications.

Robinson, John Alan. 1965. A Machine-Oriented Logic Based on the Resolution Principle. *J. ACM* 12:23–41.

Robinson, John Alan. 1979. *Logic: Form and Function.* Edinburgh: Edinburgh University Press.

Shieber, Stuart M. 1988. Separating Linguistic Analyses from Linguistic Theories. In *Natural Language Parsing and Linguistic Theories*, ed. Uwe Reyle and Christian Rohrer. 33–68. Dordrecht: Reidel.

Shieber, Stuart M., Hans Uszkoreit, Fernando C. N. Pereira, Jane Robinson, and Mabry Tyson. 1983. The Formalism and Implementation of PATR-II. In *Research on Interactive Acquisition and Use of Knowledge. SRI Final Report 1894*, ed. Barbara J. Grosz and Mark E. Stickel. 39–79. SRI International, Menlo Park.

Shoenfield, Joseph R. 1967. *Mathematical Logic.* Menlo Park: Addison-Wesley.

Smolka, Gert. 1989. Feature Constraint Logics for Unification Grammars. IWBS Report 93. IBM Deutschland, Stuttgart.

Uszkoreit, Hans. 1986. Categorial Unification Grammars. In *Proceedings of the 11th International Conference on Computational Linguistics*, 187–194. University of Bonn.

Wedekind, Jürgen. 1994. Some Remarks on the Logic of Unification Grammars. In *Constraint Propagation, Linguistic Description, and Computation*, ed. Mike Rosner, Christopher J. Rupp, and Roderick L. Johnson. 29–76. London: Academic Press.

Zeevat, Henk, Ewan Klein, and Jo Calder. 1987. An Introduction to Unification Categorial Grammar. In *Edinburgh Working Papers in Cognitive Science, Volume 1*, ed. Nicholas Haddock, Ewan Klein, and Glyn Morrill. 195–222. University of Edinburgh.

Name Index

Subject Index